During the period of intense resistance to colonisation in the Subcontinent, the use of emergency powers was correctly seen as a key method used by colonial authorities to stifle incipient nationalism and independence efforts. Virtually all leaders of decolonisation movements railed against such emergency legislation and vowed to abolish it immediately upon achieving independence. Unfortunately, too many saw the value of maintaining such laws, whether in constitutional or legislative form, to cement and perpetuate their own grip on power. In this book, Dr M. Ehteshamul Bari offers a masterful account of this phenomenon, focusing mainly on Bangladesh, which has had five states of emergency imposed since independence, but also comparing and contrasting the position with other constitutional democracies. Dr Bari provides a clear and compelling analysis of the critical need to maintain the rule of law and fundamental human rights, no matter the security challenges faced by a state. In an increasingly uncertain world, I commend this very important work without reservation to jurists, legislators and policymakers.

Professor David Weisbrot AM FAAL DLitt Chair, Australian Press Council. Former President of the Australian Law Reform Commission (1999–2009)

A wide-ranging contribution on theory of 'states of emergency', in constitutional law and in political practice – with detailed attention to British India, modern India, Pakistan and, particularly, Bangladesh. A 'standard constitutional model of emergency powers' is suggested. Dr M. Ehteshamul Bari provides an instructive analysis of how it may be possible to guard against grasping guards.

Professor Iain Stewart Honorary Fellow, Macquarie Law School, Macquarie University

Dr Bari's work is a deep exploration of emergency powers and the rights of individuals subject to those powers in Bangladesh's fragile democratic system. Notably, Bari situates the Bangladeshi law against a masterful analysis of comparable jurisdictions such as India and Pakistan thereby filling a gap in legal scholarship. Bari's work is a must-read for scholars of constitutional law in South Asia and indeed anyone interested in human rights within a multi-religious societal context.

Professor Sandeep Gopalan Pro Vice-Chancellor (Academic Innovation), Deakin University

States of Emergency and the Law

In Bangladesh, the absence of effective constitutional safeguards for governing emergency regimes has resulted in each of the five emergencies being invoked on the imprecise ground of internal disturbance. Two of these emergencies were even continued after the alleged threat posed to the life of the nation was over. Furthermore, during these five periods of emergency, either all or most of the fundamental rights guaranteed by the Constitution were suspended and the power of preventive detention was abused. Since no systematic and structured research has so far been carried out evaluating the Bangladeshi Constitution's provisions concerning the proclamation of emergency, suspension of fundamental rights and preventive detention, and the invocation of these extraordinary measures, this book will enhance knowledge by identifying the flaws, deficiencies and lacunae of the constitutional provisions concerning these exceptional measures. Consequently, based on these findings, recommendations will be put forward to rectify these defects from comparative constitutional law and normative perspectives. The outcome of this book will not only establish the best means for ensuring the maintenance of the rule of law but also for preventing undue intrusion on the fundamental human rights of individuals during emergency situations in Bangladesh.

This book will be of great interest and use to scholars and students of comparative constitutional law, human rights law and Asian law. Given the law reform analysis undertaken in this work, it will also be beneficial for the policy makers in Bangladesh and for the policy makers of constitutional polities facing similar problems with the issue of constraining the exercise of emergency powers.

Dr M. Ehteshamul Bari is a Lecturer in Law and the Director of the Deakin JD Program at Deakin University, Melbourne, Australia. He did his PhD in Law from Macquarie University, Sydney, in 2015 on an International Macquarie University Research Scholarship. Ehteshamul has published research articles on various aspects of constitutional law, human rights law and public international law in quality peer reviewed journals, such as the Oxford University Commonwealth Law Journal, San Diego International Law Journal, Commonwealth Law Bulletin and the Journal of East Asia and International Law.

Comparative Constitutionalism in Muslim Majority States
Series Editor: Javaid Rehman

This series encourages research into all aspects of comparative constitutionalism within the Muslim-Majority States of South Asia and the Middle East. Key areas of investigation include the post 9-11 implications on constitutionalism and the consequences of the Arab Spring. The studies within the series span across all aspects of constitutionalism, including constitutional rights, constitutional practices, rule of law issues, human rights, sexual rights and minorities. While the focus of the series is upon the Muslim-Majority States within the South Asia and Middle East region, the comparative critical assessment will engage a global analysis of constitutionalism and application of constitutional rights. Amidst the many cases of failed constitutionalism, there are a number of positives: this series also aims to explore and identify key successes from within the region.

Titles in the Series

States of Emergency and the Law
The Experience of Bangladesh
M. Ehteshamul Bari

States of Emergency and the Law

The Experience of Bangladesh

M. Ehteshamul Bari

Routledge
Taylor & Francis Group
LONDON AND NEW YORK

First published 2018
by Routledge

2 Park Square, Milton Park, Abingdon, Oxfordshire OX14 4RN
52 Vanderbilt Avenue, New York, NY 10017

Routledge is an imprint of the Taylor & Francis Group, an informa business

First issued in paperback 2020

British Library Cataloguing-in-Publication Data
A catalogue record for this book is available from the British Library

Library of Congress Cataloging-in-Publication Data
Names: Bari, M. Ehteshamul, author.
Title: States of emergency and the law : the experience of Bangladesh / M. Ehteshamul, Bari.
Description: New York, NY : Routledge, [2017] | Series: Comparative constitutionalism in muslim majority states | Includes bibliographical references and index.
Identifiers: LCCN 2017004156 | ISBN 978-1-138-05111-9 (hardback) | ISBN 978-1-351-68592-4 (adobe reader) | ISBN 978-1-351-68591-7 (epub) | ISBN 978-1-351-68590-0 (mobipocket)
Subjects: LCSH: War and emergency powers—Bangladesh. | War and emergency legislation—Bangladesh.
Classification: LCC KNG2650 .B37 2017 | DDC 342.5492/062—dc23
LC record available at https://lccn.loc.gov/2017004156

ISBN: 978-1-138-05111-9 (hbk)
ISBN: 978-0-367-59490-9 (pbk)

Typeset in Galliard
by FiSH Books Ltd, Enfield

Dedicated to my beloved father, late Professor M. Ershadul Bari

Contents

Acknowledgments

I am indebted to a number of individuals without whose support it would not have been possible for me to complete the writing of this book. First, I owe a profound debt of gratitude to Professor David Weisbrot AM (currently the Chair of the Australian Press Council), Professor Denise Meyerson (Macquarie University) and Associate Professor Iain Stewart (Macquarie University) for their invaluable guidance and support.

This book is dedicated to my beloved father, Professor M. Ershadul Bari, who passed away in November 2013. I will always be in awe of his vast knowledge on various branches of law, particularly Constitutional Law. I believe that witnessing his passion for Constitutional Law ultimately led me to develop a keen interest in this area. He would have been extremely proud to see the publication of this book.

I am profoundly grateful to my dearest mother, Mrs Umme Salma Atiya Bari, for her undying love and unconditional support. During the difficult times following my father's passing away, her words of wisdom and encouragement have been the driving force behind all my scholarly endeavours. I would like to thank my wonderful sister, Safia Naz, for her untiring support whenever asked. I am also thankful to my lovely wife, Samia Islam, for her constant support and encouragement.

Any errors in this book are, of course, mine alone.

Table of cases

Bangladesh

European Court of Human Rights

India

Inter-American Commission on Human Rights

International Crimes Tribunal for the former Yugoslavia

Malaysia

Pakistan

Singapore

South Africa

United Kingdom

United States of America

Table of constitutions/statutes

Bhutan

Brazil

Canada

Costa Rica

Denmark

Ethiopia

France

Germany

Greece

Hungary

India

Ireland

Israel

Macedonia

Malaysia

Namibia

Nicaragua

Panama

Pakistan

Spain

Sweden

United Kingdom of Great Britain and Northern Ireland

United States of America

Table of legislative instruments

1 Introduction

1.1 Introduction

A declaration of emergency is aimed at effectively dealing with a serious threat to the security and integrity of a nation, such as war, external aggression, armed rebellion, violent or non-violent protest, civil war, natural catastrophes or breakdown in the economy. Emergency powers should be exercised in a manner that does not risk compromising democratic values, such as respect for the rule of law and the core rights of individuals, in whose defence they are invoked (Ramraj, 2010). Thus, emergency situations pose a challenge for a democratic constitutional government to maintain an appropriate balance between competing values, namely, resorting to efficient measures for securing the integrity and cohesion of the state on the one hand, and a commitment to the maintenance of the rule of law and securing the enjoyment of the core fundamental rights of individuals on the other. However, the broad scope of certain emergency measures, such as preventive detention, often persuades the executive to upset this balance, either by resorting to the emergency measures for consolidating power by suppressing political adversaries or clinging on to these powers 'long after the conditions that triggered them have abated' (Ramraj, 2010: 38; O'Boyle, 1977).

In Bangladesh, a country which secured independence from Pakistan on 16 December 1971 through a war, the Constitution did not originally provide for an emergency framework. However, the insertion of an emergency provision via an amendment on 22 September 1973 has led to emergencies being invoked and continued, on most occasions, for purposes other than that of securing the integrity and cohesion of the state. This book, therefore, seeks to contribute from comparative constitutional law and normative perspectives towards the development of an appropriate emergency model for Bangladesh, which will not only empower the executive to effectively deal with a grave emergency but will also ensure the observance of the rule of law, respect for the core fundamental rights and minimum guarantees that mitigate the harshness of the exercise of preventive detention and other measures during emergency situations.

In this chapter, the traditional models of emergency will in the first place be briefly introduced. Second, an endeavour will be made to briefly examine the contemporary scholarly debate on emergency powers in order to provide some insight into the diversity of 'mechanisms, principles and practices' that are advocated to deal with the exigencies of emergencies (Ramraj and Guruswamy, 2013: 95). Third, light will be shed on the emergency framework contained in the *Constitution of Bangladesh*. Fourth, the objectives of this book will be outlined. Fifth and finally, an outline of the chapters of this book will be provided.

1.2 Traditional models of emergency powers

The authority for the exercise of emergency powers in order to deal with grave dangers that threaten the destruction of a nation can be traced back to various sources such as constitutions, statutes and the doctrine of necessity.

a) Constitutional model

Historically, the most common source of emergency powers has been written constitutions. Usually constitutions of most nations entrust the executive branch with the responsibility of proclaiming an emergency in order to respond to a grave threat posed to the life of the state by war, external aggression, armed conflict, natural catastrophes and financial crisis.[1] Since the vesting of unilateral power to invoke emergency in the executive involves the risk of abusing resort to such extraordinary power for purposes other than that of securing the life of the nation, the modern constitutional trend is to invest the legislature with the authority to declare an emergency upon the request or proposal of the executive branch of the government.[2] However, the gravity of an emergency may at times prevent the parliament from convening in time to proclaim an emergency, and as such it is not uncommon for these modern constitutions to take into account such a reality and consequently empower the executive to declare the emergency. But the executive power to act unilaterally with regard to a proclamation of emergency is usually constrained by the requirement that such proclamation of emergency is subject to ratification by the parliament as soon as possible.[3]

The common trend to be found in most constitutions – both past and modern – is to enumerate only the circumstances which merit a proclamation of emergency by the political organs of the government, and to abstain from making reference to any mechanisms for ensuring the effective scrutiny and timely termination of the emergency (see Sections 4.4.1, 4.4.2 and 4.4.3). Since the immediate consequences of a proclamation of emergency are the suspension of the enforcement of fundamental human rights and the use of the power of preventive detention – which entails restrictions on the right to liberty – the absence of a reliable system of checks and balances in the constitution in turn facilitates the institutionalisation of a state of emergency at the expense of the rights of individuals (see Section 2.5). For instance, in the absence of any constitutional safeguards for preventing the executive in Malaysia from stretching an emergency beyond its imperative necessity, the four emergencies proclaimed since 1964 remained in force until December 2011. Furthermore, a series of ordinary laws were enacted during the continuation of these emergencies not only to introduce changes to the legal landscape but also to erode the fundamental human rights of individuals (see Section 2.5).

b) Legislative model

The legislative model seeks to delegate special powers to the executive via legislation to respond to the exigencies of a particular emergency. The implication of such delegation of powers for dealing with an emergency by means of specific legislation, according to John Ferejohn and Pasquale Pasquino (2004), is that the legislature will ensure that the legislation eventually lapses once the emergency subsides (see Section 2.4.2.1). Thus, in principle, legislative emergency powers are temporary in nature and preserve the constitutional status quo by preventing the executive from imposing permanent changes on the legal order (see Section 2.4.2.1). However, practice shows that ordinary and temporary emergency statutes often become engrained in the ordinary legal framework, thereby contributing to the institutionalisation of a permanent emergency (see Section 2.5). For instance, in the US, the *PATRIOT Act*, which was enacted in the wake of 9/11 attacks, has been renewed repeatedly and has introduced substantial changes to the ordinary legal system (see Section 2.5).

c) The doctrine of necessity

The doctrine of necessity is founded on the assumption that extreme dangers to the life of a nation justify resort to emergency actions that would otherwise be unlawful. As F. B. Wiener (1940: 16) explains:

> Necessity calls it forth, necessity justifies its exercise … That necessity is no formal, artificial, legalistic concept but an actual and factual one: it is the necessity of taking action to safeguard the state against insurrection, riot, disorder or public calamity.

Although constitutions do not usually expressly authorise the invocation of the doctrine of necessity, some theorists, such as FM Brookfield and George Williams, do not regard its invocation as extra-constitutional. For, according to them, the invocation of the doctrine is circumscribed by the requirement of dealing with a serious threat to security of the nation and preserving the sanctity of the legal order (Brookfield, 1988; Williams, 2001). However, practice shows that, in the absence of any constraints on the authority of the executive, the doctrine can be used as a stepping stone for perpetuating power by abrogating the existing legal order. For instance, in Pakistan, on 7 October 1958 President Iskander Mirza invoked the doctrine of necessity in order to ensure his survival in office. For the invocation of the doctrine was followed by the abrogation of the country's first Constitution and the banning of all the political parties (Hasan, 1962; Kaushik, 1963). However, the 'destruction of the existing Constitution' was validated by the Supreme Court of Pakistan as being a valid consequence of the invocation of the doctrine of necessity (*State v Dosso [1958] 10 PLD (SC) 533*, 538). Thus it will be argued in this book that in the absence of any norms guaranteeing that the invocation of this doctrine will be confined to dealing with a grave threat and the preservation of the integrity of the constitutional order, the doctrine permits the exercise of unfettered power and can be properly described as extra-constitutional (see Section 2.4.3).

It is evident from the discussion above that the traditional emergency models have been concerned with empowering the executive with wide powers to deal with grave crises which threaten the survival of the state without simultaneously providing for effective mechanisms that constrain the exercise of such powers.

1.3 Contemporary scholarly debate on emergency powers

The potential of abuse of emergency powers under the traditional models has shaped the contemporary debate on emergency powers. The central issue surrounding this debate is whether *ex ante* or *ex post* mechanisms are suitable for maintaining the rule of law during emergency situations. The contemporary debate on emergency powers can be conceptualised by reference to three models: a) the extra-legal measures model, b) the court-centric model and c) the democratic formalist or constitutional model. Among these three contemporary emergency models, the extra-legal measures model advocates *ex post* checks on the exercise of emergency powers while the court-centric and democratic formalist models contend that *ex ante* checks on the powers of the executive have the merit of promoting the rule of law during emergency situations.

a) Extra-legal measures model (ELM)

The ELM, which is advocated by Oren Gross, is premised on the idea that emergencies often escape the confines of the constitutional provisions that warrant their exercise and thereby taint the entire legal order (Gross, 2003). Thus, Gross argues that in order to preserve the sanctity of the legal order and ensure the maintenance of the rule of law, the exercise of emergency powers by the executive should not be afforded any legal basis. Gross's (2003) prescription is that the executive's authority to respond to an emergency should not be circumscribed by any legal norms. It should be given the unilateral authority to decide: 1) whether a situation has attained a certain degree of gravity to be categorised as an emergency, 2) what extra-legal measures can be appropriately taken for dealing with the supposed threat, and 3) the duration of the extra-legal measures. Instead of legal constraints, Gross believes that the extra-legal measures of the executive should be subjected to *ex post* ratification by the public either through re-election of the executive or through elected representatives in the legislature (Gross, 2003; 2008). He contends that these *ex post* 'democratic-political' checks will dissuade the executive from resorting to the emergency powers as a means for subverting the rule of law.

However, it will be argued in this book that in the absence of any realistic checks on the actions of the executive during emergency situations, the ELM can be used as the vehicle for assuming arbitrary powers, which can include the abrogation or suspension of the legal order (see Section 4.2.1.1). It will further be shown that contrary to Gross's claims, the ELM involves the risk of the substitution of the rule of law by rule of man (see Section 4.2.1.2).

b) Court-centric model

David Dyzenhaus also expresses reservations about constitutionally entrenched emergency provisions. For Dyzenhaus, constitutional emergency provisions permit the judges to rely on them as the basis for scrutinising the actions of the executive during emergency situations and thereby undermine a substantive conception of the rule of law (Scheuerman, 2008). A substantive conception of the rule of law, according to Dyzenhaus (2003), can only be maintained during emergency situations when judges rely on the values and principles underpinning the common law as the benchmarks for holding the executive accountable for its breach of the rule of law. Thus it seems that rather than *ex ante* provisions in the constitution, Dyzenhaus wishes to rely on the *ex ante* checks contained in the common law system as the means for maintaining the rule of law during emergency situations.

However, this book will argue that Dyzenhaus's model overlooks the conservative contours of the common law model. For the common law system permits the executive to 'outpace' the judges by constantly expanding its powers during emergency situations (see Section 4.3.1.1.1). Furthermore, it will be argued that a substantive conception of the rule of law not only calls for judicial review of state actions during emergency situations but also requires such actions to be based on clear, precise and prospective guidelines (see Section 4.3.1.1.1).

c) Democratic formalist or constitutional model

Democratic formalists, such as Bruce Ackerman and William E. Scheuerman, contend that the absence of *ex ante* constitutional checks on the exercise of emergency powers permits the executive to resort to emergency measures as the means for subverting the rule of law and depriving individuals of their fundamental human rights. Furthermore, it is the absence of strict constitutional limits defining the scope of the exercise of emergency powers that prevents judges from vigorously scrutinising the necessity for the continuation of emergency measures beyond the circumstances which warranted their exercise (Ackerman, 2003–2004).

Democratic formalists, therefore, argue that detailed constitutional mechanisms governing the invocation, administration and termination of emergency powers offer the best solution to the problem of maintaining the rule of law and upholding fundamental human rights during emergency situations. In particular, democratic formalists stress the need for *ex ante* constitutional norms that constrain the powers of the executive to invoke and continue emergency measures by subjecting them to periodic review by increasing supermajorities of the democratically elected legislature (Scheuerman, 2006; Ackerman, 2006). Finally, they argue that detailed constitutional norms concerning emergency powers provide judges with the means to decide whether the measures taken by the executive during a state of emergency are within the parameters of these predefined norms (Ackerman, 2003–2004).

It is noteworthy that, while Gross's and Dyzenhaus's models focus primarily on the role of the executive and judges respectively, the democratic formalists seek to articulate a model whereby each of the three branches of the government – the executive, legislature and judiciary – has a significant role to play in promoting the rule of law and protecting fundamental human rights of individuals during emergencies.

This book will argue that the contemporary constitutional emergency model proposed by Ackerman and Scheuerman has the merits of not only avoiding the pathologies of emergency regimes but also of preserving the rule of law and liberties (see Section 4.3.2). For, as will be shown in Section 4.3.2, this model does not afford the executive with unfettered power during emergency situations but rather seeks to subject its power to a reliable system of checks and balances.

1.4 The emergence of Bangladesh as an independent nation and enactment of the *Constitution of Bangladesh*

During the 24 years of union with Pakistan, which became an independent dominion after partitioning of the British India on 14 August 1947, the inhabitants of Bangladesh (first as East Bengal from 1947 to 1956, and then as East Pakistan from 1956 to 1971) witnessed the Punjabi-dominated Western wing of Pakistan act so as to:

a) declare Urdu as the sole State language of Pakistan bypassing Bengali (since 1988 called Bangla) – the language of the majority population;

b) dismiss the democratically elected provisional government of East Bengal on 30 May 1954;
c) discriminate against them (the residents of Bangladesh) in recruitment and promotions in the civil services and armed forces; and
d) stimulate massive economic disparity between the two provinces.

(Ahmed, 2004)

The above occurrences aroused a sense of resentment among the Eastern Pakistanis. They began to think that their province had been downgraded to the status of being a mere colony of West Pakistan and that they had only changed their masters when India was partitioned. Faced with widespread discrimination in every sphere of governmental and public activity, East Pakistanis saw the first general election in the history of Pakistan, which was held on 7 December 1970, as their last hope of being part of a participatory democracy. In the election, the Awami League of East Pakistan won the right to form a national government as it emerged as the majority party. However, instead of appointing the leader of the Awami League, Sheikh Mujibur Rahman, as the Prime Minister, General Yahya Khan – the President and Chief Martial Law Administrator – postponed the first session of the newly constituted Constituent Assembly on 1 March 1971. This in turn sparked the first massive movement of civil disobedience in East Pakistan. Terming the movement an 'armed rebellion', Yahya ordered on 25 March 1971 a genocidal military action to put down the so-called 'armed rebellion' in East Pakistan (LaPorte Jr., 1972: 101). This led to the declaration of independence by the Eastern Wing from Pakistan on 26 March 1971.

Bangladesh ultimately emerged as an independent state on 16 December 1971, following a nine-month bloody liberation war. Unlike Pakistan, where the lawmakers carried out the process of enacting the first Constitution in a 'desultory fashion' for nine and a half years, the citizens of Bangladesh were given the Constitution on 16 December 1972 to commemorate the First Anniversary of the Victory Day of Bangladesh (Jennings, 1957; *Constitution of Bangladesh 1972* art 153(1). Thus Bangladesh got its Constitution within a year of emergence as an independent nation. In order to avoid the troubling experience of the past union with Pakistan, it was pledged in the preamble of the Constitution that

> it shall be a fundamental aim of the State to realise through the democratic process a socialist society, free from exploitation – a society in which the rule of law, fundamental human rights and freedom, equality and justice … will be secured for all citizens.

It should be pointed out here that unlike Pakistan, where respect for the Constitution has been wanting among succeeding generations of executives, as is evident from the abrogation of the 1956 and 1962 Constitutions following declarations of martial law[4] and suspension of the 1973

Constitution three times following proclamations of Martial Law and emergency,[5] the *Constitution of Bangladesh* has enjoyed continuous operation since its enactment. It was neither abrogated during the declarations of martial law on 15 August 1975 and 24 March 1982, nor has it ever been suspended. In fact, with the exception of the two declarations of Martial Law, the Constitution has been claimed to be the basis for every state action.

1.5 The emergency framework under the *Constitution of Bangladesh*

The *Constitution of Bangladesh* did not originally contain provisions concerning the proclamation of an emergency, the exercise of the power of preventive detention and suspension of the fundamental rights under any circumstances. It was claimed in the Constituent Assembly Debate (People's Republic of Bangladesh 1972: 51) that the misuse of the powers concerning emergency and preventive detention for political purposes by the Government of Pakistan (1947–1971), during the days when Bangladesh was a province of Pakistan, dissuaded the lawmakers from inserting such provisions into the Constitution.

However, these idealistic values were soon discarded by the lawmakers. Within nine months and seven days of the coming into force of the Constitution, on 22 September 1973, the *Constitution (Second Amendment) Act* was passed, inserting provisions that empowered the executive to proclaim emergencies, suspend the enforcement of the fundamental rights and exercise the power of preventive detention.

1.5.1 The power to proclaim emergency under the Constitution of Bangladesh

Article 141A of the *Constitution of Bangladesh*, as inserted by the *Constitution (Second Amendment) Act*, 1973, entrusts the President – the Head of the State – with the responsibility of proclaiming an emergency to respond to threats posed to the life of the nation by 'war or external aggression or internal disturbance'. A proclamation of emergency under the Constitution can continue to remain in force for 120 days without being approved by the Parliament. The issue of parliamentary approval arises only when there is a necessity to continue the proclamation beyond 120 days (*Constitution of Bangladesh 1972* art 141A(2)(c).

It seems that the *Constitution of Bangladesh* resembles the traditional constitutional model. For it only enumerates the circumstances that warrant the invocation of emergency, and does not contain any mechanisms for ensuring the effective scrutiny and timely termination of a proclamation of emergency. Furthermore, the Constitution does not confine the power to proclaim an emergency to circumstances that truly endanger the life of the nation. For the phrase 'internal disturbance' inserted in the Constitution as one of the grounds for invoking an emergency is not capable of precise definition (see Section 4.4.1).

The failure to limit the power to invoke emergency to grounds that achieve a certain degree of gravity in turn has allowed succeeding generations of executives to declare all the five emergencies in the history of the country – on 28 December 1974, 30 May 1981, 27 November 1987, 27 November 1990 and 11 January 2007 – due to 'internal disturbance'. It will be argued in this book that with the exception of the emergency proclaimed on 30 May 1981, following the assassination of the Head of the State by a group of army officers, the proclamations on the ground of internal disturbance were issued to deal with situations that could have been easily and properly contained under the ordinary legal framework (see Sections 5.2, 5.2.1, 5.3, 5.3.1, 5.4, 5.4.1, 5.5, 5.6 and 5.6.1). Furthermore, it will be shown that in the absence of any safeguards in the Constitution subjecting the exercise of emergency powers to a reliable system of checks and balances, and stipulating a maximum time limit on the continuation of an emergency, the emergencies declared on 28 December 1974 and on 11 January 2007 remained in force for nearly 5 years and 2 years respectively, despite the cessation of the hostilities which supposedly warranted their invocation (see Sections 5.2, 5.2.1, 5.6 and 5.6.1).

1.5.2 The power to suspend the enforcement of the fundamental rights during emergencies

Article 141C(1) of the *Constitution of Bangladesh*, as inserted by the *Constitution (Second Amendment) Act*, 1973, gives the President the *carte blanche* power to suspend the enforcement of all or any of the 18 fundamental rights guaranteed by the Constitution during a state of emergency. It is noteworthy that the lawmakers in inserting such a sweeping provision in the Constitution disregarded international human rights standards, which require the maintenance of a delicate balance between protecting national interests and safeguarding core rights during emergencies through the principles of non-derogation[6] and proportionality.[7]

Subsequently, the President of Bangladesh, after issuing a proclamation of emergency for the first time on 28 September 1974 due to 'internal disturbance', suspended the enforcement of 12 of the 18 fundamental rights (see Section 6.2.1) (Ministry of Law, 1974). The suspended rights not only included those which are considered as non-derogable under international human rights law, such as the right to life, the right not to be subjected to retroactive penal law, and the right not to be subjected to torture or cruel, inhuman or degrading punishment or treatment, but also included rights whose suspension was not strictly required for restoring normalcy, such as the right to freedom of profession or occupation and the right to property (see Section 6.2.1). This practice of suspending the enforcement of 12 fundamental rights set by the first emergency regime was adhered to by all the successive emergency regimes except the last emergency regime of 2007 (see Sections 6.2.2, 6.2.3 and 6.2.4). The last emergency proclaimed on 11 January 2007 witnessed the suspension of the enforcement of all the 18 fundamental rights, despite the fact that this emergency was supposedly declared to deal with 'internal disturbance' (see Section 6.2.5). Furthermore, it will be shown that the restrictions on the rights of the people not only continued for nearly two years in the absence of the features of a grave emergency but also that this arbitrary derogation regime was followed by the breach of the core rights of citizens, such as the rights to life and freedom from torture and cruel or inhuman or degrading treatment (see Sections 6.2.5.1, 6.2.5.2 and 6.2.5.3).

It should be stressed here that Bangladesh acceded to the *International Covenant on Civil and Political Rights* (ICCPR) in September 2000. Notwithstanding such accession, the Constitution has not been amended to incorporate into it the principles of non-derogation and proportionality.

1.5.3 The power of preventive detention under the Constitution of Bangladesh

Article 33 of the *Constitution of Bangladesh*, as amended on 22 September 1973, empowers the Parliament to enact laws concerning preventive detention. Paradoxically, this enabling clause concerning preventive detention was incorporated in the chapter on fundamental rights of the *Constitution of Bangladesh*, which guarantees a wide range of fundamental rights, including the right to liberty.

Article 33 offers only limited safeguards to detainees, such as the right of representation against the detention order and the review of the detention order by a quasi-judicial body – the Advisory Board – for mitigating the harshness of the powers concerning preventive detention. Furthermore, this Article neither confines the power of preventive detention to formally declared periods of emergency nor specifies a maximum time frame for keeping an individual in preventive custody.

This book will argue that the weaknesses of the constitutional provisions concerning preventive detention have permitted the use of the *Special Powers Act (SPA)*, 1974 – which is the permanent piece of legislation concerning preventive detention – as well as temporary laws, enacted during the emergency periods, as instruments for arbitrarily detaining enormous numbers of individuals, including political adversaries (see Section 7.3). Nevertheless, on many occasions, the Supreme Court of Bangladesh, as will be shown in Sections 7.3.1.5 and 7.3.5.1, stood between the detainee and the encroachment on his liberty by the executive. It issued release orders in respect of many of the detainees in consequence of writ petitions challenging their orders of detention. The decisions of the Supreme Court show that, in some cases, the orders of detention were passed in a casual or cavalier manner without due process of thought and consideration. The grounds themselves were vague and couched in the most general terms.

1.6 Objectives of the book

The response of a state to a public emergency is the 'litmus' test of its commitment to maintaining the rule of law and safeguarding fundamental rights, particularly those rights from which no derogation should be made (Ramraj and Guruswamy, 2013). This book will argue that, in the absence of effective constitutional safeguards in Bangladesh for governing emergency regimes, the power to invoke emergencies has been conveniently resorted to as the most effective means for substituting the rule of law with rule of man. Each of the five emergencies was invoked on the imprecise ground of internal disturbance. Two of these emergencies were even continued after the threat posed to the life of the nation ceased to exist. Such a continuance of emergency is the antithesis of the temporary nature of an emergency regime designed to fend off the extraordinary threats posed to the life of the nation. Furthermore, light will be shed on the facts that during the five periods of emergency rule in Bangladesh, either all or most of the fundamental rights guaranteed by the Constitution were suspended and the power of preventive detention under the SPA as well as under the temporary laws was misapplied and abused. Thus, this book will make it evident that the constitutional provisions concerning emergency and preventive detention laws have actually served as a means for depriving the citizens of their fundamental rights.

Since no systematic and structured research has so far been carried out evaluating the Bangladeshi Constitution's provisions concerning the proclamation of emergency, suspension of fundamental rights and preventive detention, and the invocation of these extraordinary measures, this book will enhance knowledge by identifying the flaws, deficiencies and lacunae of the constitutional provisions concerning these exceptional measures. Consequently, based on these findings, recommendations will be put forward from comparative constitutional law and normative perspectives for insertion in the *Constitution of Bangladesh* detailed norms providing for legal limits on the wide power of the executive concerning the proclamation, administration and termination of emergency. The incorporation of effective safeguards in the Constitution will ensure that emergencies are no longer resorted to as the means of discarding the rule of law and depriving individuals of their fundamental rights.

1.7 Structure of the book

Following this introductory chapter, the structure of this book is divided into seven chapters. In Chapter 2, light will first be shed on the general issues pertaining to emergency powers, i.e. the definition of emergency and necessity for the invocation of emergency. This chapter will critically examine the traditional emergency models. The possibility of abuse of the emergency powers under these traditional models will also be underscored. It will then deal with the evolution of the emergency powers and their consequent use in the Indian Subcontinent.

Chapter 3 will deal with the general issues pertaining to the immediate consequences of a proclamation of emergency, i.e. suspension of the enforcement of fundamental rights and the exercise of the power of preventive detention. In order to facilitate a systematic discussion of the issues, this chapter will be divided into two parts: Part A and Part B. In part A, an attempt will first be made to define the concept of fundamental rights. Second, following a discussion about the necessity for suspension of the enforcement of fundamental rights during emergency situations, this part will shed light on the standards contained in the ICCPR concerning derogation from human rights during emergency situations – namely, the principles of non-derogation and proportionality – and the weaknesses of the monitoring system under the ICCPR. Finally, this part will also discuss the evolution of the provisions concerning the suspension of fundamental rights during emergency, as enshrined in the Constitutions of India, Pakistan and Bangladesh. Part B will deal with the definition of preventive detention, the necessity of the power and the possibility of its abuse, and the evolution of this power in the Indian Subcontinent.

Thus Chapters 2 and 3 will seek to lay the foundation for the discussion that will be set out in the subsequent chapters of the book by identifying: a) the pathologies of emergency governments as evidenced from an examination of the traditional emergency models, and b) the similarities in the provisions concerning proclamation of emergency, suspension of fundamental rights and exercise of the power of preventive detention under the Constitutions of India, Pakistan and Bangladesh.

After gaining an insight into the traditional models concerning emergency powers and the experience of these powers in the Subcontinent – both during colonial and post-colonial periods – Chapter 4 will seek to critically engage with the contemporary scholarly debate on emergency powers. It will be argued in this chapter that the idea of fidelity to the rule of law requires the governance of emergency powers by detailed constitutionally entrenched safeguards. Consequently, this chapter will embark on the endeavour to develop a standard constitutional emergency model providing for detailed norms to deal with all the aspects of a proclamation of emergency.

In light of the standard emergency model developed in Chapter 4, Chapter 5 will examine the weaknesses of the constitutional provisions in Bangladesh concerning the proclamation, administration and termination of emergencies. Subsequently, it will be shown that these weaknesses have allowed succeeding generations of executives to invoke emergencies for purposes other than that of securing the life of the nation.

Chapter 6 will stress that in the absence of the principles of any substantive limitations, namely the principles of non-derogation and proportionality, in the *Constitution of Bangladesh* on the power of the executive to suspend the enforcement of the fundamental rights, emergencies have been used as a means for arbitrarily depriving citizens of all or the majority of their fundamental rights often for a prolonged period of time.

Chapter 7 will shed light on the lack of adequate safeguards contained in the *Constitution of Bangladesh* for mitigating the harshness of the exercise of the power of preventive detention. This chapter will argue that the weakness of the provisions concerning preventive detention has in turn facilitated the indiscriminate exercise of the power of preventive detention during the formally declared periods of emergency to detain an enormous number of individuals often without any justification. This chapter will also discuss the judicial response in preventing arbitrary encroachment on the liberty of individuals during emergency situations.

Finally, in the concluding chapter, Chapter 8, in light of the standard constitutional model of emergency and the weaknesses of the emergency framework under the *Constitution of Bangladesh*, it will be argued that a constitutionally entrenched framework providing for effective constraints on the exercise of these powers would diminish the possibility of their abuse and promote the rule of law and core rights of individuals.

1.8 References

Ackerman, B. (2003–2004) 'The Emergency Constitution', *Yale Law Journal*, 113: 1031, 1069.

Ackerman, B. (2006) *Before the Next Attack: Preserving Civil Liberties in an Age Terrorism*, New Haven, CT: Yale University Press, 80.

Ahmed, S. (2004) *Bangladesh: Past and Present*, New Delhi: SB Nangia, APH Publishing Corporation, 137, 141–142.

Brookfield, F. M. (1988) 'The Fiji Revolutions of 1987', *New Zealand Law Journal*: 251.

Cushing, T. N. (2003) 'Pakistan's General Pervez Musharraf:Deceitful Dictator or Father of Democracy?', *Penn State International Law Review*, 21: 623–624.

Dyzenhaus, D. (2003) 'Humpty Dumpty Rules or the Rule of Law: Legal Theory and the Adjudication of National Security', *Australian Journal of Legal Philosophy*, 28: 13.

Ferejohn J. and Pasquino, P. (2004) 'The Law of the Exception: A Typology of Emergency Powers', *International Journal of Constitutional Law*, 2(2): 235–236.

Gross, O. (2003) 'Chaos and Rules: Should Responses to Violent Crises Always be Constitutional', *Yale Law Journal*, 112: 1023, 1034, 1097, 1100, 1114.

Gross, O. (2008) 'Extra-Legality and the Ethic of Political Responsibility', in V. V. Ramraj (ed.), *Emergencies and the Limits of Legality*, Cambridge/New York: Cambridge University Press, 63.

Hasan, K. S. (1962) 'The New Constitution of Pakistan', *Parliamentary Affairs*, 16(2): 174–175.

International Commission of Jurists (1983) *States of Emergency – Their Impact on Human Rights: A Comparative Study by the International Commission of Jurists*, Geneva: International Commission of Jurists, 416.

Jennings, I. (1957) *Constitutional Problems in Pakistan*, London: Cambridge University Press, 22.

Kaushik, S. (1963) 'Constitution of Pakistan at Work', *Asian Survey*, 3(8): 384.
LaPorte Jr., R. (1972) 'Pakistan in 1971: The Disintegration of Nation', *Asian Survey*, 12(2): 101.
O'Boyle, M. P. (1977) 'Emergency Situations and the Protection of Human Rights: a Model Derogation Provision for a Northern Ireland Bill of Rights', *Northern Ireland Legal Quarterly*, 28(2): 164.
People's Republic of Bangladesh (1972) *Gonoporishoder Bitorko (Constituent Assembly Debate)*, vol. II, 51.
'Proclamation of Emergency' (2007) *The Dawn*, 4 November, available at www.dawn.com/news/274270/proclamation-of-emergency [Accessed 5 November 2011].
Ramraj, V. V. (2008) 'No Doctrine More Pernicious? Emergencies and the Limits of Legality', in V. V. Ramraj (ed.), *Emergencies and the Limits of Legality*, Cambridge/New York: Cambridge University Press, 27.
Ramraj, V. V. (2010) 'The Emergency Powers Paradox', in V. V. Ramraj, and A. K. Thiruvengadam (eds), *Emergency Powers in Asia*, Cambridge/New York: Cambridge University Press, 22–23, 38.
Ramraj, V. V. and Guruswamy, M. (2013) 'Emergency Powers', in M. Tushnet, T. Fleiner and C. Saunders (eds), *Routledge Handbook of Constitutional Law*, London/New York: Routledge, 95.
Scheuerman, W. (2006) 'Emergency Powers and the Rule of Law After 9/11', *The Journal of Political Philosophy*, 14(1): 76.
Scheuerman, W. E. (2008) 'Presidentialism and Emergency Government' in V. V. Ramraj (ed.), *Emergencies and the Limits of Legality*, Cambridge/New York: Cambridge University Press, 277, 284, 285.
Wiener, F. B. (1940) *A Practical Manual of Martial Law*, Harrisburg, PA: Military Service Publishing Co., 16.
Williams, G. (2001) 'The Case that Stopped a Coup? The Rule of Law and Constitutionalism in Fiji', *Oxford University Commonwealth Law Journal*, 1(1): 80.

Notes

1 See *Constitution of Azerbaijan 1995* art 112; *Constitution of Brazil 1998* arts 49(II) & (IV), 136 & 137; *Constitution of Costa Rica 1949* art 93(2)(a) & (b), art 121(6); *Constitution of the Federal Democratic Republic of Ethiopia 1995* art 93(2)(a) & (b); *Constitution of Panama 1972* art 51; *Constitution of Pakistan 1973* art 232(7); *Constitution of Paraguay 1992* art 238(7); *Constitution of Romania 1991* art 93(1); *Constitution of Bhutan 2008* art 33(1) & (2); *Constitution of India 1950* art 352(3); *Constitution of Bangladesh 1972* art 141A(1) and *Constitution of Portugal 1976* arts 137(d), 141 and 143(1).

2 See *Constitution of Greece 1975* art 48(1); *German Basic Law 1949* art 115a; *Constitution of Slovenia 1991* art 92, *Israel's Basic Law: The Government 2001* art 38(a); and *Constitution of Hungary 1949* art 19(3)(1).

3 See *Israeli Basic Law: The Government 2001* art 38(c); *Constitution of Greece 1975* art 48(2); *Constitution of Austria 1920* art 18(3); *Constitutional Act of Denmark 1953* art 23.

4 The 1956 *Constitution of Pakistan* was abrogated following the declaration of Martial Law on 7 October 1958 while the 1962 Constitution was abrogated following the proclamation of Martial Law on 25 March 1969.

5 The 1973 *Constitution of Pakistan* was first suspended on 5 July 1977 following a proclamation of Martial Law. The Constitution was also suspended following the declarations of emergency by Pervez Musharraf on 14 October 1999 and 3 November 2007 respectively.

6 The international human rights norms developed in the 1950s and 1960, such as the *European Convention for the Protection of Human Rights and Fundamental Freedoms (ECHR) 1950 (art 15(2))*, the *International Covenant on Civil and Political Rights* (*ICCPR*) *1966 (art 4(2))* and the *American Convention on Human Rights* (*ACHR*) *1969 (art 27(2))* list 4, 7 and 11 human rights respectively as non-derogable rights.

7 The ECHR (art 15(1)), ICCPR (art 4(1)) and ACHR (art 27(1)) permit states parties to derogate from only those human rights which are strictly required by the exigencies of an emergency.

2 General issues concerning the powers of emergency and the evolution of these powers in the Indo-Pak-Bangladesh Subcontinent

2.1 Introduction

It is a common feature of almost every democratic constitution of the world to contain detailed provisions concerning proclamation of emergency to tide over an actual or imminent threat to the life of nation by war, external aggression, armed rebellion, internal disturbance, natural catastrophes and breakdown in the economy. In fact, the power to proclaim an emergency, which must generally be used as a last resort, may be considered as the state's constitutional or legal right to self-defence comparable with the individual's right to self-defence under the penal law (*States of Emergency*, 1983). In this context, the immemorial words of Abraham Lincoln are worth quoting:

> Every man thinks he has a right to live and every government thinks it has a right to live. Every man when driven to the wall by a murderous assailant will override all laws to protect himself, and this is called the great right of self-defence. So every government when driven to the wall by a rebellion will trample down a constitution before it will allow itself to be destroyed. This may not be constitutional law but it is a fact.
>
> (Bonner, 1985: 2)

States of emergency are encountered with surprising frequency throughout the world. There is a general tendency to use or continue to use these powers for political purposes in the absence of a grave emergency, e.g. to repress a part of the population, to impose policies which do not enjoy popular support, or to defend an unpopular government's hold on power (*States of Emergency*, 1983). This use or lingering of the emergency and the exercise of emergency powers may turn a democratic government into a constitutional dictatorship, implying the substitution of the rule of law by rule of man. An attempt will, therefore, be made in this chapter to examine the general issues pertaining to the powers of emergency. In particular, the definition of emergency, necessity of emergency powers, traditional models of emergency powers, possibility of the abuse of emergency powers and the evolution of the emergency powers in the Indo-Pak-Bangladesh Subcontinent will be examined.

2.2 Definition of emergency

In early times, legal scholars and judges found it difficult to define the concept of emergency. For instance, in 1787, Alexander Hamilton (1948: 153) said:

> [i]t is impossible to ... define the extent and variety of national exigencies ... that endanger the safety of nations ... and for this reason no constitutional shackles can wisely be imposed on the ... extent and variety of the means which may be necessary to satisfy them.

In the same vein, Lord Dunedin observed in *Bhagat Singh & Ors v The King Emperor (1931) LR 58 IA 169*: 'A state of emergency is something that does not permit of any exact definition: it connotes a state of matters calling for drastic action (171).'

However, since the 1960s the legal authorities have not had any difficulty in defining a public emergency. For instance, in 1961, the European Court of Human Rights defined a public emergency threatening the life of the nation in *Gerard Lawless v Republic of Ireland* as 'an exceptional situation of crisis or emergency which affects the whole population and constitutes a threat to the organised life of the community of which the State is composed' (European Court of Human Rights, 1961: 56). This definition of public emergency has been almost reproduced in 'The Paris Minimum Standards of Human Rights Norms in a State of Emergency', adopted in 1984 by the International Law Association – a group of international lawyers and legal scholars – after eight years of careful deliberation to act as a guideline for states during the declaration and administration of emergencies. Article 1(b) of this instrument states:

> "Public emergency" means an exceptional situation of crisis or public danger, actual or imminent, which affects the whole population or the whole population of the area to which the declaration applies and constitutes a threat to the organized life of the community of which the state is composed.

Lord MacDermott of the Privy Council stated in 1968 in *Stephen Kalong Ningkan v Government of Malaysia [1968] 2 MLJ 238* that the natural meaning of the word (emergency) itself is capable of covering a very wide range of situations and occurrences, including such diverse events as wars, famines, earthquakes, floods and the collapse of civil government (242).

Thus, an emergency may be defined as a sudden or unexpected temporary event, either actual or imminent, which threatens the security of a state, places the existence or functioning of its institutions in a precarious position and calls for immediate additional legal actions so that normalcy can promptly be restored. The salient characteristics of a public emergency can be summarised as follows:

a) there must be a crisis or danger, actual or imminent;
b) the crisis or danger must constitute a threat to the life of the nation, i.e. the physical well-being of the population, the territorial integrity of the state or the functioning of the institutions of the State;
c) normal legal measures must be inadequate and ineffective to cope with the crisis at hand (i.e. emergency is to be used as a last resort);
d) resort to emergency powers, as contained generally in a constitution, must be needed on an immediate basis in order to tackle the situation;
e) the nature of the crisis or danger must be of temporary or provisional character; and
f) the objective of the proclamation of emergency must be to preserve the life of the nation and return, as quickly as possible, to the normal legal order.

2.3 Necessity of emergency powers

Emergency powers have become an unavoidable feature of contemporary political reality. For states may sometimes face exceptional crises or public danger, actual or imminent, like war, external aggression, rebellion, internal disturbance, civil war, natural catastrophes or breakdown in the economy which threaten their security or economic life and, as such, normal measures or restrictions provided for by ordinary law are found to be inadequate and ineffective to assure the survival of the nation. Therefore, in order to deal with such situations effectively, special powers of emergency are invoked as a 'last resort' in self-defence to preserve and protect the integrity and cohesion of the state. The right to resort to such an extraordinary power is entirely aimed at the speedy restoration of the normal legal order and, as such, no measures should deliberately be taken during an emergency which are contrary to democracy values, such as respect for the rule of law and the fundamental human rights of individuals, and are not strictly required by the exigencies of the situation. The international human rights instruments adopted in the 1950s and 1960s also recognise the right of a state to declare a public emergency in times of crisis which threaten the life of the nation, and authorise states to 'take measures ... to the extent strictly required by the exigencies of the situation, provided that such measures are not inconsistent with other obligations under international law'.[1]

2.4 Traditional models of emergency powers

The traditional sources from which the relevant authority of a democratic state derives the power to proclaim an emergency can be grouped under three models, namely, constitutional, non-constitutional and extra-constitutional.

2.4.1 Constitutional model

Under this model of emergency, it is the supreme law – the constitution – of a state which empowers either the head of the state or the Parliament to declare a state of emergency.

A number of constitutions invest the primary responsibility to declare a state of emergency in an elected President (head of the state)/Prime Minister (head of the government). The Constitutions of Azerbaijan, Bhutan, Ethiopia, Portugal, Brazil, Costa Rica, Panama, Paraguay, Romania, India, Pakistan, Bangladesh, France, Peru, Ecuador and Nicaragua are examples. Among these constitutions, the Constitutions of Azerbaijan, Bhutan, Ethiopia, Portugal, Brazil, Costa Rica, Panama, Pakistan, Paraguay, Romania, India and Bangladesh require the state of emergency invoked by the executive/head of state to be validated either by: a) prior authorisation or subsequent ratification by the legislative branch,[2] or b) the counter signature of the Prime Minister or the approval of the Government (when the head of the state is empowered by the Constitution to declare a state of emergency),[3] or c) by a combination of both (a) and (b).[4]

However, in France a mere consultation by the President with the Prime Minister, the Presidents of the Houses of Parliament and the Constitutional Council prior to declaring a state of emergency is sufficient.[5] Thus the *Constitution of France*, 1958 in Article 16 gives the President the *carte blanche* power to proclaim an emergency if there is an immediate and serious threat to the French institutions, independence of the nation, territorial integrity or the fulfilment of France's international commitments and its constitutional governmental authorities are no longer able to function normally. The Constitutions of Peru and Nicaragua, on the other hand, merely require the executive to notify the parliament of the proclamation of a state of emergency without giving any additional role to the parliament.[6] In addition to these Constitutions, which expressly empower the executive to proclaim an emergency, there are certain constitutions which are either silent on the proclamation of emergency (e.g. the *Constitution of Finland*), or make little mention of emergency (e.g. the *Constitution of Norway* speaks only of 'extraordinary circumstances, such as hostile invasion or infectious disease' when Parliament may meet outside the capital), or in which the power of the executive to proclaim an emergency is considered as implied in spite of the absence of any clear emergency clause (e.g. the *Constitution of the United States of America*).

The provisions of *Constitution of the USA*, 1787 deserves special consideration because of the 'awesome' emergency actions taken by President Abraham Lincoln in 1861 to deal with the American Civil War (Gross and Aoláin, 2006: 47). Although Article II of the *Constitution of the USA*, which deals with Presidential powers, makes no mention of emergency powers, it designates the President as the 'Commander in Chief of the Army and Navy of the United States, and of the Militia of several States' (s II). The Constitution empowers the Congress to call forth the States' militia to 'suppress Insurrections and repel invasions' and tersely provides that the 'Privilege of the Writ of Habeas Corpus shall not be suspended, unless when in cases of Rebellion or Invasion the Public Safety may require it' (art 1 ss 8 and 9). Therefore, it seems that the *Constitution of the USA* does not give the President any explicit power to declare a state of emergency but rather contemplates the exercise of emergency powers by the Congress. However, President Abraham Lincoln during the American Civil War of 1861 unilaterally enlarged the armed forces, suspended habeas corpus and spurned an order of the Chief Justice in defiance of the constitutional provisions and defended his unconstitutional actions as warranted by the necessity to preserve the Federation. As he said:

> It became necessary for me to choose whether, using only the existing means, agencies, and processes which Congress had provided, I should let the Government fall at once into ruin or whether, availing myself of the broader powers conferred by the Constitution in cases of insurrection, I would make an effort to save it, with all its blessings, for the present age and for prosperity.
>
> (Richardson, 1896–9: 78; Gross, 2011: 344)

However, such an emergency regime has never again been invoked in the United States of America.

In order to prevent the executive from unilaterally and arbitrarily declaring an emergency by exaggerating the threats posed to the life of the nation, the modern constitutional trend is to vest the primary authority for declaring a state of emergency in the legislature/parliament although, at times, the parliament is required to act upon the request or proposal of the government.[7] However, it is also common to find constitutional provisions which empower the government or the president to declare a state of emergency if the parliament cannot convene or act in time due to an emergency of great magnitude or one that deeply divides the nation. But such declaration of an emergency and any subsequent exercise of provisional legislative emergency powers by the executive are subject to a consequent prompt ratification by the parliament if they are to remain in force.[8] Thus it seems that these fall-back provisions seek to constitutionalise the sort of emergency regime that was invoked by Abraham Lincoln during the American Civil War.

Some constitutions stipulate that a 'mini-parliament' replace the legislature as the authority to take the decision regarding the proclamation of emergency. For example, Article 115a(2) of the *German Basic Law*, 1949 provides that if the Federal territory is under attack by armed force or imminently threatened with such an attack (the state of defence) and the situation inevitably calls for immediate action, and if insurmountable obstacles prevent the timely convening of the *Bundestag*, or the *Bundestag* cannot master a quorum, then the Joint Committee, which is composed of 48 members from both houses of the legislature – 32 from the *Bundestag* and 16 from the *Bundesrat* – can take the decision to proclaim an emergency by a two-thirds majority of the votes cast, including at least a majority of the members of the *Bundestag*. The *Constitution of Sweden*, 1975 provides for a similar so-called War Delegation.[9]

A common theme among most constitutional emergency framework – both past and modern – is to specify only the circumstances which can warrant the invocation of a proclamation of emergency without simultaneously providing for any effective mechanisms to constrain the exercise of emergency powers and ensure their timely termination. Furthermore, the grounds for invoking an emergency are often articulated in a broad[10] and imprecise manner.[11] Consequently, the absence of effective constitutional safeguards, as will be shown below in Section 2.5, enables the political organs of the state to 'abuse the trust the constitution has placed' in them (Ferejohn and Pasquino, 2004).

2.4.2 Non-constitutional model

2.4.2.1 Legislative model

In recent times, the legislative model of emergency powers has emerged as the preferred emergency model in some of the developed or stable democracies, such as Canada and the USA, where their respective Constitutions contain few or no provisions concerning emergency powers (Ferejohn and Pasquino, 2004). The legislative model deals with an emergency by delegating special powers to the executive through the enactment of: a) specific and temporary statutes or enabling acts (e.g. the German Enabling Acts of 1923–1924), or b) permanent legislation with an emergency flavour (e.g. the Defence of Realm Acts of the UK, and the *British Emergency Powers Act* of 1920 – which was used to proclaim a state of emergency on 12 separate occasions with the last time being in 1974). This practice implies that the emergency powers created by the statute will eventually lapse on the occurrence of a particular event (e.g. the termination of an ongoing war) or on a set date or after a set period of time, unless their renewal is sanctioned by the legislature, the clear implication being that renewal will only be sanctioned if the need for the powers continues to exist. The system of the temporary or permanent delegating statute for emergency purposes was officially justified in 1932 by the Report of the British Committee on Ministers' Powers, as follows:

> In a modern state there are many occasions when there is a sudden need for legislative action. For many such needs delegated legislation is the only convenient or even possible remedy ... It may not be only prudent

> but vital for Parliament to arm the executive Government in advance with almost plenary power to meet occasions of emergency, which affect the whole nation ... as in the extreme case of the Defence of the Realm Acts in the Great War, where the emergency had arisen; or in the Emergency Powers Act, 1920, where the emergency had not arisen but power was conferred to meet emergencies that might arise in the future ... There is in truth no alternative means by which strong measures to meet great emergencies can be made possible; and for that means the means is constitutional.
>
> (UK Committee on Ministers' Powers, 1932: 52)

The United Kingdom has one of the most recent laws on emergencies. This is the *Civil Contingencies Act*, which came into force in 2004.[12] The Act empowers the Queen (s 20(1)), as the head of state, to make emergency regulations to deal with the most serious of emergencies, namely, emergencies concerning human welfare (s 19(1)(a)), environment (s 19(1)(b)) and security (war/terrorism) (s 19(1)(c)). It is noteworthy that for the first time in the history of the UK a fall-back option has been included to cover the possibility that in times of a grave emergency the Queen may not be able to act in time. The Act, therefore, empowers the Prime Minister or a Senior Minister to make emergency regulations in such an event (s 20(2)). In order to prevent the misuse of emergency powers, the Act includes a 'triple lock guarantee' in the form of three considerations which must be taken into account before invoking emergency powers: necessity, proportionality and seriousness (Civil Contingencies Secretariat, 2004: 5). It should be further stressed here that when the Civil Contingencies Bill was introduced before the Parliament, it was accompanied by a statement of compatibility in pursuance of Section 19(1)(a) of the *Human Rights Act*, 1998. The statement read that the 'provisions of the Civil Contingencies Bill are compatible' with the rights contained in the *European Convention on Human Rights and Fundamental Freedoms*, 1950, which have been incorporated in the HRA (Civil Contingencies Bill).

An emergency regulation made in pursuance of the *Civil Contingencies Act* must be presented to the Parliament for its approval as soon as practicable (s 27(1)). Parliament has the right to make amendments to the emergency regulation and must approve it within seven days of laying (s 27(2)). The regulation shall lapse if it is not approved by the Parliament within the said seven days (s 27(2)). The duration of an emergency regulation under the Act cannot be more than 30 days from the date on which it was made (s 26(1)).

In Canada, the preamble to Section 91 of the *Canadian Constitution Act* of 1867, which empowers the parliament to make laws 'for the peace, order and good government of Canada', has been interpreted as authorising the federal parliament to enact emergency legislation. Accordingly, in 1988 the Canadian Parliament enacted the *Emergencies Act*,[13] which authorises the federal government to declare four different types of emergency, namely, 1) public welfare emergency (s 5), 2) public order emergency (s 16), 3) international emergency (s 27) and 4) war emergency (s 37). The initial duration of each of these emergencies varies from 30 days[14] up to 120 days,[15] and so does the nature and scope of permissible emergency powers granted to the federal government (Gross, 2011). A motion for confirmation of an emergency, however, must be tabled in both the Houses of the Parliament within seven sitting days of its issuance. Such a motion must contain the reasons for the proclamation of any of the four types of emergency envisaged in the *Emergencies Act*, 1988. If such a motion, according to Section 58, is rejected by either of the Houses of the Parliament, the proclamation of emergency is deemed to have been revoked on that day.

In the USA, the Congress enacted the *National Emergencies Act*, 1976 which requires public declaration of all new emergencies and subsequent reporting to the Congress by the President. It is widely believed that the consultation and reporting requirements 'largely have been diluted or ignored by Congress' (Huq, 2006).

Contemporary theorists, such as John Ferejohn and Pasquale Pasquino, provide a forceful defence of the merits of the legislative model of emergency powers. Ferejohn and Pasquino, argue that the legislative model permits closer supervision of the exercise of emergency powers by the executive than the constitutional model. For the legislature ensures that the delegation of powers to the executive by means of a statute is not stretched beyond the imperative necessities of an emergency by terminating the emergency when in its estimation 'the emergency is finished or the executive has proven untrustworthy' (Ferejohn and Pasquino, 2004: 218). Subsequently, Ferejohn and Pasquino (2004: 235) argue that the legislative model ensures the sanctity of the constitutional order by preventing the executive from imposing 'any permanent change on the legal ordering'.

However, the above arguments can be countered by pointing out that the executive might command the support of the majority in the legislature, and in turn can use its support to extend the duration of the powers concerning emergency beyond the crises which warranted their delegation. This argument is bolstered by the actual practice which, as will be discussed below in Section 2.5, reveals that the ordinary statutes concerning emergency powers often get engrained in the ordinary legal framework either through repeated renewals after each deadline or by being made permanent, thereby contributing towards the institutionalisation of a permanent emergency and undermining the viability of the legislative model in retaining the conservative nature of emergency powers. Furthermore, it should be stressed here that whereas the provisions of a written constitution concerning general emergency cannot be amended without a special and difficult process, ordinary law concerning emergency can easily be amended either by the law-making procedure at the behest of the executive or by the promulgation of an ordinance by the executive to serve its purpose.

2.4.3 *Extra-constitutional model*

2.4.3.1 Doctrine of necessity

The doctrine of necessity is derived from the maxim 'necessitas facit licitum quod alias non est licitum', which means that the necessity to deal with the exigencies of a grave threat to the life of a nation justifies the invocation of emergency measures that is otherwise not lawful. With regard to the degree of necessity that warrants such drastic measures, A. V. Dicey (1915) observes that the necessity must be 'immediate'. Mere anticipation of a grave threat is not sufficient to justify its invocation. Rather the threat must be 'actual and present' (*Ex Parte Milligan (1866) 71 US 2*, 127). Thus the doctrine, according to Dicey (1915: 539), 'comes into existence in times of invasion or insurrection when, where, and in so far as … peace cannot be maintained by ordinary means, and owes its existence to urgent and paramount necessity'.

Constitutions usually do not recognise and regulate resorting to the doctrine of necessity. In this context, the example of Switzerland is relevant. Since the *Constitution of Switzerland* does not make any reference to emergency situations that may necessitate the resort to special powers, the country has had 23 Acts providing for provisions concerning the invocation of the doctrine of necessity until 2003 when all these laws were repealed by the Government (Khakee, 2009). In 2006, the Government chose not to adopt any written rules, constitutional or legal, concerning emergency on the ground that it would risk slowing down the decision-making in emergency situations when measures would have to be taken promptly, and 'it can be feared that written rules regarding the doctrine of necessity have the psychological effect that the authorities hesitate less to use such norms in exceptional situations' (Khakee, 2009: 18–19). Therefore, the Government of Switzerland preferred to rely on an extra-constitutional and non-codified 'doctrine of necessity', which stipulates that in a severe emergency it may seize almost total power leaving the Parliament toothless.

Despite the absence of any express reference to the doctrine of necessity in constitutions, the invocation of the doctrine is not regarded by some theorists, such as George Williams and FM Brookfield, as being outside the parameters of a 'constitutional structure'. Williams (2001: 80) argues that the invocation of the doctrine is constrained by the requirement of responding to a serious crisis and preserving 'the rule of law and the existing legal order'. Brookfield (1988: 251) in the same vein notes:

> the power of a Head of State under a written Constitution extends by implication to executive acts, and also to legislative acts taken temporarily (that is, until confirmed, varied or disallowed by the lawful Legislature) to preserve or restore the Constitution.

However, practice shows that, in the absence of any express norms guiding the invocation of the doctrine of necessity, the doctrine is often invoked not to preserve the sanctity of the constitutional order but to abrogate it altogether or keep it in abeyance to suit the interests of the executive.

For instance, in Pakistan, President Iskander Mirza invoked the doctrine of necessity on 7 October 1958 to impose Martial Law throughout the country. However, the doctrine was not invoked to deal with an invasion or insurrection or to preserve the legal order but rather to ensure Mirza's survival in office. For the invocation of the doctrine of necessity was followed by the abrogation of the country's first Constitution, which was enacted in 1956, and the banning of the political parties (see Section 2.6.3.1 for details).

The above measures adopted by Mirza under the doctrine of necessity were validated by the Supreme Court of Pakistan in *State v Dosso [1958] 10 PLD (SC) 533*. Chief Justice Muhammad Munir in delivering the judgment of the Court observed:

> It sometimes happens ... that a Constitution and the national legal order under it is disrupted by an abrupt political change not within the contemplation of the Constitution ... [The] legal effect [of any such change] is not only the destruction of the existing Constitution but also the validity of the ... [new] legal order.
>
> (538)

Thus, Chief Justice Munir in essence reached the conclusion that the abrogation of the 1956 Constitution was a valid consequence of the invocation of the doctrine of necessity. This decision of the Supreme Court validating the measures taken by Mirza laid down the foundation in Pakistan for invoking the doctrine of necessity as the most efficient means for either abrogating or suspending the legal order. For, in the first place, on 25 March 1969, General Yahya invoked the doctrine of necessity for purposes other than that of dealing with a crisis of grave magnitude. The invocation was followed by the abrogation of the 1962 Constitution of Pakistan and the banning of political activities (see Section 2.6.3.2.2 for details).

Second, on 5 July 1977, General Zia-ul-Haq invoked the doctrine of necessity as a justification for suspending the 1973 Constitution and imposing Martial Law throughout Pakistan following the overthrow of the democratically elected government of Zulfikar Ali Bhutto due to widespread protest against its alleged vote-rigging in the General Election of 1977. In order to further consolidate his grip on power, General Haq placed Bhutto, who still commanded popular support, and his cabinet colleagues under protective custody. In *Begum Nusrat Bhutto v Chief of the Army Staff and Federation of Pakistan [1977] PLD (SC) 703*, the Supreme Court of Pakistan held that the measures adopted by General Haq were justified under the doctrine of necessity. It observed:

> [T]he Armed Forces of Pakistan, headed by the Chief Staff of the Pakistan Army, General Muhammad Ziaul Haq intervened to save the country from further chaos and bloodshed, to safeguard its integrity and sovereignty, and to separate the warring factions which had brought the country to the brink of disaster. It was undoubtedly an *extra-constitutional*[16] step, but obviously dictated by the highest consideration of state necessity and welfare of the people.
>
> (716)

Thus, in light of the above discussion, it can be argued that in the absence of any express norms guaranteeing that invocation of the doctrine of necessity will be confined to dealing with grave crises and the preservation of the sanctity of the constitutional order, the doctrine vests in the executive absolute and unfettered power in respect of emergency with the widest possible scope of abuse, and can be appropriately termed extra-constitutional.

2.5 The possibility of the abuse of emergency powers under the traditional constitutional and legislative emergency models

The powers of emergency carry with them the risk of abuse. Despite the notion that emergency powers are resorted to in times of grave crisis in order to end the crisis promptly by invoking appropriate measures, in the absence of any meaningful safeguards regulating their scope under the traditional models, they carry with them the disturbing and objectionable possibility of being used by the party in power for its own benefit to: a) suppress the opposition, b) impose certain unwarranted measures with a view to staying in power, and c) continue the state of emergency beyond the period of necessity when the features of grave crisis are absent.

The temporary nature of emergency has been ignored by various regimes which have invoked emergency powers. For example, being encouraged by the instances of the invocation of emergency powers granted by Article 48 of the *Constitution of the Weimar Germany*, 1919 for more than a staggering 250 times between 1919 and 1932 in order to confront major economic problems and inter-war global depression, Adolf Hitler, who ascended to the Chancellorship of Germany in 1933, proclaimed a state of emergency which lasted until the end of World War II in 1945 (Rossiter, 1948). Thus in the absence of any safeguards constraining the authority of the executive, the emergency power provided by Article 48 was resorted to as the chief mechanism for converting the Republic of Germany into a bridge leading to despotism and, ultimately, Adolf Hitler marched over this bridge to finish off the Republic (Rossiter, 1948; Gross, 2011). This is the most conspicuous instance of converting an emergency power into a stepping stone to permanent absolutism and unfettered control.

In the same vein, in Malaysia, where Article 150 of the *Federal*

Constitution has been amended on several occasions to drastically weaken the constitutional safeguards on emergency powers, emergency has been proclaimed in the whole Federation or a part thereof on four separate occasions (*States of Emergency*, 1983). It was proclaimed in 1964 throughout the Federation to deal with the hostilities from the neighbours of Malaysia during the period leading to the birth of the country (i.e. the joining of Sarawak and Sabah and the separation of Singapore); in 1966 to deal with internal jostling for power in Sarawak; in 1969 again throughout the Federation to tackle the violent communal riot that broke out in Kuala Lumpur between Malays and Chinese on 12 May 1969; and lastly, in 1977 in Kelantan to deal with the outbreak of violent political demonstrations. In the absence of any effective constitutional mechanisms for ensuring the effective scrutiny and timely termination of a proclamation of emergency, these emergencies remained in force in Malaysia until December 2011. Furthermore, these proclamations of emergency in Malaysia were used to modify the legal order by adopting a series of ordinary laws, in particular, the *Internal Security Act*, 1960, the *Emergency (Security Cases) Regulations*, 1975 and the *Societies Act*, 1966. These laws permitted prolonged detention, imposed drastic sentences for security offences, and restricted freedom of movement, freedom of association and expression, trade union rights, due process rights and political rights (*States of Emergency*, 1983). Thus the people of Malaysia became accustomed to residing under a perpetual constitutional dictatorship until 2011.

In Northern Ireland, the *Civil Authorities (Special Powers) Act* was passed in 1922 by the Parliament of Northern Ireland as emergency legislation in the context of violent conflict over the issue of the partition of Ireland to enable the government to 'take all such steps and issue all such orders as may be necessary for preserving the peace and maintaining order' (s 1). The Act, which was highly controversial due to the sweeping powers it conferred on the executive, was originally subject to annual and later quinquennial renewal (Bonner, 1985). However, in 1933 it was made permanent so that 'in a sense Northern Ireland [was] treated as being in a permanent state of emergency' (Twining, 1972: 4).

In the US, the *PATRIOT Act* was enacted by the Congress on 26 October 2001 following the 9/11 attacks to strengthen national security by broadening the scope of the powers of the law-enforcement agencies in preventing terrorist activities. This law confers broad and arbitrary powers on the executive. For instance, it concentrates wide power in the hands of the executive to capture and detain citizens and immigrants alike, without their involvement in terrorist activities, for a prolonged period of time in contravention of the 'associational First Amendment and due process rights' (Banks, 2010: 8). Despite the wideness of the powers under this Act and adverse changes it has introduced to the legal framework, e.g. relaxation of the constitutional requirement of 'the issuance of warrants based on probable cause and advance judicial review', it has been renewed repeatedly – most recently on

27 May 2011 by President Obama for a period of four years (Banks, 2010: 8; Cohen, 2011). Thus, it can be said that the Act through repeated renewals has become more or less a permanent feature of the legal system.

It, therefore, seems that the success of unconstrained emergency powers under the traditional models in dealing with crises acclimatises executives to their use, frequently leading them to cling on to these powers longer than it is necessary. Consequently, the danger is that succeeding generations of administrators inherit these powers as being efficient and unobjectionable, and do not give proper consideration to the possibility of less drastic measures being used to deal with a particular situation (O'Boyle, 1977). Hence, the real problem associated with emergency powers is one of striking the appropriate balance between the way in which a government can effectively deal with a grave emergency and, at the same time, endeavour to prevent the dangers of emergency government from occurring (O'Boyle, 1977).

2.6 Evolution of emergency powers in the Subcontinent during the colonial and post-colonial periods

2.6.1 Evolution of emergency powers in the Subcontinent during the colonial period

The historical origins of the emergency powers in the Subcontinent are to be traced back to British rule. The East India Company, which received a Charter from the British Crown as a trading entity, started doing business in India in 1613 (Mukherjee, 1973). Ultimately it managed to obtain in 1765 the entire revenue and civil administration of Bengal, Bihar and Orissa as *Dewan* (i.e. Administrator) from Emperor Shah Alam of Delhi (the then nominal ruler of India) (Bose and Bose, 1998; Mukherjee, 1973). Thereafter, by the middle of the nineteenth century, the Company succeeded in achieving its hidden objective. It became 'the undisputed ruler of India, while two-fifths of India's territory remained "independent" under the Native Rulers' (Bose and Bose, 1998: 282). However, the Subcontinent witnessed the end of the East India Company's rule in 1858 as a consequence of the *Sepoy* Mutiny, described by the Indians as the 'First War of Independence'. The British Parliament passed the *Government of India Act*, 1858, under which Queen Victoria issued a Royal Proclamation on 1 November 1858, dissolving the East India Company and assuring sovereignty over the Company's territories in the Subcontinent. Thus the year 1858 signified the beginning of England's second imperial project after the loss of its first empire in the west, with the independence of 13 former British colonies on the conclusion of the Treaty of Versailles in 1783 after eight years of the American War of Independence (Hussain, 2003). The British Parliament, which had passed statutes to regulate the affairs of the East India Company, enacted a series of laws for the governance of India. Of the statutes passed by the British Parliament, only five Acts – the *Indian Councils*

Act, 1861, the *Defence of India Act*, 1915, the *Government of India Act*, 1919, the *Government of India Act*, 1935 and the *Defence of India Act*, 1939 – contained provisions relating to emergency powers to be used in the Subcontinent.

2.6.1.1 *The Indian Councils Act, 1861*

The *Indian Councils Act*, 1861 marked the beginning of vesting the Governor-General of British India with the unilateral power of judging the existence of an emergency and, as such, the power to promulgate an ordinance for the preservation of peace and good government. The Act in Section XXIII provided that:

> it shall be lawful for the Governor-General, in cases of emergency, to make and promulgate from time to time ordinances for the peace and good government of the said territories or of any part thereof ... and every such ordinance shall have like force of law with a law of regulation made by the Governor-General in Council.

It was further provided in Section XXIII that any emergency ordinance would remain valid for a period of six months from its promulgation unless disapproved at an earlier date either by Her Majesty or superseded by ordinary legislation adopted by the Governor-General in Council.

It should be stressed here that the *Indian Councils Act*, 1861 did not specify the crises which would justify the Governor-General's resorting to his power to promulgate an emergency ordinance for the preservation of peace and good government. It did, though, provide for a maximum time limit of six months for the continuance of an emergency. The question of renewal of this time limit could not arise at all. The emergency ordinance itself would cease to exist before the period of six months if Her Majesty signified her disapproval of the ordinance or it was superseded by a law made by the Governor-General in Council.

2.6.1.2 *The Defence of India Act, 1915*

The *Defence of India Act*, which was passed on 18 March 1915, during World War I, to adapt the wartime 'emergency code' from United Kingdom for use in India, in Section 2 empowered the Governor-General to issue rules for securing the public safety and defence of British India (Alam, 1987; Kalhan et al, 2006). Thus, unlike the *Indian Councils Act*, 1861, which seemed to provide for emergency powers to ensure the defence of India from internal threats, the *Defence of India Act* provided for the exercise of emergency powers to defend India from external threats during World War I when India's very life was in jeopardy.

2.6.1.3 *The Government of India Act, 1919*

The *Government of India Act*, 1919 maintained the practice of conferring on the Governor-General of British India the absolute and unfettered authority to ascertain the existence of an emergency and the power to promulgate an ordinance for preserving peace and good government. Section 72 of the Act provided that:

> The Governor-General may, in cases of emergency, make and promulgate ordinances for the peace and good government of British India or any part thereof, and any ordinance so made shall, for the space of not more than six months from its promulgation, have the like force of law as an Act passed by the Indian legislature.

It is evident that the above provisions concerning emergency powers and their continuation were reproduced from Section XXIII of the *Indian Councils Act*, 1861. However, Her Majesty's power to signify disapproval to the continuance of an emergency ordinance for a period of six months, as had been provided for under the *Indian Councils Act*, was brought to an end. It seems that the British Parliament preferred depriving the Crown of her overseeing authority in respect of the continuance of emergency to maintain the sole decision of the Governor-General, who had also been the sole judge of the existence of emergency, in this regard uninterrupted and untouched. The Governor-General between 1921 and 1935 resorted to the power of promulgating emergency ordinances on 52 occasions (Alam, 1987).

2.6.1.4 *The Government of India Act, 1935*

The British Parliament passed the second Constitution Act, the *Government of India Act*, 1935, which incorporated into its schedule IX the provisions of Section 72 of the *Government of India Act*, 1919, under which the Governor-General of India was empowered to promulgate ordinances for the peace and good government of the country in cases of emergency. In its main body the Act under Section 102 vested the power of discretion in the hands of the Governor-General to declare that 'a grave emergency exists whereby the security of India is threatened, whether by war or internal disturbance'. Later in 1939, a new provision was added to this section with reference to the proclamation of emergency to the effect that

> [a] Proclamation of Emergency declaring that the security of India is threatened by war or by internal disturbance may be made before the actual occurrence of war or of any such disturbance if the Governor-General in his discretion is satisfied that there is imminent danger thereof.[17]

It should be stressed here that the Governor-General's power to issue a proclamation of emergency under the Act was made an independent power, not contingent on the fact that it was required to be exercised during a recess of the British Parliament when it was necessary to promulgate an ordinance for the peace and good government of the country in cases of emergency. The question of parliamentary approval of a proclamation of emergency, according to Section 102(3)(c) of the Act, arose only if it was necessary to continue it for more than six months.

Thus the modern traits of emergency emanated from the *Government of India Act*, 1935 during the colonial period in a number of ways. First, the Governor-General was invested with the unilateral power to issue a proclamation of emergency at his discretion.

Second, the *Government of India Act*, 1935 for the first time in the Subcontinent provided for the proclamation of two types of emergency, namely, emergency of war and emergency of subversion or internal disturbance. Hence the notion of emergency during the colonial period in the Subcontinent was confined to the security-oriented concept.

Third, the original 1935 *Government of India Act* provided for the proclamation of an emergency pursuant to an actual or real war/internal disturbance in which the 'security of India' was threatened. But in 1939, the Act was amended to stipulate also the imminent danger of war or internal disturbance as a ground for declaring emergency.

Finally, the unilateral declaration of emergency by the Governor-General needed the approval of the British Parliament for its continuance beyond the period of six months.

The Governor-General of the Federation of India (the Federation was declared by the *Government of India Act*, 1935) was further authorised under Section 126(5) of the Act to direct the provincial governors' exercise of their executive authority to prevent 'any grave menace to the peace or tranquillity of India or any part thereof'.

The wide and extensive emergency powers conferred on the Governor-General of British India by an Act of the British Parliament received a harsh and unfriendly remark from Sir Winston Churchill. He said that the emergency powers of the Governor-General of British India would have been 'likely "to rouse Mussolini's envy"' (Kalhan *et al.*, 2006: 131).

2.6.1.5 The Defence of India Act, 1939

On 3 September 1939, following the outbreak of World War II between Britain and Germany, the Governor-General acting under Section 102 of the *Government of India Act*, 1935 proclaimed that a grave emergency existed whereby the security of India was threatened by war (*States of Emergency*, 1983; Alam, 1987). Subsequently, the *Defence of India Ordinance* was promulgated to deal with the crisis arising out of Britain's involvement in World War II. However, in the same year, the *Defence of India Act*, 1939 was passed, repealing the *Defence of India Ordinance*. Section 2 of this new Act authorised the Government of India to exercise extensive rule-making powers with a view to securing the defence of British India, the public safety, the maintenance of public order or the efficient prosecution of war or to maintain the supplies and services essential to the life of the community.

Thus it is evident that, during the British colonial period, the Subcontinent only witnessed security-related emergencies (i.e. emergency of war and emergency of subversion). It did not experience any emergency of natural catastrophes or economic emergency. It seems that, taking into account the temporary nature of emergency, it was consistently provided that the emergency declared would remain in force for a period of six months. But the power of reducing this period of emergency, as contained in the *Indian Councils Act*, 1861, was not provided for by the *Government of India Act*, 1935. Rather the *Government of India Act*, 1935, went a step further by stipulating for extending the original period of emergency (i.e. six months), which set a new trend in the Subcontinent.

The Subcontinent was subsequently partitioned under the Indian Independence Act, passed by the British Parliament on 18 July 1947, into two independent States of India and Pakistan.[18] Later in 1971, the Eastern part of Pakistan, which had been composed of two distinct and geographically distant provinces of West Pakistan and East Bengal (from 1956 known as East Pakistan), emerged as an independent State under the name of Bangladesh. The provisions concerning emergency powers as embodied in the Constitutions of the Independent States of India, Pakistan and Bangladesh were indeed a legacy of British rule in the Subcontinent, as will be shown in the forthcoming discussion.

2.6.2 *The incorporation of emergency provisions into the Indian Constitution*

The 385-member Constituent Assembly of India, which met for the first time on 9 December 1946, adopted on 26 November 1949, after two years of deliberation, the Constitution of India to give shape and expression to the dreams and aspirations which had inspired the nationalist leaders for the long and hard struggle for freedom from British rule. Although the Constitution was adopted on 26 November 1949, it was given effect from 26 January 1950 to commemorate the declaration of independence from British rule on 26 January 1930.

The framers of the new Constitution deliberated forcefully and vigorously over the content of emergency powers for inclusion into the Constitution. Given the nascent nature of the Indian Union and democracy, strong emergency powers were considered necessary to deal with both external and internal threats (*States of Emergency*, 1983). TT Krishnamachari, a senior member of the Indian Constitutional Drafting Committee, stated on 2 August 1949 that the emergency powers were needed as a 'safety valve' for the preservation and safeguarding of the Constitution and, as such, were to be tolerated as a 'necessary evil' (Republic of India, 1949: 125). The President's power to suspend the right to move the courts for the enforcement of fundamental rights during an emergency proved more contentious. The debate centred around the issue of derogability, with emphasis on the necessity to confine the power of suspension to only a handful of rights (Republic of India, 1949). Alladi Krishnswamy Ayyar, another member of the Drafting Committee, defended the original proposal of conferring power on the President to suspend the enforcement of fundamental rights by arguing that 'a war cannot be carried on under the principles of the Magna Carta', and that 'the security of the State is more important [than] the liberty of the individual' (Republic of India, 1949: 545–547). After intense debate, the provisions concerning the proclamation of emergency were incorporated in Part XVIII of the Indian Constitution of 1950.

The original Article 352(1) of the Constitution empowered the President of India to proclaim an emergency if he was 'satisfied that a grave emergency exists whereby the security of India or of any part thereof is threatened, whether by war or external aggression or internal disturbance'. In the Constituent Assembly, the phrase 'war or external aggression or internal disturbance' was inserted in place of the proposed 'war or domestic violence' as the grounds for the declaration of emergency, at the behest of Dr Ambedkar, the Chairman of the Constitution Drafting Committee (Republic of India, 1948).

Therefore, it appears that with the exception of external aggression, the grounds for invoking emergency of war and internal disturbance by the President contained in Article 352(1) of the Indian Constitution were reproduced from the provisions of Section 102(1) of the *Government of India Act*, 1935.[19] But the proclamation of emergency on 26 June 1975 on the ground of internal disturbance and the subsequent unprecedented abuse of the emergency powers by the Government of Prime Minister Indira Gandhi's until March 1977 led the succeeding Janata Party Government to pass the *Constitution (Forty-Fourth) Amendment Act*, 1978. The Act provided for the replacement of 'internal disturbance' with 'armed rebellion' as a ground for invoking emergency (*States of Emergency*, 1983). Furthermore, originally Clause 3 of Article 352[20] of the Indian Constitution authorised the President to declare an emergency even before the actual occurrence of war or external aggression or internal disturbance.[21] This provision for issuing a proclamation of emergency in case of an imminent emergency is also reproduced from the provisions of Section 102(5) of the *Government of India Act* of 1935, as inserted by the *Government of India (Amendment) Act*, 1939, under which the Governor-General of British India was empowered to issue a proclamation of emergency even before the actual occurrence of war or internal disturbance. Moreover, following Section 102(3)(c) of the *Government of India Act*, 1935 under which a proclamation of emergency required parliamentary approval for its continuance beyond six months, it was proposed in the relevant draft Article of the Indian Constitution that the proclamation of emergency would remain valid without parliamentary approval for a period of six months. But it was due to the suggestion of Dr Ambedkar, who felt that six months was 'too long a period', that ultimately it was included in Article 352(1) of the 1950 Indian Constitution that the approval of the Parliament would be required for the continuance of the declaration of an emergency beyond two months (Republic of India, 1949; *Constitution of India 1950* art 352(2)(c). This provision of the requirement of parliamentary approval of the proclamation of emergency within two months was reduced to one month by the Indian *Constitution (Forty-Fourth Amendment) Act*, 1978 (*Constitution of India 1950* new art 352(4).

However, like the *Government of India Act*, 1935, the *Constitution of India* also does not prescribe the maximum period for which an emergency proclaimed by the President shall continue to remain in force. But unlike the *Government of India Act*, 1935, which only provided for the declaration of emergency on the grounds of (actual or apprehended) war or internal disturbance, the 1950 Indian Constitution, as amended in 1978, apart from providing for the declaration of an emergency on the grounds of war or external aggression or armed rebellion, also empowers the President in Article 360(1) to declare a financial emergency when he is satisfied that a situation has arisen whereby the financial stability or credit of India is threatened.[22] Thus, whereas the *Government of India Act*, 1935 provided for only two types of emergency – emergency of war or external aggression and subversion – out of the four kinds of emergency recognised in different jurisdictions, the *Constitution of India* recognises three types of emergency, namely, emergency of war or external aggression, emergency of subversion and economic or financial emergency. Therefore, it is evident that only the proclamation of emergency of natural catastrophes has been kept out of the domain of the President to declare under the Indian Constitution.

Hence, it is clearly apparent that in the context of the provisions concerning emergency powers no other instrument influenced the framers of the Indian Constitution as profoundly as the *Government of India* Act, 1935, the last Colonial Constitution Act. This led Alan Gledhill (1964: 3) to make the following critical comments:

> All previous Indian governments have been despotic, and the main Indian objection to the rule which ceased in 1947 was not that it was despotic, but that it was British. Despite the absorption of many Western political principles, the Indian, unless his judgment is obscured by nationalism or communalism, is prepared to concede that the ruler must be given the adequate powers to rule and to act in emergencies. We shall find, then, more willingness to entrust powers to the ruler than one would expect in a mainly British Community, and an acceleration of the centripetal tendency.

2.6.2.1 Exercise of the emergency powers in India

Since the coming into effect of the Indian Constitution in January 1950, its emergency provisions have been invoked three times: twice in 1962 and 1971 on the ground of external aggression and once in 1975 on the ground of internal disturbance. The Proclamation of Emergency declared on 25 June 1975, on the ground of the alleged threat to the security of India on account of internal disturbance, without revoking the emergency that had been proclaimed on 3 December 1971 on the ground of the threat posed to national security by the external aggression perpetrated by Pakistan, marked a watershed in the exercise of emergency powers in India.

2.6.2.1.1 THE FIRST PROCLAMATION OF EMERGENCY

The first state of emergency in India was declared on 26 October 1962 by the President, advised by the Cabinet led by Prime Minister Jawaharlal Nehru, on the ground that 'a grave situation exists whereby the security of India is threatened by external aggression', i.e. Chinese military aggression in India's north-eastern border (which later escalated into a full-scale assault on the Indian territory) (Ministry of Home Affairs, 1962). Although the invocation of the emergency power to deal with the situation in pursuance of the provisions of Article 352(1) was accepted as justified, its continuance beyond 21 November 1962, the day on which a formal cease-fire was declared by the Chinese Government bringing an end to the hostilities, led the various leaders of the opposition parties to demand quick withdrawal of the emergency. This call went unheeded. On 15 April 1963 the Prime Minister responded that 'the emergency would last a considerable time, whether there is actual fighting or not' (Schoenfeld, 1963: 235). The Prime Minister's position was further strengthened by a seven-judge Constitution bench of the Supreme Court of India in *Makhan Sing Tarsikka v State of Punjab [1964] AIR (SC) 381*, where it observed:

> How long the Proclamation of Emergency should continue … [is a matter] which must be left to the executive because the executive knows the requirements of the situation and the effect of compulsive factors which operate during periods of grave crisis, such as our country is facing today.
>
> (403)

Thus, the constitutional bench went along with the Prime Minister regarding the continuance of emergency.

After nearly three years of continuance of the first Proclamation of Emergency, India was involved in a full-scale war with Pakistan on its north-western frontier (Assam-East Pakistan border and the Rann of Kutch on the western front). The war came to an end within weeks, on 11 January 1966, when both the Indian and Pakistan Governments signed a joint declaration – the 'Tashkent Agreement' – in accordance with a United Nations Security Council resolution for the normalisation of relations between the two countries. In 1966, the Supreme Court again reiterated its inability to decide the issue of undue prolongation of the 1962 emergency in *Pol Lakhanpal v Union of India [1967] AIR (SC) 243*, stating that only the President could revoke the proclamation of emergency as the better judge of the existence of the features of a grave emergency. Thus, the Supreme Court of India failed to deal with the most obvious issue of political foot-dragging over the revocation of emergency. In February 1966, former Attorney-General of India, M. C. Setalvad, and 33 leading personalities, including former Chief Justices of India, many former High Court judges and serving Vice-Chancellors, came forward to demand and make an appeal to the Government for the revocation of the emergency forthwith, stating, *inter alia*, that 'the use of these emergency powers when the emergency has long receded is to turn a democratic government into what has been called a constitutional dictatorship' (*States of Emergency*, 1983: 177).

Eventually, the Government of India revoked the State of Emergency on 10 January 1968, more than five years after the cessation of hostilities with China and more than two years after the cessation of war with Pakistan (*Gazette of India*, 1968).

2.6.2.1.2 THE SECOND PROCLAMATION OF EMERGENCY

On 3 December 1971, as a result of the massive attack of Pakistani ground troops and air force on Indian territory from the western front as retaliation for India's support for the cause of the independence of former East Pakistan and the establishment of the independent state of Bangladesh, the President of India in pursuance of Article 352 of the Constitution issued a Proclamation declaring that 'a grave emergency exists whereby the security of India is threatened by external aggression' (*Gazette of India*, 1971). The Indian Prime Minister in her address broadcasted to the nation asserted that the 'war in Bangladesh has become a war on India. This has been [*sic*] imposed upon me, my Government and the people of India a great responsibility' (Bindra, 1981: 175).

The threat to national security, as mentioned in the Proclamation of 3 December 1971, ended on 17 December 1971 (within 15 days of the Declaration of Emergency) with the signing of an Instrument of Surrender by the Pakistani Army. The state of emergency proclaimed in 1971 was allowed nevertheless to continue in force in violation of the well-recognised principle that every exercise of emergency powers shall be confined strictly to the period of time required to deal with any threat posed to the life of the nation. More than three years after the declaration of emergency, in January 1975 a writ petition for *habeas corpus* (*Pravin Dholakia v Union of India*) was filed before the Supreme Court challenging the validity of the continuance of the emergency on the grounds that the circumstances which gave rise to the declaration of the emergency had long ceased to exist and there was no longer any threat of external aggression. A Constitutional Bench of the Supreme Court heard the arguments from March 1975 to the beginning of May 1975, i.e. before the closure of the Court for summer vacation until July 1975. But the Court could not deliver its judgment in July 1975 because of the declaration of another emergency on 25 June 1975, this time on the ground of alleged 'internal disturbance' threatening the security of India.

2.6.2.1.3 THE THIRD PROCLAMATION OF EMERGENCY (1975–1977)

The most controversial exercise of the emergency powers under the 1950 *Constitution of India* was the Proclamation issued by the President of India, on the advice of Prime Minister Mrs Indira Gandhi, declaring on 25 June 1975 that 'a grave emergency' existed whereby the security of India had been threatened by internal disturbance. This Proclamation is considered as the most controversial for the following reasons:

First, the Proclamation of 25 June 1975 was made at a time when the Emergency proclaimed on 3 December 1971, on the ground of war with Pakistan, was already in force and the powers available under the 1971 Proclamation of Emergency could have been used to deal with the alleged new situation.

Second, the 1950 *Constitution of India* did not empower the President to issue overlapping proclamations of emergency, separately on the grounds of war or external aggression and internal disturbance and, as such, apprehending the possibility of a legal challenge to the second Proclamation of Emergency of 25 June 1975, the Constitution was quickly amended to insert a new clause (4) to Article 352, empowering the President to issue overlapping proclamations of emergency with retrospective effect from 26 November 1949 (*Constitution (Thirty-Ninth Amendment) Act 1975* s 4).

Third, the manner in which Prime Minister Mrs Indira Gandhi advised the President to issue the Proclamation of Emergency on the ground of internal disturbance was highly irregular, for she did not take her Cabinet into confidence about the declaration of emergency, in violation of the requirements of the provisions of Rule 7 of the *Government of India (Transaction of Business) Rules*, 1961. Instead she invoked Rule 12 of the *Government of India (Transaction of Business) Rules*, 1961, which allowed the Prime Minister to dispense with consultation with the Cabinet in exceptional circumstances, in order to advise the President on her own to proclaim an emergency of subversion. This marked a clear departure from her earlier practice of advising the President to issue the Proclamation of Emergency of war in December 1971 (when Pakistan invaded India) after consulting the Cabinet, when she had not invoked Rule 12 of the *Transaction of Business Rules*.

Fourth, emergency on the ground of imminent threat of internal disturbance endangering the country's security was proclaimed only 13 days after the pronouncement of the judgment by Judge Jagmohan Lal Sinha of the Allahabad High Court (judgment was given on 12 June 1975), declaring Indira Gandhi's election to Parliament in 1971 from the *Raj Bareilli* constituency in Uttar Pradesh void on account of two corrupt practices (namely use of government personnel for the erection of rostrums for campaign rallies and the use of a government officer in personal election-related work), and imposing a six-year ban on her holding elected public office (Alam, 1987; Iyer, 2000). The opposition political leaders seized the moment to press for Mrs Indira Gandhi's resignation by organising street demonstrations, rallies and public meetings. On prompt appeal to the Supreme Court by the Prime Minister, the vacation judge, Krishna Iyer J, granted Mrs Indira Gandhi on 24 June 1975 a conditional stay under which she was allowed to continue as Prime Minister and attend the session of Parliament, but she was debarred from participating in the parliamentary proceedings or voting or drawing remuneration as an MP (*States of Emergency*, 1983; Ghatate, 2011). But the next day, 25 June 1975, witnessed a well-attended peaceful opposition public meeting in New Delhi, from where a call for a week-long nationwide movement of civil disobedience from 29 June 1975 was issued by prominent political leaders to exert pressure on Mrs Indira Gandhi, the head of the Congress Party Government (the party which had governed India uninterruptedly since independence) to resign (Iyer, 2000). Therefore, it is evident that in order to handle the situation with the ultimate aim of ensuring Mrs Indira Gandhi's own survival in power, emergency of subversion was declared in India on the night of 25 June 1975.

Fifth and finally, keeping in mind the Allahabad High Court's previous decision of declaring Mrs Indira Gandhi's election to Parliament invalid, retrospective amendments[23] were introduced into the *Representation of the People Act*, 1951, by the *Election Laws (Amendment) Act* 1975, empowering the President of India to condone the disqualification of a member of Parliament or a state legislative assembly from holding office (Iyer, 2000). Furthermore, pre-empting an unfavourable verdict in her appeal hearing on 11 August 1975 against the judgment of the Allahabad High Court before the Supreme Court, the *Constitution (Thirty-Ninth Amendment) Act* was passed on 10 August 1975 with unprecedented haste. All the formalities of passing the said Constitutional Bill were completed within four days of introducing the Bill before the *Lok Sabha* on 7 August 1975. The Bill was passed by the *Lok Sabha* on the same day and by the *Rajya Sabha* the next day. Ratification by the requisite number of state legislatures occurred on the following day, on 9 August 1975, and the Bill received the assent of the President on 10 August 1975. This Amendment Act incorporated a new Article 329A into the *Constitution of India*, which took away the jurisdiction of the courts to resolve disputes relating to the election of any MP who subsequently became the Prime Minister or Speaker of the *Lok Sabha* and abated any election petition relating to these functionaries which had been pending before any court (this referred to the Prime Minister's appeal before the Supreme Court). Furthermore, this Article also provided that the election of such persons to Parliament, which had previously been invalided by a court of law, would continue to be valid (Austin, 2003).

When this new Article, *inter alia*, was challenged before the Supreme Court in *Indira Nehru Gandhi v Raj Narain [1975] AIR (SC) 2299*, a majority of the Bench invalidated the provisions of Article 329A(4), purporting to eliminate judicial review of election decisions involving the Prime Minister and the Speaker. However, it upheld the validity of Mrs Indira Gandhi's election by refusing to strike down the amendments introduced into the *Representation of the People Act*, 1951,[24] which, as pointed above, nullified the effect of the judgment of the Allahabad High Court disqualifying Mrs Gandhi from holding elected office for six years. The Supreme Court of India maintained its previous tradition of refusing to scrutinise the emergency declaration.

Thus both the 1971 emergency and the 1975 emergency, which remained in force simultaneously, witnessed in 1976 the two-year extension of the duration of the House of the People – the lower House of the Parliament – through the enactment of two Acts, namely, the House of the People (Extension of Duration) Act 1976 and the House of the People (Extension of Duration) Amendment Act 1976. But the next year, Prime Minister Indira Gandhi engaged in the stratagem of holding a snap General Election on 18 March 1977, one year ahead of the scheduled date, without revoking the aforesaid two Emergency Proclamations. However, this manoeuvring did not work in Mrs Gandhi's favour as she along with most of her senior colleagues suffered a crushing defeat at the hands of the Alliance of the Opposition Parties, Janata Party, which won the election in a landslide victory. Hence Mrs Indira Gandhi, who came to power on a wave of popular support, had to pay the heavy price of being deposed from power on a wave of popular repudiation for taking India back to the days of despotic feudalism. The 1975 Proclamation of Emergency was revoked on 21 March 1977 by the Acting President, Mr B. D. Jatti, on the advice of Mrs Gandhi, given before her stepping down from the office of Prime Minister (*Gazette of India*, 1977). On 27 March 1977, six days after the assumption of power, the new Janata Party Government withdrew the 1971 Proclamation of Emergency (*Gazette of India*, 1977). Thus the two proclamations of emergency – issued in 1971 and 1975 respectively – were withdrawn by the new Government within nine days of the defeat of Mrs Gandhi in the General Elections.

2.6.3 The incorporation of emergency provisions into the Constitutions of Pakistan

Pakistan, which came into existence as an independent Dominion on 14 August 1947 after the partition of British India in pursuance of the provisions of the Indian Independence Act, 1947, has adopted three permanent

Constitutions in 1956, 1962 and 1973, within its 67-year history. The provisions concerning the proclamation of emergency occupy a prominent place in all these Constitutions, drawing heavily from the emergency provisions of the colonial constitutional framework, the *Government of India Act*, 1935. Although emergency powers were not invoked under the first *Constitution of Pakistan*, 1956, emergency was proclaimed once under the second Constitution of 1962 and once in 1971 after the abrogation of the 1962 Constitution. Pakistan also witnessed the exercise of emergency powers since 1990 on four occasions – twice in accordance with the provisions of the third Constitution of 1973 and twice while keeping the 1973 Constitution in abeyance.

2.6.3.1 Emergency powers as embodied in Pakistan's first post-colonial constitution of 1956

While India adopted its first Constitution on 16 November 1949 within about two years and four months of its independence, Pakistan took nine and a half years to enact its first Constitution after its independence, thus proving wrong the prediction of the first Governor-General of Pakistan, Quaid-e-Azam Mohammad Ali Jinnah, that Pakistan's Constitution would be framed within 18 months or two years at most (Ahmad, 1960; Ispahani, 1966). The first Constituent Assembly (elected in 1947) carried out the process of constitution-making in a 'desultory fashion for seven long years' and legal battles ensued after the dissolution of the Constituent Assembly on 24 October 1954 (Jennings, 1957: 22). The Constituent Assembly was, in reality, two bodies. First, it was a constituent assembly (the session of which was summoned by its President), which exercised its constituent powers of preparing a Constitution for Pakistan (*Indian Independence Act 1947* s 8(1). Second, it was the Federal Legislature (the session of which was convened by the Governor-General), which exercised the power to make laws for Pakistan (*Indian Independence Act 1947* s 6(1) and (6). The immediate cause of the dissolution of the Constituent Assembly by the Governor-General, Ghulam Muhammad, a retired bureaucrat, was the enactment of the *Government of India (Fifth Amendment) Act*, 1954, while he was absent from the capital Karachi. For this Act abolished his power to appoint and dismiss the Prime Minister and other Ministers. The Governor-General, in his Proclamation, issued on 24 October 1954, described this event as 'the political crisis with which the country is faced', and said that it led him with deep regret to 'the conclusion that the constitutional machinery was broken down' (*Gazette of Pakistan*, 1954). Therefore, he 'called upon the Prime Minister' Muhammad Ali Bogra, another retired bureaucrat, to reconstitute the 'cabinet with a view to giving the country a vigorous and stable administration' (*Gazette of Pakistan*, 1954). In the newly reconstituted Cabinet, the bureaucracy-dominated executive inducted General Ayub Khan, the Commander-in-Chief of the Army as the Defence Minister, which marked the beginning of the formal entry of the military into Pakistan's political arena. Furthermore, the Governor-General expressed his view that the Constituent Assembly in its present composition 'has lost the confidence of the people and can no longer function' and, accordingly, the Constituent Assembly was dissolved (*Gazette of Pakistan*, 1954).

It seems that in order to avoid public opposition to the action of dissolving the Constituent Assembly, the Governor-General in the aforesaid Proclamation considered it necessary to state his decision of declaring 'a state of emergency throughout Pakistan' (*Gazette of Pakistan*, 1954). The Proclamation of Emergency did not contain any reference to the security of Pakistan or any part thereof being threatened by real or imminent danger of war or internal disturbance. It is true that the first Constituent Assembly failed to accomplish its task of adopting the Constitution of Pakistan for more than seven years. But the Prime Minister, Muhammad Ali Bogra, who had been inducted to the office of Prime Minister after the dismissal of Khawaja Nazimuddin on 17 April 1953, expressed his optimism in the Constituent Assembly in September 1954 by stating that 'we shall be able to finalise the constitution-making completely by the end of this year' (Islamic Republic of Pakistan 1954: 503–504; Jennings, 1957). Subsequently, the Drafting Committee completed the Draft Constitution by working day and night (Islamic Republic of Pakistan 1954). Confidential copies were printed and distributed among the members in time for discussion in the meeting of the Constituent Assembly scheduled for 27 October 1954 (Bari, 2015). Thus it appears that the discord and dissension between the executive (the civilian federal bureaucracy) and the legislative branches of the Government culminated in the dissolution of the first Constituent Assembly, which resulted in further delay in the adoption of the first *Constitution of Pakistan*.

The second Constituent Assembly was composed of 80 members (of whom only 14 were members of the defunct Assembly). They were elected by the provincial assemblies on the basis of proportional representation, by means of single transferable vote. Although the Assembly's deliberation began on 7 July 1955, the debate on the emergency provisions started in February 1956. It was Mahmud Ali who first took the floor and opposed the conferment of the power of proclaiming emergency on the President on account of external aggression or internal disturbance. He referred to the issuance of the proclamation of emergency in Pakistan 'without sufficient grounds' during the previous eight years. He also opposed the inclusion of 'internal disturbance' as one of the three grounds for declaring emergency on the ground that the meaning of internal disturbance is not as precise and definite as that of war or external aggression. In support of his contention, he referred to two past incidents in which opposition to a Government's particular measure and the defeat of the Muslim League in the 1954 East Bengal Provincial Legislature Election were considered as internal disturbance for which proclamations of emergency were issued (Islamic Republic of Pakistan 1956). Accordingly, Mahmud Ali proposed an amendment to confine the grounds of proclaiming emergency to war and armed rebellion, excluding the grounds of external aggression and internal disturbance so that a *mala fide* exercise of the emergency powers could be forestalled (Islamic Republic of Pakistan 1956).

Sheikh Mujibur Rahman, who became the first President of Bangladesh in 1971 and later assumed the office of Prime Minister of the country in 1972, also opposed the inclusion of internal disturbance in the proposed Constitution as one of the grounds for proclaiming emergency, citing the removal of the United Front Party from power in the East Bengal after the March 1954 elections through the exercise of Section 92A of the *Government of India Act*, 1935 on the plea of internal disturbance (Islamic Republic of Pakistan 1956). Another member of the Assembly, Muhammad Abdul Khaleque, followed the lead of Mahmud Ali by moving the proposal to substitute 'internal disturbance' with 'rebellion' (Islamic Republic of Pakistan 1956). Abul Mansur Ahmad also supported the proposal of Mahmud Ali to authorise the proclamation of emergency in the event of war and rebellion (i.e. advocating for the exclusion of 'external aggression' as a ground and the replacement of 'internal disturbance' with 'rebellion') (Islamic Republic of Pakistan 1956). But ultimately not a single amendment proposal put forward by the Opposition was accepted. The Treasury Bench, in order to pacify and soften the Opposition, moved a proposal to qualify 'internal disturbance' as a ground for declaring an emergency with the words 'when such a disturbance proved beyond the power of the Provincial Government to control'. Another important amendment proposal introduced before the Constituent Assembly by Mr Zahiruddin was to fix a 30-day limit for laying the proclamation of emergency before the National Assembly (Islamic Republic of Pakistan 1956). This proposal was also rejected. Instead the original vague expression 'as soon as conditions make it practicable' for summoning the National Assembly by the President for laying before it the proclamation, remained intact. After years of uncertainty, the Constitution Bill was finally adopted on 29 February 1956 by the Constituent Assembly and assented to by the Governor-General on 2 March 1956. The new Constitution came into force on 23 March 1956 (*Constitution of Pakistan 1956* preamble para 14).

It should be pointed out here that the second Constituent Assembly 'authorised the final Constitution within a period of eight months and 15 days by holding one continuous session consisting of 83 meetings and without sitting as the Federal Legislature even for a single day' (Oraction, 1968: 224). But Lossiete A Oraction (1968: 104) stresses that the first Constituent Assembly should also be given credit 'for laying the foundation of the 1956 Constitution [by adopting the Objectives Resolution (the general direction), the Basic Principles Committee Report, and the 1954 Draft Constitution] upon which the second Constituent Assembly constructed the superstructure'.

Like Section 102(1) of the *Government of India Act*, 1935, which was adopted by the *Pakistan (Provincial Constitution) Order*, 1947 to serve as the provisional constitution of the country pending the framing of the new constitution by the Constituent Assembly of Pakistan, Article 191(1) of the 1956 *Constitution of Pakistan* also provided for the proclamation of two types of emergency, namely, emergency of war and emergency of internal disturbance. However, the new Constitution went further, a) by adding a new alternative ground of external aggression (i.e. invasion of Pakistan by an enemy country), and b) by providing for any threat to the financial stability or credit of Pakistan as the basis of proclaiming emergency (*Constitution of Pakistan 1956* art 194). Whereas Section 102(5) of the Government of India Act 1935, as amended in 1939, had provided for the proclamation of emergency before the actual occurrence of war or internal disturbance if the Governor-General was satisfied that there was imminent danger thereof, Article 191(7) of the 1956 Constitution empowered the President to invoke the emergency power before the actual occurrence of war or external aggression but not in case of internal disturbance. Like Section 102(3) of the Government of India Act 1935, Article 191(6) of the 1956 Constitution of Pakistan also provided for laying the proclamation of emergency before the parliament, without specifying any time limit for which it could remain in force until revoked by a subsequent proclamation.

However, during the continuance of the 1956 Constitution (March 1956–October 1956) not a single emergency was proclaimed. It was the first elected President (elected by the second Constituent Assembly on 5 March 1956 in accordance with the Constitution), Major-General Iskander Mirza, who abrogated the 1956 Constitution of Pakistan and banned political parties by proclaiming Martial Law on 7 October 1958 and appointing the Commander-in-Chief of the Army, General Ayub Khan, as the Chief Martial Law Administrator (Hasan, 1962; Kaushik, 1963).

It seems that President Mirza's ultimate objective when declaring Martial Law was to forestall the first General Election under the 1956 Constitution, scheduled for February 1959, as he did not foresee any chance of becoming President for the second time after the elections. But he was paid back with the same coin: he could not fulfil his pledge given to the nation in his Proclamation of Martial Law to 'devise a Constitution more suitable to the genius of the Muslim people', in place of the 1956 Constitution which was 'full of dangerous compromise'. For President Mirza was compelled to step down by his appointee Chief Martial Law Administrator, General Ayub Khan, only 20 days after the Proclamation of Martial Law on 27 October 1958 (Hasan, 1962; Kaushik, 1963). With Ayub Khan's assumption of the office of the President, the Pakistan Army's involvement in politics manifested distinct advances towards praetorianism.

With the abrogation of the 1956 *Constitution of Pakistan* in 1958, a very well-circulated newspaper's editorial comment, made in March 1956, came true. It had been noted that:

> We do not think that Pakistan's final and permanent Constitution has yet been written because we are convinced that when the passions and prejudices of the present die down the vision of the GRAND CONCEPTION will become clearer.
>
> ('This Great Day' 1956: 1)

2.6.3.2 The 1962 Constitution of Pakistan

In the referendum that took place on 14 February 1960, almost 96 per cent of the electorate, consisting of 80,000 members of local bodies, voted for General Ayub Khan as the President of Pakistan. This massive mandate was claimed as the mandate to enact a new Constitution of the country (Feldman, 1967). Accordingly, on 17 February 1960, the President set up a Constitutional Commission headed by the Chief Justice of Pakistan, Muhammad Shahabuddin, with ten senior justices as members. Five of them were from East Pakistan and the other five from West Pakistan. The Commission submitted its draft on 6 May 1961 to the President who along with his cabinet thoroughly examined the draft. The cabinet approved the text of the new Constitution in January 1962 and President Ayub Khan promulgated the Presidential and quasi-Federal Constitution on 1 March 1962. It came into effect on 8 June 1962 (Secretariat of the Asian-African Legal Consultative Committee, 1968; Munir, 1975).

Like the abrogated 1956 Constitution, the 1962 *Constitution of Pakistan* provided for war, external aggression and internal disturbance as the grounds for proclaiming emergency by the President, and the expression 'imminent danger of being threatened' as a precondition for the declaration of the emergency was made applicable only in cases of war or external aggression, not in case of internal disturbance (*Constitution of Pakistan 1962* art 30(1). But like the *Government of India Act*, 1935 and unlike the 1956 Constitution, the 1962 Constitution did not provide for the proclamation of financial emergency. Furthermore, unlike the *Government of India Act*, 1935 and the 1956 *Constitution of Pakistan*, the 1962 Constitution spoke only of laying a proclamation of emergency, as soon as practicable, before the National Assembly not for the approval of the Assembly but for further continuance of the emergency (*Constitution of Pakistan 1962* art 30(2).

2.6.3.2.1 FIRST PROCLAMATION OF EMERGENCY IN 1965 UNDER THE 1962 CONSTITUTION

Pakistan experienced the first Proclamation of Emergency under its permanent Constitution, the Constitution of 1962, on 6 September 1965, when President Ayub Khan declared an emergency on account of war that had broken out with India over the Kashmir dispute. The war with India ended within three weeks (17 days) and on 11 January 1966 a joint declaration, the

Tashkent Agreement, was signed by both the Indian and Pakistan Governments with a view to normalising their relationship.

However, despite the cessation of hostilities with India, the state of emergency continued to remain in force. When it was challenged, *inter alia*, in *Abdul Baqi Baluch v Government of Pakistan [1968] PLD (SC) 313* in 1968, Justice Hamoodur Rahman of the Supreme Court held that

> it cannot be said merely because hostilities have ceased, the emergency is also at an end. This is a purely political question which is outside the competence of the Courts to decide ... No Court can give a declaration that a state of war has ceased to exist when the Chief Executive does not say so.
>
> (330)

Similarly, in *MM Mansur Ali v Arodhendu Shekhar Chattarjee [1968] 71 ILR 708*, the Supreme Court of Pakistan held that the question of whether or not the circumstances which gave rise to a state of emergency had ceased to operate could only be decided by the executive.

The Supreme Court of Pakistan in both of these cases did not even put it on record that there appeared to be no justification for the continuance of the emergency proclaimed in 1965, as the circumstances, i.e. the hostilities with India, had ceased to exist for three years. Thus other than the courts, the only alternative and effective remedy that existed was to mobilise vocal public opinion against the continuance of the prolonged emergency. Ultimately, the opposition parties of Pakistan succeeded in launching a widespread political agitation against President Ayub Khan, demanding the revocation of the state of emergency that had remained in force since September 1965. President Ayub Khan ultimately gave in to the popular demand and the emergency was revoked in 1969 after four years of continuation. However, General Ayub Khan then stepped down from the Presidency, giving reasons in his letter of 24 March 1969[25] to General Yahya Khan, the Commander-in-Chief of Pakistani Army. The handing over of power to General Yahya Khan instead of the Speaker of Parliament, as required by Article 16 of the 1962 *Constitution of Pakistan*, reflected Ayub's contemptuous attitude towards the politicians.

2.6.3.2.2 PROCLAMATION OF EMERGENCY ISSUED IN 1971 AFTER THE ABROGATION OF THE 1962 CONSTITUTION OF PAKISTAN

President Ayub Khan in his letter of 24 March 1969 asked General Yahya Khan to perform his 'legal and constitutional responsibility' of saving the country from 'internal disorder and chaos'. General Yahya Khan performed his 'constitutional responsibility' not only by proclaiming Martial Law throughout the country on 25 March 1969 but also by abrogating the 1962 *Constitution of Pakistan* and temporarily prohibiting political activities. He assumed the office of the Chief Martial Law Administrator and on 31 March 1969 became the country's President (*Asma Jilani v Punjab [1972] PLD (SC) 139*, 183). President Yahya Khan's postponement of the first session of the newly constituted Constituent Assembly on 1 March 1971 triggered the first massive movement of civil disobedience in the eastern wing of Pakistan (East Pakistan) (see Section 1.3). The President described the legitimate attempt of the inhabitants of East Pakistan (known as Bengalis) to assert their rights won in the December 1970 General Election for Constituent Assembly seats as an 'armed rebellion' and on 25 March 1971 ordered a genocidal military action to put down the so-called 'armed rebellion' in East Pakistan (LaPorte Jr., 1972). This led to the declaration of independence by the Eastern Wing (now Bangladesh) from Pakistan on 26 March 1971.

In the civil war that broke out between the Bengali Nationalists and the Pakistan Army, India extended massive support to the former. As a result, hostilities between Pakistan and India began. President Yahya Khan issued a Proclamation of Emergency on 23 November 1971 in exercise of his power under the *Provisional Constitution Order*, 1969, which required that he be 'satisfied that a grave emergency exists in which Pakistan is threatened by external aggression' (*Gazette of Pakistan*, 1971). Although the war declared on 3 December 1971 came to an end on 16 December 1971 with the signing of an Instrument of Surrender between the Pakistan Army and the eastern wing of Pakistan (now Bangladesh), which saw the emergence of Bangladesh as an independent nation, the Proclamation of Emergency remained in force. President and Chief Martial Law Administrator General Yahya Khan was compelled to step down and Zulfikar Ali Bhutto, the leader of the majority party, Pakistan People's Party (PPP) (which had won 88 seats in the 1970 elections), assumed both offices on 20 December 1971. The National Assembly, which had been elected in the 1970 General Elections as a Constituent Assembly, was entrusted with the task of framing a new Constitution for Pakistan. In 1972, the Assembly adopted an interim Constitution that came into force on 21 April 1972 (*Interim Constitution of the Islamic Republic of Pakistan 1972* preamble paragraphs 1 and 3). This interim Constitution provided that the

> Proclamation of Emergency, issued on the twenty-third day of November 1971, shall be deemed to be a Proclamation of Emergency issued under this Article and any law, or rule or order made or purported to have been made in pursuance of that Proclamation shall be deemed to have been validly made'.
>
> (*Interim Constitution of the Islamic Republic of Pakistan 1972* art 139(8)

It was also provided that '[a] Proclamation of Emergency issued or deemed to have been issued under this Article shall not be called in question in any court' (*Interim Constitution of the Islamic Republic of Pakistan 1972* art 139(9).

By an order of the new President, Fazal Elahi Chaudhry (Zulfikar Ali Bhutto relinquished the offices of President on 20 April 1972 to become Prime Minister), it was declared that the Proclamation of Emergency of 23 November 1971 was still in force (*Gazette of Pakistan*, 1973). The 1971 Proclamation of Emergency remained in force until 1977 (almost six years) through the successive periodic extension of six months by the Parliament (*Gazette of Pakistan*, 1974).

The prolongation of the 1971 Proclamation of Emergency by means of periodic extension for a period of about six years, beyond the exigency of external aggression which initially gave rise to it, can hardly be justified.

2.6.3.3 The 1973 Constitution of Pakistan and the emergency provisions

The 1972 *Interim Constitution of Pakistan* was replaced about one year after its enactment by the *Constitution of the Islamic Republic of Pakistan*, which was adopted by the National Assembly on 12 April 1973 and came into force on 14 August 1973. This Constitution has been in force for more than 43 years (until July 2017) although subject to several amendments and suspension (to be referred to in Sections 2.6.3.3.1, 2.6.3.3.3, 2.6.3.3.4 and Chapter 3.9.2.2.5.2). It seems that this 1973 Constitution may be 'Pakistan's final and permanent Constitution', adopted after the 'passions and prejudices ... die[d] down' and the 'vision of the GRAND CONCEPTION' became 'clearer', as was predicted in the Dawn's editorial on 1 March 1956. The 1973 Constitution is unique for Pakistan as it was the first Constitution of the country framed by the directly elected representatives of the Constituent Assembly and was passed unanimously. However, it should be stressed here that the 1973 *Constitution of Pakistan* was profoundly influenced by the 1956 Constitution regarding the types of emergency and issuance of the proclamation of emergency. Like Article 191(1) of the 1956 Constitution, Article 232(1) of the 1973 Constitution provides that if the President is satisfied that a grave emergency exists, in which the security of Pakistan or any part thereof is threatened by war or external aggression or by internal disturbance beyond the power of a Provincial Government to control, he/she may issue a proclamation of emergency. Apart from providing for the emergency of war or external aggression and of internal disturbance, Article 235 of the 1973 Constitution also provides for the proclamation of financial emergency, following the example of Article 194(1) of the 1956 *Constitution of Pakistan*. Therefore, the discussion and comments made while comparing the provisions of the 1956 Constitution and the *Government of India Act*, 1935 will *mutatis mutandis* be applicable here.

However, unlike the *Government of India Act*, 1935, and the 1956 and 1962 Constitutions of Pakistan, the 1973 *Constitution of Pakistan* does not provide that a proclamation of emergency of war or external aggression may be made before the actual occurrence of war or any such aggression if the

President is satisfied that there is imminent danger thereof. Furthermore, unlike the *Government of India Act*, 1935, and the 1956 and 1962 Constitutions of Pakistan, which did not specify any time limit for laying the proclamation of emergency before the Parliament, Pakistan's 1973 Constitution for the first time in Article 232(7) provides that '[a] Proclamation of Emergency shall be laid before a joint sitting [of the two Houses of Parliament] which shall be summoned by the President to meet within thirty days of the Proclamation being issued'. The Proclamation 'shall cease to be in force at the expiration of two months unless before the expiration of that period it has been approved by a resolution of the joint sitting' of the Parliament (*Constitution of Pakistan 1973* art 232(7)(a). The Proclamation of Emergency may be extended by a similar resolution 'for a period not extending six months at a time' (*Constitution of Pakistan 1973* art 232(7)(b). Furthermore, unlike the 1956 and 1962 Constitutions of Pakistan, Article 232(6) of the 1973 Constitution of Pakistan empowers the Parliament during the continuance of a proclamation of emergency to extend 'the term of the National Assembly for a period not exceeding one year and not extending in any case beyond a period of six months after the Proclamation has ceased to be in force'.

2.6.3.3.1 FIRST PROCLAMATION OF EMERGENCY UNDER THE 1973 CONSTITUTION OF PAKISTAN IN AUGUST 1990

The 1973 *Constitution of Pakistan*, as pointed out earlier in 2.4.3.1, was suspended on 5 July 1977 by the then Chief of the Army Staff, General Zia-ul-Haq, after placing the entire country under Martial Law. In March 1985, he decided to restore the Constitution, and consequently issued on 2 March 1985 'The Revival of the 1973 Constitution Order 1985 (P. O. No. 14 of 1985)'. In November 1985, he persuaded the two Houses of the National Assembly, elected on a non-party basis, to pass the *Constitution (Eighth Amendment) Act*, which introduced changes, *inter alia*, to the provisions of Articles 48 and 58 of the Constitution, thereby conferring unfettered powers on the President to dissolve the National Assembly in his discretion. In particular, the amended Article 58(2) provided:[26]

> the President may … dissolve the National Assembly in his discretion where, in his opinion:
> (a) a vote of no-confidence having been passed against the Prime Minister, no other member of the National Assembly is likely to command the confidence of the majority of the members of the National Assembly …; or
> (b) a situation has arisen in which the Government of the Federation cannot be carried on in accordance with the provisions of the Constitution and an appeal to the electorate is necessary.

Thus the *Constitution (Eighth Amendment) Act* tilted the balance of power in favour of the President by giving him untrammelled discretionary powers to dissolve the National Assembly and dismiss the Prime Minister. On 29 May 1988, General Zia-ul-Haq for the first time used Article 58(2)(b) of the Constitution to dissolve the National Assembly and dismiss Prime Minister Muhammad Khan Junejo.

After the death of President General Zia-ul-Haq in August 1988, Ghulam Ishaq Khan, a former bureaucrat, Finance Minister and Chairman of the Senate (of the National Assembly), became the President of the Country for the interim period and was then elected as the regular President in December 1988. In the General Election held in November, 1988, Pakistan People's Party (PPP) managed to win 92 seats out of the 207 National Assembly seats and its leader Benazir Bhutto was invited to become the Prime Minister after her party managed to engineer a majority in the Assembly by entering into an alliance with the *Mujahir Quami Movement* (Bari, 2015). However, Ms Bhutto entered the office of Prime Minister with the clear understanding that defence and foreign policy would remain under the President's control which, later on, led her to lament 'I am in office but not in power' (Lamb, 1991: 107). Soon disagreements between the President and the Prime Minister surfaced, centring around the latter's declared aim to repeal the *Constitution (Eight Amendment) Act*, her appointments of senior military commanders (Director of Inter-Services Intelligence, Chairman of the Joint Chiefs of Staff), the use of the military to contain ethnic strife in the Prime Minister's home province of Sindh, and her resentment over the President's insistence that she inform him of all decisions that did not necessarily fall under the President's jurisdiction (for which she received 323 memos over 20 months on wide-ranging issues) (Ziring, 1991; Abbas, 1993).

The reaction of President Ghulam Ishaq Khan was to issue an Order on 6 August 1990 under amended Article 58(2)(b) of the 1973 *Constitution of Pakistan*, dissolving the National Assembly and dismissing the Prime Minister and her Cabinet (*Gazette of Pakistan*, 1990). The Order mentioned various reasons including 'corruption and nepotism in the Federal Government', failure 'to protect the Province of Sind against internal disturbances', usurping 'the authority of the provinces', and publicly ridiculing the 'Superior Judiciary' (*Gazette of Pakistan*, 1990). The last of these referred to a seminar in which the decision of the Supreme Court in 1979, disallowing appeal of the deposed Prime Minister Zulfikar Ali Bhutto against his death sentence, was termed a 'judicial murder'. These reasons led the President to form the 'opinion that the Government of the Federation cannot be carried on in accordance with the provisions of the Constitution and an appeal to the electorate is necessary' (*Gazette of Pakistan*, 1990). Thus the President did not keep in mind that Article 58(2)(a) and (b) (as stated above) provided for only the dissolution of the National Assembly, not the dismissal of the Cabinet and the Prime Minister. The President did not even care to resort to the constitutional means of asking the Prime Minister to seek a vote of no confidence, as mentioned in Article 58(2)(a) of the Constitution, before taking these actions.

On 6 August 1990, the day on which the Prime Minister and her Cabinet were dismissed, Pakistan witnessed the first Proclamation of Emergency under Article 232 of the 1973 Constitution. The Proclamation read:

> the President is satisfied that grave emergency exists in which the security of Pakistan is threatened by external aggression and by internal disturbance beyond the power of Provincial Government to control.

Thus the Proclamation speaks of real or actual external aggression and internal disturbance, which did not exist at that time in Pakistan. In fact, emergency was proclaimed to deal with the perceived agitation or disturbance that could crop up over the dismissal of the Prime Minister, the Cabinet and the National Assembly. The emergency lasted for only three months: it was withdrawn on 7 November 1990 after the holding of the General Elections (Flanz, 1999).

Although the Proclamation of Emergency of 6 August 1990 was not challenged before a court of law, the dissolution of the National Assembly by the President was challenged in *Ahmad Tariq Rahim v Federation of Pakistan [1991] PLD (Lahore) 78* before the High Court of Lahore. The Court held that the President's Order of 6 August 1990 dissolving the National Assembly and dismissing the Prime Minister and the Cabinet had 'been validly passed and is not liable to be interfered with' (90).[27]

2.6.3.3.2 SECOND PROCLAMATION OF EMERGENCY UNDER THE 1973 CONSTITUTION OF PAKISTAN IN MAY 1998

Pakistan carried out five nuclear tests on 28 May 1998 in response to India's five similar tests on 11 and 13 May, considering the Indian tests to be a security threat to the country and responding to the growing domestic pressure for such testing in order to restore 'strategic balance'. After receiving definite information about the probability of Indian attacks on Pakistan's Nuclear Installations before the dawn of 28 May 1998, the Armed Forces of Pakistan were put on red-alert for protection of the nuclear sites and territorial frontiers of Pakistan (*Farooq Ahmad Khan Leghari v Federation of Pakistan [1999] PLD (SC) 57*, 62). After carrying out the nuclear tests, President Rafiq Tarar, who became the President of Pakistan on 1 January 1998, in pursuance of Article 232(1) of the 1973 Constitution issued a Proclamation of Emergency on his satisfaction 'that a grave emergency exists in which the security of Pakistan is threatened by external aggression and by internal disturbance beyond the power of Provincial Governments to control' (*Gazette of Pakistan*, 1998).

In a surprising move, former President of Pakistan, Sardar Farooq Ahmad Khan Leghari, whom President Tarar succeeded, challenged the 1998 imposition of emergency, in *Farooq Ahmad Khan Leghari v Federation of Pakistan [1999] PLD (SC) 57*. Ajmal Mian, Chief Justice of the Supreme Court of Pakistan, rightly held that *prima facie* there was some material 'to demonstrate that at the relevant time there was "animus belligerendi" on the part of the Indian Government' and 'on the basis of which the President could issue the impugned Proclamation of Emergency on account of imminent danger of external aggression' (189–190). Over and above, Chief Justice Ajmal Mian held that notwithstanding the ouster of jurisdiction of the Court (by Article 236(2) of the 1973 Constitution, which provides that the validity of any Proclamation of Emergency issued or Order made during the continuance of an emergency 'shall not be called in question in any court'), the Court has the jurisdiction to examine whether the prerequisites provided for in the relevant provisions (of Article 232(1)) of the Constitution for the exercise of the power thereunder existed when the impugned order was passed (72, 76). The Court will, therefore, be competent to examine whether a Proclamation issued under Article 232(1) is without jurisdiction, *coram non judice* or *mala fide* (72, 178).

Thus, for the first time in the history of Pakistan, the Supreme Court took the view that the satisfaction of the President to declare emergency was not final and conclusive and, as such, was justiciable in a court of law. In fact, the Supreme Court of Pakistan echoed the views of Justice Bhagwati of the Supreme Court of India, expressed in *Minerva Mills Ltd and others v Union of India and others [1980] AIR (SC) 1789*, while dealing with the basic structure of the Indian Constitution and the amending power of the Parliament. As Justice Bhagwati observed:

> The satisfaction of the President ... is condition precedent to the exercise of [emergency] power under Article 352, clause (1) and if it can be shown that there is no satisfaction of the President at all, the exercise of the power would be constitutionally invalid ... A Proclamation of Emergency is undoubtedly amenable to judicial review though on the limited ground that no satisfaction as required by Article 352 was arrived at by the President or that the satisfaction was absurd or perverse or mala fide or based on an extraneous or irrelevant ground.
>
> (para 10)

2.6.3.3.3 FIRST PROCLAMATION OF EXTRA-CONSTITUTIONAL EMERGENCY IN PAKISTAN IN 1999

On 14 October 1999, Pakistan experienced another Proclamation of Emergency issued not by the President of the Country under Article 232(1) of the 1973 *Constitution of Pakistan*, but by General Pervez Musharraf in his capacity as the Chairman of the Joint Chiefs of Staff Committee and Chief of Army Staff 'in pursuance of deliberations and decisions of Chiefs of Staff of the Armed Forces and Corps Commanders of Pakistan Army'.[28] The whole of Pakistan was placed 'under the control of the Armed Forces' (Cushing, 2003: 623–624). This Emergency was proclaimed at a time when the 1998 Proclamation of Emergency issued by President Tarar was still in force. General Musharraf, who had been fired by Prime Minister Nawaz Sharif on 13 October 1999, while taking over the affairs of the country assumed to himself the title of 'Chief Executive', which can be compared with the office of the Prime Minister who acts as the chief executive in a parliamentary democracy (Cushing, 2003). He appointed an eight-member National Security Council as the premier governing body. Initially, in order to demonstrate that he was not power hungry, General Musharraf allowed President Tarar to 'continue in office' (Cushing, 2003: 623–624). However, General Musharraf soon consolidated his position by removing Mr Tarar from the Presidency on 20 June 2001 and installing himself as the new President of Pakistan (Burns, 2001). So long as President Tarar was in office, he was required under Article 3 of the *Provisional Constitutional Order No I* of 1999, issued by General Musharraf on the very same day after the Proclamation of Emergency, to act on and in accordance with the advice of the Chief Executive.

Unlike a typical *coup d'état*, General Musharraf preferred not to abrogate the 1973 Constitution of Pakistan but to keep it in abeyance. It seems that he took notice of Article 6 of the Constitution in deciding not to abrogate the Constitution. For Article 6 of the Constitution provided[29] that any effort to abrogate or subvert the constitution by use of force or other unconstitutional means would constitute treason. However, it should be pointed out that the 1973 Constitution did not under any of its provisions permit the suspension of the Constitution. It can be further argued that suspension of the Constitution by Musharraf could indeed be construed as subversion of the Constitution under Article 6, and, as such, Musharraf's action constituted treason.

The Proclamation of Emergency issued on 28 May 1998 was nevertheless allowed to continue, subject to the provisions of the Proclamation of Emergency of 14 October 1999 and the *Provisional Constitution Order No 1 1999*. The *Provisional Constitution Order No. I* of 1999, which provided that Pakistan would be governed as nearly as possible in accordance with the provisions of the suspended Constitution of 1973, debarred any Court, Tribunal or other authority under Article 4(1) from calling in question the Proclamation of Emergency of 14 October 1999 or any order made in pursuance thereof. It also provided under Article 4(2) that '[n]o judgment, decree, writ, order or process whatsoever shall be made or issued by any court or tribunal against the Chief Executive or any authority designated by the Chief Executive'.

Thus General Pervez Musharraf's Proclamation of Emergency of 14 October 1999 in pursuance of the decisions of Chiefs of Staff of the Armed Forces and Corps Commanders of Pakistan Army was an extra-constitutional measure of usurping executive and legislative powers suspending the 1973

Constitution of Pakistan. For the 1973 Constitution only empowers the President to declare emergency when the security of Pakistan is threatened by war or external aggression or by internal disturbance and the Chief of Army Staff General's Proclamation of Emergency contained no mention of such an exigency. Thus it is clear that Musharraf's Proclamation of Emergency did not constitute a legitimate exercise of constitutional emergency power. In fact, his Proclamation of Emergency and the *Provisional Constitution Order No I* of 1999 was not an ordinary constitutional emergency and cannot be distinguished from the declarations of Martial Law in Pakistan in 1958, 1969 and 1977 after army takeovers. Thus Musharraf set a new pattern in Pakistan – the pattern of characterising the military coup as an emergency rather than Martial Law, apparently with a view 'to make the military intervention acceptable ... [to the people of Pakistan who had witnessed several Martial Law regimes in the past] and to give it a benign political appearance to the outside world' (Maluka, 2004: 55).

The validity of the army takeover, the issuance of the Proclamation of Emergency, and the promulgation of *Provincial Constitution Order No. I* of 1999 were challenged in *Zafar Ali Shah v Pervez Musharraf, Chief Executive of Pakistan [2000] PLD (SC) 869* before the Supreme Court of Pakistan. Chief Justice Irshad Hasan Khan, who had sworn a new oath of office under the Oath of Office (Judges) Order, 2000 to uphold General Musharraf's 1999 *Provisional Constitution Order* and subsequent executive actions, delivered the judgment of the Court. He observed:

> [Since] there was no remedy provided in the Constitution to meet the situation like the present one with which the country was confronted ... [the] constitutional deviation made by the Chief of Army Staff, General Pervez Musharraf for the welfare of the people rather than abrogating the Constitution or imposing Martial Law by means of an extra-constitutional measure is validated for a transitional period on ground of State necessity and on the principle that it is in public interest to accord legal recognition to the present regime with a view to achieving his declared objectives. (1218)

Thus the Supreme Court of Pakistan, as expected, legitimised General Pervez Musharraf's military coup of 1999 through questionable jurisprudence of state necessity: the army takeover was 'extra-constitutional' but still valid under the doctrine of 'state necessity'.

2.6.3.3.4 SECOND PROCLAMATION OF EXTRA-CONSTITUTIONAL EMERGENCY IN PAKISTAN IN 2007

It may be recalled here that the 1973 *Constitution of Pakistan* empowers the President to invoke emergency powers if he is satisfied that Pakistan's security is threatened by war or external aggression or internal disturbance and that the Constitution curtails judicial review of the validity of the emergency proclamation or any order issued pursuant to it. The President can also suspend the judicial enforcement of fundamental rights. However, these traditional emergency powers do not confer on the President the power to suspend the Constitution (in fact the 1973 Constitution in Article 6(1) provides that any person who abrogates or subverts the Constitution shall be guilty of high treason) or amend its provisions to fashion structural changes to suit his objectives. It seems that taking into account these limitations, President of Pakistan and Chief of Army Staff General Pervez Musharraf issued a Proclamation of Emergency on 3 November 2007 in his capacity as the Chief of Army Staff, rather than as the President of Pakistan. For this reason, his proclamation stated, *inter alia*, that

> a situation has … arisen where the Government of the Country cannot be carried on in accordance with the Constitution and as the Constitution provides no solution for this situation, there is no way out except through emergent and extraordinary measures.
>
> (*Proclamation of Emergency 2007*, preamble para 12)

Consequently, the *Constitution of the Islamic Republic of Pakistan* was ordered to 'remain in abeyance' and the *Provisional Constitution Order No. 1* of 2007, issued just after the Proclamation of Emergency, conferred on the President, *inter alia*, the ultimate law-making authority, including unilateral authority to promulgate constitutional amendments (*Proclamation of Emergency 2007*, art 2). Thus it is evident that the emergency proclaimed in Pakistan on 3 November 2007 was also an extra-constitutional emergency, like that of General Musharraf's first emergency declared on 14 October 1999. In 1999, as mentioned earlier, General Musharraf's power base was only the armed forces, since he acted upon the deliberations and decisions of Chiefs of Staff of the Armed Forces and Corps Commanders of Pakistan Army. But in November 2007 he expanded his support base: the meetings in which the deliberations and decisions of proclaiming emergency and suspending the Constitution were taken were attended not only by the aforesaid army officers but also by key civilians, such as the Prime Minister and Governors of all the four Provinces of Pakistan (*Proclamation of Emergency 2007*, preamble paras 13 and 14).

General Musharraf's term as the President of Pakistan was scheduled to expire on 15 November 2007 and his aim was to run for re-election while still holding the office of the Chief of Army Staff. In March 2007, Musharraf considered his appointee Chief Justice Iftikhar Muhammad Chaudhury (who assumed his office on 7 May 2005) as a threat to his chance of contesting the Presidential election while holding the office of Chief of Army Staff in case of a challenge to his eligibility by any of his opponents. For the independent-minded and courageous Chief Justice Chaudhury in *Watan Party and Pakistan Steel People's Workers Union et al v Federation of Pakistan [2006]*

PLD (SC) 697 had invalidated, to the displeasure of General Musharraf, the Government's privatisation of the Pakistan Steel Mills Corporation, describing the completion of the entire process of privatisation, from the initial proposal by the Pakistani Government to the final valuation report to the eventual sale within two days, as indecent haste which cast reasonable doubt on the transparency of the whole exercise. Essentially, under the leadership of Chief Justice Chaudhury, who was suspended in March 2007 when he refused to resign although ultimately reinstated on 20 July 2007 (pursuant to the order of the Supreme Court by a 10 to 3 margin), the Supreme Court took *suo moto* notice of the enforced disappearances during Musharraf's regime and held regular hearings to determine the whereabouts of the detainees ('SC Orders Production of Man in M9 Custody' 2007). The Supreme Court traced at least 186 disappeared persons between October 2006 and November 2007 by calling high officials of intelligence agencies to testify (Amnesty International, 2008).

Therefore, in the Proclamation of Emergency of 2007, Musharraf expressed his resentment of and dissatisfaction with the Supreme Court for creating a crisis in the country and for not being loyal to his regime. Eight preambular paragraphs of the Proclamation of Emergency were devoted to criticising the judiciary for its alleged overstepping of the 'limits of judiciary authority', whereas only two preambular paragraphs made reference to 'terrorist attacks' of 'some militant groups' at 'an unprecedented level' and 'a spate of attacks on State infrastructure and on law enforcement agencies' (*Proclamation of Emergency 2007*, preamble paras 3–7, 9–11, 1–2).

It can safely be said that for the first time in the history of Pakistan a proclamation of emergency was issued mainly on the grounds that the judiciary had exercised powers transcending its jurisdiction, which is, perhaps, an unprecedented event in legal history. However, on the evening of 3 November 2007, a seven-judge bench of the Supreme Court, headed by Chief Justice Chaudhury and acting under the authority of the 1973 *Constitution of Pakistan*, annulled the Proclamation of Emergency and Provisional Constitutional Order, and directed all the judges not to take a new oath of office to uphold the new Provisional Constitution (Saleem, 2007).

Shortly after the passing of the order, Chief Justice Chaudhury and other judges who refused to take an oath to be bound by the provisions of the Proclamation of Emergency and the *Provisional Constitutional Order No I* of 2007 were placed under house arrest. General Musharraf appointed new judges who took an oath to uphold the aforesaid instruments. The post-purge 'Supreme Court' under the leadership of the new Chief Justice, Abdul Hameed Dogar, in *Wajihuddin Ahmed v Chief Election Commissioner [2000] PLD (SC) 25* overruled on 4 November 2007 the annulment order given by Chief Justice Chaudhury and validated the Proclamation of Emergency and Provisional Constitution Order invoking the doctrine of necessity. Thus under the new Chief Justice, the Supreme Court chose to acquiesce in Musharraf's extra-constitutional actions.

In July 2009, almost two years after the withdrawal of the 2007 Emergency (the Emergency was withdrawn in December 2007), the Supreme Court of Pakistan in *Sindh High Court Bar Association et al. v Federation of Pakistan [2009] PLD (SC) 5* held that Musharraf's Proclamation of Emergency in November 2007, promulgation of the Provisional Constitution Order and replacement of the Chief Justice and other judges of the Supreme Court were unconstitutional and void (12). It further held that any judge who took the 2007 oath of office violated the 1973 Constitution of Pakistan and, as such, was to be removed from his post, and all judicial appointments made in consultation with former Chief Justice Dogar were nullified. Even all orders and judgments made by any court with any unconstitutionally appointed judge were declared void (16–20). Moreover, the Supreme Court observed that Justice Chaudhury was always the constitutional Chief Justice of Pakistan (17).

Thus within a period of about two years Pakistan witnessed three judgments of the Supreme Court regarding the constitutionality of the Proclamation of Emergency in November 2007. The first and third judgments declared the said proclamation of emergency unconstitutional, while the second judgment validated General Musharraf's extra-constitutional declaration of emergency by invoking the doctrine of necessity.

2.7 The *Constitution of Bangladesh*, 1972 and the proclamation of emergency

The independence of Bangladesh was declared officially on 10 April 1971 by the issue of the 'Proclamation of Independence', which had been deemed to have come into effect from 26 March 1971. Although the instrument 'Proclamation of Independence' confirmed the declaration of independence already made on 26 March 1971, it contained 'provisional arrangements' for the governance of the People's Republic of Bangladesh. It provided that 'till such time as a Constitution is framed', the President would 'exercise all the Executive and Legislative powers of the Republic including the power to grant pardon'. This vesting of legislative power in the hands of the President instead of the Constituent Assembly empowered 'to frame' the Constitution of the country (consisting of people's representatives elected from 7 December 1970 to 17 January 1971), was contrary to the doctrine of separation of powers. Furthermore, the previous example set by the British in the Subcontinent under the *Indian Independence Act*, 1947, of allowing the Constituent Assemblies of India and Pakistan to act as the central legislatures for both the Dominions until new constitutions were framed, was not followed.

The *Constitution of Bangladesh* was ultimately adopted, enacted and given to the citizens of Bangladesh by the Constitutional Assembly on 4 November 1972, and was given effect from 16 December 1972 to commemorate the First Anniversary of the Victory Day of Bangladesh (*Constitution of*

Bangladesh 1972, last preamble para and art 153(1). The Constitution did not originally contain any provision for the declaration of an emergency. Perhaps the repeated misuse of the powers of emergency by the Governments of Pakistan (1947–1971), during the days when Bangladesh (erstwhile East Pakistan) was a province of Pakistan, discouraged the framers of the 1972 Constitution from including in it such powers, considering themselves too idealistic. There was, however, a complete change of mind within only nine months and seven days after the coming into force of the *Constitution of Bangladesh*, when on 22 September 1973, the *Constitution (Second Amendment) Act* was passed. It inserted a new Part IXA in the Constitution titled 'Emergency Provisions', providing for the declaration and continuance of emergency and the suspension of enforcement of the fundamental rights during the period of emergency. In view of the failure of the existing Government to control the rapid deterioration in the economic and law-and-order situations, such powers were perhaps considered essential to assert itself. But the then Law Minister had the complete opposite version when he said:

> these provisions for … proclamation of emergency [were] in the constitution of all democratic countries of the world … [which] were not incorporated in the Constitution when it was framed and … now this amendment was introduced to fill up that "omission".
>
> (Ahmed, 1984: 149)

Article 141A of the *Constitution of Bangladesh* empowers the head of the state – the President – to issue a proclamation of emergency which (a) requires for its validity the prior counter signature of the Prime Minister and (b) needs parliamentary approval for the continuance of the proclamation beyond 120 days.

Of the four types of emergency – emergency of war or external aggression, emergency of subversion, economic emergency and emergency of natural catastrophes – the President of Bangladesh, unlike the Presidents of India and Pakistan,[30] has been given the authority to declare only two types of emergency, namely, the emergency of war or external aggression and the emergency of internal disturbance, i.e. subversion. Thus the notion of emergency in Bangladesh has been confined to its initial security-oriented concept. In order to declare a state of emergency, Article 141A(1) of the Constitution requires that a 'grave emergency exists in which the security or economic life of Bangladesh, or any part thereof, is threatened by war or external aggression or internal disturbance'. Clause 3 of Article 141A empowers the President to proclaim an emergency before the actual occurrence of war or external aggression or disturbance if he 'is satisfied that there is imminent danger thereof', which is reproduced from the original Article 352(3) of the 1950 Indian Constitution.[31] Thus responding to an actual crisis has been supplemented with anticipating an imminent crisis.

Since the insertion of emergency provisions into the *Constitution of Bangladesh*, proclamations of emergency have been issued five times – on 28 December 1974, 30 May 1981, 27 November 1987, 27 November 1990 and 11 January 2007. In each case, these emergencies were declared on the ground of internal disturbance, never on the ground of war or external aggression. The justification for the proclamation of each of the five emergencies in Bangladesh will be discussed in detail in Chapter 5.

2.8 References

Abbas, Z. (1993) 'The Man for All Seasons', *Herald* (Karachi), 54.

Ahmad, J. D. (1960) *Speeches and Writings of Mr. Jinnah*, Lahore: Islamic Publications, 1960, 449.

Ahmed, M. (1984) *Bangladesh: Era of Sheikh Mujibur Rahman*, Dhaka: University Press Limited, 149.

Alam, Z. (1987) *Emergency Powers and Indian Democracy*, New Delhi: SK Publishers, 28, 36, 88, 95.

Amnesty International (2008) *Denying the Undeniable: Enforced Disappearances in Pakistan*, July, 5.

Austin, G. (2003) *Working A Democratic Constitution: A History of the Indian Experience*, New Delhi: Oxford University Press, 319–325.

Banks, C. P. (2010) 'Security and Freedom After September 11: The Institutional Limits and Ethical Costs of Terrorism Prosecutions', *Public Integrity*, 13(1): 8.

Bari, M. E. (2015) Suspension of the Fundamental Rights and the Unrestrained Exercise of the Power of Preventive Detention During the Successive Proclamations of Emergency in Bangladesh: A Legal Study, Doctoral Thesis, Macquarie University, Sydney, 74, 88.

Bindra, S. S. (1981) *Indo-Pak Relations*, New Delhi: Deep & Deep Publications, 175.

Bonner, D. (1985) *Emergency Powers in Peacetime*, London: Sweet & Maxwell, 2, 17.

Bose, S. K. and Bose, S. (eds) (1998) *The Indian Struggle 1920–1942*, Oxford/Delhi: Oxford University Press, 1998) 11–12, 282.

Brookfield, F. M. (1988) 'The Fiji Revolutions of 1987', *New Zealand Law Journal*, 251.

Burns, J. F. (2001) 'Pakistan's Military Ruler Declares Himslef President', *The New York Times*, available at www.nytimes.com/2001/06/21/world/pakistan-s-military-ruler-declares-himself-president.html [Accessed 10 October 2015].

Civil Contingencies Secretariat (2004) *Civil Contingencies Act 2004 (UK): A Short Guide*, 5, available at: http://webarchive.nationalarchives.gov.uk/+/www.cabinetoffice.gov.uk/media/132428/15mayshortguide.pdf [Accessed 5 September 2016].

Cohen, T. (2011) 'Obama Approves Extension of Expiring PATRIOT Act Provisions', *CNN*, available at http://edition.cnn.com/2011/POLITICS/05/27/congress.patriot.act/ [Accessed 10 April 2012].

Cushing, T. N. (2003) 'Pakistan's General Pervez Musharraf: Deceitful Dictator or Father of Democracy?', *Penn State International Law Review*, 21: 623–624.

Dicey, A. V. (1915) *Introduction to the Study of the Law of the Constitution*, London: Macmillan & Co., 539, 549, 552.

Feldman, H. (1967) *A Study of the Martial Law Administration*, London/Lahore: Oxford University Press, 1967, 108–109.

Ferejohn J. and Pasquino, P. (2004) 'The Law of the Exception: A Typology of Emergency Powers', *International Journal of Constitutional Law*, 2(2): 217–218, 235.

Flanz, G. H. (ed.) (1999) *Constitutions of the Countries of the World*, New York: Oceana Publications Inc.

Ghatate, N. M. (2011) *Emergency, Constitution and Democracy: An Indian Experience*, Delhi: Shipra Publications, 35.

Gledhill, A. (1964) *The Republic of India: The Development of its Laws and Constitution*, London: Stevens and Sons, 3.

Gross, O. and Aoláin, F. N. (2006) *Law in Times of Crisis: Emergency Powers in Theory and Practice*, Cambridge/New York: Cambridge University Press, 47.

Gross, O. (2011) 'Constitutions and Emergency Regimes', in T. Ginsburg and R. Dixon (eds), *Comparative Constitutional Law*, Cheltenham/Northampton, MA: Edward Elgar Publishing Limited, 337, 344, 348.

Hamilton, A. (1948) 'The Federalist No. 23' in A. Hamilton, J. Madison and J. Jay (eds), *The Federalist or the New Constitution*, Oxford: Blackwell, 153.

Hasan, K. S. (1962) 'The New Constitution of Pakistan', *Parliamentary Affairs*, 16(2): 174–175.

Huq, A. Z. (2006) 'Democratic Norms, Human Rights and States of Emergency: Lessons from the Experience of Four Countries' in *Democracy, Conflict and Human Society*, Stockholm: International Institute for Democracy and Electoral Assistance, 130.

Hussain, N. (2003) *The Jurisprudence of Emergency*, Ann Arbor, MI: University of Michigan Press, 23, 25.

International Commission of Jurists (1983) *States of Emergency – Their Impact on Human Rights: A Comparative Study by the International Commission of Jurists*, Geneva: International Commission of Jurists, 171–172, 177, 179, 189, 190, 201, 413, 416, 433, 451.

Islamic Republic of Pakistan (1954) *Constituent Assembly Debates*, vol. 16, no. 3121, 503–504.

Islamic Republic of Pakistan (1956) *Constituent Assembly Debates*, vol. 1, no. 79, 2795–2800, 3252–3257. (Manager of Publications, Government of Pakistan Press).

Ispahani, M. A. (1966) *Quaid-e-Azam Jinnah as I Knew Him*, Karachi: Forward Publications Trust, 106.

Iyer, V. (2000) *States of Emergency: The Indian Experience*, New Delhi: Butterworths, 153–155, 176.

Jennings, I. (1957) *Constitutional Problems in Pakistan*, London: Cambridge University Press, 3, 22.

Kalhan, A. (2010) '"Constitution" and "extraconstitution": Colonial Emergency Regimes in Postcolonial India and Pakistan', in V. V. Ramraj and A. K. Thiruvengadam (eds), *Emergency Powers in Asia: Exploring the Limits of Legality*, Cambridge/New York: Cambridge University Press, 112.

Kalhan, A., Conroy, G. P., Kaushal, M., Sam Scott Miller, S. S., and Rakoff, J. S. (2006) 'Colonial Continuities: Human Rights, Terrorism, And Security Laws in India', *Columbia Journal of Asian Law*, 20(1): 126, 131.

Kaushik, S. (1963) 'Constitution of Pakistan at Work', *Asian Survey*, 3(8): 384.

Khakee, A. (2009) 'Securing Democracy? A Comparative Analysis of Emergency Powers in Europe', Geneva: Geneva Centre for the Democratic Control of Armed Forces (Policy Paper No. 30), 18–19, available at: www.dcaf.ch/Publications/Publication-Detail?lng=en&id=99487 [Accessed 10 September 2011].
Lamb, C. (1991) *Waiting for Allah: Pakistan's Struggle for Democracy*, London: Hamish Hamilton, 107.
LaPorte, Jr, R. (1972) 'Pakistan in 1971: The Disintegration of Nation', *Asian Survey*, 12(2): 101.
Maluka, Z. M. (2004) 'Reconstructing the Constitution for a COAS President: Pakistan 1999–2002', in B. Craig (ed.), *Pakistan on the Brink: Politics, Economics and Society*, Lanham, MD: Lexington Books, 55.
Mukherjee, R. (1973) *The Rise and Fall of the East India Company*, New York: New York Monthly University Press, 224, 269.
Munir, M. (1975) *Constitution of the Islamic Republic of Pakistan*, Lahore: Law Publishing Company, 47.
O'Boyle, M. P. (1977) 'Emergency Situations and the Protection of Human Rights: a Model Derogation Provision for a Northern Ireland Bill of Rights', *Northern Ireland Legal Quarterly*, 28(2): 164–165.
Oraction, L. A. (1968) 'Constitution Making in Pakistan', Doctoral Thesis, University of Karachi, Karachi, 104, 224.
Registry of the Court: Council of Europe (1961) Strasbourg: The European Court of Human Rights, 56.
Republic of India (1948) *Constituent Assembly Debates*, vol. 7, 34–35.
Republic of India (1949) *Constituent Assembly Debates*, vol. 9, 104, 125, 531–532, 545–547.
Richardson, J. D. (1986–9) *A Compilation of the Messages and Papers of the Presidents*, vol. 6, 178.
Rossiter, C. L. (1948) *Constitutional Dictatorship: Crisis Government in the Modern Democracies*, Princeton, NJ: Princeton University Press, 60, 295.
Saleem, M. (2007) 'Seven Judges Reject PCO Before being Sent Home', *Dawn*, 4 November, 1.
Secretariat of the Asian-African Legal Consultative Committee (1968) *Constitutions of Asian Countries*, Bombay: NM Tripathi Private, 877.
'SC Orders Production of Man in M9 Custody' (2007) *Dawn*, 7 June, 1.
Schoenfeld, B. N. (1963) 'Emergency Rule in India', *Pacific Affairs*, 36(3): 235.
'This Great Day' (1956) *Dawn* (Karachi), 1 March, 1.
Twining, W. L. (1972) *Emergency Powers: a Fresh Start*, London: The Fabian Society, 4.
UK Committee on Ministers' Powers (1932) *Report of the Committee on Ministers' Powers*, London: HMSO (Cmd 4060), 52.
Williams, G. (2001) 'The Case that Stopped a Coup? The Rule of Law and Constitutionalism in Fiji', *Oxford University Commonwealth Law Journal*, 1(1): 80.
Ziring, L. (1991) 'Pakistan in 1990: The Fall of Benazir Bhutto', *Asian Survey*, 31(2): 116–117.

Notes

1 *International Covenant on Civil and Political Rights 1966* art 4(1), *European Convention for the Protection of Human Rights and Fundamental Freedoms 1950* art 15(1) and *American Convention on Human Rights 1969* art 27(1).

2 See *Constitution of Azerbaijan 1995* art 112; *Constitution of Brazil 1998* arts 49(II) & (IV), 136 & 137; *Constitution of Costa Rica 1949* art 93(2)(a) & (b); Article 121(6), *Constitution of the Federal Democratic Republic of Ethiopia 1995* art 93(2)(a) & (b); *Constitution of Panama 1972* art 51; *Constitution of Pakistan 1973* art 232(7); *Constitution of Paraguay 1992* art 238(7); and *Constitution of Romania 1991* art 93(1).

3 See *Constitution of Bhutan 2008* art 33(1) & (2); *Constitution of India 1950* art 352(3); and *Constitution of Bangladesh 1972* art 141A(1).

4 See *Constitution of Portugal 1976* arts 137(d), 141 and 143(1).

5 See *Constitution of France 1958* art 16.

6 See *Political Constitution of Peru 1993* art 137 and *Constitution of Nicaragua* art 150(9).

7 See *Constitution of Greece 1975* art 48(1); *German Basic Law 1949* art 115a; *Constitution of the Dominican Republic* art 37(7) and (8); *Constitution of Slovenia 1991* art 92; *Israel's Basic Law: The Government 2001* art 38(a), and *Constitution of Hungary 1949* art 19(3)(1).

8 See *Israeli Basic Law: The Government 2001* art 38(c), *Constitution of Greece 1975* art 48(2), *Constitution of Austria 1920* art 18(3), *Constitutional Act of Denmark 1953* art 23. Oren Gross, above n 23, 339.

9 *Constitution of Sweden 1975* art 2(1) [ch 13].

10 *Constitution of France 1958* in Article 116 merely states that the President has the authority to declare an emergency 'when the institutions of the Republic, the independence of the Nation, the integrity of its territory or the fulfillment of its international commitments are under serious and immediate threat'.

11 The Constitutions of Pakistan and Bangladesh empower the President to proclaim an emergency on the ground of internal disturbance – a phrase which does not connote any precise definition. *Constitution of Pakistan 1973* art 232(1) and *Constitution of Bangladesh 1972* art 141A(1).

12 The *Civil Contingencies Act*, which received Royal Assent on 18 November 2004, has repealed the Emergency Powers Act of 1920 and its Northern Ireland counterpart, the *Emergency Powers Act* (Northern Ireland), 1926.

13 The *Emergencies Act 1988* replaces the *War Measures Act* of 1914.

14 In case of public order emergency.

15 In case of war emergency.

16 Emphasis added.

17 Clause 5 of s 102 of the *Government of India Act 1935* as added by the *Government of India Act (Amendment) Act 1939.*

18 See *Indian Independence Act 1947* s 1(1).

19 *Government of India Act 1935* in Section 102 provided: 'Notwithstanding anything in the preceding sections of this Chapter, the Federal Legislature shall, if the Governor-General has in his discretion declared by the Proclamation … that a grave emergency exists whereby the security of India is threatened, whether by war or internal disturbance, have power to make laws for a Province or any part thereof with respect to any of the matters enumerated in the Provincial Legislative List.'

20 The original clause 3 of Article 352 has now been inserted in the explanatory note to Article 352(1) by the *Constitution (Forty-Fourth Amendment) Act 1978.*

21 The basis of internal disturbance was replaced with armed rebellion by the *Constitution (Forty-Fourth Amendment) Act 1978.*

22 A proclamation of financial emergency under Article 360(1) of the 1950 Indian Constitution requires the approval of the Parliament for its continuation beyond two months.

23 *Representation of the People Act 1951* s 8A (inserted by *Election Laws (Amendment) Act 1975* s 2) required every case in which a member of Parliament had been disqualified from holding office to be referred to the President of India who was given the power to condone such disqualification in consultation with the Election Commission. The provisions were made retrospective.

24 *Representation of the People Act 1951* s 8A (inserted by *Election Laws (Amendment) Act 1975* s 2) required every case in which a member of Parliament had been disqualified from holding office to be referred to the President of India who was given the power to condone such disqualification in consultation with the Election Commission. The provisions were made retrospective.

25 The reasons given by President Ayub Khan in his letter to the Commander-in-Chief of Pakistan Army are as follows: 'all civil administration and constitutional authority in the country has become ineffective … [I am left with no option but] to step aside and leave it to the defence forces of Pakistan, which today represent the only effective and legal instrument, to take over full control of the affairs of this country.' Quoted in *Asma Jilani v Punjab [1972] PLD (SC) 139*, 183.

26 The provisions contained in Article 58(2) were altered by Section 17 of the *Constitution (Eighteenth Amendment) Act*, 2010. Article 58(2), as amended on 2010, provides: 'Notwithstanding anything contained in clause (2) or Article 48, the President may dissolve the National Assembly in his discretion where, a vote of no-confidence having been passed against the Prime Minister, no other member of the National Assembly commands the confidence of the majority of the members of the National Assembly in accordance with the provisions of the Constitution, as ascertained in a session of the National Assembly summoned for the purpose.'

27 Ghulam Ishaq Khan again dissolved the National Assembly and dismissed the then Prime Minister Nawaz Sharif on 18 April 1993 under Article 58(2)(b) of the *Constitution of Pakistan, 1973*. The fourth and final use of Article 58(2)(b) occurred when President Farooq Leghari ousted Prime Minister Bhutto (who became Prime Minister for the second time in 1993) on 4 November 1996 and next day dissolved the National Assembly. In *Benazir Bhutto v President of Pakistan*, (1991) PLD (SC) 388, the Supreme Court upheld the dissolution. Thus under Article 58(2)(b) of the *Constitution of Pakistan 1973*, four elected governments were ousted from power within a period of eight years.

28 Full text of the Proclamation of Emergency, 1999 can be found in T. N. Cushing (2003) 'Pakistan's General Pervez Musharraf: Deceitful Dictator or Father of Democracy?', *Penn State International Law Review*, 21: 623–624.

29 This provision has been altered by *Constitution (Eighteenth Amendment) Act*, 2010, s 4(i). The amended Article 6(1) of the Constitution reads: 'Any person who abrogates or attempts or conspires to abrogate, subverts or attempts or conspires to subvert the Constitution by use of force or show of force or by other constitutional means shall be guilty of high treason.'

30 Both the Constitutions of India and Pakistan empower their respective head of state's to declare three types of emergency, i.e. emergency of war, emergency of subversion and financial/economic emergency. See *Constitution of India 1950* art 360(1) and *Constitution of Pakistan 1973* art 235(1).

31 The original clause 3 of Article 352 of the 1950 Indian Constitution has been inserted as the explanatory note to clause 1 of the Article 352 by the *Constitution (Forty-Fourth Amendment) Act 1978*.

3 Suspension of the fundamental rights and the exercise of the power of preventive detention during emergencies in the Indo-Pak-Bangladesh Subcontinent

3.1 Introduction

The immediate consequences of proclamation of an emergency are the suspension of the right to apply to the designated courts for the enforcement of all, the majority or some of the fundamental rights and the increased use of the power of preventive detention to deal with the exigencies of the situation (Rossiter, 1948; Lee, 1984). The general expectation is that as soon as the crisis which gave rise to the proclamation of the emergency is over, the suspended fundamental rights of the citizens will be restored and the government will refrain from the exercise of the power of preventive detention. However, often there is a tendency to treat the constitutional provisions concerning these powers in a somewhat casual and cavalier manner to prolong the suspension of fundamental rights and use the power of preventive detention as an instrument for detaining the political adversaries of the party in power despite the absence of the features of a grave emergency.

In this chapter, therefore, the general issues pertaining to the suspension of fundamental rights and the exercise of the power of preventive detention during declared periods of emergency in the Indo-Pak-Bangladesh Subcontinent during the colonial and post-colonial periods will be examined. In order to deal with these issues in a systematic manner, the chapter is divided into two parts, namely A and B.

In Part A, an attempt will first be made to provide a definition of fundamental rights. Second, an endeavour will be made to examine: a) the necessity to derogate from human rights during emergency situations and b) the substantive limitations, as contained in the *International Covenant on Civil and Political Rights* (ICCPR), 1966 on the right of states parties to derogate from human rights during emergency situations and the effectiveness of the monitoring system under the ICCPR for securing compliance of states parties. Third, the evolution of the guarantee of fundamental rights in the Indo-Pak-Bangladesh Subcontinent during the colonial and post-colonial periods will be discussed. Finally, the provisions concerning the suspension of fundamental rights during emergency, as enshrined in the Constitutions of India, Pakistan and Bangladesh, will also be examined.

In Part B, the definition of preventive detention, the necessity of the power of preventive detention, the abuse of the powers concerning preventive detention and the evolution of the powers relating to preventive detention in the Indo-Pak-Bangladesh Subcontinent will be examined.

Part A

3.2 Definition of fundamental rights

When certain human rights, which are understood as the inviolable and inalienable moral rights common to all individuals by virtue of their membership of the human family, are enumerated in a constitution and protected by constitutional guarantees of judicial enforcement and judicial review, they are called 'fundamental' rights (Alexy, 2006). For they protect the most fundamental interests of individuals – for instance, the interest in not being subjected to torture or cruel, inhuman or degrading punishment or treatment and the interest in enjoying freedom from discrimination on the grounds of religion, race, caste, sex etc. – and as such, have been placed beyond the power of any organ of the state, whether executive or legislative, to violate them. Such an enumeration of 'justiciable fundamental rights' in a constitution represents a fetter on legislative and executive powers by dint of judicial review. As Justice Hidayatullah of the Indian Supreme Court observed in *IC Golak Nath and others v the State of the Punjab and another [1967] 2 SCR 762:*

> declarations of the Fundamental Rights of the Citizens are the inalienable rights of the people ... [The] constitution enables an individual to oppose successfully the whole community and the state and claim his rights.
> (867)

Judge Abdul Hamid of the Federal Court of Malaysia also expressed similar views in *Beatrice Fernandez v Sistem Penerbangan Malaysia [2004] Civil Appeal No: W-02-186-96*, when he said that fundamental rights are rights guaranteed by the constitution 'for the protection of an individual against arbitrary invasion of such rights by the state' (para 14).

Fundamental rights are value-added rights; they are of a higher legal status than ordinary rights. The object of the enumeration of fundamental rights in the constitution is not to make them unalterable under any circumstances, but to invest them with legal sanction of a higher degree by making them an integral part of the fundamental law, so that they can neither be altered nor be taken away through the process of ordinary legislation by transient majorities so as to suit their own designs.[1] 'The very essence of a fundamental right', observes Chief Justice Munir of Pakistan in the case of the *State v*

Dosso [1958] PLD 533, 'is that it is more or less permanent and cannot be changed like the ordinary law' or cannot be taken away by the ordinary law (541). He also observed in the case of *Jibendra Kishore A Chowdhury and others v the Province of East Pakistan and others [1957] 9 PLD (SC) 9*:

> The very conception of a fundamental right is that it being a right guaranteed by the constitution cannot be taken away by the law and it is not only technically inartistic but a fraud on the citizens for the makers of a constitution to say that a right is fundamental but that it may be taken away by the law.
>
> (41)

Thus, a written constitution, which as the supreme law of a country is the embodiment of the will of the people, confers upon individuals fundamental rights and makes them inviolable by ordinary legislation. 'They are enjoyed as fundamental liberties – not stick and carrot privileges' (*Taw Cheng Kong v Public Prosecutor, (1998) 1 SLR 943*, 965). The fundamental rights can only be taken away by an amendment to the constitution in the manner in which the constitution provides.

The idea of incorporating certain human rights into the constitution may be traced back to the second half of the eighteenth century, after the conclusion of the revolutionary period in America and France (Phillips, 1962). The omission to include a Bill of Rights in the *Constitution of the United States*, adopted on 17 September 1787, was rectified by the addition of a Bill of Rights consisting of the first Ten Amendments to the Constitution on 15 December 1791. For it was apprehended that

> without some such declaration of rights, the Government would assume, and might be held to possess, the power of trespass upon those rights of person and property which the Declaration of Independence [of 1776] were affirmed to be unalienable... that among these [unalienable rights] are Life, Liberty and the Pursuit of Happiness'.
>
> (*American Declaration of Independence 1776*, para 1)

The historic 'Declaration of Rights of Man and of the Citizen', which is considered as the greatest contribution of the French Revolution of July 1789, contains certain rights (which had been denied by previous regimes) on the basis of the ideas of Voltaire, Montesquieu, Rousseau and John Locke. It was moved on 11 July 1789 in the French National Assembly and adopted on 26 August 1789, and 'was prefaced to the French Constitution of 1791, and was confirmed by the preambles to the Constitutions of 1946 and 1958'.[2]

However, the practice of incorporating a justiciable list of fundamental rights in the written constitutions of the new nations of the Commonwealth, being influenced essentially by American constitutionalism, has been criticised in Britain, which does not have a written constitution with constitutional guarantees of certain rights. Leading British Constitutional author Sir Ivor Jennings took pride in claiming the supremacy of the British approach to the rights of the people, where '[t]he so-called liberties of the subject are really implications drawn from the two principles that the subject may say or do what he pleases, provided he does not transgress the substantive law, or infringe the legal rights of others, whereas public authorities (including the Crown) may do nothing but what they are authorised to do by some rule of common law or statute. Where public authorities are not authorised to interfere with the subject, he has liberties' (*Halsbury's Laws of England* (1931–1942): 389). He claimed that, 'in spite of the American Bill of Rights, that liberty is even better protected in Britain than in the United States' (Jennings, 1958: 20). The attitude of Sir Ivor Jennings towards the justiciable list of liberties of the people of the United Kingdom is worth quoting:

> [T]he English constitutional lawyer ... has never tried to express, and does not think of expressing, the fundamental ideas which are implicit in his Constitution. ... An English lawyer ... is apt to shy away from a general proposition like a horse from a ghost ... On the whole the politician of tomorrow is more likely to be right than the constitutional lawyer of today ... [T]he presumption is that the constitutional guarantee of principles of civil and political liberty is unnecessary.
>
> (De Smith, 1961: 85)

In 1998 the British Parliament nevertheless proceeded towards providing a formal framework for the protection of human rights amidst growing awareness that it was no longer sufficient to rely on the common law guarantees of rights. It enacted a statutory Bill of Rights – the *Human Rights Act* (HRA), which gives 'effect to rights and freedoms guaranteed under the European Convention on Human Rights' (preamble para 1). Thus it is evident that the British Parliament preferred to retain its sovereignty by offering a weak form of protection of rights, For, in the first place, unlike fundamental rights contained in constitutions which, as pointed out above, can only be taken away by a difficult procedure – a formal amendment – the guarantees of rights contained in the HRA – an ordinary statute – can be taken away by the sovereign British Parliament at its whim through ordinary law-making procedure. Second, whereas constitutionally entrenched rights impose a fetter on legislative (and executive) powers by means of judicial review, if the British Parliament passes any legislation which contravenes any of the convention rights contained in the HRA then the judiciary is only empowered to make a declaration of incompatibility to the effect that the offending legislation 'is incompatible with a Convention right' (*HRA 1998* s 4). Furthermore, such a declaration does not affect the validity of the offending legislation.

3.3 The necessity of suspending fundamental rights during emergencies and the international standards concerning such suspension under the ICCPR

When the state's very existence is in jeopardy by virtue of severe predicaments such as war, external aggression or armed rebellion, the need for an emergency provision in the constitution and a provision permitting suspension of fundamental rights and the remedies for their enforcement during an emergency are obvious. The fundamental rights of the citizens should not obstruct the government in taking any action necessary for the preservation of the integrity and cohesion of the state. For, if the state survives, these rights also survive and if the state does not survive, these rights do not survive either. 'However precious the personal liberty of the subject may be', said Lord Atkin in *Rex v Halliday (1917) AC 260*, 'there is something for which it may well be to some extent sacrificed by legal enactment, namely national success in the war or escape from national plunder or enslavement' (271–272). In the same vein, Justice Holmes of the US Supreme Court in *Moyer v Peabody (1909) 212 US 78* remarked that:

> When it comes to a decision by the head of the State upon a matter involving its life, the ordinary rights of individuals must yield to what he deems the necessities of the moment.
>
> (85)

At the same time, the ICCPR, which is the 'most important universal instrument' on human rights with 167 state parties, attempts to strike a balance between protecting national interests and protecting individual rights during an emergency (Meron, 1986: 83). In particular, Article 4 of the ICCPR empowers States Parties to derogate from their obligations under the ICCPR during an emergency while subjecting such derogation regimes to the governance of two substantive principles, namely, non-derogation and proportionality. In this context, the observations of the Human Rights Committee (2001: para 1), a body which is entrusted with the responsibility of ensuring compliance with the standards envisaged by the ICCPR, are relevant:

> Article 4 of the Covenant is of paramount importance for the system of protection for human rights under the Covenant. On the one hand, it allows for a State party unilaterally to derogate temporarily from a part of its obligations under the Covenant. On the other hand, article 4 subjects both this very measure of derogation, as well as its material consequences, to a specific regime of safeguards.

An attempt will now be made to briefly examine these substantive limitations, namely, the principles of non-derogation and proportionality, on the right of state parties to derogate from human rights during emergency situations and the effectiveness of the monitoring system under the ICCPR in ensuring compliance of states parties with these standards.

3.3.1 The principle of non-derogation

One of the two most important principles for reducing the impact on the rights of individuals during emergency situations is the principle of non-derogation. This principle is premised on the idea that there are certain human rights that are 'too fundamental and too precious', and, as such, should remain immune to suspension even during an emergency (Iyer, 1999: 134–135). The principle of non-derogation imposes negative duties on the state apparatus during a state of emergency, i.e. the duty to secure the unhindered continuation of the non-derogable rights by refraining from the adoption of any measures which interfere with these rights.

It is generally considered that four non-derogable rights – the right to life,[3] the right not to be subjected to torture, cruel and degrading treatment,[4] the right to freedom from slavery,[5] and the right to protection from retroactive laws[6] – which are common to the *European Convention on Human Rights and Fundamental Freedoms* (ECHR), 1950,[7] the ICCPR, and the *American Convention on Human Rights* (ACHR), 1969,[8] 'express fundamental value for human beings' and, as such, bind the 'international community of states as a whole' (Koji, 2001: 930). In view of the importance of the values protected by these four non-derogable rights, it is argued that they have attained the status of *jus cogens* within international law (Oraa, 1992). The concept of *jus cogens* refers to those peremptory norms that enjoy 'a higher rank in the international hierarchy than treaty law and even "ordinary" customary rules' (*Prosecutor v. Furundzija*, IT-95-17/1, para 153; Zenovic, 2012: 19). The norms of *jus cogens* 'derive their [higher] status from fundamental values held by the international community, as violations of such peremptory norms are considered to shock the conscience of humankind and therefore bind the international community as a whole, irrespective of protest, recognition or acquiescence' (Inter-American Commission on Human Rights, 2002). The most striking consequence of this higher status is that the norms at issue are not susceptible to derogation (*Prosecutor v. Furundzija*, IT-95-17/1, para 153).

In addition to the abovementioned four non-derogable rights, Article 4(2) of the ICCPR recognises another three rights as non-derogable. These are: the right against punishment for breach of contract (art 11), the right to recognition as a person before the law (art 16), and the right to freedom of thought, conscience and religion (art 18). Thus the ICCPR envisages that the enforcement of the abovementioned seven rights should not be suspended even in the event of a grave emergency.

Since the objectives of enumerating a list of non-derogable rights are to secure the continuous operation of those rights that are: a) 'absolutely fundamental and indispensable' for promoting and protecting the dignity and worth of individuals, and b) particularly vulnerable to abuse during emergencies, it seems that the ICCPR has not succeeded in attaining such objectives (Oraa, 1992: 94). For, although freedom of thought, conscience and religion could be threatened during an emergency and, are accordingly labelled as non-derogable by the ICCPR, it is hard to imagine how the right concerning prohibition on imprisonment for breach of contract could be considered a core right, which is susceptible to abuse during crises threatening the life of a nation. It seems that at least some of these additional rights have been incorporated in the list of non-derogable rights not because they are 'among the most fundamental rights for the protection of the human being' in an emergency, but rather because their dispensation is not strictly necessary for dealing with a threat posed to the security of a nation (Oraa, 1992: 97).

Since the ICCPR, as pointed out earlier in 3.3, has the largest number of states parties, it can be strongly argued that a shorter list of non-derogable rights confined only to those fundamental human rights that are truly likely to be endangered during the continuance of an emergency, would have increased the likelihood of its acceptance and implementation by states parties, thereby strengthening the principle of non-derogation (Oraa, 1992).

3.3.2 The principle of proportionality

The exclusion of a right from the list of non-derogable rights does not mean that 'it could automatically be derogated from' during an emergency (Oraa, 1992: 94). For the principle of proportionality, which refers to the notion that 'there should be a reasonable relationship or balance between an end and the means used to achieve that end', also has to be satisfied (Kirk, 1997: 2). Article 4(1) of the ICCPR, in the same manner as Article 15(1) of the ECHR,[9] recognises the principle of proportionality by providing that States Parties are allowed to 'take measures derogating from their obligations under the present Covenant to the extent strictly required by the exigencies of the situation'. This language adopted in Article 4(1) has been interpreted as meaning that the derogating measures during a state of emergency have to be proportional to the threat posed to the life of the nation, 'both as a matter of degree and duration' (Hartman, 1981: 17). It then follows that only those rights which have a direct bearing on the emergency should be suspended and when the threat posed to the security of the nation ceases to exist, the restrictions on the enjoyment of these rights must be lifted. Furthermore, if the intensity of the situation varies, then the derogating measures should also vary accordingly.

The insertion of the phrase 'strictly required' in Article 4(1) has further strengthened the concept of proportionality as envisaged by the same. It places an implied obligation on states parties to 'act in good faith' and, as such, not use the emergency measures in derogation of the human rights contained in the ICCPR as a means for suppressing the opposition to the party in power (Hartman, 1981: 17). If the situation at hand can be contained under the ordinary legal framework, then the emergency and the restrictions on rights cannot be deemed as 'strictly required by the exigencies of the situation'.

3.3.3 The monitoring system under the ICCPR

Since states often commit the most flagrant violations of human rights during emergencies, particularly those rights from which no derogation can be made, the necessity of an effective international mechanism for protection of these rights becomes all the more important. According to J Hartman (1981), the effectiveness of any monitoring mechanism policing derogation from human rights during emergencies can be said to be contingent on four elements: a) the capability to gather relevant information concerning derogation from human rights during emergency situations; b) the ability to examine the veracity of the information received; c) the competence to pronounce objective findings; and d) the power to impose sanctions against offending parties. If an international monitoring mechanism has the above-mentioned competencies, it will further the effective implementation of the treaty rules and thereby ensure respect for the maintenance of human rights during a state of emergency.

Unlike the adjudicatory mechanism in the form of a Court under the regional instrument of ECHR,[10] which was enacted in the aftermath of World War II as the first conscious attempt to deal with the issues of emergency and their impact on human rights, the ICCPR entrusts a Committee – the Human Rights Committee (HRC)[11] – with the task of ensuring compliance of states parties with the principles of non-derogation and proportionality as enshrined in Article 4 of the Covenant.

It will now be examined whether the HRC has the competence to effectively police derogations from human rights during emergency situations under non-optional and optional procedures set out in the ICCPR.

3.3.3.1 HRC's competence under the non-optional procedures as envisaged by the ICCPR

Under the non-optional procedures set out in the ICCPR, the HRC has the following competencies:

3.3.3.1.1 COLLECTION OF INFORMATION CONCERNING DEROGATION FROM HUMAN RIGHTS

The ICCPR envisages two methods for the HRC to collect necessary information concerning derogation from human rights during emergency situations. In the first place, Article 4(3) of the ICCPR places an obligation on states parties to notify other state parties immediately of their derogation from human rights during an emergency through the 'intermediary of the Secretary-General of the United Nations'. Unlike the ECHR, which in Article 15(3) requires an explanation of the measures taken in contravention of the rights,[12] the ICCPR requires only a statement of the situation that led to the invocation of an emergency and persuaded the government to derogate from the list of treaty Articles.[13] Thus, the type of notice envisaged under Article 4(3) of the ICCPR provides very little guidance to members of the HRC as to the actual measures taken in contravention of the treaty Articles and the severity of these measures (Hartman, 1981).

Second, under Article 40 of the ICCPR, states parties are required to submit periodic reports on how they have given effect to the provisions of the Covenant for the consideration of the HRC. Usually, the first report under Article 40 is submitted '[w]ithin one year of the entry into force of the ... Covenant for the States Parties concerned'. Thereafter, states parties are required to submit reports 'whenever the Committee so requests'. Since 1981, the HRC has established a five-year schedule for submitting second and subsequent reports (HRC, 1981).

The success of any monitoring mechanism policing derogation from human rights during emergencies, as mentioned earlier in Section 3.3.3, is dependent, *inter alia*, on the ability to collect relevant information concerning derogation. However, the HRC's competence as an effective monitoring mechanism has been severely undermined due to substantial delays in the collection of necessary information. States have often refrained from submitting reports under Article 40 altogether,[14] or requested a postponement of the obligation to submit reports during an emergency so as to evade the responsibility of reporting the measures taken in contravention of the rights enumerated in the Covenant (McGoldrick, 2004). On the other hand, states reports actually submitted to the HRC often contain no relevant information.[15] Although the HRC can request additional information concerning the derogating measures from states representatives during the review of reports in the form of supplementary reports, such requests have often gone unheeded as well (Hartman, 1981). Furthermore, states reports have also revealed that state parties have either refrained from submitting notices of derogation under Article 4(3) altogether, or submitted such notices 'weeks or even months' after the proclamation of the emergency, or filed notices that were so vague as to make no attempt 'to indicate the nature and scope of the derogations actually resorted to ... or to show that such derogations were strictly necessary' (Iyer, 2000: 57; *Silva v Uruguay Comm. No. 34/1978,* para 8.2). These problems are further exacerbated by the fact that failure to notify under Article 4(3) does not have the impact of invalidating the derogation itself.

The HRC itself acknowledged the problems it has encountered in collecting information with regard to derogations, when it observed in 1981:

> [I]n the case of ... States which had apparently derogated from Covenant rights, it was unclear not only whether a state of emergency had been officially declared but also whether rights from which the Covenant allows no derogation had in fact been derogated from and further whether the other States parties had been informed of the derogations and of the reasons for the derogation.
>
> (Report of the HRC, 1981: 110)

These difficulties faced by the HRC in collecting relevant information concerning derogation from human rights during emergencies have led Hartman (1981: 41) to note:

> The article 40 report process fails as a device for fact-finding in derogation situations because it is unfocused, subject to substantial delays, and unequipped either to produce or test the veracity of relevant information.

3.3.3.1.2 REVIEW OF STATES REPORTS

The HRC's principal tool for ensuring compliance with Article 4 is the review of periodic reports from states parties. In pursuance of Article 40(4) and (5) of the ICCPR, the HRC has the following competence with regard to reviewing reports from states parties:

> 4. The Committee shall study the reports submitted by the States Parties to the present Covenant. It shall transmit its reports, and such general comments as it may consider appropriate, to the States Parties. The Committee may also transmit to the Economic and Social Council these comments along with the copies of the reports it has received from States Parties to the present Covenant.
> 5. The States Parties to the present Covenant may submit to the Committee observations on any comments that may be made in accordance with...[clause] 4 of this article.

From a bare reading of clause 4 of Article 40, it seems that the HRC does not have the authority to evaluate states parties reports with a view to highlighting the breach of standards concerning human rights during emergencies (Robertson, 1981; Hartman, 1981). Rather the HRC has the authority only to study the reports submitted by states parties and thereby make 'general comments' on the reports. Although the phrase 'general comments' is not defined, it has been interpreted to mean that the HRC may make recommendations with respect to a particular state in general terms. However, such competence does not extend to making recommendations in light of specific violations for improving the relevant laws of the states parties (Robertson, 1981; Hartman, 1981).

Due to the limitations of the language adopted in clause 4 of Article 40, the HRC has shied away from undertaking an activist role and thereby abstained from expressly pronouncing that states parties were unjustified in resorting to emergency powers or that the suspension of the enforcement of the fundamental rights was unwarranted (Meron, 1986). The soft approach adopted by the HRC has allowed states parties to evade their responsibilities concerning the maintenance of respect for human rights during emergency situations. For instance, Zambia's initial report under Article 40, which was reviewed by the HRC in 1987, did not contain any information with regard to the fact that the country was at the time under an emergency, which had been declared several years previously on imprecise grounds (HRC, 1987). The report also revealed nonfeasance with the requirement of furnishing a derogation notice under Article 4(3). However, the HRC neither held Zambia accountable for the abovementioned omissions nor sought to establish whether the standards concerning human rights as envisaged in Article 4(1) and (2) were being respected by the Zambian emergency regime.

Exacerbating the above problems concerning the review of states reports, clause 5 of Article 40 of the ICCPR does not seem to place any obligation on states parties to take any measures in connection with any recommendations that the HRC may make in 'general' terms in reviewing their reports. According to A. H. Robertson (1981: 351), the states parties 'may submit ... [their] observations on any comments that may be made' or may choose to 'ignore them completely'.

In stark contrast to the investigation method contemplated by the ICCPR, the method of investigation of derogation from human rights during emergency situations as envisaged by the ECHR is much more adversarial in nature. The European Court of Human Rights is authorised to commence 'an investigation' in pursuance of state or individual petition 'for the effective conduct of which the High Contracting Parties concerned shall furnish all necessary facilities' (ECHR art 38). Subsequently, if the Court finds that a state party has violated the standards envisaged by the ECHR, it has the authority to 'afford just satisfaction to the injured party' (ECHR art 41). Furthermore, any final decision handed down by the Court to this effect is binding on the state party concerned (ECHR art 46). The effectiveness of the adjudicatory mechanism under the ECHR is manifested in the fact that there have been no cases of total failure to file a notice of derogation under Article 15(3) (Fitzpatrick, 1994).[16]

3.3.3.1.2.1 Non-execution of the HRC's conclusions

Unlike the ECHR, which specifies a procedure for submitting the final judgment of the Court to the Committee of Ministers of the Council of Europe (COE) for securing compliance of the government concerned with the judgment,[17] the HRC's conclusions are not forwarded to any 'authoritative political organ' for ensuring compliance of the offending states parties with the conclusions (Robertson, 1981: 351). Although it might have been thought that the Economic and Social Council (ECOSOC) would play a role similar to the COE, clause 4 of Article 40 does not place any obligation on the HRC to transmit its comments on states reports to the ECOSOC. Furthermore, should the HRC submit its comments to the ECOSOC, there is no obligation on the part of the ECOSOC to make any formal recommendations to the government of the relevant state on the basis of those comments (Robertson, 1981: 351).

3.3.3.1.2.2 Inability to impose sanctions

Under Article 40 of the ICCPR, the HRC does not have any direct sanction, such as economic penalties or expulsion, at its disposal to use against states parties which commit massive violations of human rights under the guise of emergencies (Hartman, 1981). It can be strongly argued that if the HRC had been given the power of imposing sanctions on offending states, this would have had the impact of: a) changing the culture of abusing human rights during emergencies; b) limiting the opportunities for abuse of human rights during emergencies; and c) deterring other states parties from committing gross violations of human rights.

In view of the discussion above, it can be concluded that the reporting procedure envisaged under Article 40 of the ICCPR:

a) suffers from meagreness of resources in collecting and corroborating relevant information in connection with derogation from human rights during emergencies, and
b) renders the HRC incapable of pronouncing an authoritative finding of breach of human rights and imposing any sanction against offending states.

Thus, the abovementioned reporting procedure cannot be regarded as an effective and adequate adversarial mechanism for preventing abuse of human rights during emergencies.

3.3.3.2 HRC's competence under the optional procedures of the ICCPR

The HRC under the optional procedures of the ICCPR is empowered to receive interstate complaints as well as communications from individuals who claim to be victims of human rights violations by the states.

3.3.3.2.1 INTERSTATE COMPLAINTS

In pursuance of Article 41 of the ICCPR, the HRC has a 'conciliatory role' in entertaining interstate complaints with regard to derogation from human rights during emergencies (Meron, 1986: 84). However, Article 41 of the ICCPR makes interstate complaint an optional procedure. For Article 41(1) states:

> A State Party … may at any time declare … that it recognizes the competence of the Committee to receive and consider communications to the effect that a State Party claims that another State Party is not fulfilling its obligations under the present covenant.

Only those states which have recognised the competence of the HRC under Article 41 have the right to lodge a complaint with the HRC against another state party. Although 48 states have so far accepted the competence of the HRC under Article 41, this provision has not yet been invoked (HRC 2012).

Article 41 of the ICCPR specifies the procedure for two-sided negotiations between the complaining and offending state. However, if the matter is not settled after the invocation and exhaustion of 'all available domestic remedies', then either of the states may refer the matter to the HRC. In such a case, the HRC has the authority to call for 'any relevant information' in connection with the matter. Subsequently, the HRC is to exercise its good offices in an attempt to broker 'a friendly solution of the matter on the basis of respect for human rights and fundamental freedoms' as recognised in the ICCPR. If such a 'friendly solution' is not achieved then the HRC is required to submit a report, which should contain a 'brief statement of the facts'. It seems that the functions of the HRC with regard to interstate complaints are confined to the establishment of the mere facts, offering the exercise of its good offices and their consequent exercise if such a proposal is accepted. Thus, the HRC does not have the authority under Article 41 to specify any breach by the offending state of the standards concerning human rights under the ICCPR (Hartman, 1981).

Article 42 of the ICCPR provides that if a matter referred to the HRC under Article 41 is not determined to the satisfaction of the states parties concerned, then the HRC with the consent of the states may appoint an ad hoc conciliation Commission for the 'amicable solution of the matter on the basis of respect for the … Covenant'. Subsequently, if the ad hoc Commission succeeds in brokering an amicable solution between the states, then it will prepare a report containing the facts and solution reached. However, if no such solution can be reached then the report will contain the facts and the solution which the Commission had envisaged. It then remains open to the states concerned to accept or reject the contents of the report (ICCPR art 42(7c) and 7(d).

Thus it is evident that the states parties under Articles 41 and 42 are afforded with opportunities for bringing the proceedings to a complete standstill (Fitzpatrick, 1994). Furthermore, the procedures under Articles 41 and 42 fail to hold the offending state accountable for violating the standards concerning human rights. These shortcomings have led one commentator to conclude that it is 'hard to imagine a more toothless procedure [than this]' (Gandhi, 1990: 357).

3.3.3.2.2 INDIVIDUAL PETITIONS

In an attempt to provide a remedy for individuals whose rights are violated, the First Optional Protocol of the ICCPR in Articles 1 and 2 provide that the HRC has the competence to receive and consider written communications from individuals who are citizens of states that have ratified the Protocol,[18] alleging that they are victims of violations by their governments of any of the rights set out in the ICCPR. The Optional Protocol allows the admissibility of written communications instead of oral hearings and fact-finding missions. The increasing rate of ratification of the Protocol has resulted in a heavier caseload for the HRC, and this in turn has affected its ability to resolve the petitions in a timely manner (Opsahl, 1992). For instance, since 1977 the HRC has received 2144 communications from individuals. Out of these 2144 communications, only 916 communications have been resolved, while 329 communications are still pending before the HRC (HRC 2012).[19]

Under Article 5 of the Optional Protocol, the HRC can only make known its 'views', not 'decision or determinations', to the individual and state party concerned with regard to a complaint. Consequently, the HRC has refrained from determining the legitimacy of derogations from human rights. For instance, in *Salgar de Montejo v Colombia Communication No. 64/1979*, the HRC merely deplored the Colombian Government's failure to provide 'a sufficiently detailed account of the relevant facts' that could justify its derogation from human rights (para 10.3). It should also be pointed out here that the Optional Protocol does not contain any provision which places an obligation on the offending state to comply with the views of the HRC (Meron, 1986). Thus, it can be concluded that the Optional Protocol does not offer an effective remedy to individuals whose rights under the ICCPR are breached by their governments.

The limitations of the monitoring system under the ICCPR, in the form of the reporting procedure, interstate complaints and individual petitions, have often allowed states parties to use declarations of emergency as a vehicle for violating the ICCPR human rights standards with impunity.

3.4 Fundamental rights in the Subcontinent during the colonial period

Britain, after formally declaring its sovereignty over India in 1858, followed its practice of not protecting fundamental rights of individuals by constitutional guarantees. None of the Constitution Acts, for example, the *Government of India Act* of 1858, the *Government of India Act* of 1909, and the *Government of India Acts* of 1919 and 1935, enacted by the British Parliament for the governance of India, guaranteed any 'unnecessary' fundamental rights to the inhabitants of British India. In following the principles learnt at home the British repeatedly neglected the Indian demand for fundamental rights.

From the very outset of the freedom movement against the British, the Indians fought for the recognition of their basic rights and liberties. As Lokmanya B. Tilak declared to the British Government in 1895: 'Freedom is my birthright and I shall have it' (Sripati, 1997: 96). However, the idea of constitutionalised (fundamental) rights in India was first brought to the fore by the All Indian Muslim League, which was established in 1906 as the political organisation for Muslims in India, when it adopted in December 1926 a resolution 'to the effect that any scheme of the future Constitution of India should secure and guarantee ... fundamental rights' (Molla, 1988: 156). Subsequently, in December 1927 after being challenged by the then Secretary of State for India, Lord Birkenhead, to come up with a constitution containing fundamental rights, the Indian National Congress at its Madras Session undertook the task of drafting, under the leadership of Motilal Nehru, a Report demanding a 'Swaraj Constitution for India, on the basis of the Declaration of Rights' (Sripati, 1998: 433). The Motilal Nehru Committee's Report, which was published in August 1928, set out 19 fundamental rights and demanded that these rights should be 'guaranteed in a manner which will not permit their withdrawal under any circumstances' (Sharma, 2007: 30). It was further argued in the Report that the assurance of fundamental rights was 'necessary to create and establish a sense of security among those who look upon each other with distrust and suspicion' (Mishra, 2014: 743). However, the Indian demand for constitutionalised fundamental rights was met with a hostile reception from the Indian Statutory Commission (popularly known as the Simon Commission as it was chaired by Sir John Simon), which was entrusted with the responsibility of recommending constitutional reforms in British India. The Commission (1988: 22–23) categorically rejected the Indian notion of fundamental rights thus:

> Many of those who came before us have urged that the Indian constitution should contain definite guarantees for the rights of individuals in respect of the exercise of their religion and a declaration of the equal rights of all citizens. We are aware that such provisions have been inserted in many constitutions, notably in those of the European States formed after the War. Experience, however, has not shown them to be of any great practical value. Abstract declarations are useless, unless there exists the will and the means to make them effective.

The demand for the incorporation of certain fundamental rights in the future Constitution of British India suffered the ultimate setback when the Joint Select Committee on Indian Constitutional Reform, which reviewed the white paper proposals for the framing of the last pre-independence Constitution of British India, i.e. the *Government of India Act*, 1935, also rejected the notion of constitutionalised fundamental rights (Simon Commission, 1988).

Thus during almost 100 years of formal British rule in India, the Indians did not enjoy any guaranteed fundamental rights. However, the reasoning advanced by the British, as evidenced by the observations of the Simon Commission, implied an intention to protect and promote the fundamental rights of the inhabitants of British India despite the failure to expressly enumerate them in the Constitution Acts of British India. But this was a far cry from the reality. In fact, the repeated proclamations of emergency by the Governor-General of British India, coupled with the frequent abuse of the powers concerning preventive detention even in peacetime, demonstrated the British disregard towards the rights of the Indians (see Section 3.9.1 below, which will further clarify this point).

Since none of the Constitution Acts enacted by the British Parliament for governing British India contained any fundamental rights, the question of their suspension during the countless emergencies proclaimed by the Governor-General of British India under the *Indian Councils Act*, 1861, the *Defence of India Act*, 1915, the *Government of India Act*, 1919, the *Government of India Act*, 1935 and the *Defence of India Act*, 1939, did not arise at all.

3.5 Guarantee of fundamental rights in the Constitutions of India, Pakistan and Bangladesh: after the post-colonial period

It seems that the historical struggle for constitutionalised fundamental rights during the colonial period ultimately led the framers of the Constitutions of the new states of India, Pakistan and Bangladesh, on attaining independence, to significantly depart from the unwritten UK Constitution in providing for the constitutional protection of fundamental rights. These guarantees of fundamental of rights are, however, subject to curtailment during a state of emergency, as will become evident from the forthcoming discussion.

3.5.1 Fundamental rights and the 1950 Constitution of India

The *Indian Independence Act*, 1947, as pointed out earlier in Section 2.6.1.5, created a Constituent Assembly for India and entrusted it with the important task of framing the Constitution of Independent India. The absence of provisions concerning fundamental rights in the Constitution Acts enacted by the British during their rule in India influenced the Constituent Assembly, which first convened on 9 December 1946, to embark on the endeavour of providing the people of India with a Constitution based on fundamental rights. To this end, no other Constitution influenced the framers of the Indian Constitution more than the Constitution of the USA (Sripati, 1998). For the Bill of Rights provided for by the *Constitution of the USA* was perceived by the founding fathers of India as crucial to the 'achievement of a freer and fairer society' (Sripati,

1998: 418). Therefore, by following their American counterparts, the framers of the *Constitution of India*, which was enacted by the Constituent Assembly after two years of deliberation on 26 November 1949, inserted in Part III of the Constitution a comprehensive array of fundamental rights (arts 12–35). The enjoyment of these fundamental rights was effectively guaranteed by endowing the Supreme Court of India with the authority to invalidate any law inconsistent with these rights. Furthermore, perhaps most importantly, the right to move the Supreme Court for the enforcement of fundamental rights was itself made a fundamental right in terms of clause 1 of Article 32 of the Constitution, which provides: 'The right to move the Supreme Court by appropriate proceedings for the enforcement of the rights conferred by this Part [Part III] is guaranteed.'

3.5.2 The 1950 Constitution of India and provisions concerning suspension of the enforcement of the fundamental rights during a proclamation of emergency

The American Constitution (from which the framers of the Indian Constitution had 'borrowed' heavily) provides for the suspension of only one fundamental right, namely, the right to the writ of habeas corpus, by the Congress during a grave emergency, i.e. rebellion or invasion. By contrast, the Indian Constitution originally conferred on the President the absolute power to suspend the enforcement of some or all of the fundamental rights (as might be specified in the Presidential Order) guaranteed by the Constitution during the continuance of an emergency. Article 359(1) of the Constitution originally provided:

> Where a Proclamation of Emergency is in operation, the President may by order declare that the right to move any court for the enforcement of such of the rights conferred by Part III as may be mentioned in the order and all proceedings pending in any court for the enforcement of the rights so mentioned shall remain suspended for the period during which the Proclamation is in force or for such shorter period as may be specified in the order.

The only safeguard incorporated into the *Constitution of India* for the protection of fundamental rights during an emergency is that the Presidential order suspending the enforcement of fundamental rights has to be laid before the Parliament for its approval (art 359(3)). But the Constitution does not provide for a time limit for laying the said Presidential Order before the Parliament. This failure provided sufficient leeway to emergency regimes to deprive individuals of their liberties for an indefinite period of time. The decision to incorporate provisions concerning the suspension of enforcement of all or the majority of the fundamental rights enshrined in the *Constitution of India* was sought to be justified on the ground that the security of the state during a grave emergency takes precedence over the liberties of the individual.

However, the Constitution's conferral of sweeping power on the President of India to suspend the enforcement of the fundamental rights during an emergency met with a hostile response by certain members of the Indian Constituent Assembly. It was warned by a member of the Constituent Assembly, Mahavir Tyagi, that this power of the President has the potential to make a government 'become tyrannical and beastly' (Ghatate, 2011: 20). For it enables the government to take away the most basic right of the individuals to approach 'the Supreme Court for the protection of their life, honour and liberty' (Ghatate, 2011: 20). In the same vein, another member of the Indian Constituent Assembly, K. T. Shah, remarked that the suspension of the right to move the Supreme Court of India for the enforcement of the fundamental rights guaranteed by the Constitution renders all the other fundamental rights 'meaningless' (Ghatate, 2011: 20). This indiscriminate provision in Article 359 of the Indian Constitution further provoked H. V. Kamath, another member of the Indian Constituent Assembly, to observe:

> Through Fundamental Rights a great edifice of democracy is built. Surrounding that edifice is the arch of great negation and Article [359] is the keystone of this arch of autocratic reaction … the weight of negation will be so heavy that I am afraid the whole edifice will collapse.
>
> (Ghatate, 2011: 24)

These apprehensions expressed by certain members of the Indian Constituent Assembly were realised in India, particularly during the period between 25 April 1975 and 21 March 1977 when India witnessed unprecedented abuse of the powers concerning emergency and suspension of fundamental rights in the hands of the government of Mrs Indira Gandhi. This led the Government of Janata Party (a coalition of five individual parties which came to power in the General Elections held in March, 1977) to introduce an amendment, namely, the *Constitution (Forty-Fourth Amendment) Act*, 1978, to the *Constitution of India*, which, among other things, made the fundamental rights to protection against *ex post facto* laws and double jeopardy (art 20), and to life and liberty (art 21) immune from suspension during an emergency.

3.5.3 Suspension of fundamental rights during the proclamations of emergency in India

The emergency provisions as embodied in the *Constitution of India*, as mentioned earlier in Section 2.6.2.1, have so far been invoked three times: twice in 1962 and 1971 on the ground of external aggression and once in 1975 on the ground of internal disturbance. An attempt will now be made to examine the impact of the three proclamations of emergency on the enjoyment of fundamental rights in India.

3.5.3.1 Suspension of fundamental rights during the first proclamation of emergency in 1962

It may be recalled here from the discussion in Section 2.6.2.1.1 that, on 26 October 1962, following China's attack on India's northern frontier, the President of India on the advice of the Cabinet of Prime Minister Jawaharlal Nehru issued a proclamation of emergency under Article 352(1) of the Indian Constitution, declaring that a grave situation existed 'whereby the security of India was threatened by external aggression' (Ministry of Home Affairs, 1962). This proclamation of emergency was followed by the issuance of an Order by the President of India, on 3 November 1962, under Article 359(1) of the Constitution, suspending the right of any individual to move any court for the enforcement of the fundamental rights to life and personal liberty (art 21) and protection against arrest and detention (art 22) during the continuance of the emergency (*Gazette of India*, 1962). Subsequently, within only eight days of the issuance of this Order, the President on 11 November 1962 issued another Order, suspending the enforcement of the fundamental right to equality before the law as well (*Gazette of India*, 1962). In addition to these two Presidential Orders, separate Orders in the same vein were issued, on 30 October 1962 and 27 August 1965, in respect of certain foreigners (*Gazette of India*, 1962; 1965).

The suspension of the enforcement of the fundamental rights to equality before the law (as guaranteed by Article 14) and life and personal liberty (as guaranteed by Article 21) was challenged before the Supreme Court of India in *Mohammed Yaqub v State of Jammu and Kashmir [1968] AIR (SC) 765.* It was contended by the petitioner that, since a Presidential Order under Article 359(1) can only be invoked in times of an emergency, only those fundamental rights which had a nexus with the declaration of emergency could be suspended and, as such, suspension of the enforcement of the fundamental rights guaranteed by Articles 14 and 21 of the Constitution was unjustified and *ultra vires* the powers of the President. This argument was, however, rejected by the Supreme Court on the ground that Article 359(1) conferred on the President 'categorical powers' of suspending the enforcement of any of the fundamental rights guaranteed by the Constitution during the continuance of a proclamation of emergency. As Chief Justice Wanchoo observed:

> There is nothing in Article 359 which in any way limits the power of the President to suspend the enforcement of any of the fundamental rights conferred by Part III ... It follows therefore that it is open to the President to suspend the enforcement of any of the fundamental rights ... by an order under Article 359 and this Article shows that wherever

> such suspension is made it is in the interest of the security of India and no further proof of it is necessary.
>
> (768)

The hostilities with China, as mentioned earlier in Section 2.6.2.1.1, came to an end on 21 November 1962, when the Chinese Government declared a cease-fire. However, despite the cessation of the hostilities with China, both the emergency and the Presidential Orders suspending the fundamental rights lingered on despite strong opposition from various quarters. Furthermore, the prolonged suspension of the core rights of Indians, despite the absence of the features of the grave emergency which originally gave rise to their suspension, was validated by the Constitution Bench of the Supreme Court of India in *Makhan Singh Tarsikka v State of Punjab [1964] AIR (SC) 381*. The Court observed that the length of time for which the restrictions on the fundamental rights should continue is a matter which must be left to the executive determination as it is best positioned to assess the requirements of a grave crisis (403). Thus, the Court authorised the prolonged suspension of fundamental rights without taking into account the reality that the executive tendency to treat such an important issue in a cavalier and causal manner poses a serious threat to the basic values on which the democratic way of life is founded.

The Emergency, declared on 26 October 1962, 'acquired a new lease of life' following the outbreak of a war with Pakistan in April 1965 (*States of Emergency*, 1983: 177). Although the war with Pakistan came to an end on 11 January 1966, through the signing of the 'Tashkent Agreement', both the Proclamation of Emergency and the Presidential Orders suspending fundamental rights continued to remain in force.

Despite the failure of the Indian judiciary to appreciate the consequences of undue prolongation of the Presidential Order barring the enforcement of fundamental rights, the prolonged suspension of fundamental rights in India prompted the International Commission of Jurists (1967: 33) in its Bulletin of March 1967 to make the following comments:

> The International Commission of Jurists does not seek to arrogate the right of the Government to decide whether circumstances yet exist which would justify the continued suspension of fundamental rights. But such prolonged suspension of those rights, which are the very essence of a democratic form of Government, when the features of a grave emergency do not appear to exist any longer, has given rise to increasing concern in all parts of the free world where India has been looked upon as the bastion of fundamental rights and the Rule of Law in Asia.

It was not until 10 January 1968 that a Proclamation was issued by the President of India revoking the state of emergency, which also had the effect of restoring the enforcement of the suspended fundamental rights. The deprivation of the rights of the citizens of India for nearly six years despite the non-existence of the circumstances which led to their suspension is difficult to justify.

3.5.3.2 Suspension of fundamental rights during the continuance of the second proclamation of emergency

On 3 December 1971, as mentioned earlier in Section 2.6.2.1.2, the President of India proclaimed an emergency on the ground of external aggression by Pakistan on India's western border. Like the first proclamation of emergency, the second proclamation of emergency was also allowed to continue despite the cessation of hostilities with Pakistan on 17 December 1971 (within 15 days of the proclamation of emergency). Furthermore, the state of emergency was reinforced by a Presidential Order, issued on 16 November 1974, which suspended the right under Article 359(1) of the Indian Constitution to seek the assistance of the courts for the enforcement of fundamental rights to equality before the law (art 14), life and personal liberty (art 21) and protection against arrest and detention (art 22) (Gazette of India, 1974). This Order also suspended all proceedings pending before courts for the enforcement of these rights.

Thus the disturbing practice of depriving Indians of their fundamental rights despite the absence of the grave features of an emergency, which was established by the first emergency regime, continued. The emergency and the restrictions on the rights were ultimately revoked on 27 March 1977 after nearly six years of continuation.

3.5.3.3 Suspension of fundamental rights during the third proclamation of emergency in 1975

The most contentious exercise of the powers concerning suspension of fundamental rights under the Indian Constitution, as pointed out earlier in Section 2.6.2.1.3, took place during the third Proclamation of Emergency on 25 June 1975, which was issued during the continuance of the Emergency declared on 3 December 1971 on account of hostilities with Pakistan. Following the declaration of this new Emergency on the alleged ground of internal disturbance, the President of India, on 27 June 1975, issued an Order suspending the right of any person, including foreigners, to move any court for the enforcement of the fundamental rights to equality before the law (art 14), life and personal liberty (art 21) and protection against arrest and detention (art 22) during the continuance of the emergencies declared on 3 December 1971 and 25 June 1975 (*Gazette of India*, 1975). This Order barred all proceedings pending before courts for the enforcement of the aforesaid rights (*Gazette of India*, 1975 s 3(i). The cavalier attitude of the executive towards fundamental rights is evident from the fact that the Order suspending the enforcement of these rights was issued without revoking the Presidential Order of 16 November 1974 – which had been issued following the second proclamation of emergency and which had already suspended the enforcement of these rights.

Furthermore, the President by virtue of another Order, issued on 8 January 1976, for the first time in the history of emergency regimes in India also suspended the enforcement of the civil liberties (freedom of speech and expression, freedom of assembly and association, freedom of movement and residence and the freedom to practise any profession, occupation or trade) as guaranteed by Article 19 of the Indian Constitution (*Gazette of India*, 1976 s 3(i). In addition to these Presidential Orders suspending the enforcement of core rights, the *Constitution (Thirty-Eighth Amendment) Act* was passed by the deferential Indian Parliament, which inserted a new Clause 1A to Article 359 of the Constitution,[20] granting the regime of Indira Gandhi the unfettered power to make any law or take any executive action in contravention of any of the fundamental rights guaranteed by the Indian Constitution during the continuance of the Presidential Order suspending fundamental rights.

Taking advantage of the above amendment to the Constitution, which empowered the executive to impose broad restrictions on any of the fundamental rights of individuals, the government of Indira Gandhi took various arbitrary measures in contravention of international human rights standards. In particular, various torture methods were used as the means for extracting confessions from political prisoners about their alleged plots or conspiracies to oust the government (Amnesty International, 1977). The most common methods of torture used by the police were as follows:

a) hanging prisoners ‘upside down’ and consequently beating them up;
b) placing ‘lit candles’ underneath the soles of the victims’ feet;
c) tying rats inside the trousers of the victims; and
d) the ‘roller treatment’, which consisted of ‘rolling a heavy wooden or steel roller, weighed down by a number of police, over the prisoner’s legs’.

(Amnesty International, 1977: 183)

The emergency and the Presidential Order imposing restrictions on the fundamental rights of individuals were revoked on 21 March 1977.

3.5.4 *The incorporation of the provisions concerning the guarantee of fundamental rights and the suspension of their enforcement during emergency in the Constitutions of Pakistan*

Pakistan in its 67-year history has, as mentioned earlier in Section 2.6.3, adopted three Constitutions, in 1956, 1962 and 1973 respectively. Each of these Constitutions guaranteed the enjoyment of a wide range of fundamental rights and simultaneously empowered the executive to dispense with these rights in a declared state of emergency. Since no emergency was declared under the 1956 *Constitution of Pakistan*, the question of the invocation of the provisions concerning suspension of fundamental rights did not arise at all. However, the emergencies proclaimed under the 1962 and 1973 *Constitutions of Pakistan* witnessed the suspension of fundamental rights on a fairly large scale.

3.5.4.1 The Constitution of Pakistan, 1956

When Pakistan gained independence from British rule, the President of Muslim League, Muhammad Ali Jinnah, was appointed the first Governor-General of Pakistan. In his inaugural address to the Constituent Assembly, which was entrusted with the task of framing a Constitution for Pakistan, he stated:

> We are starting with this fundamental principle: that we are all citizens and equal citizens of one State ... If you change your past and work together in a spirit that every one of you ... is first, second and last a citizen of this State with equal rights, privileges and obligations, there will be no end to the progress you will make.
>
> (Chitkara, 1998: 587)

Thus, deeply embedded in his speech was the notion of securing the core rights of Pakistanis. Unlike India, where the Constituent Assembly completed the task of enacting a constitution for the people of India within two years of its establishment, the people of Pakistan had to wait for nearly nine years before the political actors settled their differences and enacted a Constitution based on fundamental rights. This Constitution, which entered into force on 23 March 1956, guaranteed a number of 'core' fundamental rights in Part II, such as the right to equality before the law (art 5), freedom from arbitrary arrest and detention (art 7), freedom of speech (art 8), assembly (art 9) and association (art 10), movement (art 11), trade, business or profession (art 12), and protection of property (art 15). Furthermore, the right to move the Supreme Court for the enforcement of the fundamental rights guaranteed by Part II of the Constitution was itself made a fundamental right (art 22).

Like Article 359(1) of the *Constitution of India*, 1950, Article 192(1) of the 1956 *Constitution of Pakistan* gave the President the unlimited and absolute power during the continuance of an emergency to issue an order suspending the right to move any court for the enforcement of such of the fundamental rights guaranteed by the Constitution as might be specified in the order. The only safeguard incorporated in the 1956 *Constitution of Pakistan* against the power of the executive to suspend the enforcement of fundamental rights also seems to be borrowed from the Indian Constitution. It merely stated that a Presidential Order suspending the fundamental rights had to be placed before the Parliament, as soon as may be, for its approval (art 191(3)). The life of the 1956 *Constitution of Pakistan*, as mentioned earlier in Section 2.6.3.1, came to an abrupt end when it was abrogated by the then President Iskander Mirza through the proclamation of a Martial Law on 7 October 1958. Since the provisions concerning emergency powers contained in the 1956 Constitution were never invoked during its lifetime, the question of suspension of the enforcement of fundamental rights did not arise either.

3.5.4.2 The 1962 Constitution of Pakistan

Following the Proclamation of Martial Law on 7 October 1958, President Mirza appointed General Ayub Khan as the Chief Martial Law Administrator who, within 20 days of the proclamation of Martial Law on 27 October 1958, ousted President Mirza from the office of the Presidency and assumed the office of the President himself (Hasan, 1962). In February 1960, President Ayub Khan formed a Constitution Commission, headed by a former Chief Justice of Pakistan, to put forward 'constitutional proposals in the form of a report' (Hasan, 1962: 174). The Commission submitted its Report for the consideration of President Ayub Khan in April 1961. However, it was not until 1 March 1962 that a new Constitution was enacted. It is worth mentioning here that, unlike the first *Constitution of Pakistan* which was given to the people after adequate deliberations before two Constituent Assemblies, the second *Constitution of Pakistan* was promulgated by President Ayub Khan himself. The 1962 *Constitution of Pakistan*, enacted by President Ayub Khan, instead of inserting fundamental rights as were provided in the 1956 Constitution, incorporated certain 'principles of law-making' which could not be enforced in a court of law. Later, the Chapter on Fundamental Rights, which guaranteed core rights such as freedom from arbitrary arrest and detention, freedom of movement, assembly, association, speech, trade, business or profession, was inserted in the Constitution (Part II, Ch 1) by the *Constitution (First Amendment) Act*, 1963. However, unlike the 1956 *Constitution of Pakistan*, which in Article 22 guaranteed the right to move the Supreme Court as a fundamental right, a newly inserted clause (c) to Article 98(2) of the 1962 Constitution, which was contained in Part IV – titled 'The High Courts' – entrusted the High Court with the responsibility of enforcing the fundamental rights of citizens. It empowered the High Court 'on the application of any aggrieved person' to issue 'an order giving such directions to any person or authority … for the enforcement of any of the fundamental rights conferred by Chapter 1 of Part II of this Constitution'.

Since the 1962 *Constitution of Pakistan* did not originally provide for guaranteed fundamental rights, Article 30 of the 1962 *Constitution of Pakistan*, which empowered the President of Pakistan to proclaim an emergency, understandably made no mention of the necessity for their suspension during an emergency. However, the introduction of certain fundamental rights in the 1962 *Constitution of Pakistan* by the *Constitution (First Amendment) Act*, 1963 necessitated the incorporation of provisions in Article 30 of the Constitution concerning the suspension of certain fundamental rights during an emergency. Consequently, the *Constitution (Fifth Amendment) Act*, 1965, among other things, inserted a new clause 10 to Article 30, which stated:

> While a Proclamation of Emergency is in force, the President may, by Order, declare that the right to move any Court for the enforcement of such of the fundamental rights conferred by Chapter 1 of Part II of this Constitution as may be specified in the Order, and any proceeding in any Court which is for the enforcement, or involves the determination of any question as to the infringement, of any of the rights so specified, shall remain suspended for the period during which the Proclamation is in force, and any such order may be made in respect of the whole or any part of Pakistan.

Thus this clause empowered the President to suspend the right to move any Court for the enforcement of such of the fundamental rights conferred by Chapter 1 of Part II of the 1962 Constitution as might be specified in the Presidential Order during the continuance of an emergency.

3.5.4.2.1 SUSPENSION OF FUNDAMENTAL RIGHTS UNDER THE 1962 CONSTITUTION DURING THE 1965 PROCLAMATION OF EMERGENCY

On 6 September 1965, Pakistan witnessed the first Proclamation of Emergency under the Constitution of 1962 when border disputes with India over the status of Kashmir turned into a full-scale war. On the same day, President Ayub Khan issued an Order suspending the enforcement of the fundamental rights to freedom from arbitrary arrest and detention (*Constitution of Pakistan 1962* ch 1 part II para 2), protection from slavery and forced labour (para 3), the freedom of movement (para 5), freedom of assembly (para 6), freedom of association (para 7), freedom of trade, business and profession (para 8), freedom of speech (para 9), property rights (para 14), and the right to non-discrimination in respect of government services (para 17). Within 10 days of the issuance of this Presidential Order, another Order was issued by President Ayub Khan suspending the enforcement of the fundamental right to equality before the law (para 15).

It seems that these Presidential Orders were issued without due thought and consideration. For the unrestrained enjoyment of fundamental rights like freedom of trade, business and profession, property rights and the right to non-discrimination in respect of government services during the continuance of the emergency could not be said to interfere with the government's effort to contain the crisis, and hence their suspension is difficult to justify.

The war with India ended after 17 days and on 11 January 1966 a joint declaration, Tashkent Agreement, was signed by both the Indian and Pakistan Governments with a view to normalising their relationship. However, both the emergency and the Presidential Orders suspending the enforcement of fundamental rights continued to remain in force until 24 March 1969. The Courts during the continuance of the 1965 Emergency refused to take notice of the prolonged suspension of fundamental rights on the basis that they did not have the competence to decide the matter due to its pure political nature and, as such, left it for the determination of the executive (*Abdul Baqi Baluch v Government of Pakistan & Others [1968] PLD (SC) 313*, 330).

It seems that President Ayub Khan was greatly influenced by the Indian Emergency Regime between 1962 and 1969. For he, like his Indian counterpart, demonstrated a tendency to treat the constitutional provisions concerning suspension of fundamental rights in a cavalier manner during the continuance of the emergency declared in 1965. Furthermore, the Courts in Pakistan followed the precedent set by the Indian Courts, during the Emergency Regime of 1962–1969, of ignoring the prolonged suspension of fundamental rights when the features of a grave emergency did not appear to exist any longer.

The Proclamation of Emergency and the Presidential Orders suspending fundamental rights ultimately came to an end when, on 25 March 1969, General Yahya Khan, the Commander-in Chief of the Pakistan Army, abrogated the 1962 Constitution in disregard of his constitutional duty by a proclamation of Martial Law throughout Pakistan (Mahmood, 1973).

3.5.4.2.2 SUSPENSION OF FUNDAMENTAL RIGHTS DURING THE PROCLAMATION OF EMERGENCY IN 1971

On 23 November 1971, President Yahya Khan declared a state of emergency on account of the war that broke out with India due to the latter's support for the cause of the independence of former East Pakistan (now Bangladesh). Since the 1962 Constitution had been abrogated by Yahya Khan in 1969, there were no fundamental rights that required suspension during the continuance of this emergency.

The war with India came to an end on 16 December 1971. However, Yahya's successor, Zulfikar Ali Bhutto – the leader of the Pakistan People's Party – decided to continue the emergency that had been declared by Yahya. In fact, this emergency was 'deemed' by Article 139(8) of the *Interim Constitution*, which was adopted by the Constituent Assembly in 1972, to be 'a Proclamation of Emergency issued under this Article'. Furthermore, the decision to continue the emergency was followed by the issuance of an Order by Bhutto, which suspended the enforcement of the safeguards relating to arrest and detention as had been guaranteed by Article 9 of the *Interim Constitution* (*Gazette of Pakistan*, 1972).

The adoption by the Constituent Assembly of the final Constitution for Pakistan, which entered into force on 14 August 1973, rendered the aforesaid Presidential Order suspending the safeguards concerning arrest and detention invalid. However, on 15 August 1973, the very next day, a Presidential Order was issued, suspending the enforcement not only of the safeguards with respect to arrest and detention (art 10), but also of the rights to freedom of movement (art 15), freedom of assembly (art 16), freedom of association (art 17), freedom of speech (art 19), freedom of trade, business or profession (art 18), property rights (arts 23 and 24), equality before the law (art 25) and the safeguard against discrimination in the services of Pakistan (art 27). The issuance of this Presidential Order at a time when the features of a grave emergency had long passed was unjustifiable. This Order was ultimately rescinded on 4 August 1974, after nearly one year of continuation (*Gazette of Pakistan*, 1973).

3.5.4.3 The 1973 Constitution of Pakistan

The 1973 Constitution, like its 1956 and 1962 predecessors, inserted an impressive 23 fundamental rights in Part II, titled 'Fundamental Rights', including the right to life and liberty (art 9), the right to equality before the law (art 25), freedom from arbitrary arrest and detention (art 10), freedom of speech (art 19), assembly (art 16) and association (art 17), movement (art 15), trade, business or profession (art 18), and protection of property (art 24). However, unlike the 1956 Constitution, the 1973 Constitution did not incorporate any provision in Part II recognising the right of an individual to move any court for the enforcement of his liberties guaranteed by the Constitution. Instead, the 1973 *Constitution of Pakistan* in Article 199(2), which is contained in Part VII titled 'The Judicature', provides that 'the right to move a High Court for the enforcement of any of the fundamental rights conferred by ... Part II shall not be abridged'.

In the same manner as the 1956 and 1962 *Constitutions of Pakistan*, the 1973 *Constitution of Pakistan* in Article 233(2) endows the President with the absolute authority to suspend the right to move any Court for the enforcement of all or any of the Fundamental Rights during an emergency. It provides:

> While a Proclamation of Emergency is in force, the President may, by Order, declare that the right to move any Court for the enforcement of such of the Fundamental Rights conferred by Chapter 1 of Part II as may be specified in the Order, and any proceeding in any Court which is for the enforcement, or involves the determination of any question as to the infringement, of any of the Rights so specified, shall remain suspended for the period during which the Proclamation is in force, and any such Order may be made in respect of the whole or any part of Pakistan.

Although the third *Constitution of Pakistan* was adopted in 1973 – seven years after the adoption of the ICCPR – it is striking that the principles of non-derogation and proportionality have not found a place in it. However, the Constitution under Article 233(3) does require a Presidential Order suspending the enforcement of fundamental rights to be laid before both Houses of Parliament for their approval within two months of the issuance of the Order. This is an improvement on the safeguards incorporated in the 1956 and 1962 *Constitutions of Pakistan*, since they merely required the Presidential Order suspending the enforcement of fundamental rights to be placed before the Parliament 'as soon as may be' for its approval.

An attempt will now be made to shed light on the impact of the proclamations of emergency issued in 1998, 1999 and 2007 in Pakistan on the fundamental rights contained in the 1973 Constitution.

3.5.4.3.1 SUSPENSION OF FUNDAMENTAL RIGHTS DURING THE PROCLAMATION OF EMERGENCY UNDER THE 1973 CONSTITUTION IN MAY 1998

The emergency powers contained in the 1973 *Constitution of Pakistan* were, as mentioned earlier in Section 2.6.3.3.2, invoked on 28 May 1998 by President Rafiq Tarar amidst the perceived threat of aggression by India in response to the nuclear tests carried out by Pakistan. On the same day as the issuance of the proclamation of emergency, a Presidential Order was also issued, suspending the enforcement of all the fundamental rights guaranteed by Part II of the 1973 Constitution. This was an unprecedented event in the history of emergency regimes in Pakistan, since the previous emergency regimes in Pakistan had preferred to take a conservative stance and confined the suspension of the enforcement to only nine fundamental rights. Perhaps in order to adhere to the precedents set by the earlier emergency regimes, President Tarar issued another Order on 13 July 1998 modifying his earlier Order of 28 May 1998. This new Order varied the earlier one by suspending only the enforcement of nine fundamental rights, namely, freedom from arbitrary arrest and detention (art 10), freedom of movement (art 15), freedom of assembly (art 16), freedom of association (art 17), freedom of trade, business or profession (art 18), freedom of speech (art 19), right to property (art 23), protection of property rights (art 24) and right to equality before the law (art 25).

The validity of these Orders was challenged before the Supreme Court of Pakistan in, *inter alia*, *Farooq Ahmad Khan Leghari v Federation of Pakistan [1999] PLD (SC) 57*. It was contended by the petitioners that the very fact that the earlier Order issued by President Tarar had to be varied by a subsequent Order indicated that they were issued by President Tarar without the application of his mind to the matter and, as such, the exercise of his power under Article 233(2) of the 1973 Constitution was unfounded. In upholding the arguments put forward by the petitioners, the Court laid down an important rule of construction to the effect that only those fundamental rights whose suspension is strictly required by the exigencies of the situation can be suspended during the continuance of the emergency. As Chief Justice Ajmal Mian observed:

> [T]he President is required to apply his mind to the question whether any order … [under Article 233(2)] is warranted. If so, to what extent. He is expected to make efforts to see that there should be minimum disturbance of the Fundamental Rights of the citizens and the enforcement of [only] those Fundamental Rights is to be suspended which have [a] direct nexus with the object to meet the situation mentioned in clause (1) of Article 232 successfully (192).

Thus, the Supreme Court of Pakistan, unlike the Indian Supreme Court during the continuance of the 1962 Emergency, took notice of the undue deprivation by the executive of the fundamental liberties of individuals during the Emergency. This was a watershed moment in the history of emergency regimes in the Subcontinent. For this nullification of arbitrary Presidential Orders by the Supreme Court of Pakistan had the effect of acting as a guide to the scope of executive powers during future emergencies in the Subcontinent.

3.5.4.3.2 SUSPENSION OF FUNDAMENTAL RIGHTS DURING THE FIRST PROCLAMATION OF EXTRA-CONSTITUTIONAL EMERGENCY IN PAKISTAN IN 1999

On 14 October 1999, as pointed out in Section 2.6.3.3.3, General Pervez Musharraf suspended the operation of the 1973 *Constitution of Pakistan* through the proclamation of an extra-constitutional emergency. A Provisional Constitutional Order issued on the same day, however, kept the Fundamental Rights guaranteed by Part II of the 1973 *Constitution of Pakistan* in operation, subject to the 'Proclamation of Emergency or any Order made thereunder' (art 2(3)).

It seems that the extra-constitutional emergency regime of General Musharraf in an attempt to distinguish itself from previous emergency regimes (which consistently dispensed with the enforcement of some or all fundamental rights during an emergency) and martial law administrations (which abrogated the Constitutions of 1956 and 1962 respectively) decided to keep the fundamental rights operative despite keeping the 1973 *Constitution of Pakistan* in abeyance.

However, when the validity of the actions taken by General Musharraf was challenged in *Zafar Ali Shah v Pervez Musharraf, Chief Executive of Pakistan [2000] PLD (SC) 869*, the Supreme Court of Pakistan stated that any derogation from fundamental rights during the continuance of the emergency was justifiable in terms of the provision contained in Article 233(2) of 1973 *Constitution of Pakistan* (see Section 3.5.4.3). It should be stressed here that

Article 233(2) of the Constitution does not recognise that there are certain rights that are too fundamental to be suspended even during the times of emergency. Thus it can be argued that the Court departed from the high threshold it had imposed, as pointed out above, in *Farooq Ahmad Khan Leghari v Federation of Pakistan* for derogation from fundamental human rights of individuals during emergency situations by preferring a literal interpretation of the provision of Article 233(2).

3.5.4.3.3 SUSPENSION OF FUNDAMENTAL RIGHTS DURING THE SECOND PROCLAMATION OF EXTRA-CONSTITUTIONAL EMERGENCY IN PAKISTAN IN 2007

On 3 November 2007, General Pervez Musharraf proclaimed another extra-constitutional emergency due to 'an unprecedented level of violent intensity posing a grave threat to the life and property of the citizens of Pakistan' (*Proclamation of Emergency 2007*, preamble para 1). The 1973 Constitution was once again kept in abeyance as the situation required 'emergent and extraordinary measures'. It was replaced with a Provisional Constitutional Order issued on the same day. However, unlike the *Provisional Constitutional Order* of 1999, which kept the fundamental rights guaranteed by the 1973 Constitution operative subject to the 1999 Proclamation of Emergency and rules made thereunder, the *Provisional Constitutional Order* of 2007 made no mention of keeping the fundamental rights guaranteed by the 1973 Constitution active. Rather, it specifically suspended the enforcement of the fundamental rights to life and liberty, freedom form arbitrary arrest and detention, freedom of movement, freedom of assembly, freedom of association, freedom of speech and equality before the law (*Provisional Constitutional Order 2007* s 2(1).

The Emergency declared on 3 November 2007 was, however, finally lifted on 15 December 2007. The Constitution of 1973 was restored and the restrictions on the enjoyment of fundamental rights were removed as well.

3.5.5 *Fundamental rights and the* **Constitution of Bangladesh,** *1972*

The 1972 *Constitution of Bangladesh* guarantees an impressive 18 fundamental rights under Part III. The remedial right to move the Supreme Court for the enforcement of fundamental rights as provided by Article 44 of the Constitution is one of the 18 fundamental rights guaranteed by the Constitution. Article 44(1), which is included in Part III entitled as 'Fundamental Rights,' provides that:

> The right to move the [High Court Division] in accordance with clause (1) of Article 102, for the enforcement of the rights conferred by this Part is guaranteed.

Article 102(1) of the 1972 *Constitution of Bangladesh* states that:

> The High Court Division, on the application of any person aggrieved, may give such directions or orders to any person or authority, including any person performing any function in connection with the affairs of the Republic, as may be appropriate for the enforcement of any of the fundamental rights conferred by Part III of this Constitution.

Thus Article 44(1) of the 1972 *Constitution of Bangladesh* is almost a reproduction of clause (1) of Article 32 of the 1950 *Constitution of India* (see Section 3.5.1). Similarly, the provisions relating to the powers of the High Court Division to enforce fundamental rights were, to a great extent, a reproduction of those contained in clause (2)(c) of Article 98 of the 1962 *Constitution of Pakistan* (see Section 3.5.4.2).

3.5.5.1 Suspension of the enforcement of the fundamental rights during the proclamation of emergency under the Constitution of Bangladesh, *1972*

The *Constitution (Second Amendment) Act*, 1973, which, as explained in Section 2.7, was passed on 22 September 1973 for the purpose of inserting provisions for the proclamation of emergency in the *Constitution of Bangladesh*, also inserted a provision for the suspension of the enforcement of fundamental rights during an emergency proclaimed at a time when the security or economic life of Bangladesh is threatened by war or external aggression or internal disturbance. Article 141C(1) of the Constitution provides:

> While a Proclamation of Emergency is in operation, the President may, [on the written advice of the Prime Minister, by order], declare that the right to move any court for the enforcement of such of the rights conferred by Part III of this Constitution as may be specified in the order, and all proceedings pending in any court for the enforcement of the right so specified, shall remain suspended for the period during which the Proclamation is in force or for such shorter period as may be specified in the order.

A perusal of this provision reveals that the President is given the unlimited and absolute power in accordance with the written advice of the Prime Minister to issue an order suspending the right to move any court for the enforcement of all or any of the 18 fundamental rights guaranteed by the Constitution.

Furthermore, the provision concerning the suspension of the enforcement of the fundamental rights during the continuance of an emergency is almost exactly reproduced from the original Article 359(1) of the 1950 *Constitution of India* and Article 30(10) of the 1962 *Constitution of Pakistan* (see sections 3.5.2 and 3.5.4.2).

The only safeguard incorporated in the 1972 *Constitution of Bangladesh* against the power of the executive to suspend the enforcement of fundamental rights also seems to be borrowed from the 1950 *Constitution of India* and the 1956 and 1962 *Constitutions of Pakistan*. It merely states that the Presidential Order suspending the fundamental rights should be placed before the Parliament 'as soon as may be' (art 141C(3)).

Since the incorporation of the provisions concerning emergency powers in Bangladesh on 22 September 1973, emergencies have been proclaimed in Bangladesh on five occasions (as mentioned in Section 2.7). The impact of each of these proclamations of emergency on the enjoyment of fundamental rights of individuals in Bangladesh will be comprehensively dealt with in Chapter 6 of this book.

Part B

3.6 Definition of preventive detention

Detention is of two types, punitive and preventive. Whereas the question of punitive detention arises after the actual commission of an offence, the question of preventive detention comes before the actual commission of a prejudicial act with a view to intercepting a person before he commits such an act. Accordingly, in case of preventive detention, no charge is formulated nor is a trial held for proving the commission of an offence: '[t]he object of preventive detention is not to punish a man for having done something' (*AK Gopalan v State of Madras [1950] AIR (SC) 27*, 91). Preventive detention is a precautionary measure taken 'against dangers ... impos[ing] some restriction on the freedom of movement of persons whom there may be any reason to suspect of being disposed to help the enemy' (*Rex v Halliday [1917] AC 260*, 269). Thus 'preventive measures, even if they involve some restraint or hardship upon individuals, do not partake in any way of the nature of punishment, but are taken by way of precaution to prevent mischief to the State' (*Rex v Halliday [1917] AC 260*, 269).

However, preventive detention is not only a precautionary measure; it is also an extraordinary measure. For a detainee's personal liberty is taken away by the executive because of the apprehension that he is about to commit acts which are detrimental to the maintenance of public order, peace, defence and security of the state or any of the matters described in the relevant statute. As Lord Atkinson in *Rex v Halliday (1917) AC 260* observed:

> Preventive justice ... consists in restraining a man from committing a crime he may commit but has not yet committed, or doing some act injurious to members of the community which he may do but has not yet done ... [P]reventive justice proceeds upon the principle that a

> person should be restrained from doing something which, if free and unfettered, it is reasonably probable he would do, it must necessarily proceed in all cases, to some extent, on suspicion or anticipation as distinct from proofs.
>
> (273, 275)

Alan Gledhill (1957: 198) observes that normally the detaining authority passes an order of preventive detention 'on information supplied by police or other public authority without taking any evidence'.

Thus the salient features of preventive detention can be summarised as follows:

i. it is detention and not imprisonment per se as the word 'preventive' is used in contradistinction to the word 'punitive';
ii. it is detention generally by an order of the executive and not by any court of law;
iii. it is generally made on the satisfaction of the executive and not after any formal enquiry as to prejudicial acts which a person detained was likely to commit;
iv. it is not a punitive but a precautionary measure; and
v. it is an extraordinary procedure.

3.7 Necessity of the power of preventive detention

The resort to the extreme power of preventive detention is generally recognised as an administrative necessity in times of grave emergencies, such as war, external aggression, subversion or civil unrest, to prevent mischief to the state. Ordinary criminal procedure requires the actual commission of an offence rather than mere suspicion of the executive in order to apprehend a person who may cause harm to the safety and security of the state during a grave crisis. However, there may be a person who indulges in activities calculated to encourage violence and public disorder and against whom a judicial trial cannot be initiated since the evidence in possession of the authorities will not be sufficient to bring a criminal charge or to secure his conviction by legal proof. In such a situation, the evidence in possession of the executive is deemed sufficient to justify the exercise of the power of preventive detention in the interest of the state. For in times of stress, it is the welfare of the state that comes first – *salus populi suprema lex* – rather than the suffering and inconvenience which may be inflicted on the suspected person. Thus the basic idea underlying the concept of preventive detention can aptly be summarised in the words of Harold Laswell (1950: 141): 'what seems unreasonable in reasonable times may look reasonable in unreasonable times.'

International and regional human rights instruments, such as the ICCPR (art 9(1)), the ECHR (art 5(1)), the ACHR (art 7(1) and (3)), and the *African Charter on Human and Peoples' Rights* 1981 (art 6), all recognise the necessity of the practice of preventive detention by state parties. But these instruments qualify the ambit of exercise of the extraordinary power of preventive detention with the requirement that such detention must not be arbitrary or unlawful.

Nevertheless, preventive detention laws contradict the basic tenets of human rights by permitting executive dispensation of the right to liberty to prevent future harmful conduct. It is a disturbing development that some of the newly independent countries of Asia and Africa have felt the necessity of empowering the legislature under the provisions of the Constitution to enact laws providing for preventive detention in times of peace to prevent anti-social and subversive elements from imperilling the welfare of the state.

3.8 Abuse of the power of preventive detention

The power of preventive detention carries with it the risk of its abuse. For instance, the government of the day may misuse this power in time of peace to suppress the opposition. For example, in Kenya, the amendment made to the first Constitution of 1963 within three years of its coming into force enabled the Government of the Kenya African National Union (KANU), a political party which ruled Kenya for nearly 40 years after its independence from British rule in 1963, to exercise the power of preventive detention under the *Preservation of Public Security Act* (PPSA) at any time without the precondition of an emergency. The PPSA was used by the KANU as the chief instrument for silencing its critics. Furthermore, in order to limit the chances of opposition political parties securing a significant foothold in Parliament, the provisions of the PPSA were used to detain prominent leaders of the opposition political parties (Mak'Ochieng, 2006).

In the Subcontinent, Indian Prime Minister Indira Gandhi under the disguise of the emergency declared on 25 June 1975 (see Section 2.6.2.1.3) used the provisions concerning preventive detention as contained in the *Maintenance of Internal Security Act*, 1971 and *Defence of India Rules*, 1971, to launch an unprecedented crackdown on opposition political leaders. The leaders had called for her resignation from the office of the Prime Minister on the ground of Allahabad High Court's invalidation of her election to the Parliament and subsequent imposition of a six-year ban on her holding public office for resorting to corrupt practices during the parliamentary elections in 1971 (Iyer, 2000; *States of Emergency*, 1983). Within 24 hours of the declaration of the emergency, a number of high-profile opposition leaders were detained (Ghatate, 2011). Congress MPs, who demanded Mrs Gandhi's resignation, were also not spared. Furthermore, newspaper editors and artists who asked the Prime Minister to step down were brought within the purview of preventive detention (Ghatate, 2011).

The disturbing use of the power of preventive detention to repress opposition political parties in various jurisdictions has led critics to label it as being equivalent to 'political detention' (Harding and Hatchard, 1993: 5). In this context, the words of Lord Shaw of Dunfermline in *Rex v Halliday (1917) AC 260* are worthy of quote:

> Vested with this power of proscription and permitted to enter the sphere of opinion and belief, they, who alone can judge as to public safety and defence, may reckon a political creed their special care, and if that creed be socialism, pacifism, republicanism, the persons holding such creeds may be regulated out of the way, although never deed was done or word uttered by them that could be charged as a crime. The inmost citadel of our liberties could be thus attacked.
>
> (293)

3.9 Evolution of the power of preventive detention in the Subcontinent during the colonial and post-colonial periods

3.9.1 Evolution of the preventive detention power in the Subcontinent during the colonial period

Contrary to the popular belief that the power of preventive detention is a 'Third World phenomenon', the historical origin of preventive detention statutes can be traced back to the British rule in the Subcontinent (Harding and Hatchard, 1993: 2, 5). First, the East India Company, which ruled the Subcontinent from 1765 to 1858, exercised the extraordinary power of preventive detention by virtue of three laws enacted by the British Parliament/Governor-General-in-Council. These were: 1) the *East India Company Act*, 1784; 2) the *East India Company Act*, 1793; and 3) the *Bengal State Prisoners Regulation*, 1818. These laws were used to maintain law and order and suppress subversive activities directed against the Company's rule (Kalhan *et al.*, 2006). Next, after the dissolution of the East India Company in 1858 and the assumption of sovereignty by Queen Victoria over the Company's territories in the Subcontinent, following the *Sepoy* Mutiny of 1857, the tradition of maintaining the extraordinary power of preventive detention to restrict political subversion was continued under: 1) the *Ingress into India Ordinance*, 1914; 2) the *Defence of India Act*, 1915; 3) the *Anarchical and Revolutionary Crimes Act*, 1919; and 4) the *Defence of India Rules*, 1939.

3.9.1.1 Preventive detention laws during the rule of the East India Company

3.9.1.1.1 THE EAST INDIA COMPANY ACT, 1784

In 1784, during the reign of King George III, the British Parliament enacted the *East India Company Act*, which was not only the first British preventive detention statute in India, but also the first of its nature in the history of civilisation (Harding and Hatchard, 1993). The Governor-General of Fort William under Section LIII of the Act was empowered:

> to issue his warrant under his hand and Seal, directed to such Peace Officers and other person as he shall think fit, for securing and detaining in custody any person or persons suspected of carrying on, mediately or immediately, any illicit correspondence, dangerous to the peace or safety of the settlement, or of the British possessions in India, or other persons whomsoever having authority in India, or with the Commanders, Governors, or Presidents of any factories established in the East Indies by any European Power, contrary to Rules and Orders of the said Company, or of the Governor General and Council of Fort William.

The Governor-General of Fort William was permitted to exercise the power of preventive detention without the precondition of a formally declared emergency against individuals on the suspicion of them being involved in activity that was considered prejudicial to the Company's rule in India, in particular, the suspicion of carrying on 'illicit correspondence'. Furthermore, the *East India Company Act*, 1784, did not prescribe a maximum period of detention and, as such, the Governor-General of Fort William could keep individuals in preventive custody for an indefinite period of time.

3.9.1.1.2 THE EAST INDIA COMPANY ACT, 1793

Like the *East India Company Act* of 1784, Section XLVS of the *East India Company Act*, 1793 empowered the Governor-General of Fort William to keep individuals in preventive custody without the prerequisite of a formally declared emergency on the suspicion of carrying on 'any illicit correspondence dangerous to the peace or safety of any of the British settlements or possessions in India'. Furthermore, it also did not stipulate the maximum period of detention of an individual in preventive custody, thus granting the Governor-General the absolute authority to detain an individual for an indefinite period of time.

3.9.1.1.3 THE BENGAL STATE PRISONERS REGULATION, 1818

In 1818, the *Bengal State Prisoners Regulation* was passed by the Governor-General-in-Council, granting the executive sweeping powers to keep individuals in preventive custody on the suspicion of them acting in a manner prejudicial to the British interest in India (Brown, 1994). In the Regulation instead of 'preventive detention' the words 'personal restraint' were used (*Bengal State Prisoners Regulation 1818* preamble). The Governor-General was empowered to place individuals 'under personal restraint' for reasons such as the 'maintenance of the alliances formed by the British Government with foreign powers, the preservation of tranquillity in the territories of native princes entitled to its protection, and the security of British dominions from foreign hostility and from internal commotion'. Like the *East India Company Acts* of 1784 and 1793, the Regulation of 1818 did not confine the Governor-General's power of preventive detention to formally declared emergency periods. Furthermore, like the Acts of 1784 and 1793, the Regulation of 1818 did not provide for any time limit on the period of preventive detention. The Regulation of 1818, which was initially applicable only in Bengal, was gradually extended throughout India.[21]

3.9.1.2 Preventive detention statutes enacted during formal British rule (1858–1947)

3.9.1.2.1 INGRESS INTO INDIA ORDINANCE, 1914

After the outbreak of World War I in Europe, the British authorities became increasingly concerned about reports that thousands of revolutionaries were entering India to launch an armed uprising against the Colonial Government. The concern of the Government was expressed in September 1914 in a press release as follows:

> The situation is one of emergency and exceptional action is justified … The Governor-General has, therefore, decided to take certain general powers of control over all persons entering India after this date.
>
> (Pati, 1998: 117)

Consequently, the *Ingress into India Ordinance* issued on 5 September 1914 authorised the Colonial Government to detain in preventive custody individuals who were considered to be 'prejudicial to the safety, interests or tranquillity' of British India (Pati, 1998: 117). Although the Ordinance did not expressly confine the exercise of the power of preventive detention to formally declared periods of emergency, it can be concluded from the above wording of the press release issued by the Government that it was the existence of an 'emergency' which for the first time in the history of British rule – both formal and informal – led to the enactment of a law providing for the exercise of the power of preventive detention.

Furthermore, like the *East India Company Acts* of 1784 and 1793, and the *Bengal Regulation* of 1818, the Ordinance of 1914 empowered the Colonial Government to detain individuals for an indefinite period of time. A total number of 370 persons were detained under the Ingress into India Ordinance, 1914, between the periods of October 1914 and December 1918 (Isemonger and Slattery, 1919).

3.9.1.2.2 THE DEFENCE OF INDIA ACT, 1915

On 18 March 1915, the *Defence of India Act* was passed by the Imperial Legislature (see Section 2.6.1.2). However, contrary to the notion that the Act was enacted to deal with the external threat posed to the life of British India due to the outbreak of World War I in a distant continent, the *Defence of India Act* was enacted to empower the Colonial Government to secure and maintain its control over the Indian Territory by putting down nationalist and revolutionary movements of Indians (Alam, 1987). Section 2(1) of the Act conferred on the Governor-General wide and arbitrary powers to frame rules for the detention of individuals considered to pose a threat to the 'public safety' and 'defence of India'. Although the *Defence of India Act* of 1915 fixed the maximum period of detention to one month, it was used in conjunction with the *Bengal Regulation III* of 1818 and the *Ingress into India Ordinance*, 1914, both of which provided for an indefinite period of detention.

3.9.1.2.3 THE ANARCHICAL AND REVOLUTIONARY CRIMES ACT, 1919 (POPULARLY KNOWN AS THE ROWLATT ACT)

As World War I was coming to an end in 1918, the British began to explore ways to retain the wartime extraordinary powers of preventive detention in British India in peacetime to suppress any form of Indian nationalist movement. With this objective in view, the British Government formed a Committee headed by Justice Rowlatt to investigate the enactment of a peacetime preventive detention law. The Committee submitted a favourable Report on 15 April 1918, emphasizing the necessity of the extraordinary power of preventive detention during peacetime in British India to deal with 'anarchical and revolutionary crimes'. Subsequently, the *Anarchical and Revolutionary Crimes Act*, popularly known as the *Rowlatt Act*, was passed on 10 March 1919.

The *Anarchical and Revolutionary Crimes Act* of 1919 empowered the Colonial Government to detain individuals in preventive custody for a period of up to 15 days on the suspicion of commission of a wide range of 'scheduled offences' (s 35),[22] which were referred to in the Act as 'anarchical and revolutionary movements'. Furthermore, the Act granted the Colonial Government the power to preventively detain for a maximum of one year any individual who failed to comply with the orders of the investigating authority to furnish security, irrespective of the fact that this might have been beyond the means of the individual concerned.

The draconian *Anarchical and Revolutionary Crimes Act*, which conferred wide and sweeping powers of preventive detention on the Colonial Government, also did not afford adequate safeguards to the detainee. Although it theoretically allowed a detainee to make representation against the detention order, the effect of this safeguard was nullified by a provision contained in the Act which empowered the investigating authority to refrain from communicating to the detainee the ground of his detention on the plea of public interest (ss 27(3) and 26(2)(b). Furthermore, the power of scrutinising the defence of any detainee lay with the same detaining authority that had passed the order of detention.

3.9.1.2.4 THE DEFENCE OF INDIA RULES, 1939

The *Defence of India Act*, 1939, which as mentioned earlier in Section 2.6.1.5, was enacted following the proclamation of an emergency in British India on 3 September 1939 due to the outbreak of World War II, granted the Government of British India wide rule-making powers. In the same year the *Defence of India Rules* were subsequently framed by the Government. These contained provisions concerning preventive detention. The necessity of new legislation at a time when several other preventive detention measures were available to the Government is difficult to justify.

Rule 26 of the *Defence of India Rules*, 1939 empowered the Colonial Government to detain any individual on the suspicion of acting in a manner 'prejudicial to defence of British India, the Public safety, the maintenance of public order, His Majesty's relations with foreign powers of Indian States, the maintenance of peaceful conditions in tribal areas or the efficient prosecution of war'. Moreover, the *Defence of India Rules*, 1939 did not stipulate any maximum period of detention of individuals, which allowed the Colonial Government to detain individuals indefinitely. Furthermore, there were no safeguards mitigating the harshness of the provision for preventive detention.

It is evident that the Colonial Government adopted one stern measure after another to repress the growing revolution against it under various statutes permitting preventive detention. Preventive detention statutes became the convenient means for the British to suppress any threat posed to the life of the Colonial Government from the nationalist movement of Indians. Furthermore, the arbitrary exercise of the extraordinary power of preventive detention was not confined to formally declared emergency periods. Consequently, detention 'became a badge of honour' for Indians (Majumdar, Raychaudhuri and Datta, 1950: 985).

3.9.2 The power of preventive detention in the Indo-Pak-Bangladesh Subcontinent

The Subcontinent was partitioned into two states of India and Pakistan in August 1947 and the eastern wing of Pakistan became an independent state in 1971 under the name of Bangladesh. It is ironical that the provisions concerning the power of preventive detention, as embodied in the Constitutions of the Independent States of India, Pakistan and Bangladesh and in statutes promulgated in accordance with these provisions, are a legacy of British rule in the Subcontinent, as will be shown in the forthcoming discussion.

3.9.2.1 *The incorporation of the power of preventive detention in the Constitution of India*

It has been claimed that the 'influx of refugees' due to the partition of the Subcontinent, 'food scarcity' and 'near famine conditions', all of which eroded the political security and financial stability of the newly independent State of India, led the members of the Indian Constituent Assembly to decide in favour of incorporating into the *Constitution of India* the extraordinary power of preventive detention to effectively contain any subversive activities (Abraham, 1993: 60). The Chairman of the Indian Constituent Assembly, Dr B. R. Ambedkar, who introduced the provisions concerning preventive detention for insertion into the Constitution of India, sought to justify the necessity 'in the present circumstances' of conferring on the executive the power to preventively detain individuals by claiming that the 'exigency of the liberty of the individual shall be placed above the interests of the state' (Abraham, 1993: 60).

It is paradoxical that the provisions concerning preventive detention are placed in Chapter III of the Indian Constitution, which guarantees a wide range of fundamental rights, so that the 'Charter of freedom' itself contains provisions for its infringement. A few months after the adoption of the Indian Constitution, Justice Mukherjee of the Indian Supreme Court disapproved the inclusion of provisions concerning preventive detention into the Constitution of India in *AK Gopalan v State of Madras [1950] SCR 88*. He stated:

> no country in the world that I am aware of has made this an integral part of their Constitution as has been done in India. This is undoubtedly unfortunate ... to make such a drastic provision in the Constitution itself, which cannot but be regarded as a most unwholesome encroachment upon the liberties of the people.
>
> (250)

Article 22(3) of the *Constitution of India* read together with Entry 3 of List I in the 7th Schedule confer on the Parliament the authority to enact laws concerning preventive detention 'for reasons connected with Defence, Foreign Affairs, or the Security of India'. Thus the framers of the Indian Constitution continued the colonial tradition of authorising the exercise of the power of preventive detention on vague grounds such as preserving the security of the state without specifying the circumstances which can pose a threat to the security of the state. As the Supreme Court of India rightly observed in the case of *AK Roy v Union of India [1982] SCR (2) 272*: 'Expressions like defence of India, "Security of India"... relations of India with foreign powers ... are not of great certainty or definiteness' (275).

Article 22 of the Indian Constitution, which provides for preventive detention, does, however, afford certain procedural safeguards to a detainee.

For instance, it provided that 'no law providing for preventive detention shall authorise the detention of a person for a longer period than three months' without the approval of an Advisory Body – a tribunal consisting of persons 'who are, or have been or are qualified to be appointed as, Judges of a High Court' (art 22(4) and art 22(4)(a)). Later in 1978, the *Constitution (Forty-Fourth) Amendment Act* reduced the period for which a person could be preventively detained without reference to an Advisory Board from three to two months (*States of Emergency*, 1983). Article 22 also requires the detaining authority to communicate to the detainee as soon as practicable the grounds on which the detention order was made. It also affords the detainee the opportunity to make a representation against the detention order (art 22(5)).

However, the above safeguards are qualified by the Indian Constitution in the same manner as the *Colonial Anarchical and Revolutionary Crimes Act*, 1918 in that the detaining authority is given the discretion to withhold the grounds of the detention order if disclosure is considered to be against the public interest (art 22(6)). The *Constitution of India* does not stipulate the maximum period for which a person could be kept in preventive custody. Rather it gives the Parliament *carte blanche* to prescribe by law the maximum period of detention.

It is also noteworthy that, maintaining the colonial tradition, the Indian Constitution also does not confine the exercise of the power of preventive detention to declared periods of emergency. It is, therefore, evident that the Indians had radically reformed their view that the exercise of the power of preventive detention during peacetime by the British was 'a very heinous offence' (Republic of India, 1949).

Since the incorporation of the 'enabling clause' concerning preventive detention into the *Constitution of India*, a number of statutes have been enacted in India providing for preventive detention. These statutes are:

1 the *Preventive Detention Act*, 1950, which was permitted to lapse in 1969;
2 the *Unlawful Activities (Prevention) Act, 1967*, as amended in 2008;
3 the *Maintenance of Internal Security Act*, 1971, which was repealed in 1978;
4 the *Conservation of Foreign Exchange and Prevention of Smuggling Activities Act*, 1974;
5 the *National Security Act*, 1980;
6 the *Terrorist and Disruptive (Activities) Prevention Act*, 1985, which was allowed to lapse in May 1995; and
7 the *Prevention of Terrorism Act*, 2002.

However, of these statutes providing for preventive detention, the *Preventive Detention Act*, 1950, the *Maintenance of Internal Security Act*, 1971, and the *Conservation of Foreign Exchange and Prevention of Smuggling Activities*

Act, 1974 deserve special attention due to their exercise during the three declared periods of emergency in India.

3.9.2.1.1 THE PREVENTIVE DETENTION ACT, 1950

On 25 February 1950, only one month after the promulgation of the Indian Constitution by the Constituent Assembly, the Indian Parliament passed the *Preventive Detention Act* (PDA) allegedly to check the 'dangerous and subversive' activities of the Communists, such as removing rails and cutting communication lines, thereby threatening the 'existence and security of India' (Ghatate, 2011).

Section 3(1) of the PDA empowered both the Central and State Governments to preventively detain individuals for a period of up to one year on the suspicion of their likelihood to engage in activities which would be 'prejudicial' to the defence of India, the security of the State, the maintenance of public order, or the maintenance of supplies and services essential to the community. Thus, the Indian Parliament followed the colonial tradition of inserting in the PDA the same vague and general grounds for invoking the extraordinary power of preventive detention.

However, the Act did afford certain safeguards to the detainee. For instance, it required the detaining authority to inform a person kept in preventive custody of the grounds for his detention within five days from the date of detention. In other words, rather than using vague phrases such as 'as soon as may be', the Act specified a time limit for informing the detainee of the reasons for detention. Furthermore, all detention orders passed in pursuance of the provisions of the PDA were made subject to the review of an Advisory Board within 30 days to 10 weeks of the date of the order. The Advisory Board, a quasi-judicial body composed of three members who 'are, have been, or are' qualified to be appointed as judges of a High Court, was not merely an ornamental body, as it had the power to reverse the detention orders passed by the Government (ss 8 and 11). Moreover, a detention order which had not been positively confirmed by the Advisory Board within 10 weeks of the detention became void.

The enactment of the PDA was sought to be justified as a necessary evil to deter those who were determined to undermine the existence and security of India (Republic of India, 1950). There was even an attempt in the Parliamentary Debates to defend the enactment of the PDA as an effective means to prevent the proclamation of emergencies (Republic of India, 1950).[23]

It should be stressed here that the PDA was enacted as a temporary measure which was scheduled to lapse on 1 April 1951. However, it was periodically renewed for nearly 19 years until it was ultimately allowed to lapse on 31 December 1969, after widespread abuse of its powers for political purposes (Ghatate, 2011).

3.9.2.1.2 THE MAINTENANCE OF INTERNAL SECURITY ACT, 1971

Within one and a half years of the lapse of the PDA, the Indian Parliament passed the *Maintenance of Internal Security Act* (MISA) on 2 July 1971, replacing the *Maintenance of Internal Security Ordinance*, which had been promulgated by the President on 7 May 1971 (Abraham, 1993). The MISA was allegedly passed 'to have the power of preventive detention to deal effectively with threats to the defence of India's security and from espionage activities of foreign agents'. But, like its predecessor, the MISA also maintained the colonial practice of empowering the Government to detain any Indian thought to be prejudicial to:

a) the defence of India, the relations of India with foreign powers, or the security of India; or
b) the security of the state or the maintenance of public order; or
c) the maintenance of supplies and services essential to the community.

(s 3(1)(a))

The MISA, like the PDA, fixed the maximum period for detaining an individual at one year. It also afforded certain safeguards to the detainee. For instance, Section 8(1) of the Act placed an obligation on the detaining authority to inform detainees of the grounds for their detention within five days in ordinary circumstances. However, this obligation could be extended to 15 days in 'exceptional circumstances', provided the reasons for invoking such exceptional circumstances were recorded in writing. Furthermore, detention orders passed by the executive were subject to the supervision of an Advisory Board, consisting of three persons who were qualified to be appointed as judges of a High Court, within 30 days from the date of detention (s 9). Detainees were given the opportunity to make representations before the Advisory Board. After considering all the relevant issues concerning the detention orders, the Advisory Board was obliged to inform the Government of its opinion as to whether there was sufficient cause for detention in each of the cases (s 11(2)).

In light of the above discussion, it can be concluded that the provisions concerning preventive detention and the safeguards designed to mitigate their harshness contained in the *Maintenance of Internal Security Act*, 1971 were effectively identical to those contained in the PDA. However, following the widespread abuse of the powers concerning preventive detention during the proclamations of emergency of 1971 and 1975, MISA was repealed by the Janata Party Government in 1978.

3.9.2.1.3 THE CONSERVATION OF FOREIGN EXCHANGE AND PREVENTION OF SMUGGLING ACTIVITIES ACT, 1974

The *Conservation of Foreign Exchange and Prevention of Smuggling Activities Act* (COFEPOSA) was passed on 13 December 1974 as an 'economic adjunct' of the MISA 1971. The Congress Government sought to justify the passing of yet another Act concerning preventive detention by putting forward the argument that economic offences posed as serious a threat to the security and defence of India as external aggression or insurrection and consequently merited the exercise of the extraordinary power of preventive detention (Iyer, 2000).

Both the Central and State Governments under the new Act were empowered to detain individuals for a maximum period of one year if they were satisfied that such orders were necessary to prevent the commission of offences connected with smuggling or prejudicial to the conservation of foreign exchange (ss 10 and 3(1). The safeguards afforded to detainees under COFEPOSA (ss 3(3) and 8(c) were identical to those contained in the MISA.

However, it is difficult to justify the enactment of the COFEPOSA by making a comparison between economic offences and external aggression. For economic offences, which are at times 'the product of arbitrary laws, of bad policies and, above all, of acquiescence, connivance and even participation by those in power', do not threaten the life of a nation in the same way as external aggression by a foreign nation (Jain, 1975). An external aggression by a foreign power violates the territorial integrity of a nation and consequently puts the life of the subjects in grave danger. The COFEPOSA continues to remain in force in India.

Thus, it is evident that India after its independence from British rule resorted to the colonial practice of not confining the exercise of the extraordinary power of preventive detention to emergency situations and extended the ambit of its exercise to peacetime. The enactment of these preventive detention statutes, closely modelled on the colonial statutes, led David Bayley (1969: 99) to observe that the use of preventive detention laws has become 'a permanent part of India's democratic experience'.

3.9.2.1.4 PREVENTIVE DETENTION LAWS ENACTED DURING THE PROCLAMATIONS OF EMERGENCY AND THE EXERCISE OF THE POWER

India, as mentioned earlier in Section 2.6.2.1, experienced proclamations of emergency on three occasions, namely in 1962, 1971 and 1975, during which times new laws providing for preventive detention were enacted in pursuance of Article 22(3) of the Constitution despite the continuance of ordinary laws governing the matter. However, these emergency laws concerning preventive custody did not contain any procedural safeguards as provided for by the Constitution, paving the way for the abuse of power by the executive arm of the government.

3.9.2.1.4.1 Preventive detention laws enacted and used during the first emergency of 1962

On 26 January 1962, the President of India, after proclaiming an emergency on account of China's attack on India, promulgated the *Defence of India*

Ordinance, which was closely modelled on the colonial wartime emergency legislation of the *Defence of India Act*, 1939. In pursuance of the provisions of Section 3 of the *Defence of India Ordinance*, 1962, the Government on 6 November 1962 subsequently promulgated the *Defence of India Rules*, 1962, which, *inter alia*, allowed it to detain any individual 'with a view to preventing him from acting in a manner prejudicial to the defence of India and civil defence, the public safety, the maintenance of public order, India's relation with foreign powers, the maintenance of peaceful conditions in any part of India, or the efficient conduct of military operations' (s 30(1)). The incorporation of provisions concerning preventive detention in the *Defence of India Rules*, when the exercise of this power on the same grounds sufficient to meet the exigencies of the situation was already permitted under a permanent piece of legislation – the PDA, 1950 – seems unjustifiable. It should be stressed here that the *Defence of India Rules*, 1962 did not afford any safeguards that were available to detainees under the PDA, 1950. For instance, they did not place any obligation on the detaining authority to furnish the grounds of detention to the detainee or to provide detainees with any opportunity for showing cause against the detention. The detention orders passed under the Rules were not subject to the supervision of an independent Advisory Board either. Furthermore, the most disturbing feature of the *Defence of India Rules*, 1962 was that they did not fix the maximum period for which an individual could be kept in preventive custody.

From the outset of the promulgation of the *Defence of India Rules*, 1962, the sweeping powers of preventive detention contained in it were exercised in an unrestrained manner. Within four months of their enactment, as many as 957 persons[24] were kept in preventive custody for political reasons (*States of Emergency*, 1983). Another 846 persons were subjected to preventive detention during the continuance of the emergency (Iyer, 2000).

3.9.2.1.4.2 Enactment of preventive detention law and its exercise during the second proclamation of emergency of 1971

The President of India, as mentioned earlier in Section 2.6.2.1.2, proclaimed an emergency for the second time in the history of India on 3 December 1971, due to the breakout of hostilities with Pakistan. The *Defence of India Act*, 1971 was passed with extreme haste by the Parliament on the same day, and, like its predecessor the *Defence of India Act*, 1962, it conferred sweeping powers on the Government to make rules for 'securing the defence of India and civil defence, the public safety, the maintenance of public order or the efficient conduct of military operations, or for maintaining supplies and services essential to the life of the community'. In the same vein as the emergency regime of 1962, the emergency regime of 1971 promulgated the *Defence of India Rules*, 1971 in pursuance of Section 3 of the *Defence of India Act*, 1971. But unlike the *Defence of India Rules*, 1962, which granted the Government sweeping powers concerning preventive detention, the *Defence of India Rules*, 1971, did not authorise the Government to pass preventive detention orders. Instead, the *Defence of India Act*, 1971 introduced an amendment to the permanent piece of preventive detention legislation – MISA – which had far-reaching implications in two ways. First, Section 6(6) of the *Defence of India Act*, 1971, inserted a new Section 17A into the MISA, empowering the Government to keep any person in preventive custody without obtaining the opinion of the Advisory Board for a period between three months and two years if the detention had been made on the grounds of the 'defence of India, relations of India with foreign powers or security of India'. This sweeping power to impose an extended period of detention was to remain in force during the continuance of the *Defence of India Act*, 1971 and the emergency of 1971. Second, the MISA, which under Section 13 originally stipulated a maximum permissible period of detention of 12 months, was amended to allow detention to continue for three years.

After the cessation of the 15-day hostilities with Pakistan, the extraordinary power of preventive detention began to be used during the continuance of emergency for political purposes, that is, to put down opposition to the Government from diverse groups such as communist extremists, national railway workers, students, peasants and industrial workers. By 1973, as many as 17,782 communist leaders were apprehended under the MISA in West Bengal alone (Iyer, 2000). Furthermore, 20,000 railway workers paid the heavy price of being detained under the MISA for organising a general strike against the Government (Iyer, 2000).

3.9.2.1.4.3 Enactment of preventive detention law and its exercise during the third proclamation of emergency (1975–1977)

The most contentious exercise of the power of preventive detention in the history of India took place during the emergency proclaimed on 25 June 1975 on the ground of 'internal disturbance', while the emergency declared on the ground of hostilities with Pakistan was still in force. Shortly after the proclamation of the emergency on account of internal disturbance, the *Defence of India Act*, 1971 was renamed the *Defence and Internal Security of India Act* to provide for the exercise of the powers contained in it for securing the internal security of India, defence of India and civil defence, the public safety, the maintenance of public order, the efficient conduct of military operations and the maintenance of supplies and services essential to the life of the community. The rules made in pursuance of the Act were likewise named the 'Defence and Internal Security of India Rules' (DISIR) (*Gazette of India*, 1975 s 3(i).

An amendment was inserted into the Rules in June 1971 empowering the Indian Government to pass orders for preventing any individual from entering any specified area or place in India, or requiring him to reside or remain in a specified place, or requiring him to report himself or notify his movements to a specified authority, or imposing restrictions in respect of his employment or business, association or communication with other persons or any dissemination or propagation by him of opinions (DISIR s 31A).

Amendments concerning preventive detention were, however, not confined to the DISIR. Drastic amendments were also introduced in the MISA restricting the right to personal liberty of Indians. These amendments to the MISA:

a) dispensed with the detainee's right to be informed of the grounds of detention (s 16A(6)(i));
b) abolished the right of the detainee to apply for bail (s 15(6));
c) permitted the attachment of the property of any person against whom an order of detention had been passed where such person failed to surrender himself before the authorities (s 15(3A));
d) made illegal the communication or disclosure by any one of any information, material or document containing the grounds of detention during the duration of emergencies declared in 1971 and 1975 respectively (s 16A(9));
e) extended the validity of the provisions allowing the Government to detain any individual without informing him of the grounds of detention and without subjecting detention orders to review by an Advisory Board for up to two years from the date of the proclamation of the emergency on the ground of internal disturbance;
f) allowed the expiry of a detention order not to be a bar on the power of the detaining authority to issue another detention order against the same person (s 14(2)).

From the very outset of the proclamation of the Emergency on 25 June 1975, the powers concerning preventive detention were used to stage an unparalleled crackdown on opposition political leaders who demanded Mrs Gandhi's resignation on account of the Allahabad High Court's invalidation of her election to Parliament. Those who were unfriendly to the ruling Congress Party were not spared either. As many as 1576 persons were detained within 24 hours of the invocation of the emergency – a third of this number were senior opposition political leaders such as Jaiprakash Narayan, Moraji Desai, Atal Bihari Vajpayee, L. K. Advani, Charan Singh, Madhu Dandavate, Jyotirmoy Basu, Madhu Limaye, and Piloo Modi (Iyer, 2000; *States of Emergency*, 2000; Ghatate, 2011). These detainees also included Congress MPs, such as Chandra Shekhar, Ram Dhan and Sher Singh, who demanded the resignation of the Prime Minister. An Official Commission of Inquiry – the Shah Commission, formed on 28 May 1977 to investigate the 'excesses, malpractices and misdeeds' perpetrated during the emergency of 1975 – concluded that during the continuation of the emergency from 25 June 1975 to 21 March 1977 an astounding 110,806 persons – 34,988 under the MISA and 75,818 under the DISIR – were kept in preventive custody. The indiscriminate exercise of the power of preventive detention during the emergency regime of 1975 led observers to rightly note that '[t]here was [*sic*] neither criteria nor a basis for the detentions … during the Emergency' (Dayal and Bose, 1978: 37–39).

3.9.2.1.4.4 *The Supreme Court of India's deferential attitude towards the challenge of the exercise of the power of preventive detention during the emergencies*

When challenges were made to the detention orders and constitutionality of preventive detention laws during declared periods of emergency, the Indian Supreme Court consistently adopted a deferential attitude. For instance, in *Mohan Chowdhury v Chief Commissioner of Tripura [1963] AIR (SC) 173*, a detainee contended that since Article 32 of the Indian Constitution, which conferred the right to approach the Supreme Court for the enforcement of other fundamental rights, was kept operative during the continuance of emergency of 1962, he had the right to challenge the constitutional validity of the *Defence of India Rules*, 1962 on the ground that it infringed his right to liberty. The Supreme Court rejected this argument on the ground that maintaining such a challenge involved the invocation of Article 21, which guaranteed the right to personal liberty, the enforcement of which had been specifically dispensed with by the Presidential Order issued on 3 November 1962. The court observed:

> Unquestionably, the Court's power to issue a writ in the nature of Habeas Corpus has not been touched by the President's Order, but the petitioner's right to move the Supreme Court for a writ of that kind has been suspended by the Order of the President.
>
> (174)

Similarly, when in *Haradhan Saha v State of West Bengal [1974] AIR (SC) 2154* the validity of the MISA was challenged on the grounds that it violated Articles 19 (protection of certain rights including the right to move freely throughout India, freedom of assembly and association), 21 (protection of life and personal liberty), and 22(5) (protection against arrest and detention) of the *Constitution of India*, the Supreme Court of India rejected the arguments. It held, *inter alia*, that it would be far-fetched to invoke Article 19 in cases where a person has been lawfully deprived of his liberty, because any effect that the imprisonment would have on his other freedoms, such as the right to move freely within the country or to assemble peacefully or to associate with others, was, in the nature of things, unavoidable. The Court found that the restrictions imposed by MISA were reasonable.

During the continuance of the Emergency of 1975, the Supreme Court of India once again demonstrated its reluctance to scrutinise the detention orders. In this regard, the decision of the Supreme Court of India in the case of *Additional District Magistrate, Jabalpur v Shivakant Shukla [1976] AIR (SC) 1207* (popularly known as the *Habeas Corpus Case*) proved to be the most controversial. The case concerned appeals from the decisions of 10 High Courts, namely, the High Courts of Allahabad, Andhra Pradesh, Bombay, Delhi, Karnataka, Madras, Madhya Pradesh, Punjab, Haryana and Rajasthan, in which the petitioners, who were preventively detained under the MISA, challenged the validity of their detention through writs of *habeas corpus*. In all of the 10 proceedings, the detaining authorities raised preliminary objections that the petitioners had no *locus standi*. For the Presidential Order issued on 27 June 1975, which suspended in pursuance of Article 359 of the Constitution the enforcement, *inter alia*, of the right to protection of life and personal liberty as guaranteed by Article 21, was a bar for the petitioners to invoke the jurisdiction of the High Court under Article 226 of the Constitution and to ask for writs of *habeas corpus*. The High Courts of the abovementioned 10 States had rejected these arguments, holding that though the petitioners had no right to move the court to enforce their fundamental rights under Article 21, they were nevertheless entitled to argue that the order of their detention was 'not under or in compliance with law or was *mala fide*'. The constitutional bench of five judges of the Supreme Court of India by a majority overruled the decisions of the High Courts. Chief Justice A. N. Ray, who delivered the majority judgment, held that:

> In view of the Presidential Order dated 27th June, 1975 under clause (1) of Article 359 of our Constitution no person has any locus standi to move any writ petition under Article 226 before a High Court for habeas corpus or any other writ or order or direction to challenge the legality of an order of detention on the ground that the order is not under or in compliance with the Act [MISA] or is illegal or is vitiated by mala fides factual or legal or is based on extraneous considerations … Article 21 is the sole repository of rights to life and personal liberty against the State. Any claim to a writ of habeas corpus is enforcement of Article 21 and, is therefore, barred by the Presidential Order.
>
> (1234)

It is submitted that the right to test the validity of an order of preventive detention for compliance with the provisions of the MISA exists independently of the suspension of the enforcement of a fundamental right during an emergency. To hold that an order of preventive detention which is vitiated by *mala fides* cannot be challenged during the proclamation of an emergency is in violation of settled jurisprudence regarding ouster clauses even in India. For instance, in *G Sadanandan v State of Kerala [1966] AIR (SC) 1925*, the Supreme Court held that the Courts always retain jurisdiction to set aside *mala fide* orders, even where a statute contains a conclusive ouster clause (i.e. expressly excluding such a jurisdiction). Furthermore, it is difficult to agree with the view that Article 21 is the sole repository of the right to life and personal liberty; in fact, according to the Supreme Court of India in the 1950 case of *AK Gopalan v State of Madras [1950] SCR 88*, the Article merely recognises the existence of the right to life and personal liberty and affords protection against its unlawful deprivation. As it held, the right to life and personal liberty is an 'inherent birthright of man' (254). Yet the Supreme Court in the *Habeas Corpus* Case gave the executive arm of the

Government *carte blanche* in the matter of the exercise of emergency and preventive detention measures.

3.9.2.2 Incorporation of the provisions concerning preventive detention into the Constitutions of Pakistan

In its 67-year history, Pakistan, as pointed out earlier in Section 2.6.3, has adopted three Constitutions in 1956, 1962 and 1973. Each of the three Constitutions contained provisions concerning preventive detention, following in the footsteps of the 1950 Indian Constitution.

3.9.2.2.1 THE 1956 CONSTITUTION OF PAKISTAN

Like the Indian Constitution, Pakistan's first Constitution, adopted in 1956 after more than nine years of gaining independence from British rule, inserted provisions concerning preventive detention in Part II, titled 'Fundamental Rights'. Article 7(4) of the Constitution, read with Entry 18 of the Federal List and Entry 5 of the Provincial List in the 5th Schedule, empowered the Parliament to enact laws concerning preventive detention for similar reasons connected with 'defence', 'foreign affairs, or the security of Pakistan,' and the 'maintenance of public order,' without confining the exercise of such power to formally declared periods of emergency. Like its Indian counterpart, the 1956 *Constitution of Pakistan* did not prescribe the maximum period for which an individual could be kept in preventive custody. This granted the Parliament significant leeway to enact laws providing for preventive detention for an indefinite period of time.

The Constitution did, however, extend certain procedural safeguards to mitigate the harshness of the power of preventive detention. For one thing, the Constitution imposed an obligation on the detaining authority not to detain anyone for a period exceeding three months without the scrutiny of the detention order by an 'appropriate Advisory Board' (art 7(4)). Rather than allowing the executive to choose the formation of the Advisory Board, the 1956 *Constitution of Pakistan* empowered the Chief Justice of Pakistan to constitute such a body (art 7(4)). The detainee was entitled to be communicated the grounds of his detention. But no specific timeframe was provided for informing the detainee of the reasons for his apprehension. Instead the vague expression 'as soon as may be' was used. This granted the detaining authority the wide power of withholding the grounds of detention for an indefinite period of time. Detainees were, however, afforded the opportunity to make a representation before the Advisory Board against their detention orders (art 7(5)).

The life of the 1956 *Constitution of Pakistan*, as mentioned earlier in Section 2.6.3.1, came to an abrupt end on 7 October 1958 through the Proclamation of a Martial Law by the President of the country, Major General Iskander Mirza.

3.9.2.2.2 THE CONSTITUTION OF PAKISTAN, 1962

On 1 March 1962, the Martial Law Regime of Ayub Khan adopted a new Constitution for Pakistan which, as pointed out earlier in 3.5.4.2, instead of inserting fundamental rights originally incorporated certain 'Principles of Law-Making' which could not be enforced in a court of law. Contained in the 'Principles of Law-Making' was the power to enact laws providing for preventive detention 'in the interest of the security of Pakistan or public safety' (Principles of Law-Making No. 8(2)(a). The 1962 Constitution in the same manner as its 1956 predecessor did not stipulate the maximum period of preventive detention, which undoubtedly left the door wide open for the executive to fix by law the detention of individuals for an indefinite period of time.

Like the 1956 Constitution, the 1962 *Constitution of Pakistan* also afforded identical safeguards – the right to be informed of the grounds of detention by the detaining authority as soon as practicable, and the right not to be kept in preventive custody for a period exceeding three months without concurrence of an Advisory Board (Principles of Law-Making Numbers 8(2)(b) and (c). But unlike the 1956 Constitution, which specifically allowed the Chief Justice of Pakistan to choose the members of the Advisory Board, the 1962 Constitution spelt out the composition of the Advisory Board. The Advisory Board was to be composed of a judge of the Supreme Court nominated by the Chief Justice of Pakistan and a nominee of the President, that is, a civil servant, who could hardly be expected to be independent of the influence of the executive (Principles of Law-Making No. 8(2)(c).

Unlike the 1956 Constitution, which allowed the detainee to make a representation against the detention order, the 1962 Constitution dispensed with this right. However, later in 1963, the *Constitution (First Amendment) Act* afforded the detainee the right to make representations against the order of detention (Fundamental Rights No. 2(5). It is pertinent to mention here that the *Constitution (First Amendment) Act*, 1963, which (as pointed out earlier in Section 3.5.4.2) inserted certain fundamental rights in Part II of the 1962 *Constitution of Pakistan*, placed the abovementioned provisions concerning preventive detention in Part II of the Constitution, titled Fundamental rights (Fundamental Rights No. 2(4) and (5).

The 1962 Constitution of Pakistan suffered the same fate as its predecessor when it was abrogated on 25 March 1969 through the declaration of a Martial Law.

3.9.2.2.3 THE CONSTITUTION OF PAKISTAN, 1973

Pakistan's third Constitution which is still in force was, as pointed out earlier in Section 2.6.3.3, adopted by the National Assembly on 12 April 1973 and came into force on 14 August 1973. Like its predecessors of 1956 and 1962, the 1973 *Constitution of Pakistan* also places the provisions concerning preventive detention in Part II titled 'Fundamental Rights'. Article 10(4) of the 1973 Constitution empowers the Parliament to make laws concerning preventive detention to deter activities 'prejudicial to the integrity, security or defence of Pakistan or any part thereof, or external affairs of Pakistan, or public order, or the maintenance of supplies or services'. Thus the British practice of permitting preventive detention for vaguely defined purposes was continued even by the 1973 Constitution of Pakistan.

However, the 1973 *Constitution of Pakistan* affords improved safeguards to detainees compared to its 1956 and 1962 predecessors. First, Article 10(5) of the 1973 Constitution originally imposed an obligation on the detaining authority to furnish the grounds of detention to the detainee 'as soon as may be, but not later than one week' from the date of detention. In this way, the tradition of not specifying a time limit for communicating the grounds of detention was done away with. Second, the period of three months, during which the executive could detain a person without the concurrence of an Advisory Board under the 1956 and 1962 Constitutions of Pakistan, was originally reduced to one month by Article 10(4) of the 1973 *Constitution of Pakistan*. But the *Constitution (3rd Amendment) Act*, 1975 altered these safeguards. The effect of this amendment will be discussed below in 3.9.2.2.5.2.

There are improvements concerning the composition of the Advisory Board as well. The 1973 Constitution returned the power to constitute the Advisory Board to the Chief Justice of Pakistan. It also specifies the composition of the Board and dispenses with the requirement of the inclusion of a civil servant as a representative of the executive on the Advisory Board. It confines the membership of the Board to three persons – a Chairman and two members – each of whom is or has been a Judge of the Supreme Court or a High Court (art 10(4)). Unlike the 1956 and 1962 *Constitutions of Pakistan*, which did not specify the maximum period of detention, the 1973 Constitution in Article 10(7) stipulates that no person can be detained for more than eight months in the case of a person detained for acting in a manner prejudicial to public order, and 12 months in any other case. Thus, the 1973 Constitution prescribes a specific time limit beyond which detainees are not allowed to be kept in preventive custody by the detaining authority. It is therefore evident that the 1973 Constitution significantly liberalised the provisions concerning preventive detention in comparison to its 1956 and 1962 predecessors.

3.9.2.2.4 PREVENTIVE DETENTION STATUTES IN PAKISTAN

In Pakistan, six statutes have been adopted since independence in 1947 permitting the exercise of the power of preventive detention. They are:

1 the *Public Safety Ordinance*, 1949, which was allowed to lapse in 1951;
2 the *Public Safety Ordinance*, 1952, which was repealed in the same year;

3 the *Security of Pakistan Act*, 1952;
4 the *Maintenance of Public Order Ordinance*, 1960;
5 the *Anti-Terrorism Act*, 1997; and
6 the *Protection of Pakistan Act*, 2014.

Of these statutes, the provisions concerning preventive detention enshrined in the *Security of Pakistan Act*, 1952 and the *Maintenance of Public Order Ordinance*, 1960 deserve special attention due to their exercise during declared periods of emergency in Pakistan.

3.9.2.2.4.1 The Security of Pakistan Act, 1952

The *Security of Pakistan Act* (SPA) was initially enacted as temporary legislation, being supposed to come to an end in 1955. But its life has been extended from time to time and it is still in force in Pakistan today. Initially, Section 3(1) of the SPA authorised the Government to detain individuals in order to prevent them from acting in a manner prejudicial to the 'defence', 'external affairs', the 'security of Pakistan or any part thereof', or the 'maintenance of supplies and service essential to the community or 'the maintenance of public order'. In 1956, the grounds of maintenance of supplies and service essential to the community and maintenance of public order were omitted by the *Adaption (Security Laws) Order*, 1956. In 1962, with the adoption of yet another Constitution, the SPA was further amended to confine the exercise of power of preventive detention only in the interest of the 'security of Pakistan' (*Preventive Detention Laws (Amendment) Act 1962* s 2(1). It seems that this amendment to SPA was preferred with a view to bringing it into conformity with the 1962 *Constitution of Pakistan* which, as pointed out above, envisaged the exercise of the power of preventive detention only for reasons connected with the security or public safety of Pakistan.

After the enactment of Pakistan's third Constitution in 1973, the SPA, 1952 was subjected to further amendments which can be summarised as follows:

a) no person detained for reasons connected with 'defence', 'external affairs' or the 'security of Pakistan or any part thereof' can be kept in preventive custody beyond three months without the scrutiny of an Advisory Board (s 6A);
b) the detainee has been given the rights to be heard in person by the Advisory Board and to consult a legal practitioner (s 6A);
c) the composition of the Advisory Board was brought in line with that as envisioned by the 1973 Constitution in Article 10(4). Hence, the Advisory Board would now be appointed by the Chief Justice of Pakistan and consist of a Chairman and two members, each of whom is or has been a Judge of the Supreme Court or a High Court; and
d) the communication of the grounds to the detainee and the review of detention order by the Advisory Board were made mandatory.

3.9.2.2.4.2 Maintenance of Public Order Ordinance, 1960

The *Maintenance of Public Order Ordinance* (MPOO) was enacted in 1960 to be applicable to West Pakistan only. Since the liberation of the eastern wing of Pakistan in 1971, the Ordinance is now applicable to the whole of Pakistan.

The broad and vaguely worded MPOO in Section 3 authorises the government to 'detain suspected persons' for up to six months with a view to preventing any person from acting in any manner prejudicial to 'public safety or the maintenance of public order'. The explanation to Section 3 provides that black-marketing or hoarding or smuggling shall be deemed as being prejudicial to the 'maintenance of public order'.

Thus the MPOO brought within its purview offences which could have been dealt with adequately by the ordinary criminal law framework, such as the *Hoarding and Black-Market Act*, 1948 or the *Sea Customs Act*, 1878 or the *Land Customs Act*, 1925. In 1964, the Government assumed further sweeping powers when it appended another explanation by an amendment to Section 3 of the MPOO to the effect that any member of an association which has been declared unlawful should be deemed as acting in a manner prejudicial to the 'maintenance of public order'. As a result, the MPOO was able to be used for ordinary and political purposes to suit the designs of the government of the day.

However, the MPOO does afford certain safeguards to detainees in the same manner as the SPA, 1952. For instance, it provides for the communication of grounds to detainees and the formation of an Advisory Board to scrutinise detention orders.

3.9.2.2.5 ENACTMENT OF PREVENTIVE DETENTION LAWS AND THEIR EXERCISE DURING THE PROCLAMATIONS OF EMERGENCY IN PAKISTAN

Altogether Pakistan has, as discussed in Section 2.6.3, experienced proclamations of emergency on seven occasions between 1954 and 2007. The enactment of preventive detention laws and their exercise during the emergencies declared in 1965, 1969 and 2007 deserve special attention because the exercise of the power of preventive detention during these three declared periods of emergency has proved to be the most contentious in the history of Pakistan.

3.9.2.2.5.1 Enactment of Preventive Detention Law and its exercise during the emergency declared in 1965

On 6 September 1965, as noted in Section 2.6.3.2.1, President Ayub Khan proclaimed an emergency throughout Pakistan due to armed conflict that broke out with India. The Proclamation of Emergency was followed by the promulgation of the *Defence of Pakistan Ordinance*, 1965, which empowered the Government to make rules for maintaining the 'defence', 'public safety', and 'security of Pakistan'.

The Ordinance of 1965 in Section 3 authorised the executive to frame rules concerning preventive detention under which Rules were framed by the Government relating to preventive detention. Rule 32 stated:

> (1) The ... Government, if satisfied with respect to any particular person, that with a view to preventing him from acting in a manner prejudicial to the security, the public safety or interest or the defence of Pakistan, the maintenance of public order, Pakistan's relations with any other powers, the maintenance of peaceful conditions in any part of Pakistan, the maintenance of essential supplies and services or the efficient prosecution of war, it is necessary so to do, may make an order ...
> (b) directing that he be detained;

The Ordinance of 1965 did not provide the procedural safeguards to detainees that were envisaged by the 1962 *Constitution of Pakistan.* Numerous people were detained in preventive custody in pursuance of Rule 32 of the Ordinance. The enactment of such arbitrary rules concerning preventive detention can hardly be justified when similar powers were already available to the Government under two regular laws concerning preventive detention, namely, the SPA, 1952 and MPOO, 1960, sufficient to meet the exigencies of the situation. It is obvious that the executive arm of the Government did not want to extend the safeguards that were enshrined in these permanent laws concerning preventive detention to the detainees.

The war with India, which gave rise to the promulgation of the abovementioned rule concerning preventive detention, came to an end within 17 days but both the emergency and the arbitrary and wide rules were continued until 1969.

3.9.2.2.5.2 Enactment of Preventive Detention Law and its exercise during the emergency proclaimed in 1971 after the abrogation of the 1962 Constitution of Pakistan

The 1962 Constitution of Pakistan, as mentioned earlier in Section 2.6.3.2.2, was abrogated by General Yahya Khan through the proclamation of a martial law on 25 March 1969. When President Yahya Khan refused to allow the inhabitants of East Pakistan (known as Bengalis) to form the Government after winning the majority in the General Elections for Constituent Assembly held in December 1970, they proclaimed independence from Pakistan in 1971 and to deal with the situation the regime issued the *Martial Law Regulation No 78* (PLD, 1971). This Regulation, among other things, granted the executive the following wide powers concerning preventive detention to put down the Bengali Nationalists:

> (1) The Chief Martial Law Administrator or Martial Law Administrator or a Deputy Martial Law Administrator authorized by the Martial

> Law Administrator concerned in this behalf, if satisfied with respect to any particular person, that with a view to preventing him from acting in a seditious manner or in a manner prejudicial to the security, the public safety or interest or the defence of Pakistan, the maintenance of public order, Pakistan's relations with any other power, the maintenance of peaceful conditions in any part of Pakistan, the maintenance of essential supplies and services, it is necessary to do, may make an order, …
> (b) directing that he be detained;

The above provisions concerning preventive detention were reproduced exactly from those of Rule 32 of the Defence of Pakistan Rules, 1965. The *Martial Law Regulation No. 78* did not afford any safeguards concerning preventive detention. Consequently, thousands of Bengalis were detained and persecuted under the provision of this Regulation. Some of these detainees were even brutally slaughtered by the Pakistan Military Regime.

On 23 November 1971, the Military Regime of Pakistan proclaimed an Emergency on account of hostilities that broke out with India due to India's support for the cause of Bangladesh's Independence. The proclamation was quickly followed by the issuance of the *Defence of Pakistan Ordinance*, 1971 on the same day, which empowered the Government to make rules to guarantee the 'security', 'public safety or interest' and 'the defence of Pakistan', or the 'efficient conduct of military operations or prosecution of war', or 'maintaining supplies and services essential to the life of the community' (*Gazette of Pakistan*, 1971). Unsurprisingly, Rules were framed in pursuance of the Ordinance of 1971, which bestowed on the Martial Law Regime very wide powers concerning preventive detention. In particular, Rule 32 provided that:

> Where with respect to any person the … Government is of opinion that, for the purpose of preventing him from acting in a manner prejudicial to Pakistan's relation with foreign powers, or to the security, the public safety or interest, the defence of Pakistan or of any part thereof, the maintenance of supplies and services essential to the life of the community, the maintenance of peaceful conditions in any part of Pakistan, or efficient conduct of military operations or prosecution of war, it is necessary so to do, it may make an order …
> (b) directing that he be detained;

Although the emergency was proclaimed on account of a war with India, the targets of preventive detention powers were again Bengalis until 16 December 1971 when Bangladesh gained its independence.

The war with Bangladesh ended on 16 December 1971 and the Martial Law Regime was replaced by the Civilian Administration of Zulfikar Ali Bhutto, leader of the Pakistan People's Party, which won 88 seats in the

1970 elections. The emergency declared in 1971 and the *Defence of Pakistan Ordinance*, 1971 and the Rules concerning preventive detention enshrined therein were nevertheless continued despite the adoption of a new Constitution which contained liberalised provisions, as pointed out earlier in Section 3.9.2.2.3, concerning preventive detention. Subsequently, these powers began to be used by the regime of Zulfiqar Ali Bhutto for political purposes to strengthen its grip on power. Furthermore, a number of amendments were made to the 1973 *Constitution of Pakistan* reducing the safeguards in respect of preventive detention.

First, the *Constitution (Third Amendment) Act*, 1975, which was adopted in February 1975, changed Article 10 of the 1973 Constitution in the following ways:

a) it extended the period for which a person could be detained without reference to an Advisory Board from one month to three months (art 10(4)); and
b) the timeframe of one week within which the detaining authority was required to communicate the grounds of detention to the detainee was increased to 15 days (art 10(5)).

Second, the *Constitution (Fourth Amendment) Act*, 1975, arbitrarily abolished the jurisdiction of the High Courts, preventing them from scrutinising executive orders of preventive detention. Furthermore, this amendment took away the authority of High Courts to grant bail in preventive detention cases. The validity of this amendment was challenged before the Supreme Court of Pakistan in the case of *Pakistan v United Sugar Mills Ltd [1977] PLD (SC) 397*. It was argued by the petitioner that the amendment unconstitutionally took away the High Courts' judicial powers and, as such, contravened the principle of separation of powers. Although the Court agreed that 'it is not disputed that power of making final decision[s] remains with the High Courts and [is] not transferred to the executive', it nevertheless denied the petition on the ground that the 'power to afford interim relief [i.e. bail] has not been entirely taken away; its operation has [merely] been curtailed' (411). The Court in denying this petition regrettably took a narrow view of the concept of separation of powers. It observed:

> It is also important to observe that our Constitution, like many other modern written Constitutions, does not provide for rigid separation of powers. Indeed there is no direct provision in that behalf except that the Constitution by various provisions provides for the setting up of the principal institutions for the exercise of the sovereign powers of the State in the appointed field. In actual practice in all modern Governments, separation is only functional to subserve the practical necessity of an efficient and enlightened Government by providing for checks and balances

> to avoid abuse of public power. Nowhere … the principle is pushed to its logical conclusion so as to create watertight compartments within the Government.
>
> (411)

Third, the *Constitution (Fifth Amendment) Act*, which was passed in September 1976, deprived the High Courts of the power to offer any remedy whatsoever to detainees in the exercise of their writ jurisdiction.[25] The validity of this amendment was also challenged. In the case of *Jehangir Iqbal v Pakistan [1979] PLD (Peshawar) 67*, the petitioner argued that the Parliament of Pakistan had abused its legislative power by eliminating the jurisdiction of the High Courts to offer any relief in preventive detention cases (69). However, the High Court of Peshawar, maintaining the practice established by the Supreme Court of Pakistan of deferring to the executive, upheld the constitutionality of the amendment on the ground that the ouster of the Courts' jurisdiction was not in violation of fundamental rights as those rights were expressly suspended by a valid proclamation of a state of emergency (74). Thus the Court failed to appreciate the fact that the *Constitution of Pakistan*, 1973 envisaged the enjoyment of the right to enjoy the protection of law and to be treated in accordance with law independently of the Chapter on Fundamental Rights.[26]

Defending the attack on the judiciary, Zulfiqar Ali Bhutto remarked that '[i]n a system of parliamentary democracy sovereignty could belong to the legislature alone' (Noorani, 1977: 1017). He went further, blaming the judiciary for the amendments to the Constitution and saying that the exercise of the writ jurisdiction by High Courts has been 'the biggest show on the Broadway' (Noorani, 1977: 1017).

Amnesty International in its Report on Pakistan in 1976 reported that the abovementioned amendments coupled with Defence of Pakistan Ordinance, 1971 and the Rules concerning preventive detention paved the way for the regime of Mr Bhutto to detain several thousand political adversaries with a view to perpetuating its rule in the absence of a grave emergency threatening the life of the nation. Calling attention to the similarities with the exercise of these powers in India, Lewis M. Simons observed:

> Beneath a translucent gloss of political stability, Prime Minister Zulfiqar Ali Bhutto is wiping out civil liberties and waging a campaign of repression in Pakistan as ruthlessly as Indian Premier Indira Gandhi is destroying democracy next door.
>
> (Noorani, 1977: 1016)

The emergency declared in 1971 as well as the *Defence of Pakistan Ordinance*, 1971 and the Rules enacted in pursuance of it were ultimately revoked in 1977.

3.9.2.2.5.3 Exercise of the Power of Preventive Detention during the extra-eonstitutional emergency of 2007

It may be recalled here that, as discussed in Section 2.6.3.3.4, President Pervez Musharraf proclaimed an extra-constitutional emergency in Pakistan on 3 November 2007 to deal with the paralysis of the government and its law enforcement agencies allegedly due to the Supreme Court's interference. However, rather than promulgating a *Defence of Pakistan Ordinance*, as was done during the emergencies proclaimed in emergencies in 1962 and 1971, so as to assume extraordinary powers concerning preventive detention, President Musharraf decided to rely on the permanent law of MPOO, 1960 to preventively detain those who posed a threat to his rule.

The primary target of MPOO was not the major leaders of opposition political parties, such as Benazir Bhutto or Nawaz Sharif. Rather, it was the lawyers and human rights activists who took to the streets of Pakistan to protest against the unceremonious dismissal of Chief Justice Iftikhar Chaudhry and seven other judges of the Supreme Court by Musharraf and to demand their reinstatement. Resort was specifically made to Section 16 of the MPOO, titled, 'Dissemination of Rumors etc.'. which prohibits speech that 'causes or is likely to cause fear or alarm to the public' or 'which furthers or is likely to further any activity prejudicial to public safety or the maintenance of public order'. As many as 2,000 lawyers and human rights activists were detained under the MPOO within 48 hours of the proclamation of the emergency. Several thousand more were detained during the continuation of the emergency until 15 December 2007 (Kronstadt, 2007).

It can be concluded that President Musharraf used the law concerning preventive detention as an instrument for detaining his adversaries – in this case lawyers and human rights activists – with a view to strengthening his grip on power.

3.9.2.3 The Constitution of Bangladesh, *1972 and the power of preventive detention*

The 1972 *Constitution of Bangladesh*, which in Article 32 guarantees that 'No person shall be deprived of life or personal liberty save in accordance with law', did not originally contemplate any kind of preventive detention and hence the question of providing for restrictions on legislation in respect of preventive detention did not arise. Perhaps the repeated misuse of the powers of preventive detention by the Governments of Pakistan (1947–1971), during the days when Bangladesh (erstwhile East Pakistan) was a province of Pakistan, discouraged the framers of the 1972 Constitution from including in it such powers. Article 33 of the Constitution, which contained safeguards as to arrest and detention, originally stated:

> (1) A person who is arrested shall not be detained in custody unless he has been informed of the grounds of his arrest, nor shall he be

denied the right to consult and be defended by a legal practitioner of his choice.

(2) Every person who is arrested and detained in custody shall be brought before a Court within twenty-four hours of his arrest (excluding the time required to transport him to the Court), and shall not be further detained save by order of the Court.

(3) Nothing in the foregoing clauses shall apply to an enemy alien.

Later, on 22 September 1973, due to the rapid deterioration in the economic and law-and-order situations the *Constitution (Second Amendment) Act*, 1973 replaced this original Article 33 of the Constitution with a new one, which adds two additional clauses to the original Article 33. The newly inserted clauses (4) and (5) not only empower the Parliament to pass laws relating to preventive detention but also provide for certain safeguards to mitigate the harshness of such laws by imposing restrictions on legislative power. The inserted clauses (4) and (5) of Article 33 state:

(4) No law providing for preventive detention shall authorise the detention of a person for a period exceeding six months unless an Advisory Board consisting of three persons, of whom two shall be persons who are, or have been, or are qualified to be appointed as, Judges of the Supreme Court and the other shall be a person who is a senior officer in the service of the Republic, has, after affording him an opportunity of being heard in person, reported before the expiration of the said period of six months that there is, in its opinion, sufficient cause for such detention.

(5) When any person is detained in pursuance of an order made under any law providing for preventive detention, the authority making the order shall, as soon as may be, communicate to such person the grounds on which the order has been made, and shall afford him the earliest opportunity of making a representation against the order.

The provisions concerning preventive detention contained in the 1972 *Constitution of Bangladesh* and the permanent and temporary laws in Bangladesh, the exercise of the power of preventive detention during the declared periods of emergency, and the judicial response to the exercise of such power shall be examined in an in-depth manner in Chapter 7 of this book.

3.10 References

Abraham, C. M. (1993) 'India- An Overview' in A. Harding and J. Hatchard (eds), *Preventive Detention and Security Law: A Comparative Survey*, Dordrecht/Boston: Martinus Nijhoff Publishers, 60, 61.

Alam, Z. (1987) *Emergency Powers and Indian Democracy*, New Delhi: SK Publishers, 28.

Alexy, R (2006) 'Discourse Theory and Fundamental Rights', in Menendez, A. J. and Eriksen, E. O. (eds), *Arguing Fundamental Rights*, Dordrecht: Springer, 15, 18.

Amnesty International (1976) *Islamic Republic of Pakistan: An Amnesty International Report Including the Findings of a Mission to Pakistan: Report*, 53.

Amnesty International (1977), *Report*, 183.

Austin, G. (1999) *Working a Democratic Constitution: The Indian Experience*, New Delhi: Oxford University Press, 508.

Bayley, D. (1969) *The Police and Political Development in India*, Princeton, NJ: Princeton University Press, 99.

Brown, J. (1994) *Modern India: The Origins of an Asian Democracy*, Oxford/New York: Oxford University Press, 202.

Communication No. 64/1979, UN Doc CCPR/C/OP/1 (1985), available at http://hrlibrary.umn.edu/undocs/newscans/64-1979.html [Accessed 28 December 2016].

Chitkara, M. G. (1998) *Converts Do Not Make a Nation*, New Delhi: SB Nangia, APH Publishing Corporation, 587.

Dayal, J. and Bose, A. (1978) *The Shah Commission Begins*, New Delhi: Orient Longman, 37–39.

De Smith, S. A. (1961) 'Fundamental Rights in the New Commonwealth', *International and Comparative Law Quarterly*, 10: 85.

Fitzpatrick, J. (1994) *Human Rights in Crisis: The International System for Protecting Rights During States of Emergency*, Philadelphia, PA: University of Pennsylvania Press, 97, 196.

Gandhi, P. R. (1990) 'The Human Rights Committee and Derogation in Public Emergencies', *German of Yearbook of International Law*, 32: 357.

Ghatate, N. M. (2011) *Emergency, Constitution and Democracy: An Indian Experience*, Delhi: Shipra Publications, 20, 24, 36, 142, 144.

Gledhill, A. (1957) *Pakistan: The Development of its Laws and Constitutions*, London: Steven & Sons, 198.

Halsbury's Laws of England (1931–1942) second ed., London: LexisNexis Butterworths, 389 (Para 435).

Harding, A. and Hatchard, J. (1993) 'Introduction', in A. Harding and J. Hatchard (eds), *Preventive Detention and Security Law: A Comparative Survey*, Dordrecht/Boston: Martinus Nijhoff Publishers, 2, 5, 6.

Hartman, J. F. (1981) 'Derogation from Human Rights Treaties in Public Emergencies', *Harvard International Law Journal*, 22(1): 5, 17, 20, 36, 40, 41–42, 48.

Hasan, K. S. (1962) 'The New Constitution of Pakistan', *Parliamentary Affairs*, 16(2): 174.

Home Office White Paper 1997, *Rights Brought Home: The Human Rights Bill*, London: HMSO (Cm 3782) 1.4, available at www.gov.uk/government/uploads/system/uploads/attachment_data/file/263526/rightspdf [Accessed 7 October 2011].

Human Rights Committee (1981) *General Comment 5(13)*, UN Doc A/36/40, para 2.

Human Rights Committee (1981) *Report of the Human Rights Committee*, 36 UN GAOR Supp. (No. 40), UN Doc A/36/40, 41, 110.

Human Rights Committee (1987) *Consideration of Reports Submitted by States*

Parties under Article 40 of the Covenant: Zambia, UN Doc CCPR/C/SR.776, November, paras 4–7;

Human Rights Committee (2001) *General Comment 29: States of Emergency*, U.N. Doc. CCPR/C/21/Rev.1/Add.11, para 1, available at http://hrlibrary.umn.edu/gencomm/hrc29.html [Accessed 5 April 2014].

Human Rights Committee (2012) *Report of the Human Rights Committee*, vol 1, 103rd sess & 104th sess, UN Doc A/67/40, 15–16, 79, 195–197.

Inter-American Commission on Human Rights (2002) *Michael Domingues v. United States*, Case 12.285, Report No. 62/02: Decision Overview, Newark: The International Justice Project, available at www.internationaljusticeproject.org/pdfs/dominguesoverview.pdf [Accessed 5 May 2014].

International Commission of Jurists (1967) 'Inroads Into Fundamental Rights in India', *ICJ Bulletin*, 29: 33.

International Commission of Jurists (1983) *States of Emergency – Their Impact on Human Rights: A Comparative Study by the International Commission of Jurists*, Geneva: International Commission of Jurists, 176, 177, 180, 189.

Isemonger, F. C. and Slattery, J. (1919) *An Account of the Ghadr Conspiracy (1913–1915)*, Lahore/ Punjab: Superintendent, Government Printing, 147.

Iyer, V. (1999) 'States of Emergency – Moderating their Effects on Human Rights', *Dalhousie Law Journal*, 22: 134–135.

Iyer, V. (2000) *States of Emergency: The Indian Experience*, New Delhi: Butterworths, 57, 138, 140, 157.

Jain, G. (1975) 'Erosion of the Rule of Law: Suspension of Fundamental Rights', *The Times of India* (Bombay), 20 November, Editorial.

Jennings, I. (1958) *Approach to Self-Government*, Cambridge: Cambridge University Press, 20.

Johansen, J. and Rosen, P. (2010) 'The Notwithstanding Clause of the Charter', Background Paper No BP-194-E, Ottawa: Library of Canadian Parliament Research Publications, available at www.parl.gc.ca/content/lop/researchpublications/bp194-e.htm#arguments (Accessed 15 June 2014).

Kalhan, A., Conroy, G. P., Kaushal, M., Miller, S. S., and Rakoff, J. S. (2006) 'Colonial Continuities: Human Rights, Terrorism, and Security Laws in India', *Columbia Journal of Asian Law*, 20(1): 125.

Kirk, J. (1997) 'Constitutional Guarantees, Characterisation, and the Concept of Proportionality', *Melbourne University Law Review*, 21: 2.

Koji, T. (2001) 'Emerging Hierarchy in International Human Rights and Beyond: From the Perspective of Non-derogable Rights', *European Journal of International Law*, 12(5): 928, 930.

Kronstadt, K. A. (2007) *CRS Report for Congress: Pakistan's Political Crisis and State of Emergency*, Report, Congressional Research Service, Washington, 6.

Lasswell, H. D. (1950) *National Security and Individual Freedom*, New York: McGraw-Hill, 141.

Lee, H. P. (1984) *Emergency Powers*, Sydney: The Law Book Company Limited, 1.

Mahmood, M. (1973) *The Constitution of the Islamic Republic of Pakistan*, 1973, Lahore: Pakistan Law Times Publications, 33.

Majumdar, R. C., Raychaudhuri, H. C., and Datta, K. (1950) *An Advanced History of India*, London: Macmillan, 1985.

Mak'Ochieng, M. (2006) 'Sparse Role for Kenya's Media during the Reign of Daniel arap Moi', *Ecquid Novi: African Journalism Studies*, 27(1): 79–80.

McGoldrick, D. (2004) 'The Interface between Public Emergency Powers and International Law', *International Journal of Constitutional Law*, 2(2): 391.

Meron, T. (1986) *Human Rights Law Making in the United Nations: A Critique of Instruments and Process*, Oxford: Clarendon Press, 83, 84, 85, 90.

Mishra, A. K. (2014) *50 Leading Cases of Supreme Court of India*, Discount Book Store, 743.

Molla, M. K. U. (1988) 'The Influence of the US Constitution on the Indian Subcontinent: Pakistan, India and Bangladesh', in Starr, J. B. (ed.), *The United States Constitution: Its Birth, Growth and Influence in Asia*, Hong Kong: Hong Kong University Press, 156.

Noorani, A. G. (1977) 'Anatomy of Repression', *Economic and Political Weekly*, 25 June, 1016–1017.

Opsahl, T. (1992) 'The Human Rights Committee', in P. Alston (ed.), *The United Nations and Human Rights: A Critical Appraisal*, Oxford: Clarendon Press, 422.

Oraa, J. (1992) *Human Rights in States of Emergency in International Law*, Oxford: Clarendon Press, 94, 96, 97 125.

Pati, B. (1998) *India and the First World War*, New Delhi: Atlantic Publishers & Distributors Pvt. Ltd, 117.

Phillips, O. W. (1962) *Constitutional and Administrative Law*, London: Sweet & Maxwell, 13–14.

Republic of India (1949) *Constituent Assembly Debates*, vol. ix, 1949, 1505–1508.

Republic of India (1950) *Parliamentary Debate*, vol. II, part II, 1950, 874–876

Robertson, A. H. (1981) 'The Implementation System: International Measures' in L. Henkin, *The International Bill of Rights: The Covenant on Civil and Political Rights*, New York: Columbia University Press, 350–351.

Rossiter, C. L. (1948) *Constitutional Dictatorship: Crisis Government in the Modern Democracies*, Princeton, NJ: Princeton University Press, 5, 11.

Sharma, B. K. (2007) *Introduction to the Constitution of India*, New Delhi: Asoke K Ghosh, Prentice-Hall of India Private Ltd, 30.

Simon Commission (1988) *Report of the Indian Statutory Commission: Recommendations*, vol. 2, New Delhi: Arvind K Mittal Logos Press, 22–23.

Sripati, V. (1997) 'Human Rights in India: Fifty Years After Independence', *Denver Journal of International Law and Politics* 26(2): 96.

Sripati, V. (1998) 'Toward Fifty Years of Constitutionalism and Fundamental Rights in India: Looking Back to See Ahead', *American University International Law Review*, 14(2): 417, 418, 433.

The All Pakistan Legal Decisions (1971) 'Central Statutes', 275–276.

United Nations Treaty Collection, *Chapter IV: Human Rights*, available at https://treaties.un.org/Pages/ViewDetails.aspx?mtdsg_no=IV-4&chapter=4&lang=en [Accessed 10 March 2014].

Zenovic, P. (2012) 'Human Rights Enforcement Via Peremptory norms – A Challenge to State Sovereignty', Riga: Riga Graduate School of Law (RGSL Research Papers No. 6, 19.

Notes

1 An exception to this notion can be found in the notwithstanding clause contained in the Canadian constitutional arrangement. Section 33(1) of the *Canadian Charter of Rights and Freedoms* empowers the Parliament and

Provincial Legislatures to enact legislation overriding a number of rights, including core rights, such as the right to life, the right not to be subjected to any cruel and unusual treatment or punishment, the rights to freedom of conscience and religion. The Canadian approach to constitutionally entrenched rights has been the subject of much criticism due to its inconsistency with the very objective of incorporating rights within a constitution. See Johansen J., and Rosen, P. (2010) 'The Notwithstanding Clause of the Charter', Background Paper No BP-194-E, Library of Canadian Parliament Research Publications, available at www.parl.gc.ca/content/lop/researchpublications/bp194-e.htm#arguments (Accessed 15 June 2014).

2 In fact, on 25 September 1789, Congress transmitted to State Legislatures 12 proposed amendments, two of which, having to do with Congressional representation and Congressional pay, were not adopted. The remaining 10 amendments became the Bill of Rights.

3 *European Convention for the Protection of Human Rights and Fundamental Freedoms* (ECHR) *1950* art. 2; ICCPR art. 6; *American Convention on Human Rights* (ACHR) *1969* art. 4.

4 ECHR, art. 3; ICCPR, art. 26; ACHR, art. 5.

5 ECHR, art. 4; ICCPR, art. 26; ACHR, art. 6.

6 ECHR, art. 7; ICCPR, art. 26; ACHR, art. 9.

7 ECHR, art. 15(2).

8 ACHR, art. 27(2).

9 ECHR in Article 15(1) states that a state party 'may take measures derogating from its obligations under this Convention to the extent strictly required by the exigencies of the situation'.

10 The European Court of Human Rights under the ECHR.

11 The HRC is composed of 18 members. See ICCPR, art. 28.

12 ECHR in Article 15(3) states: 'Any High Contracting Party availing itself of this right of derogation shall keep the Secretary General of the Council of Europe fully informed of the measures which it has taken and the reasons therefor.'

13 ICCPR in Article 4(3) states 'Any State Party to the present Covenant availing itself of the right of derogation shall immediately inform the other States Parties to the present Covenant, through the intermediary of the Secretary-General of the United Nations, of the provisions from which it has derogated and of the reasons by which it was actuated'.

14 For instance, Equatorial Guinea's initial report, which was due on 24 December 1988, has not been submitted in 23 years (as at 30 March 2012); Somalia's initial report, which was due on 23 April 1991, has not been submitted in 20 years (as at 30 March 2012); Grenada's initial report, which was due on 5 December 1992, has not been submitted in 20 years (as at 30 March 2012); Côte d'Ivoire's initial report, which was due on 25 June 1993, has not been submitted in 20 years (as at 30 March 2012); Malawi's initial report, which was due on 21 March 1995, was submitted after 18 years on 21 May 2013; Haiti's initial report, which was due on 30 December 1996, was submitted after 16 years on 3 December 2012; South Africa's initial report, which was due on 9 March 2000, was submitted after 14 years on 26 November 2014; Bangladesh's initial report, which was due on 6 December 2001, was submitted after nearly 14 years on 19 June 2015. Human Rights Committee (2012) *Report of the Human Rights Committee*, Volume 1, 103rd sess & 104th sess, UN Doc A/67/40, 15–16; Human Rights Committee (2013) *Consideration of reports submitted by States parties under article 40 of the Covenant: Côte d'Ivoire*, UN Doc CCPR/C/CIV/1; Human Rights Committee (2013) *Consideration of reports submitted by States parties under article 40 of the Covenant: Haiti*, UN Doc CCPR/C/HTI/1; Human

Rights Committee (2015) *Consideration of reports submitted by States parties under article 40 of the Covenant: South Africa*, UN Doc CCPR/C/ZAF/1; Human Rights Committee (2015) *Consideration of reports submitted by States parties under article 40 of the Covenant: Bangladesh* UN Doc CCPR/C/BGD/1.

15 For instance, the *Initial USSR Report*, UN Doc CCPR/C/1/Add.2.

16 However, the effectiveness of the European Court of Human Rights as an implementation organ has often been marred by the adoption of the deferential concept of 'margin of appreciation'. The Court used this concept for the first time in the case of *Handyside v United Kingdom* (5493/72 [1976] ECHR 5). This concept has subsequently been reaffirmed in a number of subsequent cases. For instance, in the cases of *Brannigan and McBride v The United Kingdom*, and *Ireland v The United Kingdom*, it was held by the Court that: 'By reason of their direct and continuous contact with the pressing needs of the moment, the national authorities are in principle in a better position than the international judge to decide both on the presence of such an emergency and on the nature and the scope of derogations necessary to avert it. In this matter Art.15 (1) leaves the authorities a wide margin of appreciation'. *Brannigan and McBride v The United Kingdom* (14553/89; 14554/89 [1993] ECHR at 43) and *Ireland v The United Kingdom* (5310/71 [1993] ECHR at 48).

However, the root of the concept of 'margin of appreciation' can be traced back to the to Cyprus Report. In this report, two principles were established: a) that the former European Commission, which was abolished in 1998, had 'the competence and duty' to examine the merits of a declaration of a state of emergency by a state party, and b) that 'some margin of appreciation' must be afforded to a government in evaluating the legality of its claim of derogation from human rights. Cyprus Case [1958–1959] Yearbook of the European Convention on Human Rights 182 (European Commission on Human Rights) (Report); Report of the European Commission on Human Rights, Lawless Case, [1960–1961], ser. B, 82.

17 Under Article 46(2) of the ECHR, the Committee of Ministers is to supervise the execution of the Court's judgments.

18 115 states have so far ratified the First Optional Protocol. United Nations Treaty Collection, available at https://treaties.un.org/Pages/ViewDetails.aspx?src=IND&mtdsg_no=IV-5&chapter=4&clang=_en (Accessed 14 April 2014).

19 The residual 899 communications have either been declared inadmissible or discontinued or withdrawn.

20 *Constitution (Thirty-Eighth Amendment) Act 1975* s 7. The newly inserted clause 1A to art 359 was given retrospective effect from 26 November 1949.

21 Madras by *State Prisoners Regulation*, 1819, Bombay by *State Prisoners Regulation*, 1827, Punjab by Act IV of 1872, Santhal Pargnas by Regulation III of 1872, Agra by Act XV of 1874, Central Provinces by Act XX of 1875, Oudh by Act XVIII of 1876, Ajmer by Regulation III of 1877, Chittagong Hill Tracts by Regulation I of 1890, North Western Frontier Province by Regulation VII of 1901, British Baluchistan by Regulation II of 1913, Panth Piploda by Regulation II of 1929, District of Khondamals by Regulation IV of 1936 and Angul District by Regulation V of 1936.

22 The scheduled offences under Section 34(1) of the Act included sedition, waging war against the government, attempting or conspiring to wage war, collecting arms with the intention of waging war, abetting mutiny, promoting enmity between different religious, racial, or linguistic groups, and causing criminal intimidation.

23 As Thakur Das Bhargava argued:

> All the same, we must realize that there is an emergency. So far as the emergency is concerned, there can be no two opinions in this country … This is a situation which is not an emergency as envisaged in Article 352 of this Constitution which is a more serious affair … Under Article 359 all the fundamental rights must remain in suspense when the emergency is declared under Article 352. Thus this Bill is designed to avert that emergency. We do not want that emergency to overtake us. This in only intended to avert that emergency so that we may be able to control the situation. By doing so the emergency can averted (898).

24 Most of these 957 persons were members of the Indian Communist Party.

25 *Constitution (Fifth Amendment) Act 1975* provided that: '(3A) A High Court shall not make under its writ jurisdiction:

a) an order prohibiting the making, or suspending the operation, of an order for the detention of any person under any law providing for preventive detention;
b) an order for the release on bail of any person detained under any law providing for preventive detention;
c) an order for the release on bail, or an order suspending the operation of an order for the custody, of any person against whom a report or complaint has been made before any court or tribunal, or against whom a case has been registered at any police station, in respect of an offence, or who has been convicted by any court or tribunal;
d) an order prohibiting the registration of a case at a police station, or the making of a report or complaint before any court or tribunal, in respect of an offence; or
e) any other interim order in respect of any person referred to in any of the preceding paragraphs.

26 *Constitution of Pakistan 1973* in Article 4 states: '(1) To enjoy the protection of law and to be treated in accordance with law is the inalienable right of every citizen, wherever he may be, and of every other person for the time being within Pakistan. (2) In particular:– a) no action detrimental to the life, liberty, body, reputation or property of any person shall be taken except in accordance with law; b) no person shall be prevented from or be hindered in doing that which is not prohibited by law; and c) no person shall be compelled to do that which the law does not require him to do.'

4 Devising and developing a standard emergency model

4.1 Introduction

Recent scholarly debate on emergency powers has been dominated by theorists belonging to two competing models, the extra-legal model and the legal model. The extra-legal model is based on the premise that it is not possible for the framers of constitutions to foresee all conceivable emergencies and, as such, constitutional provisions concerning emergency powers will obviously fail to address the exigencies of a particular emergency (Gross, 2003). The scepticism of this model with regard to constitutionally entrenched emergency provisions has led critics to label it as being influenced by the work of Carl Schmitt, who also insisted that constitutional norms are incapable of constraining emergency powers and, as such, only the absolute form of emergency rule is possible.

On the other hand, the alternative model to the extra-legal model, i.e. the legal model, is premised on the idea that emergencies can indeed be effectively governed by constitutional or legal norms. This model can be further subcategorised into the 'democratic formalist model' and the 'liberal common lawyer model' (Scheuerman, 2006: 74). The democratic formalist model is based on the assumption that it is possible to effectively govern emergencies by enumerating *ex ante* provisions in the constitution, while the liberal common lawyers are of the opinion that the common law contains the resources for effectively constraining the exercise of emergency powers (Scheuerman, 2006; Dyzenhaus, 2006a).

Having made an in-depth study in preceding chapters of the traditional models of emergency, general issues concerning the exercise of the power of suspension of the fundamental rights and of preventive detention during emergencies, and the experience of frequent abuse of these powers both during the colonial and post-colonial period in the Subcontinent, an attempt will first be made in this chapter to evaluate the above contemporary models of emergency powers. It will next be argued that the idea of fidelity to the rule of law advises that whatever responses are made to the exigencies of a particular emergency, such responses should be found and limited within the confines of the constitution. For arbitrary action is the complete antithesis of the rule of law and the hallmark of a model democracy is the maintenance of the rule of law and protection of the core rights of individuals. Finally, an attempt will be made to design a standard constitutional model governing the core issues concerning the proclamation, continuance and termination of emergency powers with a view to reducing the scope of their abuse.

4.2 Extra-legal model

Oren Gross is the proponent of the 'Extra-Legal Measures Model' (ELM). He argues that constitutional norms cannot satisfactorily contain or regulate emergencies. Gross bases his arguments on two supposed facts. First, Gross believes that every attempt to incorporate provisions concerning emergency powers within a constitutional framework has escaped the confines of these provisions (Gross, 2003). Second, statutes passed during emergencies proclaimed in pursuance of constitutional provisions often remain in the statute books even beyond the crises which gave rise to them. Furthermore, courts of law are susceptible to the criticism that they 'impede war efforts' and, as such, in times of crises they adopt a highly deferential attitude when asked to review governmental actions and decisions (Gross, 2003: 1034). Consequently, the emergency-related statutes and decisions of the courts handed down in deference to the executive become integrated into the normal system of laws, and in turn poison the entire legal order.

Gross, therefore, argues that in order to prevent the legal order from becoming contaminated and thereby to ensure fidelity to the rule of law, emergency powers should not be provided with any legal basis. His ELM would inform government officials that they are entitled to act extra-legally when in their estimation such measures are necessary for protecting the nation and the public in the face of calamity, provided that they 'openly and publicly' acknowledge their action as being external to law (Gross, 2003: 1023). Furthermore, according to Gross, 'no limits – certainly no legal limits' can be imposed on officials in controlling their deviation from the norms of the constitutional order (Gross, 2008: 71).

The only safeguard Gross (2003: 1100; 2008: 63) envisages against executive abuses under the ELM is by placing reliance on the ethical concept of the 'moral and political' responsibility of the public to take a stand on the issue of extra-legal action of the government through direct or indirect *ex post* ratification. By direct ratification Gross refers to the returning to office by the public of the elected officials who had acted extra-legally during the emergency and who had 'openly and candidly' disclosed the nature of their actions to the public. On the other hand, indirect ratification, according to Gross (2003), refers to the ratification of the extra-legal actions of the executive during a state of emergency by the public through their elected representatives in the legislature.

Thus, Gross (2008: 79), under his model, seeks to portray the executive as the saviour which risks itself 'on the justice of … [its] country' to rescue the nation from the exigencies of a grave emergency by overstepping the limits of legality.

4.2.1 Criticism of the extra-legal measures model

Gross's ELM is, however, not free from imperfections. An attempt will now be made to examine these limitations.

4.2.1.1 Resemblance to Carl Schmitt's legal scepticism

Carl Schmitt (2005) was a harsh critic of liberal democracy and attempted to demonstrate the impossibility of emergency powers being effectively contained by constitutional norms. As William Scheuerman (2006: 61) notes: '[f]or Schmitt, liberal democracy and emergency power are akin to water and oil: they simply do not mix.'

Schmitt contended that constitutional framers can never successfully anticipate the novelty of future emergencies. Consequently, he argued that since the exigencies of an emergency cannot be circumscribed factually, the response of the executive to these exigencies cannot be made to conform to preformed constitutional or legal norms. Thus, during an emergency the executive is entitled to step beyond the confines of the constitution and assume absolute power – even if it means the suspension of the entire legal order – to bring the emergency to a conclusion (Schmitt, 2005). Furthermore, according to Schmitt (2005), the actions taken by the executive during an emergency – no matter how illegal – should be deemed legal.

It seems that Gross accepts elements of Carl Schmitt's legal scepticism to build his own account of an emergency model. For he, like Schmitt, as has been pointed out in Section 4.2, also believes that constitutional norms cannot satisfactorily contain or regulate emergency situations and, as such, the exigencies of an emergency requires the executive to step outside the confines of legality. In this context, David Dyzenhaus (2006a: 50) observes:

> [i]t might seem ... that the only conclusion to be drawn by someone committed to ... the rule of law is Schmitt's. One should concede that, in the state of exception or emergency, law recedes leaving the state to act unconstrained by law. Just this conclusion is reached ... by Oren Gross.

Gross, however, offers certain arguments in rejecting the claims that his model resembles that of Schmitt. He argues that his model does not advocate the authoritarian conclusions of Schmitt. First, he points out that even though the executive is permitted to exceed the limits of legality, unlike on Schmitt's account which deems such transgression as legal, its actions under the ELM remain illegal or extra-legal (Gross and Aoláin, 2006). Furthermore, the executive itself is required to expressly acknowledge the extra-legal character of its actions during the continuation of an emergency. Second, Gross asserts that the ELM, by contrast with Schmitt's theory, recommends keeping the 'legal and constitutional norms' intact during an emergency (Gross and Aoláin, 2006: 170). Third, in contrast to Schmitt's theory, which does not offer any mechanisms for ensuring the accountability of the executive during a crisis, Gross believes that ELM subjects the actions of the executive during an emergency to mechanisms of direct or indirect *ex post* ratification by the public (Gross and Aoláin, 2006).

However, there are reasons to doubt Gross's response.

First, although Gross maintains that the executive's actions during an emergency remain illegal, history demonstrates that there is a general tendency to insist that its unconstrained authority during a crisis is warranted by the constitution itself. For instance, following the wave of popular repudiation in the US of the invasion of Cambodia by the US and Vietnamese forces in 1970, President Richard Nixon defended in an interview with David Frost his approval of the controversial and largely illegal 'Huston Plan', 'which advocated the systematic use of wiretappings, burglaries or so-called black bag jobs, mail opening and infiltration against anti-war groups and others', by saying:

> [W]hen the President does it, that means it is not illegal ... If the President, for example, approves something because of the national security, or in this case because of a threat to internal peace and order of significant magnitude, then the President's decision in that instance is one that enables those who carry it out, to carry it out without violating a law.
>
> (Frost, 1977: A16)

Similarly, following the 9/11 attacks, President Bush's adoption of certain draconian measures, such as indefinite detention, the establishment of Guantanamo Bay and the enactment of the *PATRIOT Act*, essentially tore away the liberal veils of executive power and, consequently, diminished civil liberties (Scheuerman, 2006). These measures, however, were sought to be justified as being within the confines of the US Constitution under the 'war powers' doctrine of the Federal Government. Thus, it seems that Gross discounts the idea that during an emergency the executive can always call upon the 'best and brightest' lawyers to 'stretch the legalisms' in order to cover its transgressions (Ackerman, 2006: 90).

Furthermore, in view of the abovementioned instances it seems that Gross's proposal is not very realistic either as he does not explain why prudent state officials would openly acknowledge the extra-legal nature of their actions during emergency.

Second, as opposed to Gross's assertion that his ELM contains mechanisms for ensuring the accountability of the executive during an emergency, his model risks condoning executive abuses during a state of emergency. For neither direct or indirect *ex post* ratification can function as effective checks preventing the executive from abusing its powers during emergencies for the following reasons:

a) Gross's idea of direct *ex post* ratification as an effective deterrent to prevent executive abuse would seem to be an unsound proposition. For the executive during an emergency can paint a grim picture exaggerating the threats posed to the life of the nation and subsequently manipulating public opinion in its favour. As Dyzenhaus (2005: 72–73) notes:

   > [i]f the Extra-Legal Measures model were public, as it must be if it is to promote deliberation, the expectation would be generated of after-the-fact validation of illegal official acts. In an atmosphere of fear that expectation would likely to be met rather easily, especially when the threat is, or is claimed to be, a constant one and the government successfully manipulates public opinion.

   Consequently, following Gross's logic, it can be argued that the abuses committed by the Bush administration, in particular the torture of prisoners in Abu Gharib and Guantanamo Bay, were condoned by the public in 2004 through the re-election of Mr. Bush to White House and, as such, went unpunished. Thus John Yoo, who served Bush Jr's administration as the Deputy Assistant US Attorney General, opined after the 2004 presidential elections that the debate surrounding the issue of legality of the treatment of prisoners in Abu Gharib and Guantanamo Bay had been settled by the public's referendum on the matter in the elections (Mayer, 2005).[1]
b) With regard to indirect *ex post* ratification Gross believes that an appeal to the legislature to ratify the actions of the government might lead to public deliberation and subsequently persuade the legislative branch to take an effective stand when confronted with the issues connected with the emergency. This proposition might seem overly optimistic about the role of the legislature as it discounts the reality that the government might command the support of the majority in the legislature, who in turn might be willing to indemnify the executive in respect of abuses during an emergency. As A. V. Dicey (1982: 144) observed, the expectation of the executive that its conduct will be indemnified by the legislature 'has not been disappointed' as a matter of 'history and experience' (Gross, 2008: 71).

   For instance, on 30 March 1960, the Government of South Africa resorted to emergency powers after police at Sharpeville had shot

> dead 67 and injured over 180 unarmed Africans protesting at the pass laws (Bonner, 1985). Subsequently, on 5 July 1961, the *Indemnity Act 61* was enacted to commence with retrospective effect from 21 March 1960, the day on which the Sharpeville incident took place. The Act indemnified the executive from liability for the excesses that had been committed in the suppression of the 'internal disorder' of 21 March 1960 and thereafter.

Third, contrary to Gross's claims, the ELM which allows the executive to act extra-legally during an emergency might tempt it to suspend the normal legal order during an emergency. For the ELM does not contain any guarantees that will prevent it from suspending the legal order if it feels that such an extreme measure is a necessity to effectively deal with the emergency.

Thus, despite Gross's reservation about Schmitt's account, his ELM finds a way to accommodate some of Schmitt's theoretical claims, i.e. that emergency powers are incapable of being effectively contained by constitutional norms and the executive in turn should be permitted to step outside the legal order to respond to emergency situations, without attempting to endorse his authoritarian conclusions. However, a detailed evaluation of the ELM reveals that in the absence of any efficacious mechanisms the executive under the ELM, similar to Schmitt's account, can also run wild by exercising powers arbitrarily – which can even involve the suspension of the existing legal order. Thus, it can be argued that a model such as the ELM, which allows the executive to assume unfettered power and has the impact of condoning executive abuses committed during the continuation of an emergency, cannot maintain its claim of ensuring fidelity to rule of law. It essentially risks the substitution of the rule of law by rule of man.

4.2.1.2 The ELM also has the effect of creating bad precedents

Gross's assertion that it is justifiable to permit the executive to step publicly beyond the tenets of the rule of law as it prevents the legal order from being contaminated by controversial legal precedents seems to overlook the dangerous proposition that if lawlessness is once 'publicly embraced', it may 'escalate uncontrollably' (Ackerman, (2003–2004): 1044). For without the existence of any realistic checks for preventing abuse under the ELM, succeeding generations of executives may seek to resort to these powers as being an efficient means of perpetuating their rule by suppressing any opposition. In this context, the observations of Niccolò Machiavelli (1950: 203) are worthy of note: '[I]f the practice is once established of disregarding the laws for good objects, they will in a little while be disregarded under the pretext for evil purposes.' Since preventing lawlessness is one of the fundamental goals of the rule of law in a democratic society, it can therefore be argued that the ELM jeopardises the rule of law.

4.3 The legal model

Despite Schmitt's scepticism about maintaining the rule of law during emergencies and the acceptance of his arguments (with certain modifications) by theorists such as Oren Gross, for some theorists it nevertheless remains possible for the exercise of emergency powers to be both effective and legally constrained. In this context, it is necessary to discuss the theories advocated by theorists belonging to two competing models, namely, the liberal common lawyers and the democratic formalists.

4.3.1 The liberal common lawyer model

The liberal common law model is premised on the traditional common law position, namely that the judiciary is the best institution for upholding the values and principles associated with human dignity and freedom. David Dyzenhaus is the principal proponent of this school of thought.

4.3.1.1 David Dyzenhaus's court-centric emergency model

Dyzenhaus has reservations about constitutionally entrenched emergency powers. According to him, constitutional emergency powers are articulated even by the best constitutional craftsman in a manner that gives rise to a 'prerogative state', which can dispense with legal constraints in times of crises (Dyzenhaus, 2006a; 2006b; Scheuerman, 2006). Subsequently, he argues that judges often find that explicit provisions concerning emergency written down in the constitution offer them 'convenient pegs … [on which] to hang their reasoning' (Dyzenhaus, 2006a: 75). However, 'if judges take too seriously the pegs' while reviewing executive actions during an emergency – which Dyzenhaus refers to as preferring a 'positivistic attitude', namely 'constitutional positivism' – they render themselves a disservice as it not only weakens their reasoning but also undermines the rule of law (Dyzenhaus, 2006a: 16, 75; Morss, 2009). For, according to Dyzenhaus (2006a: 191), constitutional positivism denotes dualism – 'a dualism between the rule-of-law state, which deals with ordinary matters, and the prerogative state, which responds to the emergency'. In other words, Dyzenhaus contends that constitutional positivism undermines the rule of law by treating it as sufficient for ordinary times but insufficient for times of grave threat to security of the state.

Dyzenhaus's prescription is that instead of having recourse to constitutional positivism, judges should find the source of the limits on the powers of the executive and legislature during emergency situations in the common law constitution, which is an 'evolving or living constitution' containing 'values and principles to do with human dignity and freedom … [and] also presuppos[ing] that judges are the ultimate guardians of these values' (Dyzenhaus, 2006a: 190; 2003: 13). According to him, if the judges rely on the values embedded in the common law constitution during emergency situations to devise 'controls on public actors which ensure that their decisions comply with the principle of legality', they are said to uphold a 'substantive conception of the rule of law' (Dyzenhaus, 2007: 168).

However, as Dyzenhaus (2006a) concedes, the role of the judiciary during states of emergency when called upon to scrutinise executive excesses even in countries like the USA and UK has been marred by the invocation of the controversial doctrine of judicial deference. The adoption of a deferential attitude of upholding executive actions by the judiciary in times of crisis is generally defended by resort to 'judicial mechanisms' such as the political question doctrine, which is the claim that certain questions relating to emergency powers are not 'justiciable or amenable to judicial review' (Dyzenhaus, 2006a: 19). The historical origins of such deference can be traced to the US Supreme Court decisions in the cases of *Ex Parte Quirin (1942) 317 US 1* and *Korematsu v United States (1944) 323 US 214.*

Ex Parte Quirin involved the determination by the Supreme Court of the justiciability of President Roosevelt's proclamation during World War II that took away the rights of eight individuals (one of whom was a US citizen), who arrived on the East Coast by two German Submarines, wearing German military uniforms, and who were accused of espionage activities to be prosecuted in the federal courts. The Presidential proclamation subjected them to the jurisdiction of military tribunals in accordance with the law of war instead of a trial before the federal courts (44). The Supreme Court refused to scrutinise the proclamation of the President on account of his declaration of an all-out war against Germany. This judgment remains in the record books as one of the darkest hours of American judicial history. For, within one week of the Court's decision, six of the eight detainees, including the US citizen, were executed.

Korematsu v United States was decided by the Supreme Court in the aftermath of the devastating Japanese attacks on Pearl Harbour. It involved a challenge by Fred Korematsu, an American citizen of Japanese descent, to the constitutionality of an Exclusion Order, which was issued in pursuance of a Presidential Order[2] granting the military commanders the authority to circulate such Exclusion Orders at their 'discretion' with respect to people of Japanese origin residing in their districts. The Supreme Court maintained its previous practice of adopting a deferential attitude. As Justice Hugo Black delivering the majority judgment observed:

> [W]e cannot reject as unfounded the judgment of the military authorities and of Congress that there were disloyal members of that population, whose number and strength could not be precisely and quickly ascertained. We cannot say that the war-making branches of the Government did not have ground for believing that in a critical hour such persons could not readily be isolated and separately dealt with, and

> constituted a menace to the national defense and safety, which demanded that prompt and adequate measures be taken to guard against it.
>
> (216, 223)

Thus, the US Supreme Court in *Korematsu* demonstrated a deferential attitude without appreciating the fact that the exclusion order was passed arbitrarily without the evidence of any collaboration on the part of the Japanese Americans with the enemy. Furthermore, it did not take into account that judicial deference had the impact of converting an isolated instance of executive intemperance into an established constitutional practice. As Justice Jackson in his dissenting opinion observed:

> The principle then lies about like a loaded weapon ready for the hand of any authority that can bring forward a plausible claim of an urgent need ... A military commander may overstep the bounds of constitutionality, and it is an incident. But if we review and approve, that passing incident becomes the doctrine of the Constitution. There it has a generative power of its own, and all that it creates will be in its own image.
>
> (246)

In the same vein in the UK, the Home Secretary ordered during World War II the detention of Mr Robert Liversidge in pursuance of Regulation 18B of the *Defence (General) Regulations*, 1939, which authorised the Secretary to detain an individual if he had 'reasonable cause to believe ... [such] person to be of hostile origins or associations' (*Liversidge v Anderson*, [1942] AC 206). The House of Lords in *Liversidge v Anderson* was confronted with the question whether Regulation 18B should be given a subjective or objective interpretation. An objective interpretation of the Regulation would have enabled the Court to ask for particulars pertaining to the grounds for passing the detention order against Mr Liversidge with a view to test its validity. However, the House of Lords by a majority held that the circumstances of a wartime emergency constrained them to interpret the Regulation subjectively and, as such, they had to accept the Secretary's contention that Mr Liversidge was a risk to national security. Lord Atkin in his famous dissent pointed out that the phrase 'reasonable cause' as used in the Regulation had only one possible interpretation in common law and statute, namely, that judges have the authority to test the grounds for a decision to ensure that it was made fairly. Thus, the majority of the House of Lords in deferring to the executive 'say-so' demonstrated that they were 'more executive minded than the executive'.

In South Africa, where during the apartheid era declarations of emergency were used to stage a crackdown against opponents, the judiciary refused to take notice of the executive abuses during the declared periods of emergency by invoking the doctrine of judicial deference. For example, in the case of

Rossouw v Sachs (1964) 2 SA 551 (A), the Appellate Division, the then highest court in South Africa, overruled the decision of the Cape Provincial Division to the effect that the non-granting of reading and writing materials to Albie Sachs, an 'unconvicted' person who had been detained under Section 17(1) of *Act 37* of 1963[3] (popularly known as the '90-day Detention Law'), would amount to a punishment, which could not have been the intention of the Legislature. The Appellate Division reasoned that granting Albie Sachs access to reading and writing materials would undermine the very object of Section 17, which was to exert psychological pressure on the detainee with a view to induce him to speak (560–561). Thus the Court in effect created a sense among the security forces that they could abuse the human rights of individuals with impunity. This case marked the beginning of the South African judiciary's complicity in the executive attempt to institutionalise a permanent state of emergency during apartheid (Mathews and Albino, 1966).

Despite the 'dismal' judicial record during emergencies, which undermines his argument for maintaining a central role for the judiciary during emergencies, Dyzenhaus argues that one should take heart from the dissenting opinions of judges in cases such as *Liversidge* and *Korematsu*. For these dissents, according to Dyzenhaus, demonstrate that it was open to the majority of the judges in these cases to decide differently and uphold the rule of law. Dyzenhaus (2006a: 63–64) argues that these dissents in turn have the potential of influencing future judges to uphold the rule of law in times of crisis in 'full awareness of the past, so with complete benefit of foresight'. However, Dyzenhaus (2009; 2007: 166) himself concedes that the actual response of the judiciary in the present 'era of human rights and constitutionalism' has also been 'dismal'.

In the US, particularly following the 9/11 terror attacks in 2001, the Supreme Court handed down a series of judgments in deference to the executive. Among these cases, the case of *Hamdi v Rumsfeld (2004) 124 S.Ct. 2633* is worthy of discussion. Yaser Edam Hamdi, a dual citizen of the United States and Saudi Arabia, was seized in Afghanistan during American combat operations in late 2001. The US Government claimed that he was 'closely associated' with Al Qaeda and 'affiliated with a Taliban military unit' and, as such, he was detained as an 'enemy combatant' (2633–2637). However, Hamdi's father claimed that he was an inexperienced aid worker and not an 'enemy combatant' as claimed by the US officials. He filed a petition for a writ of habeas corpus on his son's behalf, seeking a hearing to enable Hamdi to contest the allegations against him, and release him from United States custody. The two issues that were raised in the petition were as follows: (1) could the United States detain its citizens as enemy combatants without charging them with a crime and, if so, for how long; and (2) if a detainee contested his enemy combatant status, what manner of habeas corpus review, if any, was he entitled to receive?

With regard to the first question, the US Supreme Court upheld the aggressive theory of exclusive executive authority as advanced by the President's lawyers to the effect that the President acting as the Commander in Chief could detain Hamdi for the duration of the war on terror as he was best equipped to make that decision. Thus the Supreme Court in deferring to the Presidential Authority made Hamdi vulnerable to the grim 'prospect of perpetual detention' (2641). In response to the second question, the Supreme Court decided against granting Hamdi his day in court, despite the fact that the Congress had not exercised its authority under the Constitution to suspend habeas corpus due to 'Rebellion or Invasion' threatening the Public Safety (2643–2652; Constitution of the USA 1787 art I s 9). Rather the Supreme Court in following the controversial *Ex Parte Quirin* precedent granted Hamdi only a 'meaningful opportunity' of refuting his designation as an 'enemy combatant' before a military tribunal (2651). The majority led by Justice O'Connor held:

> Quirin was a unanimous opinion. It ... provid[es] us with the most apposite precedent that we have on the question of whether citizens may be detained in such circumstances. Brushing aside such precedent – particularly when doing so gives rise to a host of new questions never dealt with by this Court – is unjustified and unwise.
>
> (2669, 2643)

The UK was not immune to judicial deference either in the aftermath of 9/11. In this context, the 2002 decision of the House of Lords in *Secretary of State for the Home Department v Rehman [2001] UKHL 47* is relevant. The petitioner, Mr Rehman, a Pakistani national had entered the UK on 9 February 1993, having obtained a work permit to act as an imaminister in Oldham until 9 February 1997. Subsequently, his work permit was extended until 7 January 1998. However, his application for 'indefinite leave to remain in the United Kingdom' was refused by the Home Secretary on the ground that he was associated with a Muslim terrorist organisation and had encouraged Muslims in the UK to engage in terrorist training. It was therefore contended that Mr Rehman's deportation was necessary in the interests of 'national security'. The House of Lords in delivering its judgment took notice of the decision of the Special Immigration Appeals Commission in hearing Mr Rehman's appeal under Section 2(1)(c) of the *Special Immigration Appeals Commission Act*, 1997, against the letter of refusal issued by the Secretary of State. The Commission in its decision of 20 August 1999 held that the Home Office had failed to establish that 'the appellant was, is, and is likely to be a threat to national security' (point 5). The House of Lords also took into account the fact that the Home Secretary in his open statement himself acknowledged that '[t]he Security Service assesses that ... Mr. Rehman and his United Kingdom-based followers are unlikely to carry out any acts of violence in this country' (point 1 para 4). But the House of the Lords succumbed to the executive determination by taking a broad view of what could constitute a threat to national security, 'taking into account the executive's policy with regard to national security'. As Lord Slynn observed:

> [E]ven though the Commission has powers of review both of fact and of the exercise of the discretion, the Commission must give due weight to the assessment and conclusions of the Secretary of State in the light ... of Government policy and the means at his disposal of being informed of and understanding the problems involved. He is undoubtedly in the best position to judge what national security requires ... The assessment of what is needed in the light of changing circumstances is primarily for him. (point 26)

Thus, judiciaries in times of declared or undeclared periods of emergency have demonstrated a willingness to defer to the executive without taking into account that the extraordinary action may not be proportional to the threats posed to the life of the nation or that the circumstances which gave rise to the emergency may no longer be in existence. These instances of deference lead Dyzenhaus (2006a: 63) to remark:

> [O]ne day, and I hope the day is not too far off, judges will have to reckon with the fact that when they had the opportunity to stand up for the rule of law, they decided to take the path of South Africa's Appellate Division during apartheid, or of the majority of the House of Lords during the [second] world ... [war], or the American Supreme Court in Korematsu.

Despite these concessions, he nevertheless remains optimistic that judges will carry out their duty to uphold the rule of law during emergencies. For, if they fail to carry out their duty, they will also fail to clarify to the people what constitutes responsible government – government in compliance with the rule of law (Dyzenhaus, 2006a).

Dyzenhaus's continued optimism regarding the role of the judiciary in examining the measures taken during emergencies stems from the decision of the House of Lords in *A v Secretary of State for the Home Department [2004] UKHL 56*, popularly known as the *Belmarsh* decision. The petitioners, who were detained in Belmarsh prison, challenged Section 23 of the *Anti-Terrorism, Crime and Security Act* (2001), which allowed the government to detain indefinitely only non-nationals who were considered to be a risk to national security but could not be deported due to the risk of them being tortured in their home country. The detainees contended that the UK was not under an emergency as claimed by the government and that the indefinite detention of the non-citizens was not strictly required by the exigencies of the situation. They further argued that the provisions concerning detention as contained in the *Anti-Terrorism Act* were discriminatory in contravention of Article 14 of the *European Convention for the Protection of Human Rights and Fundamental Freedoms*, 1950, as incorporated in the *Human Rights Act* (1998) (HRA), which prohibits discrimination on various grounds including national origin. The Court of Appeal led by Lord Woolf followed the decision laid down in *Rehman* in holding that it had no other option but to defer to the government in national security matters (*Belmarsh [2004] QB 335*, 359–360).

On appeal, the House of Lords held that while it accepted that there existed an emergency as claimed by the executive branch of the government, the detention of the non-citizens was disproportionate, i.e. not strictly required by the exigencies of the crisis, and discriminatory. However, *Belmarsh* is not free from defects.

First, while the House of Lords found that the treatment of non-citizen detainees was in breach of the HRA, it nevertheless deferred to the executive contention of an ongoing emergency three years after the 9/11 attacks. Such deference to the executive cannot be justified in view of the admission of the Secretary for the Home Department that a terrorist attack was not imminent. Thus, the *Belmarsh* decision cannot be seen as a complete departure from the culture of judicial deference.

Second, Dyzenhaus himself concedes that in delivering the judgment in *Belmarsh*, the House of Lords did not overrule its previous deferential and controversial decision in *Rehman*.

Notwithstanding the abovementioned issues concerning *Belmarsh*, Dyzenhaus is of the opinion that the *Belmarsh* decision 'might seem to put a stop' to the trend of deferring to the executive in matters of national security as evidenced in the case of *Rehman* (Dyzenhaus, 2006a: 174).

4.3.1.1.1 CRITICISM OF DAVID DYZENHAUS'S COURT-CENTRIC ACCOUNT

The following arguments may be put forward to show the inadequacies of Dyzenhaus's account. First, Dyzenhaus in articulating a court-centric emergency model, does not seem to take into account the conservative orientation of the common law tradition, which renders the courts incapable of effectively scrutinising the executive abuse of emergency powers. As Scheuerman (2008: 277) notes:

> Congenital structural tendencies, which drive the ... [executive] incessantly to expand emergency discretion means that the courts always lag behind, its review powers always outpaced in an institutional competition which the courts cannot possibly win; before our cautious common law judges have even begun to grapple with the ramifications of the last round of ... emergency decrees, the executive has already undertaken new ones.

Second, Dyzenhaus does not take into account that the rule of law 'demands not only judicial review', but also sufficiently specific and objective legal norms which form the basis for any state action (Scheuerman, 2008: 285). The 'dismal' record of the judiciary during emergency situations might be attributed to the reality that constitutions in most cases remain silent as to the permissible limits of executive action during declared states of emergency and the maximum period of emergency.[4] Consequently, judges, in the absence of explicit constitutional provisions for guidance in deciding whether the circumstances which gave rise to the emergency are over, might feel that they are left with no other option but to hold that the executive is in the best position to make this judgment.

However, Dyzenhaus, as pointed out earlier in Section 4.3.1.1, discounts the merits of constitutionally entrenched emergency provisions by generalising their flaws. It seems that such generalisation overlooks the merits of detailed constitutional provisions providing for effective prospective constraints on the power of the executive with regard to the proclamation, administration and termination of emergency. Detailed constitutional provisions provide judges with the means to stand up to the executive during the continuation of an emergency and thereby uphold the rule of law. In this context, Scheuerman (2008: 283) points out that constitutional emergency provisions provide for 'demanding institutional tests by means of which the polity can at least minimise the executive's tendency to try to monopolise … judgments [about the necessity for invoking emergency powers]: emergency rules are made strictly dependent on other institutional actors'. Thus, detailed constitutional emergency provisions have the merit of dispensing with the constitutional dualism that Dyzenhaus refers to (see Section 4.3.1.1). For detailed constitutional provisions governing the exercise of emergency powers guard against a 'prerogative state', which can use emergencies as a means for dispensing with the rule of law.

In light of the foregoing discussion, it can be argued that Dyzenhaus's preference for an overtly court-centric approach for maintaining the rule of law in times of crisis despite its overwhelming 'dismal' record has the potential of exacerbating the pathologies of emergency governments.

4.3.2 Democratic formalist model

The democratic formalist model, as defended by Bruce Ackerman and William Scheuerman, is premised on the idea that even if the exigencies of a particular emergency may seem ungovernable, the response to these exigencies can nevertheless be governed by developing a set of constitutional provisions. Justice Davis of the US Supreme Court is said to have laid down the basis for this school of thought in *Ex parte Milligan (1866) 71 US 2*, when he observed:

> The Constitution … is a law for rulers and people, equally in war and in peace, and covers with the shield of its protection all classes of men, at all times, and under all circumstances. No doctrine, involving more

> pernicious consequences, was ever invented by the wit of man than that any of its provisions can be suspended during any of the great exigencies of government. Such a doctrine leads directly to anarchy or despotism, but the theory of necessity on which it is based is false; for the government, within the Constitution, has all the powers granted to it, which are necessary to preserve its existence.
>
> (120–121)

Consequently, democratic formalists critique the idea that constitutions, such as that of the USA, are better off without an elaborate set of emergency provisions and that reliance should primarily be placed on the judges to prevent the executive from abusing power during an emergency (Ackerman, 2003–2004). They do not discount the virtues of judicial intervention during an emergency. Rather they question whether judicial checks are sufficient to ensure fidelity to the rule of law given the judiciary's historical tendency to defer to the executive during emergency situations (Scheuerman, 2006).

Democratic formalists, therefore, put forward two claims in support of a constitutional framework of emergency powers providing for mechanisms that will act as a check on politicians from exploiting momentary panic to impose long-lasting limitations on people's liberty. First, they argue that constitutional emergency powers help maintain the rule of law by subjecting the exercise of these powers to legal devices manifesting the essential legal virtues of 'clarity, publicity, generality, prospectiveness and stability' (Scheuerman, 2006: 76). Second, the elected legislature, which is the formal avenue for 'free-wheeling democratic deliberation and debate', is best suited to scrutinise the exercise and continuation of emergency powers (Scheuerman, 2006: 76). It is argued that such a constitutional framework of emergency powers will provide the judges with the means to intervene effectively to check potential executive abuses during an emergency (Ackerman, 2003–2004).

4.4 Developing a constitutional model of emergency powers

After evaluating the merits of the 'Extra-Legal' and liberal common law emergency models, it seems that the best solution to the problem of maintaining the rule of law during emergencies is put forward by the democratic formalists, who seek to advocate the governance of these powers by detailed constitutionally entrenched norms. For, as will be argued below, the incorporation of effective mechanisms within the constitution creates useful prospective guidelines for the proclamation, administration and termination of emergency, which in turn contribute to the creation of a precise separation between ordinary and emergency situations. Such mechanisms also provide the objective standards for scrutinising the actions of the emergency government so that they do not risk compromising the democratic nature of the society in whose defence it is fighting.

In light of this, an attempt will now be made from comparative constitutional law and normative perspectives to devise a standard constitutional model for governing the proclamation, administration and termination of a state of emergency, which should contain the following provisions concerning:

a) the circumstances which merit a proclamation of emergency;
b) the nature of the authority to proclaim and ratify a proclamation of emergency;
c) the mechanisms for ensuring the effective scrutiny of a state of emergency and its timely termination;
d) the principles of non-derogation and proportionality for diminishing the possibility of unjustified restrictions on the rights of individuals; and
e) the safeguards for preventing the possibility of abuse of the powers concerning preventive detention and simultaneously guaranteeing the humane treatment of individuals kept in preventive custody.

4.4.1 Enumerating the circumstances in the constitution which merit a proclamation of emergency

Generally, there are two types of disturbing trends that can be found in a number of national constitutions in respect of incorporating the grounds for proclaiming an emergency. First, some constitutions contain wide and broad grounds for invoking emergency. Second, some constitutions empower the executive to proclaim a state of emergency on the imprecise grounds of social unrest or internal disturbance. Both these approaches are problematic as they are easily susceptible to manipulation by the executive for purposes other than that of securing the life of the nation.

The classic example of allowing 'broadest grants of emergency powers to the executive'[5] can be found in the *Constitution of France*, 1958, which in Article 16 empowers the President to declare a state of emergency

> when the institutions of the Republic, the independence of the Nation, the integrity of its territory or the fulfilment of its international commitments are under serious and immediate threat, and when the proper functioning of the constitutional public powers is interrupted.

Taking advantage of these broad powers concerning emergency, the then French President Jacques Chirac on 8 November 2005 proclaimed a state of emergency to repress French youths of Arab and African origin who took to the streets protesting against the Government's failure to address the systematic racial discrimination and chronic unemployment directed towards their community (Landler, 2005; 'State of Emergency Declared in France' 2005). The Prime Minister acknowledged the failure of the Government to build an effective 'integration model' that was not susceptible to allegations of bias and discrimination. However, despite these acknowledgments, the proclamation of emergency was followed by resort to a 50-year old law that was enacted during the war against Algeria and which authorised the enforcement of night-time curfews for up to 12 days from the date of the proclamation. As many as 8000 police officers and another 1500 reservists as reinforcements were deployed to areas where curfews were imposed to put down the protesters. Several other stern measures, such as the establishment of fast track tribunals to try and sentence numerous minors to prison or detention centres, were also taken (Landler, 2005; 'State of Emergency Declared in France' 2005). The state of emergency was withdrawn after three months of its imposition. The situation in France following the protests by the youth in 2005 was by no means comparable to that of a war and thereby worthy of warlike measures dating approximately 50 years back. Thus, when broad powers concerning the proclamation of emergency are enshrined in the Constitution, it enables the executive to blur the distinction between warlike situations and protests against certain unpopular governmental policies.

On the other hand, when a Constitution provides for social unrest or internal disturbance as a ground for proclaiming an emergency, then what constitutes social unrest or internal disturbance in a particular case would to a large extent depend upon the personal assessment or judgment of the individual authority concerned. A wide range of situations, such as mass demonstrations in order to express discontent or opposition to certain governmental actions, violent riots which do not assume the characteristics of an armed conflict, and isolated and sporadic acts of violence can be brought within the purview of the expression 'social unrest' or 'internal disturbance'. Consequently, when these vague phrases are inserted in constitutions as grounds for invoking a state of emergency, it makes resort to extraordinary powers of emergency extremely convenient for the executive in dealing with situations that could easily be contained under the ordinary legal framework. An emergency declared on the grounds of social unrest or internal disturbance also has the disturbing impact of worsening and perpetuating situations that are inherently volatile and explosive. The European Commission in the *Greek Case YBECHR 12* of 1969 took notice of this reality when it refused to uphold the contention of the Greek Military Junta that the existence of social unrest incited by the Communist Party was sufficient to invoke the declaration of an emergency on 21 April 1967, holding that no evidence was adduced by the Junta before the Commission to demonstrate any attempt of 'displacement of the lawful Government by force of arms by the Communists and their allies' (73). In the same vein, the imprecise ground of internal disturbance, which owes its origin to colonial legislation, as pointed out in Section 2.6.2, was inherited by the Constitutions of the Subcontinent,[6] which in turn proved to be extremely counter-productive for these newly established democracies. For this vague ground has been indiscriminately used by subsequent regimes in these jurisdictions, as discussed in Sections 2.6.2.1.3, 2.6.3.3.1 and 2.6.3.3.2, to invoke emergency with the ulterior motive of suppressing opposition to these regimes and perpetuating their rule. Although the emergency in India invoked by Indira Gandhi on 25 June 1975 on the vague ground of internal disturbance to ensure her own survival in power persuaded the succeeding Parliament to learn a lesson from the history and replace 'internal disturbance' with 'armed rebellion' as a ground for invoking emergency, the Constitutions of Pakistan and Bangladesh have retained internal disturbance as a ground for declaring emergency, despite widespread abuse of the said ground without the realisation that '[n]ot every disturbance ... qualifies as a public emergency which threatens the life of the nation' (Human Rights Committee, 2001: para 2).

It is, therefore, evident that a list of concrete circumstances, which capture a certain degree of gravity, putting the life of the nation and its subjects under serious risk, should be enumerated in constitutions as grounds for invoking emergency. Formulating such a concrete list is, however, by no means an easy task. The International Law Association (ILA) expressed some scepticism during the Paris Conference of 1984 about the possibility of precisely specifying the circumstances for invoking an emergency, when it observed:

> It is ... [not] possible to stipulate *in abstracto* what particular type or types of events will automatically constitute a public emergency ... taking into account the overriding concern for the continuance of a democratic society.
>
> (1984: 59)

However, a study prepared by the UN Commission on Human Rights in 1961, together with the literature on the issue encapsulating the grounds which are mentioned in national constitutions, provides some guidance as to the grounds which can justify a valid proclamation of emergency threatening the life of the nation. In this context, the following grounds are relevant:

a) international conflict, war, war of national liberation, invasion (UN Commission on Human Rights, 1964; Marks, 1982; Oraa, 1992);
b) 'rebellion' (UN Commission on Human Rights, 1964: 257);
c) 'natural or public calamity or disaster' (UN Commission on Human Rights, 1964: 257);
d) 'danger to the economic life of the country or parts' of the country or economic crises (UN Commission on Human Rights, 1964: 257).

Furthermore, recent statutes concerning emergency demonstrate an admirable attempt to outline the precise grounds for invoking an emergency. In this context, the *Civil Contingencies Act* (2004) of the UK, as pointed out earlier in Section 2.4.2.1, signifies an endeavour in Part II to outline the circumstances which merit the invocation of an emergency rather than consigning this important issue to the discretion of the executive. Part II singles out:

a) threats of 'serious damage to human welfare in the United Kingdom or in a Part or region' (s 19(1)(a));
b) threats of 'serious damage to the environment of the United Kingdom or of a Part or region' (s 19(1)(b));
c) 'war, or terrorism, which threatens serious damage to the security of the United Kingdom' (s 19(1)(c)).

The abovementioned grounds, as contained in the UN Study of 1961, various constitutions and recent legislation, coupled with the hindsight of past emergencies make it easier to envisage the events which merit a proclamation of emergency in the future. The gravity of these events, as will be shown below, ensures that they are not reduced to abstract notions but rather are 'transformed into tangible, real and probable events' ('Responding to Terrorism: Crime, Punishment, and War', 2002; Gross, 2003: 1039).

a) War or external aggression

The most serious threat to the life of a nation can come in the form of war or external aggression, i.e. the attempt by another state to destroy, occupy or take control over a country. In such a situation, the integrity and cohesion of the state must be preserved by resorting to emergency powers, which include the conversion of the peacetime political and social order of the state into a 'wartime fighting machine', overpowering the 'skill and efficiency of the enemy' and dispensing with some or all of the civil liberties of the citizens who face the 'grim horror of national enslavement' (Rossiter, 1948: 6).

During the drafting stage of the *International Covenant on Civil and Political Rights* (ICCPR), several representatives to the UN Commission on Human Rights in discussing the grounds which merited inclusion in Article 4 for the proclamation of emergency vigorously attempted to suppress any mention of war. For it was felt 'that the Covenant should not envisage, even by implication, the possibility of war, as the UN was established with the object of preventing war' (A/2929, 1952: 67). However, it was soon realised that war poses the greatest threat to the life of a nation. Thus, the expression 'public emergency' as incorporated in Article 4 of the Covenant is fully applicable to war (A/2929, 1952).

Taking into account the seriousness of war as a ground, provisions concerning the right of the head of a state or parliament to declare a state of emergency due to war or external aggression can be found in modern constitutions such as the Constitutions of Portugal (art

19(2)), Greece (art 48(1)), Germany (art 115a(1)), South Africa (art 37(1)(a)), India (art 352(1)), Pakistan (art 232(1)) and Bangladesh (141A). Emergency legislation, such as the *Civil Contingencies Act* (2004), as mentioned above, and the *Canadian Emergencies Act* (1988), enacted by the Parliaments in the UK and Canada also recognise the right of the executive to proclaim an emergency in times of war or external aggression.

b) Armed rebellion

Armed rebellion is the second kind of crisis which merits a declaration of a state of emergency by the executive or parliament. An emergency on the ground of armed rebellion is declared when the internal political actors of a nation openly resist their constitutional government and disrupt the life of the country by engaging in violent and armed insurrection against certain policies of the government, to effect certain far-reaching demands, which, among other things, can be based on linguistic, religious or racial lines (Rossiter, 1948). The International Crimes Tribunal for the former Yugoslavia provided a definition of the term in similar vein in *The Prosecutor v Dusco Tadic IT-94-1-A 1995*, when it observed that there exists an armed rebellion 'whenever there is ... protracted armed violence between governmental authorities and organised armed groups' (para 70).

Thus it seems that an emergency on the ground of 'armed rebellion' can only be declared when hostilities between the governmental and non-governmental forces attain a certain level of intensity, e.g. when the nature of hostilities induces the government to deploy military forces against the rebels instead of the ordinary law enforcing agencies, i.e. the police forces (*The Prosecutor v. Fatmir Limaj IT-03-66-T 2005*, para 135–170).

The precise nature of the term 'armed rebellion', as opposed to internal disturbance or social unrest, has persuaded the framers of constitutions, such as the 1937 *Constitution of Ireland* (art 28) and the 1950 *Constitution of India* (new 352(4), as amended in 1978, to recognise it as a ground for invoking emergency.

c) Natural catastrophes

By natural catastrophe is meant epidemics, famines, tornadoes, typhoons, cyclones, avalanches, volcanic eruptions, drought and fire, 'in which the day-to-day patterns of life are – in many instances – suddenly disrupted and people are plunged into helplessness and suffering and, as a result, need protection, clothing, shelter, medical and social care, and other necessities of life' (*A Handbook of Red Cross Disaster Relief*, 1976: 13). In recent times, natural catastrophes such as floods, hurricanes, earthquakes and even heavy rainfalls, which adversely affect the lives, health, and private property of the inhabitants of a nation or any part thereof and put the public infrastructure at risk, have also merited the declaration of a state of emergency. Emergencies proclaimed on the ground of national disasters expand the state's ability to free up funds and cut through bureaucratic red tape to expedite and dispatch resources and emergency personnel to emergency areas. Certain constitutions, e.g., the *Political Constitution of Peru*, 1993 (art 137(1)), the *Constitution of the Republic of South Africa*, 1996 (37(1)(a)), and the *Constitution of Azerbaijan*, 1995 (art 112), and recent emergency legislation, such as the *Canadian Emergencies Act*, 1988 (s 5) and the British *Civil Contingencies Act*, 2004 (ss 19(1)(a) and (b), 19(2) and 19(3)), acknowledge the right of the executive to declare a state of emergency due to natural catastrophes. A recent example of a declaration of state of emergency due to natural disasters can be found in the United States of America, where on 28 October 2012 an emergency was declared in New Jersey due to the devastation caused by Hurricane Sandy (The White House, 2012). A year earlier, in 2011, an emergency was declared on 26 August in the seven states along the east coast of the US from North Carolina to Connecticut ahead of the arrival of Hurricane Irene, and in Central Peru, emergency was declared on 22 November due to damage caused by heavy rains ('Hurricane Irene: Emergency declared in seven US states' 2011; 'Emergency Declared Due to Rains in Central Peru' 2011).

d) Economic crisis

A breakdown in the economy of a nation may deprive millions of persons of their employment and means of earning a living for themselves and their families and in the process generate widespread want and suffering among the citizens. It is, therefore, now acknowledged that an economic crisis can be as direct a threat to a nation's continued and constitutional existence as war or subversion. Article 48 of the *Constitution of Weimar Germany*, 1919, was invoked on many occasions between 1922 and 1933 to deal with economic or financial crisis (Rossiter, 1948). Provisions concerning economic or financial emergency can also be found in modern constitutions, such as the *Constitution of India* (art 360(1)) and the *Constitution of Pakistan* (art 235(1)). Both these Constitutions empower their respective head of state to declare a financial or economic emergency to protect and safeguard the financial stability of their countries. Sometimes an economic emergency is also dealt with by legislative enactments, e.g. the *Minnesota Mortgage Moratorium Law* was passed in 1933 by the Minnesota Legislature in response to the homeowner 'emergency' generated by the great American Depression of the 1930s.

If national constitutions confine the proclamation of a state of emergency to the abovementioned grounds, which carry specific and clear-cut connotations, they can go a long way to diminish the possibility of any abuse of the power to resort to such an extraordinary measure.

4.4.2 Naming the authority in the Constitution with the power to proclaim and ratify an emergency

It is needless to say that genuine emergencies do occur. Therefore, it is imperative that the Constitution should explicitly stipulate which governmental organ is competent to expeditiously and decisively proclaim a state of emergency.

Modern constitutions invest the task of proclaiming an emergency with the political organs of the government, i.e. either the executive or the legislature, as they are better positioned than the judicial organ to assess whether the facts of a particular situation constitute a serious threat. There is a greater tendency among modern constitutions, as pointed out in Section 2.4.1, to invest the primary responsibility and authority to declare a state of emergency with the legislature,[7] in order to avoid the possibility of the abuse of such a power by the executive for political purposes. But in times of an emergency of great magnitude requiring prompt action, the legislature may not be able to convene immediately without serving proper notice or muster the necessary quorum indispensable for proclaiming an emergency. It is, therefore, not uncommon for modern constitutions to deal with this reality by enumerating provisions that empower the government or the head of the state to declare a state of emergency in the event of the inability of the legislature to convene to make such a declaration due to the exigencies of the grave threat looming over the nation.[8]

Therefore, since an emergency requires severe measures to deal with the threats affecting a nation and since inordinate delay in responding to such threats may result in the destruction of the nation, it is contended that only the executive (the head of the state or the head of the government) is capable of responding swiftly and decisively to the exigencies of a grave situation (Dyzenhaus, 2012). For it possesses the necessary means and resources, e.g. the reports of the intelligence agencies, for ascertaining the gravity of the circumstances threatening the life of the nation.

However, the executive authority to act unilaterally with regard to the proclamation of emergency should be reserved for the shortest possible time. It is contended that the proclamation of emergency should be subject to a prompt ratification by the legislature. If the legislature is not in session then it should be convened preferably within 14 days of the proclamation for deliberation as to whether the emergency should be ratified or not (Ackerman, 2006; *Constitution of Spain 1978*, art 116(2). The idea underlying such a ratification is that a serious issue such as the proclamation of emergency should be shared by the executive with a body that represents the interests of all segments of the nation (*States of Emergency*, 1983). Such an arrangement has a twofold effect. First, it ensures that a grave emergency is responded to by the executive promptly. Second, requiring the legislature to ratify a proclamation of emergency has a salutary effect on the executive with regard to the possibility of abuse of such powers for political purposes.

Thus, it is evident that, of the two political branches, the executive is better placed to act swiftly to counter the grave dangers and, as such, an ideal emergency model enshrined in the constitution should empower the executive with the responsibility of invoking a state of emergency. However, such a power should be qualified by subjecting the proclamation of emergency to a prompt ratification by the legislature in order to obviate the possibility of abuse of such powers by the executive.

4.4.3 Incorporating mechanisms in the Constitution for the timely withdrawal of emergency

The general tendency to be found in modern constitutions is to provide for only the circumstances which merit a proclamation of emergency and to remain silent as to the termination of the emergency. The absence of a provision in the constitution for the termination of emergency as soon as the circumstances which gave rise to it are adequately contained provides the executive with significant leeway to take steps towards the institutionalisation of the emergency. It is, therefore, submitted that a constitution should contain a reliable system of checks and balances so that an emergency does not continue beyond the circumstances which gave rise to it.

Given the poor record of the judiciary, as pointed out earlier in Section 4.3.1.1, formalists believe that the legislature should be entrusted with the responsibility of overseeing the timely completion of the emergency (Roach, 2008). For this approach ensures meaningful deliberation concerning resort to the extraordinary powers and, as such, better reconciles with the concept of democracy. Furthermore, it does away with the executive tendency to shroud its extraordinary actions under the veil of secrecy (Scheppele, 2006; Roach, 2008). An attempt will be made in the subsequent sections to explore how the legislature can play the role of policing emergencies. It will also be examined whether other innovative devices can be incorporated within the constitutional framework to ensure that the emergency is not prolonged unnecessarily.

4.4.3.1 Legislature as the authority to bring an end to the emergency

A proclamation of emergency, as pointed out earlier in Section 4.3.2.2, should be subject to a prompt ratification of the parliament within 14 days from such proclamation. However, during an emergency, the executive might dissolve the parliament in order to avoid obtaining such a ratification. For instance, the *Weimar Constitution* in Article 25 empowered the

President of the Republic to dissolve the Parliament during a state of emergency. This power was arbitrarily exercised during the lifetime of the Weimar Republic in order to obviate the possibility of any scrutiny of the astounding 250 proclamations of emergency between 1919 and 1932 (Scheppele, 2004). Some modern constitutions, taking into account the experiences of the past, therefore categorically take away the power of the executive to dissolve the legislature during an emergency.[9] Furthermore, some constitutions even provide for the automatic extension of the life of the legislature during an emergency threatening the life of the nation.[10] Thus a provision for the unhindered continuation of the legislature during a state of emergency should be contained in the constitution in order to invest it with the responsibility of not only ratifying the proclamation of emergency but also ensuring that it does not continue beyond the cessation of the hostilities which gave rise to it.

After the initial ratification, it is generally expected that the proclamation of emergency should be subject to periodic review by the legislature. However, it should be stressed here that such an arrangement may lose its efficacy if the party in power has the support of the requisite number of members in the legislature. Therefore, the constitution should provide for stricter guidelines with regard to the extension of the proclamation of the emergency by the legislature.

In this context, resort may be had to the idea of incorporating the device of 'supermajoritarian escalator', as put forward by Bruce Ackerman and discussed below.

4.4.3.1.1 'SUPERMAJORITARIAN ESCALATOR' MODEL AND ITS EVALUATION

It seems that Bruce Ackerman developed his model of 'supermajoritarian escalator' from the *Constitution of South Africa*. Article 37(2)(b) of the South African Constitution empowers the Parliament at the first instance to approve a proclamation of emergency for a period not exceeding three months through a simple majority, and thereafter any further extension of the proclamation of emergency requires 'a supporting vote of at least 60 per cent of the members of the Parliament'. Ackerman, however, believes that the South African model of supermajority is not developed to its fullest potential. For, this model envisages only a simple two-step process – first, approval by a simple majority, then by 60 per cent, without the possibility of any stricter adjustments. The South African model, therefore, remains susceptible to abuse since in that country a single political party wins the majority of the parliamentary seats in the general elections (Ackerman, 2006).[11]

Consequently, Ackerman (2006) proposes a model on which a proclamation of emergency should be placed before the legislature for its endorsement within 14 days and thereafter be subjected to repeated renewals every two months, requiring each such renewal to be amenable to the approval of a larger majority of legislators – 60 per cent for the first two months, 70 per cent for the next two and 80 per cent for each subsequent two-month interval. The advantage of the 'supermajority escalator model' is that it not only contributes towards the timely revocation of emergency powers but also acts as an effective check on any potential abuse of emergency of powers. As Ackerman (2006: 81) argues:

> The president knows that he will have a tough time sustaining supermajorities in the future, and this will lead him to use his powers cautiously. The public will bridle if his underlings run amok, acting in arbitrary ways that go beyond the needs of the situation. So the ... check of supermajorities not only makes the emergency regime temporary but makes it milder while it lasts.

However, the 'supermajoritarian escalator' model as developed by Ackerman is not free from deficiencies. In the first place, his version of the 'supermajoritarian escalator' can be best described as a weak version of the model. For, he sets the first escalating cascade of supermajority at only 60 per cent which does not even constitute two-thirds of the total members of the legislature and the difference between a simple majority and 60 per cent is too narrow and, as such, can be masterminded by the executive without much difficulty. For instance, if the legislature is composed of 300 members, then 60 per cent of the total number means the support of 180 members. Thus even if the executive commands the support of only a simple majority – 151 out of the 300 members – then it will require the support of only an additional 29 members for extending the period of the emergency, which can be garnered by persuading the legislators belonging to smaller parties and independent legislators to vote in favour of the extension. The executive can influence the support of such members by painting a grim picture of the threats looming over the nation. It then follows that such an arrangement provides the executive with significant leeway to impose broad measures incommensurate with the threats posed to the life of the nation. For the executive will be aware that the imposition of such wide measures will be difficult to justify at a later point due to the increasing supermajorities (Posner and Vermeule, 2007).

Second, Ackerman's 'supermajoritarian model' does not envisage a maximum period of emergency. Rather it relies entirely on the legislators to bring an end to the emergency. It does not acknowledge the possibility that a political party might command the support of three-quarters (75 per cent) or four-fifths (80 per cent) of the total number of members of the legislature.[12] Ackerman's model, therefore, in such a scenario grants the executive the option of perpetuating the emergency rule with the support of the overwhelming majority in the legislature and after a while people will become accustomed to the emergency rule to such an extent that it may become the ordinary machinery of the government.

4.4.3.1.2 THE POSSIBILITY OF A STRONGER SUPERMAJORITARIAN ESCALATOR MODEL

The abovementioned problems therefore suggest the incorporation within the constitutional framework of a stronger version of the 'supermajoritarian escalator', requiring the issue of the renewal of a proclamation of emergency after the first two months to be approved by two-thirds of the total number of members of the legislature. The subsequent escalator due for the continuation of emergency beyond four months should require the support of three-quarters (75 per cent) of the legislators. Since the objective of the 'supermajoritarian escalator' is to prevent the executive attempting to stretch an emergency beyond its absolute necessity by making it easy for a small minority of legislators to oversee the timely termination of the emergency, it can be strongly argued that only a strong version of the 'supermajoritarian model' can attain such an objective. For example, if the Malaysian Constitution had contained a strong version of the 'supermajoritarian escalator', then the Malaysian Opposition Parliamentarians would have been able to bring an end to the four emergencies declared in 1964, 1966, 1969 and 1977, all of which remained in force until December 2011, despite the fact the UMNO-led Coalition had, with the exception of the general elections of 2008 and 2013, always enjoyed a two-thirds majority in the Parliament.

4.4.3.2 Stipulation of a time limit in the constitution on the continuation of emergency

Finally, with regard to the question as to the fate of a proclamation of emergency after receiving the assent of three-quarters of the legislators for continuation beyond four months, the constitution should fix the maximum period of emergency at six months. Thus, a proclamation of emergency and the consequent emergency measures after securing two extensions from the pre-requisite supermajorities of the Parliament should come to an end on the completion of six months. For given the resources available to the executive during an emergency to counter the threats posed to the security of the nation, it is extremely unlikely that in today's world any crisis threatening the life of the nation can remain in existence beyond six months (*States of Emergency*, 1983). However, if the threat posed to the life of the nation does continue for more than six months, it nevertheless remains open to the executive to proclaim a fresh emergency. The principal objective is to ensure that executive action during a state of emergency is governed by the rule of law. Prescribing a time limit on the continuation of the emergency provides notice to everyone concerned that the executive cannot manipulate the continuation of an emergency for political purposes beyond the six-month period. In this context, the constitutional arrangement in Poland, a country which like South Africa also had a distressing experience with states of emergency during the 1980s, is relevant. For the present *Constitution of Poland* contains even stricter standards as it sets the maximum period for the continuance of a state of emergency at 150 days (five months) in order to prevent the undue lingering of these powers beyond the cessation of hostilities which gave rise to them (art 230(1) and (2)).

4.4.3.3 The possibility of incorporating other forms of checks and balances in the constitution

In addition to the abovementioned system of check and balances, the constitution can also provide for the establishment of a quasi-judicial commission headed by a retired chief justice after the revocation of the emergency to inquire into any excesses committed by the emergency regime. Such commissions can bring to the fore a lot of sensitive information concerning the emergency regime that was concealed from the public during the continuation of the emergency in the interests of 'national security.' It therefore has the potential of acting as a weak form of safeguard in order to prevent potential executive abuses. For the executive will be aware that any excesses committed by it during the continuation of the emergency will be made public by the Commission once the emergency is over. For example, in India, after the termination of the traumatic emergency rule of Indira Gandhi on account of internal disturbance, a Commission headed by Justice J. C. Shah was appointed by the Government in 1978 to investigate the abuses committed by Mrs Gandhi's emergency regime. The findings of the Commission, which were published in the form of a report, sent shockwaves around the country and the world. For the gravity of the excesses committed was unknown due to strict censorship guidelines that were in place during the emergency regime (Iyer, 2000).

4.4.3.4 The role of the judiciary under the democratic formalist model

The democratic formalist or constitutional model retains a role for the judges as well. It is contended that the incorporation of the abovementioned checks and balances concerning the response to emergencies within the constitutional structure has the impact of taking some of the pressure off the judges in managing 'front-line' legal responses during emergencies (Ackerman, 2003–2004: 1044).

For instance, even if the executive is unwilling to respect the legislature's refusal through the 'supermajoritarian escalator' to extend an emergency or the maximum period of emergency, the judiciary will not have to come up with complicated arguments in deferring to the executive's contentions. Rather, the judges will be in a position to hold the executive accountable. For the constitution itself provides them with the basis in 'clean and clear' terms to scrutinize the executive's breach of the rule of law' (Ackerman, 2003–2004: 1068). As Ackerman (2006: 1069) argues:

> The supermajoritarian escalator [coupled with the maximum time limit] will have a salutary impact on the behavior of judges ... Judges tend to exploit ambiguities in the constitutional text to minimize energetic inquiry during the period of most acute crisis. ... The key point for ... [them] is that they are off the hook, that the legislature has taken responsibility for terminating the emergency in a highly public fashion. Once the legislature has taken the lead, judges will resume their normal role ... [of] providing due process of law.

Thus it can be argued that the incorporation of the said checks and balances concerning emergency within the constitution restores the judiciary's role as the guardian and protector of the rule of law during an emergency.

4.4.4 Incorporating the standards concerning human rights within the constitutional framework

In light of the weakness, as noted earlier in Section 3.3.3, of the international treaty-based monitoring system, the standards concerning human rights, such as the principles of non-derogation and proportionality, should be implemented within the constitutional framework of every nation (Fitzpatrick, 1994). It can be argued that if the principles of non-derogation and proportionality are complemented by the abovementioned elaborate mechanisms in the constitution then the possibility of abuse of human rights during emergencies would be obviated.

First, the enumeration of the circumstances which truly merit a proclamation of emergency would ensure that the executive would not be able to resort to the extraordinary powers concerning emergency for unjustifiable purposes to impose unwarranted restrictions on fundamental rights. Second, the incorporation of the provisions concerning the strong version of the 'supermajoritarian escalator' in the Constitution would ensure that the parliament is not subordinate to the wishes of the executive and can act as an effective check against its attempt to use a state of emergency as a vehicle for imposing unnecessary restrictions on the rights of individuals. Thus, entrusting a competent, active and informed organ like the parliament through the device of 'supermajoritarian escalator' to oversee the scrutiny of emergency measures might help to ensure the implementation of the principle of proportionality in practice, and thereby secure the continuous operation of those fundamental rights which do not have any direct nexus with an emergency. Fourth, even if the parliament fails to perform its requisite duties, the existence of a time limit on the continuation of an emergency would mean that the restrictions on the fundamental rights would be lifted after a finite period of time. Fifth and finally, the enumeration of these safeguards in the Constitution would provide the judiciary with the benchmarks for examining the constitutionality and necessity of derogations from human rights during emergency situations. As Tom Hickman (2005: 659) aptly notes, a carefully designed derogation model 'creates a space between fundamental rights and the rule of law. While governments are permitted to step outside the human rights regime their action remains within the law and subject to judicial supervision.'

It is noteworthy that there is a greater tendency among drafters of modern constitutions to work towards the liberalisation of the provisions concerning emergency by incorporating standards against which the constitutionality of the invocation of emergency and its impact on human rights can be judged. For instance, the *Constitution of Namibia*, 1990 not only makes a number of fundamental rights non-derogable[13] during a state of emergency but also subjects the exercise of emergency powers to certain safeguards.

In the first place, the *Constitution of Namibia* confines the power to invoke emergency to certain clearly defined circumstances, such as national disaster or 'during a state of national defence' (art 26(1)). Second, a proclamation of emergency and the consequent emergency measures under the Constitution will lapse within seven days if not ratified by the National Assembly in session, or otherwise within 30 days, by a vote of two-thirds of all its members (art 26(2)(a) and (b)). Finally, emergency measures under the Constitution can only be extended by a vote of two-thirds of the members of the Assembly for no more than six months at a time (26(3). The addition of these safeguards to the non-derogable rights in the *Constitution of Namibia* makes it difficult for the executive to continue an emergency with a view to imposing unwarranted restrictions on the fundamental rights of citizens.

The present *Constitution of South Africa*, which was adopted in 1996 after South Africa had experienced between 1948–1994 a number of emergencies which severely eroded human rights, lists in a tabular form a number of rights from which no derogation can be made even during an emergency threatening the life of the nation.[14] The *Constitution of South Africa* also contains certain safeguards so that emergencies cannot be resorted to and continued with a view to imposing arbitrary restrictions on fundamental rights. For instance, the Constitution confines the invocation of emergency to circumstances such as 'war, invasion, general insurrection, disorder, natural disaster'; stipulates who has the authority to declare a state of emergency; and subjects the emergency measures and their continuation to the scrutiny of the Parliament through, as pointed out above in Section 4.4.3.1.1, the device of 'supermajoritarian escalator' (s 37(1) and (2)).

4.4.5 *Incorporation of safeguards concerning preventive detention within the constitutional framework*

The exercise of the power of preventive detention is an extraordinary measure. For it entails the deprivation of an individual's right to liberty without any finding of guilt and without the possibility for the individual to have his day in court whereby a finding of guilt or innocence would be handed down (see Section 3.7). It is therefore evident that the exercise of this power involves a 'serious denial of human rights' (*States of Emergency*, 1983: 429). Consequently, the International Commission of Jurists (ICJ) and the Special Rapporteur on States of Emergency have opined that preventive detention should only be permissible during a state of emergency threatening the life of a nation (Fitzpatrick, 1994). However, international human rights law does not stipulate that the exercise of the power of preventive detention can be warranted only by a grave emergency. The Human Rights Committee in its general comment on Article 9, which deals with the issue of preventive detention, also did not avail of the opportunity to suggest that preventive detention should be confined to emergencies. Subsequently, the absence of any such guarantee has allowed executives to exercise the power indiscriminately, as pointed out earlier in Section 3.8, to keep the critics of their policies behind bars even during peacetime.

Furthermore, international human rights law, rather than providing for adequate safeguards to prevent abuse of the power of preventive detention, merely advocates for the protection of the right to be free from arbitrary deprivation of the right to liberty (Londras, 2011). During the drafting stage of the ICCPR, the United States and France proposed that some of the 'most fundamental guarantees against arbitrary detention and some minimum rights of due process' should be made non-derogable under any circumstances (Oraa, 1992: 106; Hartman, 1985; US and French Draft, 1949). However, the proposal did not see the light of the day, as the United Kingdom objected to it on the ground that the exigencies of a grave emergency may require the suspension of these guarantees (UK Proposal, 1949; Hartman, 1985). Consequently, human rights scholars argue that the absence of guarantees concerning preventive detention has facilitated the violation of fundamental human rights, including non-derogable rights such as the right to life and freedom from torture. The conditions associated with preventive detention which have been said to facilitate such violation of fundamental human rights include:

a) Indefinite or prolonged detention: Indefinite or prolonged detention often leads to inhuman treatment, death and certain form of torture. For instance, a US Senate Report, which was published on 9 December 2014, on the techniques employed to interrogate individuals who were detained indefinitely in Guantanamo Bay revealed that detainees were frequently subjected to various methods of torture during interrogation. The most commonly employed torture methods were waterboarding, sleep deprivation for more than a week at a time, and rectal hydration or rectal feeding (Kutsch, 2014). The indefinite detention and consequent torture in Guantanamo Bay not only caused the death of detainees but also had an adverse psychological impact on the detainees, leading a number of them to suffer from 'hallucinations, paranoia, insomnia' and to attempt at 'self-harm and self-mutilation' (Kutsch, 2014).

Furthermore, a report concerning the *Belmarsh* case published on 13 October 2004 by 11 Consultant Psychiatrists and one Consultant Clinical Psychologist revealed that indefinite detention caused 'serious damage to the health of eight of the detainees' (Amnesty International, 2004; Zayas, 2005). It is also not uncommon, particularly in developing nations, for detainees to lose their lives due to prolonged detention in the unhealthy conditions of the prison (see Section 7.2.5.1).

b) Detention incommunicado: Detention incommunicado – which refers to 'non-publication of the names of persons detained, denial of access to a court or to a lawyer, [and] denial of visits by family members' – makes a detainee non-existent for the outside world as he is deprived of all communication with family, friends and lawyers (*States of Emergency*, 1983: 430). Consequently, such detention makes it easier for detaining authorities to torture the detainees as it excludes the possibility of the information concerning such violation of the fundamental human right of detainees being made public. Such torture in extreme cases also leads to the death of detainees ('The Present State of Emergency in Argentina', 1983).
c) Laws which condone excesses committed by detaining officials by giving them immunity: Laws which grant immunity to officials for the excesses they commit in their treatment of the detainees create a sense among them that violating the fundamental human rights of detainees is an acceptable form of behaviour which is endorsed by the state (*States of Emergency*, 1983).

Since the incorporation of guarantees against arbitrary preventive detention in the human rights treaties through a protocol is not politically feasible, major studies[15] on human rights during emergencies has concluded that: 1) at a bare minimum the following guarantees concerning preventive detention should be entrenched in national constitutions, and 2) the following guarantees should also be made non-derogable during states of emergency.

a) Limiting the exercise of the power of preventive detention to formally declared emergencies: The ICJ, as pointed out above, in a comprehensive study on states of emergency carried out in 1981, advocated preventive detention should only be exercised during an emergency to protect a nation from threats to its security and public order. As soon as the emergency is revoked, the power to preventively detain individuals should come to an end. In 1989, the ICJ (1989: para 66) in an oral intervention before the 41st Session of the United Nations Sub-Commission on Prevention of Discrimination and Protection of Minorities, reiterated its above stance, when it stated: '[T]he I.C.J has, ever since its congress in Lagos ..., recommended: that it [preventive detention] only be adopted during an officially declared state of emergency which threatens the life of the nation.'

Furthermore, the ICJ stated that the discretion to exercise the power during an emergency, should not be unlimited. Rather the Constitution or the legislation concerning preventive detention should specify the grounds which can warrant the exercise of the power to preventively detain individuals (*States of Emergency*, 1983; Oraa, 1992).

It can be argued that, confining preventive detention to formally declared emergency periods would ensure that the liberty of individuals is not taken away in an arbitrary manner at the whim of the executive during peacetime. Individuals would be dealt with under the ordinary criminal law framework during times of peace and stability.

b) Right of the detainee to be informed of the grounds: A detainee should be informed within seven days of his/her detention of the grounds which led the detaining authority to conclude that relevant prejudicial acts might be committed by the detainee if he were not preventively interned (Oraa, 1992; Harding and Hatchard, 1993; *Paris Minimum Standards 1984*, art 5(2)(a). This would enable the detainee to make effective representation against the detention. In order to further aid the detainee in making an effective representation, the grounds supplied to the detainee should be sufficient and articulated in clear terms that can be understood by a layman. Failure to do so would defeat the very objective of extending the right to the detainee to make a representation against the detention order. In this context, the observations of Chief Justice Kania of the Supreme Court of India in the case of *State of Bombay v Atma Ram Shridhar Vaidya [1951] AIR (SC) 157* are noteworthy:

> [I]f the representation has to be intelligible to meet the charges contained in the grounds, the information conveyed to the detained person must be sufficient to attain that objective … Without getting information sufficient to make a representation against the order of detention, it is not possible for the man to make the representation. Indeed, the right will be only illusory but not a real right at all.
> (161–162)

c) Right to make representation against detention order: A detainee should be afforded the opportunity to make representations against his detention order before a review body headed by a person of judicial standing within 10 to 30 days of their detention (*Constitution of South Africa 1996* s 37(6)(e); *Paris Minimum Standards 1984* art 5(2)(d). The review body should have the authority to recommend the release of a detainee if it considers that continued detention is not conducive for the purposes of dealing with the threats to the security of the nation and such a decision of the body should be binding on the government (Oraa 1992; Harding and Hatchard, 1993).

d) Access to judicial review: The authority of the judiciary to examine the lawfulness of the detention in pursuance of writ of habeas corpus during an emergency should not be ousted by the constitution or permanent or temporary piece of legislation concerning preventive detention. The three major human rights instruments, namely the ICCPR (art 9(4)), ECHR (art 5(4)) and ACHR (art 7(6)), also recognise this remedy.

The judiciary in turn should adopt an objective test in assessing the 'reasonableness of executive satisfaction' for detaining an individual in preventive custody. The objective test, in this context, refers to the willingness of the judiciary to 'scrutinise the allegations of fact as well as grounds for the detention' with a view to ascertaining whether or not the detention order is necessary to prevent an individual from committing activities prejudicial to the security of a nation (Harding and Hatchard, 1993). In this context, the observations of Justice Hamoodur Rahman in *Mir Abdul Baqi Baluch v Government of Pakistan [1968] PLD (SC) 313* are pertinent. As he observed:

> What the court is concerned with is to see that the executive or administrative authority had before it sufficient materials upon which a reasonable person could have come to the conclusion that the requirements of law were satisfied. It is not uncommon that even high executive authorities act upon the basis of information supplied to them by their subordinates. In the circumstances, it cannot be said that it would be unreasonable for the Court, in the proper exercise of its constitutional duty, to insist upon a disclosure of the materials upon which the authority acted so that it should satisfy itself that the authority had not acted in an 'unlawful manner'.[16]

e) Access to lawyer and family members: Since detention incommunicado, as pointed out previously, facilitates torture and ill-treatment of detainees, it is contended that detainees should be given adequate opportunity for having 'as much contact as possible with "the outside world"', in particular, with lawyers and family members (*States of Emergency*, 1983). In this context, the specific proposal of the *Siracusa Principles on the Limitation and Derogation Provisions in the International Covenant on Civil and Political Rights*, 1984 is relevant. For it proposes that individuals should not be kept in preventive custody incommunicado for more than three to seven days.
f) Stipulating the maximum period of preventive detention: Since the life of a proclamation of emergency should come to an end after six months, the constitution of a nation should also fix the maximum period for keeping persons in preventive custody at six months rather than providing for indefinite periods of detention. In this context, the observations of the Inter-American Commission on Human Rights (1982: 337) are worthy of note:

> no domestic or international legal norm justifies, merely by invoking this special power [of preventive detention], the holding of detainees in prison for long and unspecified periods, without any charges being brought against them for violation of Law of National Security or another criminal law, and without their being brought to trial so that they may exercise the right to a fair trial and to due process of law.

It can be argued that providing for a time limit on keeping a person in preventive custody contributes towards striking a better balance between protecting national interests and protecting the liberty of individuals.

g) Right to monetary compensation: Finally, the constitution of a nation should contain a provision providing for monetary compensation for an unlawful deprivation of the right to personal liberty, particularly in cases of flagrant abuse of the power of preventive detention. In this context, the provision contained in clause 5 of Article 9 of the ICCPR is worthy of quote: 'Anyone who has been the victim of unlawful ... detention shall have an enforceable right to compensation.' The provision for providing compensation would have a salutary effect on the executive. As Ackerman (2006: 54) notes:

> The emergency administration should be obliged to pay these costs out of its own budget, and this prospect will concentrate the bureaucratic mind on what is most vital in a democracy. The arbitrary stockpiling of suspects in prison will come with a price, and one that all of us will pay in taxes. The security forces will have new incentives to spend time and energy determining who has been snared by mistake.

The present *Constitution of South Africa*, which was enacted in 1996, represents the most recent endeavour to offer specific guarantees for obviating the possibility of abuse of the powers concerning preventive detention during a state of emergency. The guarantees against arbitrary detention find expression in Section 37(6) and (7) of the *Constitution of South Africa* in the following manner:

> 6) Whenever anyone is detained without trial in consequence of a derogation of rights resulting from a declaration of a state of emergency, the following conditions must be observed:
>
>   a) An adult family member or friend of the detainee must be contacted as soon as reasonably possible, and informed that the person has been detained.
>   b) A notice must be published in the national Government Gazette within five days of the person being detained, stating the detainee's name and place of detention and referring to the

emergency measure in terms of which that person has been detained.

c) The detainee must be allowed to choose, and be visited at any reasonable time by, a medical practitioner.

d) The detainee must be allowed to choose, and be visited at any reasonable time by, a legal representative.

e) A court must review the detention as soon as reasonably possible, but no later than 10 days after the date the person was detained, and the court must release the detainee unless it is necessary to continue the detention to restore peace and order.

f) A detainee who is not released in terms of a review under paragraph (e), or who is not released in terms of a review under this paragraph, may apply to a court for a further review of the detention at any time after 10 days have passed since the previous review, and the court must release the detainee unless it is still necessary to continue the detention to restore peace and order.

g) The detainee must be allowed to appear in person before any court considering the detention, to be represented by a legal practitioner at those hearings, and to make representations against continued detention.

h) The state must present written reasons to the court to justify the continued detention of the detainee, and must give a copy of those reasons to the detainee at least two days before the court reviews the detention.

7) If a court releases a detainee, that person may not be detained again on the same grounds unless the state first shows a court good cause for re-detaining that person.

In addition to the abovementioned guarantees, Section 37(5)(c) of the *Constitution of South Africa* also makes certain guarantees concerning preventive detention non-derogable during a state of emergency. These non-derogable guarantees, *inter alia*, include the right to be informed of the grounds of detention (s 35(3)(a)), the right to challenge the legality of the detention before a court of law (s 35(2)(d)), and the right to be represented by a legal practitioner (s 35(3)(f)).

Although the *Constitution of South Africa* neither confines the exercise of the power of preventive detention to formally declared periods of emergency nor stipulates a maximum period for keeping a person in preventive custody, it provides an example of the realisation that protecting the national security of a nation does not necessarily require the complete surrender of the liberty of individuals. Rather a delicate balance can be struck between protecting national interests and simultaneously maintaining respect for an individual's right to protection from arbitrary preventive detention. These guarantees in turn also have the merit of diminishing the likelihood of torture and mistreatment of detainees in compliance with the relevant international human rights standards.

4.5 The advantages of incorporating detailed safeguards concerning emergency in the constitution

It should be stressed here that if the emergency model devised above, providing for legal limits on the power of the executive as to the proclamation, administration and termination of emergency, is incorporated into a constitution, then it would not only reduce the possibility of the abuse of the emergency powers but also ensure: a) the maintenance of rule of law, in which it is the law that governs through the instrumentality of man, and not the man independently of or above the law;[17] and b) the enjoyment of the core rights of individuals.

If the constitution contains detailed provisions concerning the exercise of emergency powers then the judiciary will find it difficult to adopt a highly deferential attitude when called upon to scrutinise the merits of the continuance of the emergency by arguing that the question is essentially 'political' and, hence, should be left to the executive judgment (Dyzenhaus, 2006a; Gross, 2011: 347). Conversely, the absence of these safeguards in the constitution concerning emergency powers essentially provides the executive with the necessary ammunition to convert itself into what Clinton Rossiter (1948: 8) called a 'fascist dictator'. For instance, Adolf Hitler took advantage of Article 48 of the *Weimar Constitution*, 1919, which did not stipulate the grounds for declaring emergency or provide for a legal framework for regulating emergency powers, by proclaiming an emergency in 1933 which remained in force for nearly 12 years. In the same vein in Poland in 1981, in the absence of express provisions concerning the proclamation of emergency and explicit constraints on the exercise of such powers, an emergency was declared by the military rulers, not to deal with an actual crisis threatening the life of the nation but to stage a massive crackdown on the pro-democracy Solidarity labour movement, which had carried out numerous strikes since August 1980 challenging the Communist Polish government ('1981: Military crackdown on Polish people', 1981). A series of arbitrary laws was imposed by the regime, with instruction to the newly formed Military Council for National Salvation to shoot anyone breaking the new laws. Although the emergency was officially lifted in 1983, the arbitrary and extraordinary laws continued to remain in force till 1989. Thus, in this context, the observations of Machiavelli (1950: 203) are worthy of note: '[N]o republic will be perfect if she has not by law provided for everything, having a remedy for every emergency, and fixed rules for applying it.'

In conclusion, it seems impossible to agree with the views of Carl Schmitt, the German fascist legal theorist, who argued for the abandonment of 'exaggerated formalism of the rule of law' in times of grave threats posed to the security and well-being of the state (Dyzenhaus, 2006a: 34). It also seems difficult to accept some of the arguments put forward by contemporary theorists, such as that the exigencies of an emergency require the executive to rule with lawlessness (Gross), which has Schmittian overtones, or that an overt reliance should be placed on the judiciary, despite its poor record, to police emergencies (Dyzenhaus). The latter approach essentially downplays the merits of innovative constitutional mechanisms. These models also, as has been argued above, involve the risk of discarding the rule of law during emergencies.

Having devised from a comparative constitutional law perspective a standard model for governing the proclamation, administration and termination of a state of emergency for incorporating into a constitution, an attempt will be made in the subsequent chapters to use the model as a yardstick to examine:

a) the provisions of the *Constitution of Bangladesh 1972* concerning the grounds for proclaiming emergency, the justification of the emergencies proclaimed on five occasions, and the continuation of some of the proclamation of emergencies even after the threat posed to the life of the nation was over to perpetuate the survival of the party in power;
b) the provisions of the *Constitution of Bangladesh* concerning suspension of the enforcement of fundamental rights during emergency situations, and the impact of the five proclamations of emergency in Bangladesh on the enjoyment of the fundamental rights of individuals; and
c) the provisions concerning preventive detention as enshrined in the *Constitution of Bangladesh* and Bangladeshi statutes (both permanent and temporary), the exercise of the power of preventive detention during the five declared periods of emergency, and the judicial response to the exercise of such power.

4.6 References

Ackerman, B. (2003–2004) 'The Emergency Constitution', *Yale Law Journal*, 113: 1031, 1044, 1068–1069.

Ackerman, B. (2006) *Before the Next Attack: Preserving Civil Liberties in an Age of Terrorism*, New Haven, CT: Yale University Press, 54, 90.

Adams, C. F. (ed.) (1851) *The Works of John Adams*, vol. 4, Boston: Little, Brown and Co, 106.

Amnesty International (2004) 'UK Lord Ruling: Three Years Too Late for Internees' (Press Release), 16 December, available at www.amnesty.org.uk/press-releases/uk-lords-ruling-three-years-too-late-internees [Accessed 5 April 2013].

A/2929 (1952) UN Doc. E/CN. 4/SR., 330, 66, 67 (para 39).

Bonner, D. (1985) *Emergency Powers in Peacetime*, London: Sweet & Maxwell, 17.

Cassidy, J. (2014) 'America's Shame: What's in the Senate Torture Report', *The New Yorker*, 9 December, available at www.newyorker.com/news/john-cassidy/americas-shame-whats-senate-torture-report [Accessed 20 December 2014].

Dicey, A. V. (1915) *Introduction to the Study of the Law of the Constitution*, London: Macmillan & Co., 144.

Dyzenhaus, D. (2003) 'Humpty Dumpty Rules or the Rule of Law: Legal Theory and the Adjudication of National Security', *Australian Journal of Legal Philosophy*, 28: 13.

Dyzenhaus, D. (2005) 'The State of Emergency in Legal Theory', in V. V. Ramraj, M. Hor, K. Roach and G. Williams (eds), *Global Anti-Terrorism Law and Policy*, Cambridge/New York: Cambridge University Press, 72–73.

Dyzenhaus, D (2006a) *The Constitution of Law: Legality in a Time of Emergency*, Cambridge/New York, Cambridge University Press, 16, 19, 34, 50, 63, 64, 75, 174, 190, 191.

Dyzenhaus, D. (2006b) '*Schmitt v Dicey*: Are States of Emergency Inside or Outside the Legal Order', *Cardozo Law Review*, 27(5): 2014.

Dyzenhaus, D. (2007) 'Cycles of Legality in Emergency Times', *Public Law Review* 18: 166, 168.

Dyzenhaus, D. (2009) '*Liversidge v Anderson* in Peter Cane & Joanne Conaghan, The New Oxford Companion to Law', Oxford Reference, available at www.oxfordreference.com/view/10.1093/acref/9780199290543.001.0001/acref-9780199290543-e-1359 [Accessed 4 February 2013].

Dyzenhaus, D. (2012) 'States of Emergency', in M. Rosenfeld and A. Sajó (eds), *Oxford Handbook of Comparative Constitutional Law*, Oxford: Oxford University Press, 445.

'Emergency Declared Due to Rains in Central Peru' (2011) *Latin American Herald Tribune*, 22 November, available at http://laht.com/article.asp?CategoryId=14095&ArticleId=351568 [Accessed 2 February 2013].

Fitzpatrick, J. (1994) *Human Rights in Crisis: The International System for Protecting Rights During States of Emergency*, Philadelphia, PA: University of Pennsylvania Press, 45, 77–78.

French Draft (1949) UN Doc. E/CN.4/324.

Frost, D. (1977) 'I have impeached myself', *The New York Times*, 20 May, A16, reproduced in 'Great Interviews of the 20th Century' (2007) *The Guardian*, 7 September, available at www.guardian.co.uk/theguardian/2007/sep/07/greatinterviews1 [Accessed 2 April 2013].

General Secretariat, Organisation of American States (1982) *The IACHR: Ten Years of Activities (1971–1981)*, Washington, DC: General Secretariat, Organisation of American States, 337.

Gross, O. (2003) 'Chaos and Rules: Should Responses to Violent Crises Always be Constitutional', *Yale Law Journal*, 112: 1023, 1034, 1039, 1097, 1100, 1114.

Gross, O. (2008) 'Extra-Legality and the Ethic of Political Responsibility', in V. V. Ramraj (ed.), *Emergencies and the Limits of Legality*, Cambridge/New York: Cambridge University Press, 63, 71, 73, 79.

Gross, O. (2011) 'Constitutions and Emergency Regimes', in T. Ginsburg and R. Dixon (eds), *Comparative Constitutional Law*, Cheltenham/Northampton, MA: Edward Elgar Publishing Limited, 347.

Gross, O. and Aoláin, F. N. (2006) *Law in Times of Crisis: Emergency Powers in Theory and Practice*, Cambridge/New York: Cambridge University Press 170.

Harding, A. and Hatchard, J. (1993) 'Introduction', in A. Harding and J. Hatchard (eds), *Preventive Detention and Security Law: A Comparative Survey*, Dordrecht/Boston: Martinus Nijhoff Publishers, 8–9.

Hartman, J. (1985) 'Working Paper for the Committee of Experts on the Article 4 Derogation Provision', *Human Rights Quarterly*, 7: 115–118.

Hickman, T. R. (2005) 'Between Human Rights and the Rule of Law: Indefinite Detention and Derogation Model of Constitutionalism', *Modern Law Review*, 68: 659.

'Hurricane Irene: Emergency declared in seven US states' (2011) *BBC News*, 26 August, available at www.bbc.co.uk/news/world-us-canada-14669374 [Accessed 2 February 2013].

Human Rights Committee (2001) *General Comment 29: States of Emergency*, U.N. Doc. CCPR/C/21/Rev.1/Add.11, para 2, available at http://hrlibrary.umn.edu/gencomm/hrc29.html [Accessed 5 April 2014].

International Commission of Jurists (1983) *States of Emergency – Their Impact on Human Rights: A Comparative Study by the International Commission of Jurists*, Geneva: International Commission of Jurists, 429, 430, 433, 459, 461.

International Commision of Jurists (1983) 'The Present State of Emergency in Argentina', in *States of Emergency – Their Impact on Human Rights: A Comparative Study by the International Commission of Jurists*, International Commission of Jurists, 28.

International Law Association (1984) *Paris Report*, 59.

Iyer, V. (2000) *States of Emergency: The Indian Experience*, New Delhi: Butterworths, 152, 171–176.

Kutsch, T. (2014) 'Summary: Key Findings in CIA Torture Probe', *Al Jazeera America*, 9 December, available at http://america.aljazeera.com/articles/2014/12/9/torture-report-excerpts.html [Accessed 20 December 2014].

Landler, M. (2005) 'France Declares State of Emergency to Curb Crisis', *The New York Times*, 8 November, available at, www.nytimes.com/2005/11/08/international/europe/08cnd-france.html?pagewanted=all&_r=0 [Accessed 5 May 2013].

League of Red Cross Societies (1976) *A Handbook of Red Cross Disaster Relief*, Geneva: League of Red Cross Societies, 13.

Lillich, R. B. (1985) *The Paris Minimum Standards of Human Rights Norms in a State of Emergency 1984* art 5(2)(d), 'Current Developments: The Paris Minimum Standards of Human Rights Norms in a State of Emergency', *American Journal of International Law*, 79: 1072–1079.

Londras, F. (2011) *Detention in the 'War on Terror': Can Human Rights Fight Back?*, Cambridge/New York: Cambridge University Press, 36.

Machiavelli, N. (1950) *The Prince and The Discourses* (translated by Luigi Ricci and Christian Edward Detmold), New York: The Modern Library, 203.

Marks, S. (1982) 'Principles and Norms of Human Rights Applicable in Emergency Situations' in Karel Vasak (ed), *International Dimensions of Human Rights*, Westport, CT: Greenwood Press, 175–213.

Martinez, J. S. (2006) 'Inherent Executive Power: A Comparative Perspective', *Yale Law Journal*, 115: 2496.

Mathews, A. S. and Albino, R. C. (1966) 'The Permanence of the Temporary: An Examination of the 90- and 180-Day Detention Laws', *South African Law Journal*, 83: 43.

Mayer, J. (2005) 'Outsourcing Torture', *The New Yorker*, 14 February, available at www.newyorker.com/magazine/2005/02/14/outsourcing-torture [Accessed 5 April 2013].

Morss, J. R. (2009) 'Facts, Threats and Reds: Common Law Constitutionalism and the Rule of Law', *Deakin Law Review*, 14(1): 81.

Note (2002) 'Responding to Terrorism: Crime, Punishment, and War', *Harvard Law Review*, 115(4): 1230.

Oraa, J. (1992) *Human Rights in States of Emergency in International Law*, Oxford: Clarendon Press, 30–31, 106, 108, 109, 113.

Posner, E. A. and Vermeule, A. (2007) *Terror in the Balance: Security, Liberty and the Courts*, Oxford: Oxford University Press, 168.

Roach, K. (2008) 'Ordinary Laws for Emergencies and Democratic Derogations from Rights' in V. V. Ramraj (ed.), *Emergencies and the Limits of Legality*, Cambridge/NewYork: Cambridge University Press, 234.

Rossiter, C. L. (1948) *Constitutional Dictatorship: Crisis Government in the Modern Democracies*, Princeton, NJ: Princeton University Press, 6, 8, 41–53.

Scheppele, K. L. (2004) 'Law in a Time of Emergency: States of Exception and the Temptations of 9/11', *University of Pennsylvania Journal of Constitutional Law*, 6: 1008.

Scheppele, K. L. (2006) 'Small Emergencies', *Georgia Law Review*, 40: 858.

Scheuerman, W. E. (2006) 'Emergency Powers and the Rule of Law After 9/11', *The Journal of Political Philosophy*, 14(1): 61, 68, 74, 75, 76, 77–78.

Scheuerman, W. E. (2008) 'Presidentialism and Emergency Government', in V. V. Ramraj (ed.), *Emergencies and the Limits of Legality*, Cambridge/New York: Cambridge University Press, 277, 283, 285.

Schmitt, C. (2005) *Political Theology, Four Chapters on the Concept of Sovereignty* (translated by George Schwab), Chicago: University of Chicago Press, 6, 12–13.

'State of Emergency Declared in France' (2005) *Fox News*, 8 November, available at www.foxnews.com/story/0,2933,174868,00.html [Accessed 5 May 2013].

The White House: Office of the Press Secretary (2012) 'President Obama Signs New Jersey Emergency Declaration', 28 October, available at www.whitehouse.gov/the-press-office/2012/10/28/president-obama-signs-new-jersey-emergency-declaration [Accessed 2 February 2013].

UK Proposal (1949) UN Doc E/CN.4/SR.126, 4–5.

UN Commission on Human Rights (1964) *Study of the Right of Everyone to be Free from Arbitrary Arrest and Detention and Exile*, New York: United Nations, 257.

US Draft (1949) UN Doc. E/CN.4/325.

Zayas, A. (2005) 'Human Rights and Indefinite Detention', *International Review of the Red Cross*, 87(857): 19.

'1981: Military Crackdown on Polish People' (1981) *BBC News*, 13 December, available at http://news.bbc.co.uk/onthisday/hi/dates/stories/december/13/newsid_2558000/2558955.stm [Accessed 3 February 2014].

Notes

1 Mr Yoo remarked that '[t]he issue is dying out. The public has had its referendum.'

2 The Presidential Order was confirmed by the Congress on 21 March 1942.

3 Act 37 of 1963 in Section 17(1) stated: Notwithstanding anything to the contrary in any law contained, any commissioned officer … may … without warrant arrest … any person whom he suspects upon reasonable grounds of having committed or intending … to commit any offence under the Suppression of the Communism Act … or the Unlawful Organizations Act … or the offence of sabotage, or who in his opinion is in possession of information relating to the

commission of such offence … and detain such person … for interrogation … until such person has in opinion of the Commissioner of Police replied satisfactorily to all questions at the said interrogation, but no such person shall be so detained for more than ninety days on any particular occasion when he is so arrested.

4 For example, *Constitution of the USA* 1787.

5 J. S. Martinez, (2005–2006) 'Inherent Executive Power: A Comparative Perspective', *Yale Law Journal*, 115: 2496.

6 *Constitution of India 1950;* 1956, 1962 and 1973 *Constitutions of Pakistan;* and *Constitution of Bangladesh 1972*, as amended in 1973.

7 See *Constitution of Greece 1975* art 48(1); *German Basic Law 1949* art 115a; *Constitution of the Dominican Republic* art 37(7) and (8); *Constitution of Slovenia 1991* art 92; *Constitution of Macedonia 1991* art 125(4); *Israel's Basic Law: The Government 2001* art 38(a); *Constitution of Hungary 1949* art 19(3)(1) and *Constitution of Hungary 2011* art 48(1)(b).

8 See *Israeli Basic Law: The Government 2001* art 38(c); *Constitution of Greece 1975* art 48(2); *Constitution of Austria 1920* art 18(3); *Constitutional Act of Denmark 1953* art 23; and *Constitution of Hungary 2011* art 48(3).

9 See *Constitution of France 1958* art 16(5*); Constitution of Spain 1978* art 116(5); *Constitution of Hungary 2011* art 48(7); and *Constitution of Paraguay 1992* art 288(9).

10 See *German Basic Law 1949* art 115*; Constitution of Greece 1975* art 53; and *Constitution of Poland* 1997 art 228.

11 The African National Congress Party has been ruling South Africa by securing more than 60 per cent of seats of the 400-seat National Assembly in each of the general elections since 1994. For instance, in the recently held elections on 7 May 2014, it won 249 seats, which constitutes 62.15 per cent of the total members of the National Assembly.

12 For instance, in the General Elections of 2008, the Awami League led Alliance won three-quarters of the 300 parliamentary seats in Bangladesh.

13 *Constitution of Namibia 1990* art. 24(3). These non-derogable rights include the right to life (art. 6), prohibition of torture or cruel, inhuman or degrading treatment or punishment (art. 8), prohibition of slavery and forced labour (art. 9), freedom from discrimination (art. 10), right to fair trial (art. 12), right to family (art. 14), rights of child (art. 15), right to administrative justice (art. 18), cultural rights (art. 19), freedom of speech and expression (art. 21(1)(a)), freedom of thought, conscience and belief (art. 21(1)(b)), freedom to practise any religion (art. 21(1)(c), and freedom of association (art. 21(1)(e)).

14 *Constitution of South Africa 1996* s 37(5). The rights envisaged as non-derogable by the *Constitution of South Africa* are as follows: the right to equality with respect to discrimination on the grounds of race, colour, ethnic or social origin, sex, religion or language (s 9), right to human dignity (s 10), right to life (s 11), freedom and security of the person (s 12), freedom from slavery, servitude and forced labour (s 13), right of children (s 28), and, right of arrested, detained and accused persons (s 35).

15 *States of Emergency – Their Impact on Human Rights: A Comparative Study by the International Commission of Jurists* (1983) Geneva: International Commission of Jurists; *Paris Minimum Standards of Human Rights Norms in a State of Emergency, 1984; and Siracusa Principles on the Limitation and Derogation Provisions in the International Covenant on Civil and Political Rights*, E/CN.4/1985/4, 1984.

16 Quoted in *Aruna Sen v Government of the People's Republic of Bangladesh & Others [1974] 3 CLC (HCD) 1*, 15.

17 Hence the ideal of rule of law is often expressed by the phrase 'government of laws, and not of men'. C. F. Adams (ed.) (1851) *The Works of John Adams*, vol. 4, Boston: Little, Brown and Co, 106.

5 The emergencies proclaimed in Bangladesh on five occasions from 1974 to 2007 and their justification

5.1 Introduction

The proclamation of an emergency is a formal attempt to establish a system of rule in times of grave crises. It serves as a notice to all whom it may concern that the situation demands strong measures and restrictions broader than those ordinarily enforced by the civil authorities. A proclamation of emergency may also have a certain emotional value in that it suggests to the ordinary citizens that the state has taken effective measures to restore normalcy as soon as possible.

It may be recalled here from the discussion in Sections 2.6.2, 2.6.3.1 and 2.6.3.2 that, although the 1950 *Constitution of India* and 1956 and 1962 Constitutions of Pakistan contained provisions recognising three types of emergency – emergency of war, emergency of subversion and financial emergency – the Constitution Drafting Subcommittee of the Constituent Assembly of Bangladesh did not consider it necessary to provide for provisions in the *Constitution of Bangladesh* empowering either the executive or the legislature to proclaim any kind of emergency whatsoever. Furthermore, not a single member of the Assembly ever spoke about the necessity of incorporating any provision into the Constitution concerning the proclamation of emergency. Rather, it was claimed in the Constituent Assembly Debate that the repeated misuse of emergency powers and preventive detention laws during the days when Bangladesh was a Province of Pakistan discouraged them from including such provisions in the Constitution (People's Republic of Bangladesh, 1972). However, after only nine months and seven days of the coming into force of the *Constitution of Bangladesh*, the Government realised the necessity for inserting a new Part IXA in the Constitution, titled 'Emergency Provisions', providing for the declaration and continuance of emergency and suspension of enforcement of the fundamental rights during such a proclamation. The then Law Minister argued that provisions concerning emergency were contained in the constitutions of almost all the democratic countries around the world, and hence that it was necessary to incorporate provisions concerning emergency in the Constitution to fill up the void that was left in the Constitution during its framing stage (Ahmed, 1984).

Article 141A of the *Constitution of Bangladesh*, as inserted by the *Constitutional (Second Amendment) Act*, 1973, empowers the Head of the State, who has the constitutional obligation to safeguard the territorial integrity of the country, to proclaim only two types of emergency in respect of security-oriented matters, namely, the emergency of war or external aggression and the emergency of internal disturbance. It speaks of the President's 'satisfaction' as to the existence of 'a grave emergency... in which the security or economic life of Bangladesh or any part thereof is threatened by war or external aggression or internal disturbance' (art 141A(1)). Thus, two sets of qualifying words have been used in the *Constitution of Bangladesh* for the valid exercise of the power to proclaim an emergency, namely, a) the satisfaction of the President, and b) the emergency which exists must be grave, thus importing an element of degree having reference to the magnitude, imminency and seriousness of the threat to the security or economic life of Bangladesh. The Presidential satisfaction as to the necessity of emergency action need not await the actual occurrence of war, external aggression or internal disturbance. The President is empowered to proclaim an emergency before the actual occurrence of war or any such aggression or disturbance if he is satisfied that there is imminent danger of such event (art 141A(3)). Thus, the executive as a matter of political expediency can exercise the power of proclamation of emergency in pursuance of the Constitution. As Justice Bhagwati of the Indian Supreme Court in *State of Rajasthan v Union of India [1978] SCR (1)* observed: 'The satisfaction of the President is a subjective one [test] and cannot be tested by reference to any objective tests' (1). It might be based on a political judgment founded on the assessment of diverse factors such as national and international situations, intelligence reports, ambassadors' reports, etc.

It seems that the framers of the *Constitution of Bangladesh* failed to limit the power to proclaim a state of emergency solely to clearly defined circumstances that put the life of the nation and its subjects under a grave threat. For, despite the imprecise nature of the phrase 'internal disturbance' and its subsequent abuse during colonial and post-colonial periods, this ground has been inserted in the *Constitution of Bangladesh* as one of the grounds for invoking a state of emergency (see Section 4.4.1 and Sections 2.6.1.5, 2.6.2.1.3, 2.6.3.3.1 and 2.6.3.3.2). Consequently, this ground, as will be argued below, made it extremely convenient for the succeeding generations of executives to proclaim emergency for purposes other than that of securing the life of Bangladesh.

It should also be stressed here that the *Constitution of Bangladesh*, as elaborated in Section 2.7, does not contain any reliable system of checks and balances for overseeing the effective scrutiny of a state of emergency and its subsequent timely termination. One of the closest things to a safeguard envisaged by the *Constitution of Bangladesh* against any possibility of abuse of emergency powers is a requirement that the proclamation of emergency must be countersigned by the Prime Minister.[1] However, since pursuant to

Article 48(3) of the Constitution, the President, as the ceremonial Head of the State, performs all his functions – except the appointments of the Prime Minister and the Chief Justice – on the advice of the Prime Minister, the requirement of the countersignature of the Prime Minister for securing the validity of the emergency can hardly be considered as a safeguard for preventing any abuse concerning the resort to this power. Rather this requirement can properly be described as a procedural formality. Thus, it seems that the validity of the proclamation of emergency can only be challenged on the ground of the *mala fide* exercise of power but the proof of the circumstances on which the *mala fides* of the executive could be exhibited is a difficult matter.

The Constitution also stipulated the requirement of parliamentary endorsement for the continuation of an emergency beyond 120 days (see Section 5.7 below for the changes introduced to this provision in 2011).[2] The requirement of parliamentary approval of an emergency for its continuation beyond 120 days in essence meant that an emergency could continue without any scrutiny for four months. Furthermore, the Constitution did not contain any mechanism for requiring such renewal to be approved by a larger majority of legislators, which in turn made it very easy for the executive to secure such renewal, as it commanded the support of the majority in the Parliament. In addition, the Constitution did not contain any provision for preventing the dissolution of the Parliament by the executive during an emergency with a view to avoid obtaining such approval altogether.

Since the incorporation of the provisions concerning emergency into the *Constitution of Bangladesh* on 22 September 1973, emergencies have been proclaimed on five occasions – on 28 December 1974, 30 May 1981, 27 November 1987, 27 November 1990, and 11 January 2007 – on the ground of internal disturbance. The following discussion will reveal that all the states of emergency proclaimed, except that promulgated on 31 May 1981 following the assassination of the Head of the State, were unjustified. In fact, the emergency powers were abused as a means to remain in power by suppressing the opposition.

5.2 The first proclamation of emergency issued in December 1974

Sheikh Mujibur Rahman, who had assumed the office of Prime Minister on 11 January 1972 with unprecedented popular support, found it difficult to transform this support into the political strength and preparedness needed to function as the head of the government. Consequently, on 28 December 1974, a year and three months after the insertion of emergency provisions into the *Constitution of Bangladesh*, he advised President Muhammadullah to proclaim a state of emergency throughout the country on the ground of internal disturbance. The Proclamation of Emergency, as published in the *Gazette of Bangladesh Extraordinary*, provided that

> [w]hereas the President is satisfied that a grave emergency exists in which the security or economic life of Bangladesh are threatened by internal disturbance; Therefore ... the President is pleased hereby to issue the Proclamation of Emergency.

It is striking that Mujib, who, as pointed out earlier in Section 2.6.3.1, in the Pakistan Constituent Assembly debate vehemently opposed the insertion of internal disturbance in the 1956 *Constitution of Pakistan* as a ground for invoking emergency because of the likelihood of the abuse of this power for political purposes, had a complete change of heart in the 1970s. Insertion of internal disturbance as a ground for proclaiming emergency into the amended *Constitution of Bangladesh* in 1973 was not only acceptable to him, but he also advised the President to declare an emergency on the wide and vague ground of internal disturbance. Neither the first proclamation of emergency nor the *Emergency Powers Ordinance*, which was issued following the proclamation of emergency, specified the compelling circumstances which led to the declaration of emergency on 28 December 1974.

The *Emergency Powers Ordinance* (1974 s 2) empowered the Government to make 'such rules as appeared to it to be necessary or expedient for ensuring the security, the public safety, and interest and for protecting the economic life of Bangladesh or for maintaining supplies or services essential to the life of the community'. Within six days of assuming the power of making rules under the Ordinance, 1974, the Government assumed wide and extensive powers to deal with the alleged crisis by formulating and adopting the Emergency Power Rules.

5.2.1 *Justification of the proclamation of emergency on 28 December 1974*

It is widely believed that the emergency was declared on 28 December 1974 because of the failure of Sheikh Mujib's Awami League Government to combat rapid inflation, food shortages, famine, smuggling and black-marketeering, which came to pervade the life of the nation (Ziring, 1992). Misappropriation of foreign grants, aids and relief goods only added to the suffering of the people. From September 1973 onwards, political violence was on the increase and the Awami Leaguers often became the targets of violent attacks for their alleged corruption and association with the Government of the day. Sheikh Mujib himself estimated that by 1974 more than 3000 members of the Awami League, including five Members of the Parliament, had been killed (Franda, 1982). However, it seems that the murders of a Member of the Parliament and a Union Council Chairman on 25 December 1974 at the time of offering *Eid* prayers coupled with the threats of large-scale industrial unrest by five labour organisations from 18 January 1975 gave Mujib the pretext to advise the President to proclaim an emergency.

Against a decreased popularity due to the failure to effectively govern the country, Mujib in a deliberate move chose to assume more powers as the most effective means of dealing with the deteriorating economic and law and order situations of the country. Within one month of the proclamation of emergency, the Awami League Government of Mujib began taking measures to retain power permanently. Mujib used the overwhelming support of the Members of the Parliament[3] to get the *Constitution (Fourth Amendment) Act* passed on 25 January 1975, which is considered as the most drastic amendment to the *Constitution of Bangladesh*. For it introduced fundamental changes in the Constitution and abolished the spirit of liberal democracy in Bangladesh. It is pertinent to mention here that Mujib had constantly expressed his commitment to parliamentary democracy during the days of Pakistan (August 1947– March 1971). Subsequently, only a day after his return from Pakistan to independent Bangladesh he issued the *Provisional Constitution of Bangladesh Order* on 11 January 1972, which introduced parliamentary democracy in Bangladesh to give effect to the 'aspiration of the people' manifested in the first General Elections of Pakistan held in December 1970 (preamble para 4). However, it seems that he had a change of mind.

First, by getting the *Constitution (Fourth Amendment) Act*, 1975, passed by the Parliament, he replaced parliamentary democracy with a presidential form of government centring on an all-powerful executive, namely, the President, on the American pattern without, however, its checks and balances. The President was to be elected directly by the people but no such election was considered necessary in the case of Premier Mujib, who would automatically enter upon the office of President of Bangladesh and 'shall, as from such commencement hold office as President of Bangladesh as if elected to that office under the Constitution as amended by this Act [the *Constitution (Fourth Amendment) Act*]' (s 35). Even the procedure for the impeachment of the President on the charge of violating the Constitution or of grave misconduct, and for his removal from office on the grounds of physical or mental incapacity, were made unusually difficult, rendering it almost impossible for Parliament to act. An initiative to move a motion for the President's impeachment or removal needed the support of at least two-thirds of the total number of Members of the Parliament and had to be passed by at least three-quarters of total number of members.[4] It is striking that the office of the President created by the supreme law of Bangladesh, i.e. the Constitution, required such a difficult process for impeachment or removal, while the amendment of any provision of the supreme law requires merely the support of at least two-thirds of the total number of Members of the Parliament. Furthermore, there was hardly any possibility of securing the support of at least three-quarters of the total number of Members of the Parliament to get the impeachment or the removal procedure passed, as there were only eight Members of the Parliament belonging to the opposition.

Second, the original Article 80(5) of the Constitution provided that a Bill passed by the Parliament was to be presented to the President for his assent to become a law (an Act of Parliament). But Section 12 of the *Constitution (Fourth Amendment) Act* empowered the President to declare that 'he withholds assent therefrom'. This was virtually a power of veto, although the word 'veto' was not used in the Act. Unlike the 1962 *Constitution of Pakistan*, which contained elaborate provisions in such a case to make a Bill into an Act of the Parliament,[5] the *Constitution (Fourth Amendment) Act* did not provide for any procedure to convert a Bill, to which Presidential assent was initially withheld, into a law. Thus, the law-making procedure was left virtually at the will of the President.

Third, the *Constitution (Fourth Amendment) Act* curtailed the independence of both the higher and lower judiciary. The President was freed from the obligation of consulting the Chief Justice in appointing the puisne judges of the Supreme Court of Bangladesh and was also empowered to remove such judges of the Supreme Court on grounds of misbehaviour or incapacity in accordance with his own will (ss 16 and 15). He was further invested with the power to appoint, control and discipline persons employed in the judicial service, and magistrates exercising judicial functions (s 19).

Fourth, the *Constitution (Fourth Amendment) Act* gave the President the power of declaring Bangladesh a one-party state in order to give full effect to any of the 'Fundamental Principles of State Policy' of socialism, nationalism, secularism, and democracy, which are not judicially enforceable (s 23). Consequently, President Mujib issued on 24 February 1975 an order introducing the one-party system in Bangladesh. Upon the formation of a single national party, known as the Bangladesh *Krishak Sramik Awami* League (BAKSAL) – the Bangladesh Peasants and Workers National Party – all political parties in the country were dissolved. A person would not be qualified for election as President or as a Member of the Parliament if the National Party did not nominate him as a candidate. The President was given the sole authority to decide all matters pertaining to the nomenclature, program, membership, organisation, discipline, finance and functions of the National Party. The party was to be headed by the President himself. On 6 June 1975, President Mujib issued the Constitution of the BAKSAL, which provided him with absolute power to control and oversee the functions all the high-ranking officials of the party. He headed all the high-powered committees of the National Party, including the 15-member (national) Executive Committee, which was at the head of the BAKSAL, and consisted of four of Mujib's close relatives, 10 of his associates and Mujib himself.

Thus the structure of the National Party formally recognised the fact that Mujib was the undisputed leader and key figure of the country. It should be kept in mind that the provision for the National Party was first provided by the supreme law itself and its constitution was announced by an *Extraordinary Gazette Notification*. Mujib used the phrase 'second revolution' to describe this political manoeuvre. It seems that the objective of the second revolution was not to rebuild the nation but to secure the systematic obliteration of any opposition to Mujib's regime. This transformation of Mujib from an ardent supporter of liberal democracy into an absolute dictator came as a profound shock to the politically conscious citizens of Bangladesh.

Since the politics of the second revolution created a suffocating political atmosphere, in which a peaceful and constitutional change of government was almost impossible, eventually a group of 47 Army officers carried out a coup in the early morning of 15 August 1975 and assassinated Mujib. Consequently, the whole of Bangladesh was placed under Martial Law on 15 August 1975 (*Proclamation of Martial Law 1975*). Martial Law was declared in Bangladesh at a time when the country was peaceful and already under an emergency, which, as mentioned earlier, had been imposed on 28 December 1974. But the emergency powers were evidently considered by the relevant authorities to be inadequate to obviate any public opposition to the extra-constitutional act of overthrowing a legitimate civilian regime by means of a *coup d'état*. After the unconstitutional declaration of Martial Law in August 1975, the 1974 constitutional declaration of emergency and the emergency measures receded to the background. However, while Martial Law was withdrawn on 6 April 1979, the proclamation of emergency was revoked after nearly five years of continuance on 27 November 1979. Thus the emergency proclaimed on 28 December 1974 remained in force for nearly five years despite the cessation of the threat which gave rise to the emergency.

In very specific circumstances, as argued in detail in Section 4.4.1, the declaration of a state of emergency can be a legitimate constitutional method to take prompt preventive measures in times of crises threatening the life of the nation. But as it entails restrictions on the fundamental rights of the citizens, it must be used with utmost care and as a means of last resort only. The threat to the life of the nation by the crisis must not only be actual or imminent. In addition, the normal measures or restrictions permitted for the maintenance of public safety, health and order must be plainly inadequate for addressing the crisis. Since there existed no exceptional crisis to justify the use of the constitutional expression 'grave emergency', it can be strongly argued that the emergency declared on 28 December 1974 was unjustified. In fact, the enactment of the *Constitution (Fourth Amendment) Act*, 1975, within a month of the convenient proclamation of emergency on the vague and wide ground of 'internal disturbance', revealed that the party in power proceeded in a calculated manner to assume dictatorial power to perpetuate its survival in power by suppressing the opposition.

5.3 The second proclamation of emergency in May 1981

Bangladesh witnessed a proclamation of emergency for the second time in its history on 30 May 1981 – within only one and a half years of the termination of the first emergency. President Ziaur Rahman, who on 3 June 1978 had become the first popularly elected President of the country since its independence, was assassinated by a faction of the Army on 30 May 1981 while on an official visit to Chittagong (Ziring, 1992; 'Assassination of President Zia' 1981). The Army faction was led by Major General Manzoor, a freedom fighter and the then Commanding Officer of the Army's 24th Division based in Chittagong, who was apparently jealous of Zia (Ziring, 1992; 'Bangladesh: General Shaukat Ali Retired' 1981). Subsequently, Manzoor announced on Chittagong radio that he had formed a Revolutionary Council to run the affairs of the country. He also declared himself to be the supreme commander of the armed forces and the chief of the civilian administration ('Assassination of President Zia' 1981). Manzoor was able to successfully isolate Chittagong from the rest of Bangladesh.

In order to deal with this grave situation, Vice-President Abdus Sattar, who had succeeded Ziaur Rahman as Acting President under Article 55(1) of the *Constitution of Bangladesh*, proclaimed a nationwide emergency, citing a threat to the country's security from 'internal disturbances' (Bangladesh Gazette, 1981). However, unlike the first proclamation of emergency, as will be shown below, the second emergency was not proclaimed to suppress opposition to the government of the day with a view to securing its survival in power.

5.3.1 Justification of the proclamation of emergency on 30 May 1981

General Zia's assassination on 30 May 1981 brought to an end the longest period of political stability in Bangladesh since its independence from Pakistan. Not only was the country's President killed in the attempted coup but the rebel army officers also gained control of the main port and second largest city of Bangladesh, Chittagong. They had announced the formation of a Revolutionary Council for governing the nation. There were also calls made via Chittagong radio to members of the armed forces throughout the country to join their cause in establishing an efficient and 'incorruptible' administration ('Assassination of President Zia' 1981: 16099). Thus the situation prevailing in the country assumed the necessary gravity for it to be properly compared to that of an armed rebellion, as defined in Section 4.4.1, and, as such, required immediate and stern measures for its containment. However, since the *Constitution of Bangladesh*, as amended on 22 September 1973, does not recognise armed rebellion as a ground for invoking an emergency, Acting President Sattar was constrained to proclaim an emergency on 30 May 1981 on the ground of internal disturbance to adequately deal with the situation.

Following the proclamation of emergency, Sattar went live on Dhaka radio to order the 'misguided Army men' to surrender by 6 am on 1 June 1981. He further warned that the failure to meet this deadline would result in 'stern action' being taken against them by the loyal armed forces ('Assassination of President Zia' 1981). The failure of the rebels to abide by this deadline saw the government troops move in on them. Consequently, 48 hours after the beginning of the rebellion, the government was able to put the rebellion down and regain control of Chittagong.

Despite successfully putting down the rebellion, the government decided to continue the emergency. In a parliamentary session convened on 3 June 1981 after the assassination of Zia, opposition Members of the Parliament called on the government to withdraw the emergency as soon as possible, warning that the indefinite continuation of the emergency would impede the growth of democracy. In response, Prime Minister Shah Azizur Rahman assured the house that the emergency would not continue for a single day beyond its imperative necessity ('Assassination of President Zia' 1981). However, the very next day, President Sattar, while speaking to the media, hinted that the continuance of the emergency was necessary to prevent any further strikes aimed at undermining Bangladesh's endeavour to sustain democracy. He remarked:

> [w]e shall never forget the unshakable faith and loyalty of the late President towards democratic ideals and values have [*sic*] restored democracy in this country. It is, therefore, our sacred responsibility to preserve democracy and strengthen democratic process at all costs.
> ('Assassination of President Zia' 1981: 16099)

In the same press brief, Sattar further pledged that the emergency would not be used as an instrument for victimising any political party ('Bangladesh: General Shaukat Ali Retired' 1981).

President Sattar also announced that a Presidential election would be held within 180 days of Zia's assassination. Thus, it seems that the government deemed it fit to continue the emergency to prevent any further insurrection from disrupting the democratic transition of power through the Presidential election that was scheduled to be held on 15 November 1981.

Furthermore, although the *Constitution of Bangladesh*, as mentioned earlier in Section 5.1, required parliamentary approval of a proclamation of emergency for its continuance beyond 120 days, the government, with a view to bestowing a further sense of legitimacy on the proclamation of emergency, placed it before the Parliament for approval only 40 days after its invocation on 9 July 1981. In seeking the Parliament's approval of the proclamation, Prime Minister Shah Azizur Rahman remarked that the situation in the country still warranted the proclamation of an emergency. In line with the previous assurances of the Acting President, he also sought to assure that the decision to continue the emergency was not designed to hinder the electoral activities of the political parties. There was also reiteration of the commitment not to continue the emergency 'even an hour' beyond its requirement ('Bangladesh: Parliament Approves Emergency' 1981: 16179). It seems that in view of these assurances, the Parliament decided to approve the proclamation of emergency.

After nearly 111 days of continuation, the government on 21 September

1981 deemed it appropriate to withdraw the proclamation of emergency as the threat that gave rise to it had ceased to exist. Thus, unlike the first emergency, which remained in force for nearly five years and was used to systematically crush the opposition to Mujib's regime, the emergency of 1981 was not used as an instrument for suppressing political activities. Furthermore, the emergency regime afforded the Parliament an opportunity to signify its assent to the proclamation of emergency.

Hence, in view of the above facts, it can be argued that the resort to the second proclamation of emergency was justified in light of the spirit of the constitutional provisions concerning emergency.

5.4 The third proclamation of emergency in November 1987

General H. M. Ershad, the Chief of Army Staff, had emphatically ruled out the possibility of a military takeover after Zia's assassination and instead pledged his loyalty to the civil administration in ensuring a seamless constitutional and democratic transition of power through the Presidential election of November 1981. Drawing on the experiences of Martial Law in Pakistan since its independence from British rule, Ershad remarked to the Indian media:

> Martial Law is never the answer. Pakistan of course is continuing with one after another. But does it ultimately pay? It does not. The Army's role is different from running an administration. If you get involved in this, ultimately you destroy the Army.
>
> ('Bangladesh: Rioting Over Executions' 1981: 16300)

However, it seems that Ershad was waiting for a more opportune time. For only 12 days after the election of Justice Sattar as President on 27 November 1981, Ershad publicly put forward the idea of creating a mechanism through which the Army could share power with the civilian government so that coup attempts or the possibility of any form of Army adventurism would come to an end (Kemaluddin, 1982a: 1982b). Sattar originally sought to fend off Ershad's demands but soon realised Ershad's motives. Hence, in order to appease Ershad, he formed a National Security Council, consisting of the President, the Vice-President, and the ministers for finance, foreign affairs, industry and home affairs, as well as the Chiefs of the Army, Navy and Air Force. However, Ershad was unhappy with the composition of the Council as he felt that the Chiefs of the armed forces were overshadowed by the presence of civilian ministers. Furthermore, in an attempt to foil the possibility of any coup, Sattar discharged a number of military officers from service. This last event gave Ershad the convenient premise to depose the democratically elected President Sattar and impose Martial Law throughout the country in a bloodless coup on 24 March 1982 (Heitzman and Worden, 1988).

After more than four years of the imposition of Martial Law, on 7 May 1986 a general election was held in which Ershad's newly established Jatiya Party obtained a majority of the seats of the Parliament. The Awami League contested the election despite earlier announcing that it would boycott it. Another major political party, Bangladesh Nationalist Party, preferred not to contest the election. There were widespread accusations that the election was 'rigged' (Maniruzzaman, 1994: 84; 'Bangladesh: Parliamentary Elections' 1986: 19039). Without paying any heed to these accusations, Ershad sought to become a civilian President by contesting and winning by landslide a controversial Presidential ballot, which was boycotted by the major opposition political parties and according to observers was participated in by only 10 to 30 per cent of the electorate (Heitzman and Worden, 1988).

At the end of October 1987, Sheikh Hasina, the leader of the Awami League, and, Begum Khaleda Zia, the leader of the Bangladesh Nationalist Party (BNP), had come to the conclusion that they had to work together to depose Ershad and thereby prevent the institution of a permanent 'garrison state' (Heitzman and Worden, 1988: 203). They took their protests to the streets. Ershad's response was akin to that of Mujib in December 1974, namely, the declaration of an emergency on the vague ground of internal disturbance on 27 November 1987. As with the Proclamation of Emergency of 1974, the Proclamation of Emergency of 1987 did not specify the circumstances that led to the invocation of emergency. Furthermore, in line with the *Emergency Powers Ordinance*, 1974, the *Emergency Powers Ordinance* issued following the declaration of emergency on 27 November 1987 empowered the government to 'make such rules as it thinks expedient for the purpose of maintaining the security and interests of the state and population or of preserving the public order or of keeping the economic life unimpaired or of securing the supply of goods and services essential to the life of the community' (s 3(1)). Thus the Ordinance sought to imply that the emergency was invoked because the country's security and economic life was under threat.

An attempt will now be made to examine whether the emergency proclaimed on 27 November 1987 was justified.

5.4.1 Justification of the proclamation of emergency on 27 November 1987

On 28 October 1987, Begum Khaleda Zia and Sheikh Hasina, leaders of two major opposition parties, announced a detailed programme to bring down the 'autocratic' regime of Ershad and restore democracy in Bangladesh ('Bangladesh: Opposition Leaders Join Forces' 1987). Consequently, between 10 and 12 November 1987, in what was termed as the 'final showdown', the opposition parties were able to bring thousands of supporters into the streets to force the resignation of Ershad. On 10 November 1987 alone, 50 persons were injured in clashes between the police and demonstrators. Ershad's immediate response was to order the arrest of Khaleda Zia and Sheikh Hasina on 11 November 1987 ('Bangladesh: Opposition Leaders Arrested' 1987).

On 13 November 1987, Ershad said that riots and strikes would not force him to resign from office. He promised to take even stricter action against the opposition. He stated:

> I will not tolerate any nonsense from the Opposition. We have had enough of it. I cannot allow vandalism to continue. I can be very tough and I will survive this challenge.
>
> ('Bangladesh: Opposition Leaders Arrested' 1987: 19795–19796)

He also hinted that he would take extraordinary steps to normalise the situation. However, despite these warnings and the internment of the two opposition leaders, the opposition agitation continued in the form of dawn-to-dusk strikes and a civil disobedience movement. These opposition protests brought the country to a standstill. Finally, on 27 November 1987, after days of protests that saw hundreds being wounded and at least 12 losing their life, and a fresh call from the opposition parties for a non-stop 72-hour strike across the country, Ershad took the extraordinary action that he had earlier referred to on 13 November 1987 ('Bangladesh: Opposition Agitation' 1988). He declared an emergency on 27 November 1987 on the flimsy ground of internal disturbance to deal with the protests demanding his resignation, which he described as being tantamount to 'terrorism' ('Bangladesh: Opposition Leaders Arrested' 1987: 19796). However, it seems that the emergency was declared by Ershad to suppress the political opposition that had threatened to bring down his five-and-a-half-year long rule. For, in the first place, the declaration of emergency was followed by the imposition of curfews in five major cities, namely, Dhaka, Chittagong, Khulna, Rajshahi and Narayanganj. In addition to the police, Ershad also deployed paramilitary forces to enforce the curfew and ensure that the opposition could no longer continue their protests in the streets.

Second, Ershad used the emergency ordinance to bar the newspapers from reporting 'anything against the emergency' (*Emergency Powers Ordinance 1987* s 3(2)(1)(h). Ershad's Information Minister advised the media that while they could not report anything against the government, they were nevertheless 'free' to report on developmental activities of the government ('Bangladesh Bans Protect Coverage' 1987). In order to secure compliance with this requirement, the *Emergency Powers Ordinance* empowered Ershad's regime to confiscate and close down the 'printing-houses' of any newspaper failing to meet the governmental expectations (s 3(2)(1)(i) and (j)). Thus, Ershad used the emergency as an instrument for systematically shutting down all democratic avenues for criticising his rule.

Third, after successfully putting down the opposition, Ershad sought to secure a fresh mandate from the electorate through sham parliamentary elections during the continuation of the emergency. Consequently, on 7

December 1987 Ershad dissolved the Parliament and called for elections on 3 March 1988 in pursuance of Article 123(3) of the *Constitution of Bangladesh*, which requires an election of members of Parliament to be held 'within ninety days after Parliament is dissolved'. But the main opposition parties, namely the Awami League and the BNP, echoed their earlier commitment of refusing to contest any elections held under the supervision of the 'corrupt and repressive' regime of Ershad (Ziring, 1992: 208). The opposition parties, however, underestimated Ershad's manoeuvring skills. For, although Ershad himself banned all political activities during the continuation of the emergency, he nevertheless allowed the formation of a number of political parties with a view to securing their participation in the elections and thereby creating a domestic and puppet opposition in the Parliament. Subsequently, according to his design, in the controversial elections of 3 March 1988, Ershad's Jatiya Party won 251 of the 281 seats that were contested in the 300-member Parliament, while the combined opposition of 73 small parties, which were established with Ershad's blessing, managed to secure only a handful of seats (Ziring, 1992). Since the proclamation of emergency of 27 November 1987 was not placed before the Parliament for its approval for continuation beyond 120 days as required by Article 141A(2) of the *Constitution of Bangladesh*, the proclamation of emergency became inoperative on 27 March 1987.

In light of the above discussion, it is evident that the major political parties of Bangladesh in November 1987 in exercise of their democratic right took to the streets to demand the resignation of an administrator, Ershad, who had assumed power by extra-constitutional means, deposing the democratically elected regime of Justice Sattar. However, the protests carried out by the opposition political parties in the country did not attain the seriousness of a 'grave emergency' that could justify the resort to the proclamation of an emergency under the *Constitution of Bangladesh*. Nor can it be said that the prevailing situation could not have been contained by the deployment of the ordinary law enforcement agencies. But clinging on to power by any means possible meant everything for Ershad. He himself remarked on 27 November 1987 that he would preserve his nearly six-year rule with 'the last drop of … [his] blood' ('Bangladesh: Opposition Leaders Arrested' 1987). It thus seems that the proclamation of an emergency on the ground of internal disturbance was deemed by Ershad as the appropriate measure to deal with the opposition protests and thereby sustain his continued survival in power.

5.5 The fourth proclamation of emergency on 27 November 1990 and its justification

Although Ershad managed to hold parliamentary elections during the continuation of the emergency declared on 27 November 1987, the elections did not bestow on Ershad's regime a sense of legitimacy in the eyes of the citizens of Bangladesh. For the boycott of the elections by the major opposition parties rendered the result of the elections 'meaningless' for the people of Bangladesh (Baxter, 1998: 114). But rather than seizing the moment as the discontent of the people grew, the Alliance between the Awami League and BNP split, due to the leaders of the two parties blaming each other for the failure of the movement in November 1987 to dislodge Ershad from office (Bangladesh: Renewed Opposition Campaign, 1989). It ultimately came down to the students of the University of Dhaka, who set aside their own political ideologies to unite under the banner of All-Party Students Union and subsequently press for Ershad's resignation and the holding of a free and fair election under the supervision of a neutral interim government. This show of unity by the students 'shamed' the leaders of the two opposition parties to once again join the common cause of bringing down the autocratic regime of Ershad (Bari, 2015).

The movement to force out Ershad from office gained momentum in October 1990. Indefinite strikes paralysed life across the country. Ershad thought that he could fend off the fresh threats to his regime by proclaiming yet another emergency on 27 November 1990 on the vague ground of internal disturbance. Thus within a period of three years Bangladesh witnessed the invocation of two emergencies on the ground of internal disturbance to deal with the threats posed to the rule of Ershad. The *Emergency Powers Ordinance*, which was framed following the declaration of the emergency on 27 November 1990 in the same language as the *Emergency Powers Ordinance* of 1987, sought to justify the proclamation of emergency on the grounds of threat to the security and economic life of Bangladesh. It read that the emergency was declared 'for the purpose of ensuring the security and the interests of the state and the population, and for the purpose of maintaining public order and protecting the economic life, and for the purpose of ensuring the maintenance of supplies and services essential for the life of the community' (preamble para 1).

In the same manner as in 1987, Ershad attempted to use the emergency as an instrument for barring political activities and the newspapers from publishing anything against his regime. Allegedly six people died, 3000 were wounded and 5000 were arrested after the imposition of the emergency ('Bangladesh Chief Offers Concession to Opposition' 1990). However, Ershad misread the magnitude of discontent against him in November 1990 and he was mistaken in thinking that the declaration of the emergency would once again prove sufficient for suppressing the opposition to his rule. For, unlike November 1987, in 1990 people from all walks of life – doctors, lawyers, university teachers, journalists, workers and employees – took to the streets to force Ershad out of office. Furthermore, top government officials (civil servants) declined to carry out their official duties under the authority of Ershad ('Bangladesh: President Ershad Resigns' 1991).

In the wake of the above developments which saw members of all sections of society unite in demanding Ershad's resignation, Ershad gave in to the popular demand and resigned on 6 December 1990 after more than eight years in office. Ershad's resignation was followed by the swearing in of Chief Justice Shahabuddin Ahmed as the Acting President. One of the first orders of business for Justice Ahmed's interim government, which was entrusted with the responsibility of holding free and fair parliamentary elections, was to revoke the emergency on 6 December 1990 ('Bangladesh: President Ershad Resigns' 1991).

In view of the discussion above, it can be concluded that although the emergency proclaimed on 27 November 1990 was short-lived – it continued for only 10 days – it was declared not to deal with an actual threat to the security of Bangladesh but rather to deal with the political threat posed to the party in power and, as such, cannot be justified.

5.6 The fifth proclamation of emergency in January 2007

When the Government of Bangladesh Nationalist Party (BNP) completed its five-year term on 28 October 2006, violent protests, sponsored and led by the Bangladesh Awami League (BAL), broke out in the country over the possibility of the immediate past Chief Justice of the country, Justice K. M. Hasan, heading the Non-Party 'Care-taker' Government ('Bangladesh Power Shift Postponed' 2006).[6]

The BAL alleged that Justice K. M. Hasan, who was constitutionally destined to take over as the Chief Adviser of the Caretaker Government in October 2006 in his capacity as the last retired Chief Justice of the country, was biased towards the BNP. They put forward three claims in support of their allegation. First Justice Hasan, according to the BAL, had served as the International Affairs Secretary of the BNP in 1979 ('K. M. Hasan Was Involved in BNP Politics' 2006). Second, the convention of appointing the most senior Judge of the Appellate Division of the Supreme Court of Bangladesh as the Chief Justice of Bangladesh was violated for the first time by the regime of the BNP on 23 June 2003 when Justice K. M. Hasan was appointed as the Chief Justice of Bangladesh in supersession of two fellow colleagues. The BNP Government at the time justified this supersession by describing it as a corrective measure aimed at providing redress to the earlier injustice that had been perpetrated on Justice K. M. Hasan, who had been superseded twice by the Previous BAL Government (1996–2001) in being elevated to the Appellate Division. Third and finally, following Justice Hasan's retirement on 26 January 2004 as the Chief Justice of Bangladesh, the BNP regime had raised the retirement age of Supreme Court judges from 65 to 67 with a view to ensuring that Justice J. R. Mudasser Husain, who had succeeded Justice Hasan as the Chief Justice, would continue as the Chief Justice beyond the General Elections scheduled on 22 January 2007,[7] making Justice Hasan the first option to head the 'Care-taker' Government as the last retired chief justice.

Amidst the violence that had been instigated by the BAL, Justice K. M.

Hasan declined to accept the position of the Chief Adviser. The BAL claimed Justice Hasan's refusal as a victory of its violent agitation. However, without exhausting the four alternative options for appointing the Chief Adviser of the 'Care-taker Government', as laid down in former Article 58C of the Constitution,[8] after Justice Hasan's reluctance to head the 'Care-taker' Government, President Iajuddin Ahmed offered himself as a candidate for the office of the Chief Adviser in addition to the responsibilities of the Presidency. It seems that President Iajuddin made such an offer in pursuance of the provisions of the former Article 58C(6) of the *Constitution of Bangladesh*, which empowered the President to take over the position of the Chief Adviser once all options concerning the appointment of the same were exhausted. The President was able to secure the endorsements of the major political parties except that of the BAL. The BAL's reservation about President Ahmed's neutrality stemmed from the fact that he was elected to the office of the President of the Country on a BNP ticket ('Bangladesh's Controversial Ex-President Iajuddin Ahmed Passes Away' 2012).

Notwithstanding these issues, President Iajuddin assumed the office of the Chief Adviser. However, the BAL again staged violent opposition to the Caretaker Government headed by Iajuddin (Liton, 2006). It laid down a number of demands, which it felt were necessary for the regime to implement in order to prove its impartiality in holding credible general elections. These demands included: a) the removal of the Chief Election Commissioner, Justice M. A. Aziz; b) re-constitution of the Election Commission; and c) rectifying the flaws in the voter list ('Hasina Declares Tougher Action' 2007). The Caretaker Government in order to demonstrate its seriousness in holding the elections in a credible manner sent Justice M. A. Aziz on leave and set the date for the General Elections on 22 January 2007.

The BAL in December 2006 nevertheless announced that it would boycott the polls due to the failure of the 'Care-taker' regime of Iajuddin to prove its impartiality by accepting all their demands and its alleged favouritism towards the BNP ('Hasina Declares Tougher Action' 2007). It intensified its violent campaign against the regime with a view to preventing the scheduled elections from taking place on 22 January 2007. In light of the magnitude of the violence coupled with mounting pressure from western diplomats, in particular that of the then US Ambassador and British High Commissioner, Chief of Army Staff along with other senior Army personnel persuaded President Iajuddin on 11 January 2007 to step down from the position of the Chief Adviser and proclaim an emergency for the fifth time in the history of Bangladesh, yet again on the ground of 'internal disturbance' (International Crisis Group (ICG), 2008).[9]

The Presidential Order, which was issued on 11 January 2007 notifying the Proclamation of Emergency, did not make any attempt to encapsulate the circumstances which constituted the 'internal disturbance'. Rather the Order merely stated:

> [a]s it is to the President's satisfaction that a grave emergency exists in which the security or economic life of Bangladesh is threatened by internal disturbance, a Proclamation of Emergency was issued throughout the country until further order under articles 141A(1), (2), (3), 141B, 141C(1), (2) and (3) of the Constitution.

Furthermore, the *Emergency Powers Ordinance*, which was issued on 12 January 2007, in the same vague manner as the four emergency ordinances of the past reproduced that the invocation of an emergency was warranted

> for the purpose of ensuring the security and the interests of the state and the population, and for the purpose of maintaining public order and protecting the economic life, and for the purpose of ensuring the maintenance of supplies and services essential for the life of the community. (preamble para 2)

5.6.1 Justification of the emergency declared in January 2007

It seems that the immediate reasons for the declaration of the emergency were the indefinite strikes called for by the BAL between October 27 and 11 January 2007 that rendered the economy of the country stagnant. The foreign diplomats saw an intervention by the Army as the only viable option for protecting their developmental investments in the country and, as a result, they induced the Army to pressurise Iajuddin to declare the emergency on 11 January 2007 (ICG, 2008).

The proclamation of emergency was followed by the installation of a new 'Care-taker' Government headed by former Governor of the Bangladesh Bank, Fakhruddin Ahmed. However, his appointment as the Chief Adviser was not made after the exhaustion of all of the provisions concerning the appointment of the head of the Caretaker Government as had been enshrined in the *Constitution of Bangladesh*. The political unrest that was used as a premise to proclaim an emergency on the ground of 'internal disturbance' on 11 January 2007 came to an end as soon as the new military-backed 'Care-taker' regime of Fakhruddin took oath of office ('Grand Alliance Calls Off All Programmes' 2010). But despite the cessation of the hostilities which allegedly gave rise to the 'grave emergency', the emergency was continued and the parliamentary elections, scheduled to be held on 22 January 2007, were deferred indefinitely. Moreover, the new Chief Adviser, Fakhruddin, ordered the deployment of 60,000 soldiers throughout the country 'in aid of the civilian administration' to preserve order (Fair, 2007: 1). However, as will be shown below, the emergency was continued beyond its imperative necessities by an unelected interim regime backed by the armed forces for purposes other than that of securing the life of the nation.

First, the new 'Care-taker' regime instead of announcing a timeframe for holding the parliamentary elections, sought to make a number of policy decisions, which *inter alia* included reconstituting the Election Commission and the Anti-Corruption Commission, implementing a voter identification card system, cleansing the prevalent corruption in politics, and separating the judiciary from the executive (CA Vows to Transfer Power Through Polls at Earliest, EC to be Reconstituted, Flawless Electoral Roll to be Prepared' 2007; Jahangir, 2009). These were in direct contravention of the provisions concerning the functions of the 'Care-taker' Government as had been enshrined in the *Constitution of Bangladesh*, for the *Constitution* stipulated that the 'Care-taker' regime would only carry on 'the routine functions of such government' and 'not make any policy decision'.[10] Its principal constitutional mandate was to provide necessary assistance to the Election Commission in 'holding the general election of members of parliament peacefully, fairly and impartially' within 90 days of the dissolution of the Parliament.[11] Thus it seems that the continuation of the emergency was considered a necessity by the military-backed 'Care-taker' regime for sustaining the façade of its 'Care-taker' tag. For the *Emergency Powers Ordinance* made it virtually impossible to challenge in a court of law any action of the regime taken in 'good faith' for preserving the 'interests of the state and the population'.[12] In other words, the emergency enabled the regime to justify its policy decisions by claiming that such policy decisions were necessary in the very interests of the state and the population, and, as such, they were not amenable to review by any court of law. Therefore, in essence, the regime felt it necessary to continue the emergency with a view to using it as a shield against any challenge to its constitutionality.

Second, it might be recalled here from the discussion in Sections 5.3, 5.3.1, 5.4, and 5.4.1, that the Generals in the Bangladesh Army have always had a keen interest in stepping outside the boundaries of the cantonment and governing the country. The political unrest between October 2006 and January 2007 and the consequent green signal from the western diplomats presented the Army with such an opportunity once again. Consequently, the continuation of the emergency beyond its imperative necessity was considered indispensable for the realisation of the Army's ambition of governing the country.

Chief Adviser Fakhruddin's decision to deploy 60,000 soldiers throughout the country despite the cessation of the political crisis and the appointment of the 10 members of Fakhruddin's 'Care-taker' government, most of whom were former senior officials of the Army,[13] first gave rise to the suspicion that the new Caretaker regime was instituted to carry out the design of the Army. This suspicion gained further momentum when current and former Army professionals were appointed to key positions in the public services as well. In particular, the Election Commission, which is a constitutional body entrusted with the responsibility of holding the general elections, was reconstituted and a retired Army officer Brigadier General M. Sakhawat Hossain, was appointed as one of the two Commissioners. Furthermore, the Army was entrusted with the important task of preparing the new voter list (Asian Human Rights Commission, 2008).

The Anti-Corruption Commission (ACC) was also militarised. Lieutenant General (retired) Hasan Mashud Chowdhury, the then immediate past Chief of Army Staff, received appointment as the Chairman of the Commission, while Colonel Hanif Iqbal was appointed to the second most important position of the Commission, namely, the Director General (Asian Human Rights Commission, 2009). But the independence of the Commission in pursuing corruption cases was substantially curtailed by the establishment on 8 March 2007 of the National Coordination Committee on Corruption and Serious Crime (NCC), which was headed by Lieutenant General Masud Uddin Chowdhury, the then Principal Staff Officer of the Army (Karim, 2013). For the NCC was given the ultimate authority to identify the persons against whom corruption cases were filed while the ACC was to faithfully prosecute those persons identified by the NCC.

Third, the continuance of the emergency was considered a necessary evil by the military- backed regime for crushing the two mainstream political parties of the country. The Chief of Army, General Moeen U. Ahmed, in a speech on 3 April 2007 signalled the possibility of the rise of a third political force rather than a return to the status quo, when he stated:

> The roadmap to democracy lies, I presume, with objectives as envisioned by the government … within [an] affordable time frame that will steer the country away from escapism and build [a] strong foundation of validity on democracy … We do not want to go back to an elective democracy where corruption in society becomes all pervasive, governance suffers in terms of insecurity and violation of rights, and where political criminalisation threatens the very survival and integrity of the state.
>
> ('Bangladesh to Have Own Brand of Democracy' 2007: 1)

The above observations of the Army Chief brought to the fore the fear that Bangladesh was perhaps sliding towards formal military rule following in the footsteps of Pakistan. For, in Pakistan, as had been pointed out in Section 2.6.3.3.3, General Pervez Musharraf had risen to power through the proclamation of an emergency in 1999. Subsequently, Musharraf used the emergency as an instrument to systematically annihilate the political parties on charges of corruption and send the leaders of two major political parties, Benazir Bhutto and Nawaz Sharif, into exile (Gall, 2007a; 2007b).

This fear gained further momentum when the military-backed 'Caretaker' regime sought to implement the 'minus-two' formula. The formula involved sending the leaders of the BNP and the Awami League, Begum Khaleda Zia and Sheikh Hasina, into exile. It was announced by the regime in mid-April, that Begum Zia would be sent to Saudi Arabia while Sheikh Hasina who had gone to the USA on a family visit, would not be allowed to return to the country ('Bangladesh: The Minus-Two Solution' 2007). Furthermore, with a view to prevent Hasina from re-entering the country, the regime filed cases implicating her in the deaths that had occurred during the political unrest between October 2006 and January 2007 (Fair, 2007).

Furthermore, in order to give full effect to the plan of the Chief of the Army, the NCC created a list of high-profile politicians belonging to the two main political parties of the country, who were apparently perceived as a threat to the regime's desire to perpetuate its rule, to be arrested on charges of corruption. Subsequently, the joint forces arrested these prominent politicians. By the end of the year 2007, the regime had arrested as many as 150 senior politicians, as well as businessmen (who were associated with the two political parties either in an official or unofficial capacity) and officials (who were beneficiaries of the political governments), while another 78 were arrested during the course of the year 2008 (Bureau of Democracy, Human Rights, and Labour, 2008: 2009). However, the regime could not take the risk of indulging in the time-consuming process of trying them in the ordinary courts of law in pursuance of the *Anti-Corruption Commission Act*, 2004, and the *Money Laundering Prevention Act*, 2002.[14] Rather, since the *Emergency Power Rules*,[15] which were promulgated on 25 January 2007, allowed the regime to treat corruption and money laundering related offences as serious offences, it established Speedy Tribunals – headed by specially appointed judges – under *the Speedy Trial Tribunal Act* of 2002 to prosecute them on charges of corruption. These tribunals were convened in the corridors of the Parliament of Bangladesh, which now stood dissolved.

Neither members of the media nor the general public were allowed to be present in the trials. Most of the arrested politicians were sentenced to 13 years in prison by the Speedy Tribunals (Bureau of Democracy, Human Rights, and Labour, 2008). In some cases, the jail sentences were accompanied by orders of seizure of property acquired through corruption. It, therefore, seems that the emergency was used by the regime to impose jail sentences on senior politicians of the country with a view to preventing them from contesting in the next general elections, thereby implementing its political agenda.

5.6.1.1 The challenge to the constitutionality of the 2007 emergency and the eventual termination of the emergency

Before discussing the challenge to the constitutionality of the emergency proclaimed on 11 January 2007, it is appropriate to provide a brief introduction to the structure and function of the superior judiciary of Bangladesh.

Part VI, Chapter I of the *Constitution of Bangladesh*, titled 'THE JUDICIARY', having pyramidal structure, contains provisions concerning composition, jurisdiction, appointment and removal of judges of the Supreme Court – the highest court of law in Bangladesh. As to the composition of this court, the Constitution in Article 94(1) states that '[t]here shall be a Supreme Court for Bangladesh (to be known as the Supreme Court of Bangladesh) comprising the Appellate Division and the High Court Division'.

The High Court Division (HCD) has been given original and appellate jurisdictions and powers by the Constitution, while the Appellate Division (AD) has been provided with the authority 'to hear and determine appeals from judgments, decrees, orders or sentences of the High Court Division' (arts 101 and 103).

In July 2008, for the first time in the history of emergency regimes in Bangladesh, the constitutionality of the emergency proclaimed on 11 January 2007 was challenged after more than one and a half years of its continuation in *M Saleem Ullah and Others v Bangladesh Writ Petition No 5033 (2008)*. The HCD of the Supreme Court of Bangladesh after an initial hearing issued a *rule nisi* demanding an explanation from the military-backed regime as to why the emergency declared on 11 January 2007 should not be declared unconstitutional. The Court also asked the regime to provide its roadmap and timeframe for handing over power to a government elected through free, fair and credible general elections.

However, the military had by this time come to the realisation that its aspiration of formally taking the helm of the country through the imposition of a possible martial law could not materialise. For the foreign dignitaries, who had once encouraged the military to play a leading role in ending the political stalemate in the country, had now signalled their unwillingness to support a formal military takeover. The diplomats felt that while the initial intervention by the Army was necessary, the systematic slide towards formal military rule by annihilation of the politicians had the impact of further undermining their developmental investments in Bangladesh (ICG, 2008). The Chief of Army Staff, General Moeen U. Ahmed, was apparently also told that the imposition of Martial Law would result in Bangladeshi soldiers being banned from serving in UN peacekeeping missions (Wolven, 2007). It should be pointed out here that a total of 128,545 members of the Bangladesh Armed Forces have served as UN peacekeepers, making the country the biggest contributor to UN peacekeeping missions ('Bangladesh in UN Peacekeeping Mission'). The high pay scale under the UN scheme is particularly attractive to these soldiers ('UN Peacekeeping Gets Bangladesh $1 BN in Three Years' 2012). Thus it seems that General Moeen realised that his ambition of imposing Martial Law would not receive the support of the mid-ranking officers of the armed forces, who faced the prospect of losing lucrative opportunities of serving the UN peacekeeping missions.

Consequently, before the HCD could decide in detail the merits of the challenge to the invocation of the emergency, the state of emergency which had lasted for almost two years was ultimately lifted on 17 December 2008, rendering ineffective the case instituted in July 2008.

The foregoing discussion reveals that the political impasse between October 2006 and January 2007 required a political solution. This is evident from the fact that the political unrest came to an end as soon as the new 'Care-taker' regime was installed. Therefore, the emergency was declared and subsequently continued beyond the hostilities so as to:

a) justify the 'Care-taker' Government's unconstitutional hold on power for nearly two years; and,
b) realise the military's desire of eventually instituting a formal military rule in Bangladesh by persecuting the senior leadership of the two mainstream political parties following Pakistan's example.

It goes without saying that the emergency was invoked and continued for political purposes rather than for securing the life of the nation and, as such, cannot be justified.

5.7 The impact of the *Constitution (Fifteenth Amendment) Act* 2011 on the provisions concerning emergency in the *Constitution of Bangladesh*, 1972

Following the landslide victory in the parliamentary elections that were eventually held under the supervision of the military-backed 'Care-taker' regime on 29 December 2008, the Government of BAL established a Parliamentary Special Committee for Constitutional Amendment (Global Legal Monitor, 2013). It was expected that this Committee, taking into account the traumatic experience of the emergency of 2007–2008, would recommend an amendment to the *Constitution of Bangladesh* that, among other things, would limit the power to proclaim an emergency to circumstances that truly attain a degree of gravity and endanger the very life of the nation. It was also expected that the proposed amendment would provide for innovative mechanisms aimed at eliminating the possibility of any abuse of the extraordinary powers concerning emergency. However, the Committee's proposal fell well short of these expectations.

The *Constitution (Fifteenth Amendment) Act*, 2011, which was passed following the recommendations of the Parliamentary Committee and which repealed the chapter on 'Non-Party Care-taker Government' contained in the *Constitution of Bangladesh*, introduced limited changes to Article 141A of the *Constitution*. Prior to the enactment of the Amendment Act of 2011, Article 141A of the *Constitution of Bangladesh* read as follows:

> Proclamation of Emergency
> (1) If the President is satisfied that a grave emergency exists in which the security or economic life of Bangladesh, or any part thereof, is threatened by war or external aggression or internal disturbance, he may issue a Proclamation of Emergency:
> Provided that such Proclamation shall require for its validity the prior counter signature of the Prime Minister.
> (2) A Proclamation of Emergency
> (a) may be revoked by a subsequent Proclamation;
> (b) shall be laid before Parliament;

> (c) shall cease to operate at the expiration of one hundred and twenty days, unless before the expiration of that period it has been approved by a resolution of Parliament:
> Provided that if any such Proclamation is issued at a time when Parliament stands dissolved or the dissolution of Parliament takes place during the period of one hundred and twenty days referred to in sub-clause (c), the Proclamation shall cease to operate at the expiration of thirty days from the date on which Parliament first meets after its re-constitution, unless before that expiration of the said period of thirty days a resolution approving the Proclamation has been passed by Parliament.
> (3) A Proclamation of Emergency declaring that the security of Bangladesh, or any part thereof, is threatened by war or external aggression or by internal disturbance may be made before the actual occurrence of war or any such aggression or disturbance if the President is satisfied that there is imminent danger thereof.

After the amendment, Article 141A of the Constitution reads as follows:

> Proclamation of Emergency
> (1) If the President is satisfied that a grave emergency exists in which the security or economic life of Bangladesh, or any part thereof, is threatened by war or external aggression or internal disturbance, he may issue a Proclamation of Emergency for one hundred and twenty days:
> Provided that such Proclamation shall require for its validity the prior counter signature of the Prime Minister.
> (2) A Proclamation of Emergency
> (a) may be revoked by a subsequent Proclamation;
> (b) shall be laid before Parliament;
> (c) shall cease to operate at the expiration of one hundred and twenty days;
> Provided that if any such Proclamation is issued at a time when Parliament stands dissolved or the dissolution of Parliament takes place during the period of one hundred and twenty days referred to in sub clause (c), the Proclamation shall cease to operate at the expiration of thirty days from the date on which Parliament first meets after re constitution, unless before that expiration of the said period of thirty days a resolution approving the Proclamation has been passed by Parliament or at the expiration of one hundred and twenty days, whichever occurs first.
> (3) A Proclamation of Emergency declaring that the security of Bangladesh, or any part thereof, is threatened by war or external aggression or by internal disturbance may be made before the actual occurrence of war or any such aggression or disturbance if the President is satisfied that there is imminent danger thereof.

The changes introduced to Article 141A by the Amendment of 2011 can be summarised as follows:

a) the President was authorised to issue a proclamation of emergency for a period of 'one hundred and twenty days' as the words 'for one hundred and twenty days' were added after the word 'Emergency' in clause (1);[16]
b) the stipulation of parliamentary approval of the proclamation of emergency for its continuation beyond 120 days was done away with. For the words 'unless before the expiration of that period it has been approved by a resolution of Parliament' contained in sub-clause (c) of clause (2) were omitted;[17] and
c) after the words 'passed by parliament' contained in the proviso to clause (2), the words 'or at the expiration of one hundred and twenty days, whichever occurs first' were added.[18]

Thus the *Constitution (Fifteenth Amendment) Act* sought to impose an overall time limit of 120 days on the continuation of an emergency declared in pursuance of Article 141A of the Constitution. However, the Amendment of 2011 did not introduce any safeguards for reducing the possibility of any abuse of the extraordinary powers concerning emergency. For instance, the new amendment did not replace the ground of internal disturbance with a ground that would be less susceptible to abuse by the executive for political purposes. Furthermore, there was no attempt made by the Amendment of 2011 to curtail the unilateral power of the executive to proclaim an emergency by subjecting the proclamation of emergency to a prompt ratification by the parliament within 14 days of its invocation. Neither did the new amendment introduce any mechanism in the Constitution to subject a proclamation of emergency to periodic review by increasing supermajorities of the Parliament, as can be found in the *Constitution of South Africa*, 1996 (see Section 4.4.3.1.1).

The requirement of parliamentary approval for the continuation of an emergency beyond 120 days was done away with. However, the notion that an emergency could not continue beyond 120 days was nullified by changing the proviso to clause (2) of Article 141A. For the insertion of the words 'or at the expiration of one hundred and twenty days, whichever occurs first' by the Amendment at the end of the proviso to clause (2) of Article 141A makes it possible for the life of an emergency proclamation to be extended by the Parliament before the expiry of the period of 120 days.

It seems that enabling the President to proclaim an emergency for 120 days, and bestowing the sole power on the Parliament to extend the continuation of an emergency beyond 120 days were designed perhaps to prevent an extra-constitutional regime, such as that of the military-backed caretaker regime of 2007–2008, from clinging on to emergency powers beyond the imperative necessities when the Parliament stood dissolved. However, while such an objective may have been attained, the Constitution after the amendment still leaves the door wide open for democratically elected governments to abuse the power concerning resort to the extraordinary power of emergency and its subsequent continuation. For under the present scheme, the President can still proclaim an emergency on the advice of the Prime Minister on the ground of internal disturbance. Moreover, the emergency can continue for 120 days without the necessity of it being promptly ratified by the Parliament. Only the Parliament can approve the continuation of the emergency beyond 120 days. But securing such an approval seems to be an easy task as the executive commands the support of the majority in the Parliament.

5.8 References

Ahmed, M. (1984) *Bangladesh: Era of Sheikh Mujibur Rahman*, Dhaka: University Press Limited, 149.

Armed Forces Division, 'Bangladesh in UN Peacekeeping Mission', available at www.afd.gov.bd/index.php/un-peacekeeping/bangladesh-in-un-mission [Accessed 5 January 2017].

Asian Human Rights Commission (2008) 'The State of Human Rights in Bangladesh', Hong Kong (Working Paper No AHRC-SPR-008-2008), 22.

'Assassination of President Zia' (1981) *Asian Recorder*, 2–8 July, 16099.

'Bangladesh Bans Protect Coverage' (1987) *The New York Times*, 29 November, available at www.nytimes.com/1987/11/29/world/bangladesh-bans-protest-coverage.html [Accessed 5 April 2014].

'Bangladesh Chief Offers Concession to Opposition' (1990) *The New York Times*, 4 December, available at www.nytimes.com/1990/12/04/world/bangladesh-chief-offers-concession-to-opposition.html [Accessed 5 April 2013].

'Bangladesh: General Shaukat Ali Retired' (1981) *Asian Recorder*, 16–22 July, 16123.

'Bangladesh: Opposition Leaders Join Forces' (1987) *Asian Recorder*, 26 November– 2 December, 19752.

'Bangladesh: Opposition Agitation' (1988) *Asian Recorder*, 15 January– 21 January, 19827.

'Bangladesh: Opposition Leaders Arrested' (1987) *Asian Recorder*, 24 December–31 December, 19795–19796.

'Bangladesh: Parliament Approves Emergency' (1981) *Asian Recorder*, 20–26 August, 16179.

'Bangladesh: Parliamentary Elections' (1986) *Asian Recorder*, 20–26 August, 19039.

'Bangladesh: Political Stalemate' (1988) *Asian Recorder*, 25–31 March, 19935.

'Bangladesh Power Shift Postponed' (2006) *BBC*, 28 October, available at http://news.bbc.co.uk/2/hi/south_asia/6093300.stm [Accessed 9 April 2013].

'Bangladesh: President Ershad Resigns' (1991) *Asian Recorder*, 7–13 January, 21519.

'Bangladesh: Renewed Opposition Campaign' (1989) *Asian Recorder*, 1–7 January, 20364.

'Bangladesh: Rioting Over Executions' (1981) *Asian Recorder*, November 5–11, 16300.

'Bangladesh to Have Own Brand of Democracy' (2007) *The Daily Star*, 3 April, 1.
'Bangladesh: The Minus-Two Solution' (2007) *The Economist*, 8 September, 66.
'Bangladesh's Controversial Ex-President Iajuddin Ahmed Passes Away' (2012) *The Times of India*, 12 December 2012, available at http://articles.timesofindia.indiatimes.com/2012-12-10/south-asia/35725921_1_interim-government-bnp-sheikh-hasina [Accessed 5 March 2013].
Bari, M. E. (2015) 'Suspension of the Fundamental Rights and the Unrestrained Exercise of the Power of Preventive Detention During the Successive Proclamations of Emergency in Bangladesh: A Legal Study', Doctoral Thesis, Macquarie University, Sydney, 296.
Baxter, C. (1998) *Bangladesh: From a Nation to a State*, Boulder, CO: Westview Press, 114.
Bureau of Democracy, Human Rights, and Labour (2008) *Country Report on Human Rights Practices: Bangladesh, 2007*, Washington, DC: US Department of State, available at www.state.gov/j/drl/rls/hrrpt/2007/100612.htm [Accessed 1 January 2011].
Bureau of Democracy, Human Rights, and Labour (2009) *Country Report on Human Rights Practices, 2008*, Washington: US Department of State, available at www.state.gov/j/drl/rls/hrrpt/2008/sca/119132.htm [Accessed 1 January 2011].
'CA Vows to Transfer Power Through Polls at Earliest, EC to be Reconstituted, Flawless Electoral Roll to be Prepared' (2007) *The Daily Star*, 22 January, 1.
Fair, C. C. (2007) 'On the Issues: Bangladesh', *United States of Institute of Peace*, 27 April, available at www.usip.org/publications/the-issues-bangladesh [Accessed 3 February 2013].
Franda, M. (1982) *Bangladesh: The First Decade*, New Delhi: South Asian Publishers, 54.
Gall, C. (2007a) 'Pakistan Edgy as Ex-Premier Is Exiled Again', *The New York Times*, 11 September 2007, available at www.nytimes.com/2007/09/11/world/asia/11pakistan.html?ref=pervezmusharraf&_r=0 [Accessed 1 January 2011].
Gall, C. (2007b) 'Bhutto Announces Date of Return to Pakistan', *The New York Times*, 15 September, available at www.nytimes.com/2007/09/15/world/asia/15pakistan.html?ref=pervezmusharraf [Accessed 1 January 2011].
Global Legal Monitor (2013) 'Bangladesh Special Parliamentary Committee on Constitution Formed', *Library of Congress*, 13 August, available at www.loc.gov/lawweb/servlet/lloc_news?disp3_l205402154_text [Accessed 9 January 2017].
'Grand Alliance Calls Off All Programmes' (2007) *The Daily Star*, 13 January, 1, available at http://archive.thedailystar.net/2007/01/13/d7011301096.htm [Accessed 11 January 2013].
'Hasina Declares Tougher Action' (2007) *The Daily Star*, 11 January, 1.
Heitzman, J. and Worden, R. L. (1988), *Bangladesh: A Country Study*, Washington, DC: Federal Research Division, Library of Congress, 40, 169, 203.
International Crisis Group (ICG) (2008) *Restoring Democracy in Bangladesh: Asia Report No. 151*, 7, 9, available at www.crisisgroup.org/~/media/Files/asia/south-asia/bangladesh/151_restoring_democracy_in_bangladesh [Accessed 5 February 2013].
Jahangir, J. (2009) 'Bangladesh's Fresh Start', *Journal of Democracy*, 20: 49.
Karim, M. R. (2013) *Role of a Section of the Bangladesh Armed Forces during the*

Caretaker Government of 2007–8: A Review, Dhaka: Transparency International Bangladesh, 6.

Kemaluddin, S. (1982a) 'Bangladesh: the Generals are Posed to Take Over as Sattar Says, Changing of the Guard', *Far Eastern Economic Review*, 19 March, 12.

Kemaluddin, S. (1982b) 'Bangladesh, Ershad's New Order', *Far Eastern Economic Review*, 20 August, 16.

'Lt Gen (rtd) Mashud Made ACC Chief' (2007) *The Daily Star*, 19 January, 1.

Liton, S. (2006) 'President sworn in as Chief of Caretaker Govt', *The Daily Star*, 30 October, 1.

Liton, S. (2008) 'Emergency Out, Rights In', *The Daily Star*, 17 December, 1.

Maniruzzaman, T. (1994) *Politics and Security of Bangladesh*, Dhaka: University Press Ltd, 84.

People's Republic of Bangladesh (1972) *Gonoporishoder Bitorko* (Constituent Assembly Debate), vol. II, 51.

Sarkar, A. (2013) 'Backlog of Cases', *The Daily Star*, 18 March, available at http://archive.thedailystar.net/beta2/news/backlog-of-cases/ [Accessed 5 March 2014].

Staff Correspondent (2006) 'KM Hasan Was Involved in BNP Politics', *The Daily Star*, 21 September, 1.

Staff Correspondent (2006) 'President offers to be Chief Adviser', *The Daily Star*, 29 October, 1.

'UN Peacekeeping Gets Bangladesh $1 BN in Three Years' (2012) *Agence France-Presse (AFP)*, 26 April, available at www.google.com/hostednews/afp/article/ALeqM5jhHDpwZ5cI16mW6quhSYf_4dDx0g [Accessed 3 January 2017].

Wolven, S. (2007) 'Bangladesh: The Adolescence of an Ancient Land', Washington, DC/ Stockholm/Yangon/Chengdu: Institute for Security & Development Policy, 47.

Ziring, L. (1992) *Bangladesh: From Mujib to Ershad: An Interpretive Study*, Dhaka: University Press Limited, 86, 141, 208, 210.

Notes

1 Article 141A(1) of the Constitution provides that a proclamation of emergency 'shall require for its validity the prior counter signature of the Prime Minister'.

2 Article 141A(2) of the Constitution provided that a proclamation of emergency 'shall cease to operate at the expiration of one hundred and twenty days, unless before the expiration of that period it has been approved by a resolution of Parliament'. This provision has been altered by the *Constitution (Fifteenth Amendment) Act 2011*. The effect of this Amendment is discussed in detail above in Section 5.7.

3 Sheikh Mujib's Awami League won by a landslide in the first general elections held in Bangladesh on 7 March 1973 by securing 293 out of 300 seats in the Parliament.

4 The difficult process of impeaching the President of Bangladesh as had been envisaged by Section 4 of the *Constitution (Fourth Amendment) Act 1975* has been done away with by the *Constitution (Twelfth Amendment) Act 1991*, which reintroduced parliamentary democracy in Bangladesh.

5 See *Constitution of Pakistan 1962* art 27.

6 The idea of a Non-Party 'Care-taker' Government was incorporated into the *Constitution of Bangladesh* through the *Constitution (Thirteenth Amendment)*

Act 1996 due to the distrust that exists between the two main political parties, i.e. the BNP and the BAL, with regard to conducting a free, fair and impartial under the supervision of a political government. The Constitution, as amended by the *Constitution (Thirteenth Amendment) Act*, therefore, provided that a Non-Party 'Care-taker' Government, headed by the last retired Chief Justice and 10 Advisers appointed by the President among eminent citizens of the country, would be established within 15 days of the dissolution of the Parliament with the principal mandate of assisting the Election Commission in conducting the General Elections in a free, fair and impartial manner within 90 days of the dissolution of the Parliament. *Constitution of Bangladesh* former Articles 58C(1), 58C(2) & (3) and 58D(2) read with Article 123(3).

The chapter on 'Care-taker' Government was repealed from the *Constitution of Bangladesh* by the *Constitutional (Fifteenth Amendment) Act* on 3 July 2011. *Constitution (Fifteenth Amendment) Act 2011*, Act XIV of 2011, s 21.

7 Justice Mudasser Husain retired from office on 28 February 2007.

8 The four alternative constitutional options available to President Iajuddin for appointing the Chief Adviser were as follows:
First, the *Constitution of Bangladesh* in former Article 58C(3) provided that in the event of the reluctance of the last retired Chief Justice to hold the office of Chief Adviser, 'the President shall appoint as Chief Adviser the person who among the retired Chief Justices of Bangladesh retired next before the last retired Chief Justice'.

Second, in the event of the unwillingness or unavailability of the last two retired Chief Justices to assume the office of the Chief Adviser, the *Constitution of Bangladesh* in former Article 58C(4) provided that 'the President shall appoint as Chief Adviser the person who among the retired Judges of the Appellate Division retired last'.

Third, if the immediate past Judge of the Appellate Division of the Supreme Court was not available or willing to accept the position of the Chief Adviser, the Constitution in former Article 58C(4) stipulated that 'the President shall appoint as Chief Adviser the person who among the retired Judges of the Appellate Division retired next before the last such retired Judge'.

Finally, if no such Judge of the Appellate Division was available or willing to assume the office of the Chief Adviser, the next constitutional option for the consideration of the President was to search for under former Article 58C(5) of the Constitution a consensus candidate after consultation, 'as far as practicable with the major political parties' for appointment as the Chief Adviser.

9 Circular Issued by the Office of the President, 11 January 2007.

10 *Constitution of Bangladesh* in former Article 58D(1) provided that 'The Non-Party Care-taker Government shall discharge its functions as an interim government and shall carry on the routine functions of such government with the aid and assistance of persons in the services of the Republic; and, except in the case of necessity for the discharge of such functions it shall not make any policy decision.'

11 *Constitution of Bangladesh* in former Article 58D(2) stated that 'The Non-Party Care-taker Government shall give to the Election Commission all possible aid and assistance that may be required for holding the general election of members of parliament peacefully, fairly and impartially.' This provision contained in Article 58D(2) should be read with Article 123(3) of the *Constitution of Bangladesh* which states that 'A general election of members of Parliament shall be held within ninety days after Parliament is dissolved.'

12 Section 6(2) of Emergency Powers Ordinance 2007 read together with the second preambular para of the Ordinance.

13 For instance, Major General (retired) M. A. Matin, who was once the head of the Directorate General of Forces Intelligence (DGFI), was made the Adviser for the Ministry of Home Affairs; Major General (Retired) Ghulam Quader, former head of the National Security of Intelligence, was entrusted with the responsibility of overseeing the affairs of the Ministry of Communications; Major General (retired) ASM Matiur Rahman, a former physician in the Army, was made the Adviser for Ministry Health. In addition to these former Army professionals, another retired Army Officer Brigadier General (retired) M. A. Malek was appointed as the Special Assistant to the Chief Adviser for Ministries of Social Welfare and Telecommunications. See Asian Human Rights Commission, 'The State of Human Rights in Bangladesh' (Working Paper No AHRC-SPR-008-2008, Asian Human Rights Commission, 2008) 22.

14 In the lower and higher judiciary of Bangladesh, there is a backlog of an awesome number of cases. According to one estimation, approximately 2.3 million cases are pending with both the lower and higher judiciary. See Ashutosh Sarkar, Backlog of Cases (2013) *The Daily Star*, available at http://archive.thedailystar.net/beta2/news/backlog-of-cases/ (Accessed 25 April 2014).

15 *Emergency Power Rules 2007*, SRO Law No. 15/2007, rs 15, 18(1) & (2).

16 See *Constitution (Fifteenth Amendment) Act 2011* s 41(a).

17 See *Constitution (Fifteenth Amendment) Act 2011* s 41(b).

18 See *Constitution (Fifteenth Amendment) Act 2011* s 41(c).

6 Impact of the five proclamations of emergency in Bangladesh on the fundamental rights of individuals*

6.1 Introduction

The extraordinary measure of suspension of the remedies for enforcement of some of the fundamental rights of the citizens is justified when the state's very life is in danger due to overwhelming crises which cannot be contained by ordinary measures. Typically, rights concerning liberty, freedom of movement, freedom of thought, conscience and speech, and freedom of assembly are curtailed during the period of an emergency (Fitzpatrick, 1994). For if these rights are allowed to be enjoyed in an unrestrained manner, they might interfere with a government's effort to contain the threat posed to the life of the nation. However, experience demonstrates, as elaborated in Sections 3.5.3.1, 3.5.3.2, 3.5.3.3, 3.5.4.2.1, 3.5.4.2.2, 3.5.4.3.1, and 3.5.4.3.3, that emergency situations are commonly characterised not only by the suspension of the above-mentioned fundamental rights but also the suspension of the most important fundamental rights, such as the right to life and the prohibition on torture (Meron, 1986; Fitzpatrick, 1994). The functioning of the national courts in securing the unhindered enjoyment of the core human rights during emergencies has often been unsatisfactory (see Section 3.5.3.1 and Section 4.3.1.1).

In this chapter, an attempt will first be made to examine the provision concerning the suspension of the enforcement of fundamental rights during emergency situations under the *Constitution of Bangladesh*, 1972. After that, attention will be turned to the main focus of this chapter, which is the scrutiny of the impact of the five proclamations of emergency in Bangladesh on the enjoyment of the fundamental rights of the citizens.

6.2 Suspension of the enforcement of the fundamental rights during emergencies under the *Constitution of Bangladesh*

The *Constitution of Bangladesh*, as amended by the *Constitution (Second Amendment) Act*, 1973, does not make any attempt to strike a balance between the necessity for overcoming an emergency and restoring order in the country and simultaneously maintaining respect for the fundamental human rights of individuals during such an emergency. For the Constitution, as pointed out earlier in Section 3.5.5.1, confers on the President the unfettered power to suspend the enforcement of all or any of the 18 fundamental rights guaranteed by Part III of the Constitution in order to deal with an emergency threatening the life of the nation. Article 141C(1) of the Constitution, provides:

> While a Proclamation of Emergency is in operation, the President may, on the written advice of the Prime Minister, by order, declare that the right to move any court for the enforcement of such of the rights conferred by Part III of this Constitution as may be specified in the order, and all proceedings pending in any court for the enforcement of the right so specified, shall remain suspended for the period during which the Proclamation is in force or for such shorter period as may be specified in the order.

Therefore, the Constitution does not recognise the reality that there is a core of rights which are considered too important to be suspended even during an emergency. Although Bangladesh acceded to the ICCPR on 6 September 2000, its Constitution has not been amended to incorporate into it the seven non-derogable rights contained in the ICCPR.

An attempt will now be made to examine the impact of the five proclamations of emergency in Bangladesh on the fundamental rights of the citizens.

6.2.1 Suspension of fundamental rights during the first proclamation of emergency in 1974

It may be recalled here from the discussion in Sections 5.2. and 5.2.1 that Prime Minister Sheikh Mujibur Rahman in an attempt to perpetuate his survival in power advised the President on 28 December 1974 to declare an emergency on the ground of internal disturbance. The proclamation of emergency was followed by the issuance on the same day of a Presidential Order in pursuance of Article 141C(1) to the effect that:

> the right of any person to move any court for the enforcement of the rights conferred by articles 27 [right to equality before the law], 31 [right to protection of law], 32 [right to life and personal liberty], 33 [right to be safeguarded from arbitrary arrest and detention], 35 [rights to protection from *ex post facto* penal law, and, from torture or cruel, inhuman, or degrading punishment or treatment], 36 [right to freedom of movement], 37 [right to freedom of assembly], 38 [right to freedom of association], 39 [right to freedom of thought and conscience, and of speech], 40 [right to freedom of profession or occupation], 42 [rights to

> property] and 43 [right to protection of home and privacy of correspondence] of... [the] Constitution, and all proceedings pending in any court for the enforcement of the said rights, shall remain suspended for the period during which the Proclamation of Emergency issued under clause (1) of Article 141A thereof on the 28th December, 1974, is in force.

The Order had a tremendous impact on individual rights, suspending the enforcement of 12 of the 18 fundamental rights guaranteed by the Constitution. It is noteworthy that the emergency regime in disregard of the international human rights standards not only suspended those rights which are considered non-derogable, such as the right to life, the right not to be subjected to retroactive penal law, and the right not to be subjected to torture or cruel, inhuman or degrading punishment or treatment, but also dispensed with some rights (freedom of profession or occupation and rights to property) which could not be said to have any direct bearing on the emergency declared to deal with the alleged internal disturbance.

6.2.1.1 The deprivation of the power of the High Court Division to enforce the fundamental rights during the continuation of the emergency

Article 44 of the *Constitution of Bangladesh*, 1972, as mentioned earlier in Section 3.5.5, grants an individual the remedial right of moving the High Court Division (HCD) of the Supreme Court for the enforcement of the fundamental rights. Furthermore, this right is also one of the 18 fundamental rights guaranteed by the Constitution due to its inclusion in Part III of the Constitution entitled 'Fundamental Rights'. However, the *Constitution (Fourth Amendment) Act*, which, as mentioned earlier in Section 5.2.1, was passed on 25 January 1975 to concentrate dictatorial powers in the hands of Sheikh Mujib, took away the guarantee afforded to citizens to move the HCD of the Supreme Court for the enforcement of the fundamental rights by replacing the original Article 44 with a new one. The new Article 44, as inserted by Section 3 of the *Constitution (Fourth Amendment) Act*, 1975, stated that: 'Parliament may by law establish a constitutional court, tribunal or commission for the enforcement of the rights' conferred by Part III of the Constitution. Furthermore, Section 17 of the Fourth Amendment Act also altered the provisions of the original Article 102(1) of the Constitution so as to omit the original jurisdiction of the HCD to give directions or orders to any person or authority for the enforcement of any of the 18 fundamental rights guaranteed by the Constitution.

Therefore, the emergency regime through the Fourth Amendment Act deprived the Superior Judiciary of Bangladesh of its authority to enforce the fundamental rights of its citizens, which is 'a unique and unprecedented departure from the normal constitutional pattern followed elsewhere' (Munim, 1975: 333). It is submitted that the HCD due to its original jurisdiction under the *Constitution of Bangladesh* was more likely to play an efficient role in enforcing the fundamental rights that remained in force during the emergency than a constitutional court, tribunal or commission established under an ordinary law to give effect to the designs of Mujib's dictatorial regime. It may seem that the emergency regime of Mujib did not want to take the risk of allowing the HCD to enforce the fundamental rights of the individuals that remained in operation during the continuance of the emergency, and, as such, removed such a possibility through a sweeping constitutional amendment.

6.2.1.2 Reinstatement of the authority of the High Court Division (HCD) to enforce the fundamental rights and the eventual removal of the restrictions on the 12 fundamental rights by the Martial Law regime

Bangladesh, as mentioned earlier in Section 5.2.1, was placed under Martial Law on 15 August 1975, following Mujib's assassination on the same day by a group of army officers. The Martial Law regime in a notable move substituted the new Article 44 of the Constitution with the original Article 44 to restore the right of citizens to move the HCD of the Supreme Court for the enforcement of the fundamental rights (Proclamation Order No. IV 1976). Furthermore, the Martial Law regime restored the HCD's authority under Article 102(1) of the Constitution, which, as mentioned above, was omitted by Section 17 of the *Constitution (Fourth Amendment) Act*, 1975, to give directions or orders to any person or authority for the enforcement of any of the fundamental rights conferred by Part III of the Constitution (*Second Proclamation (Tenth Amendment) Order*, 1977).

It should be stressed here that although the Martial Law regime took the necessary measures for restoring the right of individuals to move the HCD under Article 44 and the power of the HCD to issue directions or orders to any individual or authority for the enforcement of the fundamental rights, the Proclamation of Emergency and the Presidential Order suspending the enforcement of 12 of the 18 fundamental rights were not revoked by it. In this connection, clause (f) of the Proclamation of Martial Law, which was issued on 20 August 1975, is of relevance. For it categorically stated that

> all Acts, Ordinances, President's Orders and other Orders, Proclamations, rules, regulations, bye-laws, notifications and other legal instruments in force on the morning of the 15th August, 1975, shall continue to remain in force until repealed, revoked or amended.

Nevertheless, the restoration of the original provisions of Articles 44 and 102(1) of the Constitution and the amendment of certain provisions of the *Emergency Power Rules*, 1975 relating to preventive detention[1] were interpreted by the HCD as the revocation of the Proclamation of Emergency and the Presidential Order suspending fundamental rights. As Justice Bandrul Haider Chowdhury in *Haji Joynal Abedin v the State [1978] 30 DLR 371* observed:

> It will be seen that Article 33 [which deals with safeguards as to arrest and detention][2]... was mentioned in the Presidential Order dated 28.12.74. Article 33(4)(5) of the Constitution prohibits any law providing for preventive detention unless it ensures four things in case of preventive detention, namely, (1) right to be informed regarding the grounds of his detention, (2) right of the representation, (3) reference to Advisory Board and (4) action upon the report of the Advisory Board. These rights are essentially rights within the concept of fundamental rights... [If] the Proclamation and Presidential Order dated 28.12.74 is still in force then the rights mentioned in Article 33(4)(5) are not available ... By amendment of the Emergency Powers Act [*sic*] on 18.8.77 communication of the grounds of the detention order and constitution of Advisory Committee and a reference thereto and the action upon the report of this Advisory Committee have been provided for. As already been noted these are essential concepts within the fundamental rights. If these rights are available by amendment of the Emergency Powers Act [*sic*] then the fundamental rights have been reconferred. If not, how was it necessary for a regime during Martial Law to confer the rights upon the citizens which have been taken away by the Proclamation of Emergency under Constitution. Either the Proclamation of Emergency and Presidential Order is dead or alive. If it is dead then the rights have reappeared. If it is not, the rights simply are not there. Assuming that these Proclamations and Orders are still alive then how this Emergency Powers Act [*sic*] was amended for bringing into the conception of fundamental rights and how correspondingly Articles 44 and 102 of the Constitution were amended by Martial Law Order for the enforcement of these rights? ... Re-conferment of those two provisions in its original character and colour by [the] Second Proclamation (7th Amendment) Order dated 28.5.76 which was reiterated by the Second Proclamation (10th Amendment) dated 27.11.77 bringing the entire jurisdiction in its original position and introducing the provisions of Article 33 into the Emergency Powers Act [*sic*], the opinion is the fundamental rights which were taken away... have been reconferred by these two Martial Law Proclamations. If Article 33 had been reconferred there is not doubt that other rights are also available because proclamation said that such proclamation is in force until it is amended, revoked and repealed. It is a case of repeal by implication ... [Therefore] the fundamental rights have reappeared and Article 44 has given guarantee for the enforcement of these rights through the machinery of Article 102 of the Constitution.
>
> (391–392)

It can be argued that Justice Chowdhury had misconstrued the effects of the restoration of the original provisions of Articles 44 and 102(1) of the Constitution. Arguably, the restoration of these provisions in the Constitution allowed a citizen to move the HCD for directions or orders for the enforcement of only those fundamental rights which were not suspended by the Presidential Order of 28 December 1974. Thus the proposition that the enjoyment of the 12 suspended fundamental rights was restored as a consequence of the reinstatement of the above-mentioned original provisions in the Constitution seems far-fetched and unsound. Furthermore, the argument that the 12 fundamental rights remained inoperative is bolstered by the fact that the politicians of the time made clear that their participation in the parliamentary elections scheduled for early 1979 was contingent, among many other things, on the restoration of the suspended fundamental rights. Consequently, after four years of continuous restrictions on the majority of fundamental rights, President and Chief Martial Law Administrator, Major General Ziaur Rahman, issued an order on 27 December 1978 revoking the suspension of the enforcement of the 12 fundamental rights (Bari, 2015). Although the restrictions on fundamental rights were lifted on 27 December 1978, the emergency continued for another 11 months until 27 November 1979.

6.2.2 Suspension of fundamental rights during the second proclamation of emergency in 1981

An emergency was proclaimed, as mentioned in Section 5.3, for the second time in Bangladesh on 30 May 1981, following an armed rebellion, which involved the assassination of President Ziaur Rahman. The proclamation of emergency on the ground of internal disturbance was followed by a Presidential Order issued in accordance with Article 141C(1) of the Constitution. This Order suspended:

a) the right of any person to move any court for the enforcement of the rights conferred by Articles 27, 31, 32, 33, 35, 36, 37, 38, 39, 40, 42, and 43 of the Constitution; and
b) all proceedings pending in any court for the enforcement of the above-mentioned rights.

Thus, the emergency regime of 1981 suspended the enforcement of the same 12 fundamental rights that were suspended by the first emergency regime of 1974. Although the security and integrity of the country, as pointed out earlier in Sections 5.3 and 5.3.1, were truly threatened by an armed rebellion, the derogation from fundamental rights, which are generally deemed non-derogable, as pointed out earlier in Section 6.2.1, and from those rights which could not be said to have any direct nexus with the threat posed to the life of nation, is hard to justify. It may seem that the emergency regime in concentrating all its attention on restoring normalcy imitated the arbitrary derogation patterns adopted by the first emergency of 1974 without any serious thought or consideration. However, unlike the emergency regime of Mujib, the second emergency did not introduce any amendment to the Constitution taking away the jurisdiction of the HCD of the Supreme Court of Bangladesh to enforce the fundamental rights that remained in operation. Furthermore, unlike the continuation of the suspension of the fundamental rights for four years during the first emergency, the restrictions on the fundamental rights during the second emergency were short-lived, being lifted on 21 September 1981 after continuation for three months and 21 days.

6.2.3 Suspension of fundamental rights during the third proclamation of emergency in 1987

An emergency was declared in Bangladesh due to 'internal disturbance' for the third time on 27 November 1987, as mentioned earlier in Sections 5.4 and 5.4.1, with a view to crushing the threat posed to General Ershad's rule from the two major opposition parties, the BAL and BNP. Like the proclamations of emergency of 1974 and 1981, the declaration of emergency on 27 November 1987 was followed by the issuance of a Presidential Order, which suspended the enforcement of the same 12 fundamental rights that remained unenforceable during the continuation of the first and second emergency.

The fact that the emergency was declared for purposes other than that of securing the life of Bangladesh is manifested in the measures taken by the regime following the suspension of fundamental rights, which among other things, included the issuance of prohibitory orders banning all political activities, including processions, demonstrations, meetings, and strikes, and the imposition of a strict press censorship (*Emergency Powers Ordinance 1987* s 3; Bureau of Democracy, Human Rights and Labour, 1987).

It can be concluded that the restrictions on the majority of the fundamental rights under the pretext of an emergency were considered necessary by Ershad to bring an end to the pro-democracy movement of the opposition parties, which had threatened to bring down his rule. The emergency and the consequent restrictions on rights came to an end on 27 March 1987 after the threat to Ershad's rule was adequately contained.

6.2.4 Suspension of fundamental rights during the fourth proclamation of emergency in 1990

Ershad, as pointed out earlier in Section 5.5, within a space of three years proclaimed yet another emergency on the ground of internal disturbance on 27 November 1990. Like the emergency of 1987, Ershad also sought to use the emergency of 1990 as the efficient vehicle for oppressing the popular movement to oust him from power. Following the previous three patterns of dispensing with 12 fundamental rights during declared periods of emergency, a Presidential Order suspending the enforcement of the same 12 fundamental rights was issued on the same date as the declaration of the emergency.

Prohibition orders banning all kinds of political activities were once again issued in pursuance of the Emergency Powers Ordinance. Consequently, scores of political activists and student leaders, as pointed out earlier in Section 5.5, were arrested by the regime. However, these arbitrary measures did not deter the populace from taking to the streets demanding Ershad's resignation. Furthermore, the imposition of a strict press censorship also failed to yield the desired result for Ershad. For the publication of all newspapers was stopped during the continuance of the emergency due to the refusal of journalists to work under the censorship (Bureau of Democracy, Human Rights and Labour, 1990). The emergency and the restrictions on the fundamental rights were subsequently lifted on 5 December 1990 after the fall of Ershad's regime.

6.2.5 *Suspension of fundamental rights during the fifth proclamation of emergency in 2007*

A state of emergency was declared for the fifth time in Bangladesh on the ground of internal disturbance, as described in Sections 5.6 and 5.6.1, on 11 January 2007 following the political deadlock surrounding the appointment of the head of the interim 'Care-taker' Government. Subsequently, taking advantage of the lacuna in the Constitution, which does not provide any guidelines as to which of the 18 fundamental rights should remain stalwart in the face of a declared emergency, the President issued an order suspending the rights of the citizens to move any court for the enforcement of all the 18 fundamental rights guaranteed by the *Constitution of Bangladesh* (*Emergency Powers Ordinance 2007*). This was an unprecedented event in the history of the emergency regimes in Bangladesh. For all the previous four emergency regimes, as pointed out in the previous sections, had established the pattern of suspending the enforcement of 12 of the 18 fundamental rights. It seems that the emergency regime did not take into account the fact that Bangladesh in September 2000 had acceded to the ICCPR, which required it to be respectful to the non-derogable rights as enshrined in the Covenant and suspend only those rights whose suspension was strictly required by the exigencies of the situation. Furthermore, the government in fulfilment of Bangladesh's obligation as a state party to the ICCPR was required to immediately notify the UN Secretary-General of its derogation from the provisions of the Covenant.[3] Such a notice was never submitted by the emergency regime and nor was there any request from the UN Secretary-General's Office or the Human Rights Committee asking the government to fulfil its obligation under the Covenant.

Due to the lack of any effective mechanisms within the *Constitution of Bangladesh* for scrutinising the executive actions during a state of emergency, many of the suspended rights were grossly violated with impunity. An attempt will now be made to briefly underscore some these abuses.

6.2.5.1 *Arbitrary and unlawful deprivation of life*

The *Constitution of Bangladesh*, 1972, as pointed out earlier in Section 6.2.1, guarantees the right to life in Article 32.[4] This right receives protection from Article 6(1) of the ICCPR to the effect that: 'Every human being has the inherent right to life. This shall be protected by law. No-one shall be arbitrarily deprived of his life.' Furthermore, the ICCPR, as mentioned earlier in Section 3.3.1, makes this right immune from suspension even during an emergency threatening the life of the nation. However, the *Constitution of Bangladesh* does not provide any such guarantee for the continued operation of this right during an emergency.

Consequently, taking advantage of the suspension of the enforcement of this right along with the other rights guaranteed by the Constitution following the imposition of the emergency on 11 January 2007, as many as 315 persons were killed extra-judicially by the law enforcement agencies during the continuation of the emergency (Asian Human Rights Commission, 2008). The emergency regime labelled these killings as 'crossfire killings', 'gunfights', or 'encounter killings' in an attempt to imply that these persons were members of criminal groups who were engaged in exchanges of gunfire with the law enforcement agencies (World Organisation Against Torture, 2008).

The official cover-up of these killings was very much in line with the spirit of the *Emergency Powers Ordinance*, 2007, which in Section 6(1) provided that:

> no action, done by a person in *good faith*, according to this ordinance or any rule under this Ordinance or any provision under such rule, may be challenged in civil or criminal court.

Consequently, the law enforcement agencies were never held to account for their actions in a court of law.

6.2.5.2 *Arbitrary arrests*

In pursuance of Section 3 of the *Emergency Powers Ordinance*, 2007, the government framed the *Emergency Power Rules* on 25 January 2007, which in Rule 16(2) empowered the law enforcement agencies to 'arrest without warrant and take legal actions against any person'. Furthermore, Rule 19D of the *Emergency Power Rules* precluded the authority of 'any court or tribunal' to release a detainee on bail during the continuance of an enquiry, investigation, or trial against him for an offence under the *Emergency Powers Rules*, notwithstanding the provisions contained in Sections 497 and 498 of the *Code of Criminal Procedure* (CrPc), 1898, which empower the HCD or Court of Session to release an accused on bail.[5] Consequently, an astounding 500,000 individuals were arbitrarily arrested during the continuance of the emergency (Asian Human Rights Commission, 2008). The Inspector General of Police told the media on 9 June 2008 that since the proclamation of the emergency an average of 1,667 persons were being arrested everyday. He further admitted that these arrests were deliberately executed under the *Emergency Power Rules* with a view to precluding the authority of the courts to release the suspects on bail (Asian Human Rights Commission, 2008).

Thus it seems that the trend of arbitrarily arresting an enormous number of individuals everyday, even when the alleged hostilities which gave rise to the emergency had ceased to exist was continued with a view to instituting a reign of terror, and thereby perpetuating the rule of the military-backed 'Care-taker' regime at the expense of one of the most important fundamental rights of individuals – the right to liberty. Furthermore, these arrests took place notwithstanding the fact that the prisons in Bangladesh did not have enough space to accommodate so many persons. The arrest of 500,000 persons by the law enforcement agencies was more than 1441 per cent of the official capacity of the prisons in Bangladesh, which is 34,681.[6]

6.2.5.2.1 JUDICIAL RESPONSE TO SUCH ARRESTS

The HCD on many occasions ordered the release of prisoners on bail notwithstanding the ouster, as pointed out earlier, of its jurisdiction under Rule 19D of the *Emergency Power Rules*. This position of the HCD was first articulated in *Moyezuddin Sikder v State [2007] 59 DLR (HCD) 287*. In this case, a businessman who had been imprisoned for allegedly conspiring to create an artificial fuel shortage by storing 50,000 litres of fuel in the compound of his business challenged the validity of Rule 19D. The HCD relying on comparative constitutional law decisions held that the HCD, which is a creature of the Constitution and a Division of the highest court of law in Bangladesh, cannot be equated with subordinate courts and in the absence of explicit wording ousting its jurisdiction, it could not be said that the HCD was 'intended to be covered by operation' of Rule 19D of the *Emergency Powers Rules* (296). The following observations of the Court are relevant in this regard:

> [W]e cannot conceive for a moment, that the framers of the said Rules, in their wisdom, can afford to be oblivious of the grim reality *that a stream of highest magnitude, flowing from the Everest cannot be blocked altogether without the risk of devastation, it can be kept open by a sluice gate not by a floodgate, though*[7]... Therefore ... the framers of the said

> Rules, deliberately refrained from using the expression to include the Supreme Court within the ambit of Rule 19Gha [D] of the said Rules ... [W]e are of the opinion, that the framers of the said Rules did not intend to include the Supreme Court within the ambit of Rule 19Gha [D] ... Therefore, this Court can entertain applications under section 498 of the Code of Criminal Procedure despite Rule 19 Gha [D] of the said Rules, even with a *non-obstante* expression.
>
> (297)

Thus, the HCD essentially held that the phrase 'any court or tribunal' employed in subordinate legislation such as the *Emergency Powers Rules* could not curb the inherent authority of the HCD under Section 498 of the CrPc to entertain an application for bail, even during an emergency threatening the life of the nation.

But when the government challenged the decision of the HCD in *State v Moyezuddin Sikder [2008] DLR (AD) 82*, the Appellate Division (AD) of the Supreme Court adopted overtly formalist reasoning and overturned the decision of the HCD. It held that since Section 498 of the CrPc empowers the HCD to grant bail and the *Emergency Powers Rules* in Rule 19D expressly restricted the operation of Section 498, the term 'any court' therefore included the HCD. As it observed:

> In Rule 19(Gha) [D] expression ... ['any court or tribunal'] specifically refers to all courts and it is not necessary to name the Courts by specific names. Nothing can be more specific than ... ['any court or tribunal'] to oust the jurisdiction of the High Court Division and therefore, the ouster is by specific words and not by implications ... It is pertinent to mention here that section 498 provides for jurisdiction of the High Court Division and the Sessions Judge in granting bail under Section 498 and application under section 498 cannot be entertained by another Court, other than the High Court Division and the learned Sessions Judge and therefore when the law makers mentioned Section 498 they knew they were ousting the jurisdiction of the High Court Division and the learned Session Judge in entertaining applications under section 498 and therefore, the ouster has been deliberately done with manifest intention and by express words. Non-mention of the names of the Courts is irrelevant for the purpose.
>
> (88)

The formalist underpinnings of the decision of the AD are further evidenced by the observation that '[t]he question whether the law makers have disregarded justice and sound policy in framing 19(Gha)[D] is not for the Court to decide' (89).

The AD not only adopted a highly deferential attitude in contravention of its judicial responsibility of deciding 'the Constitutionality of the law', but it also criticised the HCD for its lengthy judgment focusing on constitutional questions (89). It observed:

> The High Court Division is not to embark upon interpretation of law and scrutiny of intricate question of law far less Constitutional questions, while deciding bail petitions and should decide petitions expeditiously. (90)

The AD in delivering its decision did, however, leave a small window of opportunity open for the HCD to release a prisoner on bail for any offence under the *Emergency Powers Rules* when the facts exhibited 'a case of without jurisdiction, *coram non judice* or malafide' (89). It is evident that the AD significantly increased the threshold required for a suspect to gain an efficacious remedy in the form of bail. The deferential decision of the AD incensed the legal fraternity. Rafiqul Hauque, one of the most senior lawyers of the country, who was an outspoken critic of the military-backed regime, termed the decision a 'black chapter' in the history of the country's judiciary ('SC Strikes Down HC Jurisdiction for Granting Bail in EPR Cases' 2008). He further implied that the judges of the AD were unduly influenced by the military-backed regime. For he stated that 'an army major had been occupying a room on the second floor of the Supreme Court and had been deciding which case was to be heard by which judge' (Asian Legal Resource Centre, 2008: 12).

Despite the decision of the AD in the above-mentioned case approving the ouster of the jurisdiction of the HCD to release prisoners on bail barring few exceptions, the HCD in exercise of its inherent power under Section 561A of the CrPc to 'secure the ends of justice' continued to release individuals detained under the *Emergency Powers Rules* on bail.[8] In *AKM Reazul Islam v State [2008] 13 BLC (HCD) 111*, the HCD forcefully held that it should not wash its hands when no effective remedy is left at the disposal of the petitioner and consequently should interject in such a case in order to fulfil its responsibility of furthering 'the cause of justice' (119).

6.2.5.3 Torture and cruel or inhuman or degrading treatment

The *Constitution of Bangladesh* in Article 35(5) prohibits 'torture or cruel, inhuman, or degrading' punishment or treatment. Perhaps to further demonstrate its seriousness in ensuring protection from torture and cruel, inhuman or degrading treatment or punishment under any circumstances, Bangladesh in 1998 acceded to the *Convention Against Torture and other Cruel, Inhuman, or Degrading Treatment or Punishment* (CAT). The CAT in Article 2(2) contains a non-derogation clause which states that: 'No exceptional circumstances whatsoever, whether a state of war or a threat of war, internal political instability or any other public emergency, may be invoked as a justification of torture.' Bangladesh, as mentioned earlier in Section 6.2, is also a party to the ICCPR, which in Article 4(2) makes the right not to be subjected to 'torture or to cruel, inhuman or degrading treatment or punishment' non-derogable during an emergency.

Nevertheless, despite Bangladesh's accession to the above-mentioned treaties in 1998 and 2000 respectively, the emergency regime of 2007 suspended the right not to be subjected to torture or cruel, inhuman, or degrading treatment or punishment along with the other 17 fundamental rights guaranteed by the Constitution. The suspension of this right facilitated the military-backed emergency regime in using various methods of torture as the most effective means of coercing false confessions of guilt from the politicians belonging to the two major political parties with a view to barring them from contesting the next general elections and thereby implementing its political agenda of staying in power indefinitely.

The most common methods of torture used by the law enforcement agencies in the various torture cells operated by them were:

> a) hanging persons from the ceiling by their wrists and beating them up mercilessly;
> b) electric shocks;
> c) pouring very hot water over the victim's head with a view to scalding it; and
> d) insertion of 'nails or needles under the fingernails or toenails or other sensitive parts of the body'.
>
> (Asian Human Rights Commission, 2008: 25)

One of the high-profile victims of the torture by the law enforcement agencies was Mr. Tareque Rahman, the then Senior Joint-Secretary-General of the BNP and also the son of the former Prime Minister Begum Khaleda Zia, who was detained by the regime on charges of corruption. He was tortured to the extent that his spine was broken rendering him unable to walk for several months ('BNP Tells AL: Keep Off Tarique' 2013).

6.2.5.4 Challenge to the constitutionality of suspending all the fundamental rights during the 2007 emergency and the subsequent termination of the emergency

In *M Saleem Ullah and Others v Bangladesh* – the case in which, as pointed out earlier in Section 5.6.1.1, the constitutionality of the proclamation of emergency was challenged – the constitutionality of the extraordinary measure of suspension of all the fundamental rights was also challenged. The HCD after an initial hearing issued a *rule nisi* asking the military-backed regime to explain why the emergency declared on 11 January 2007 and the consequent restrictions on the fundamental rights should not be declared unconstitutional. However, the emergency and the restrictions on the fundamental rights were lifted on 17 December 2008 before the Court could decide the merits of the constitutionality of the challenges.

In conclusion, it seems absolutely unjustifiable that for the purpose of dealing with 'internal disturbance', which did not exist after 12 January 2007, the citizens of Bangladesh were deprived of enjoying all their fundamental rights for nearly two years.

6.3 References

Asian Human Rights Commission (2008) 'The State of Human Rights in Bangladesh', Hong Kong: Asian Human Rights Commission (Working Paper No AHRC-SPR-008-2008), 23, 24, 25, 30.

Asian Legal Resource Centre (2008) 'Bangladesh: The Prolonged State of Emergency is Resulting in Widespread Violations of Human Rights, A Written Statement Submitted to the 7th Session of the Human Rights Council', Hong Kong: Asian Legal Resource Centre (Working Paper No ALRC-CWS-07-001-2008), 12.

'Bangladesh Chief Offers Concession to Opposition' (1990) *The New York Times*, 4 December, available at www.nytimes.com/1990/12/04/world/bangladesh-chief-offers-concession-to-opposition.html [Accessed 3 June 2013].

Bari, M. E. (2015) 'Suspension of the Fundamental Rights and the Unrestrained Exercise of the Power of Preventive Detention During the Successive Proclamations of Emergency in Bangladesh: A Legal Study', Doctoral Thesis, Macquarie University, Sydney, 325.

Bureau of Democracy, Human Rights and Labour, US Department of State (1987) *Annual Human Rights Report: Bangladesh*, 1114.

Bureau of Democracy, Human Rights and Labour, US Department of State (1990) *Annual Human Rights Report: Bangladesh*, 1392.

Fitzpatrick, J. (1994) *Human Rights in Crisis: The International System for Protecting Rights During States of Emergency*, Philadelphia, PA: University of Pennsylvania Press, 37.

International Centre for Prison Studies (2015) *World Prison Brief: Bangladesh*, August, available at www.prisonstudies.org/country/bangladesh [Accessed 10 January 2017].

Meron, T. (1986) *Human Rights Law Making in the United Nations: A Critique of Instruments and Process*, Oxford: Clarendon Press, 86.

Munim, F. K. M. A. (1975) *Rights of the Citizen under the Constitution and Law*, Dhaka: Bangladesh Institute of Law and International Affairs, 333.

'SC Strikes Down HC Jurisdiction for Granting Bail in EPR Cases' (2008) *Financial Express*, 24 April, 1.

Staff Correspondent (2013) 'BNP Tells AL: Keep Off Tarique', *bdnews24.com*, 24 May, available at http://bdnews24.com/politics/2013/05/24/bnp-tells-al-keep-off-tarique [Accessed 5 January 2017].

World Organisation Against Torture (2008) *Severe Human Rights Violations under the State of Emergency*, Report, Geneva: World Organisation Against Torture, 15 February, available at www.refworld.org/docid/47d796771c.html [Accessed 9 January 2017].

Notes

* A significantly edited and truncated version of this chapter has been published in a refereed journal. For details, see M. E. Bari (2014) 'The Unjust Exercise of Emergency Powers in Bangladesh and Their Consequent Impact on the Fundamental Rights: A Critical Appraisal', *Jurisprudence (Jurisprudenija)*, 21(2): 578–598.

1 The amendment of the provisions concerning preventive detention in the *Emergency Power Rules* will be discussed in the next chapter.

2 The provisions concerning art 33 of the Constitution have been briefly discussed in Section 3.9.2.3.

3 *International Covenant on Civil and Political Rights (ICCPR) 1966*, art 4(3).

4 *Constitution of Bangladesh 1972* in Article 32 states: 'No person shall be deprived of life … save in accordance with law.'

5 *Code of Criminal Procedure 1898* in Section 497 provides:

> '(1) When any person accused of any non-bailable offence is arrested or detained without warrant by an officer in charge of a police-station, or appears or is brought before a Court, he may be released on bail, but he shall not be so released if there appear reasonable grounds for believing that he has been guilty of an offence punishable with death or transportation for life:
> Provided that the Court may direct that any person under the age of sixteen years or any woman or any sick or infirm person accused of such an offence be released on bail.
> (2) If it appears to such officer or Court at any stage of the investigation, inquiry or trial, as the case may be, that there are not reasonable grounds for believing that the accused has committed a non-bailable offence, but that there are sufficient grounds for further inquiry into his guilt, the accused shall, pending such inquiry, be released on bail, or, at the discretion of such officer or Court, on the execution by him of a bond without sureties for his appearance as hereinafter provided.
> (3) An officer or a Court releasing any person on bail under subsection (1) or subsection (2) shall record in writing his or its reasons for so doing.
> (4) If, at any time after the conclusion of the trial of a person accused of a non-bailable offence and before judgment is delivered, the Court is of opinion that there are reasonable grounds for believing that the accused is not guilty of any such offence, it shall release the accused, if he is in custody on the execution by him of a bond without sureties for his appearance to hear judgment delivered.
> (5) The High Court Division or Court of Session and, in the case of a person released by itself, any other Court may cause any person who has been released under this section to be arrested and may commit him to custody.'

Code of Criminal Procedure in Section 498 states:

> 'The amount of every bond executed under this Chapter shall be fixed with due regard to the circumstances of the case, and shall not be excessive; and the High Court Division or Court of Session may, in any case, whether there be an appeal on conviction or not, direct that any person be admitted to bail, or that the bail required by a police-officer or Magistrate be reduced.'

6 The data concerning the official capacity of the prisons in Bangladesh was collected from the website of the International Centre for Prison Studies. See International Centre for Prison (2015) Studies, *World Prison Brief: Bangladesh*, August, available at www.prisonstudies.org/country/bangladesh (Accessed 10 January 2017).

7 These sentences were underlined by Justice Nozrul Islam Chowdhury, who delivered the judgment of the Court.

8 *Code of Criminal Procedure 1898* in Section 561A states:

> 'Nothing in this Code shall be deemed to limit or affect the inherent power of the High Court Division to make such orders as may be necessary to give effect to any order under this Code, or to prevent abuse of the process of any Court or otherwise to secure the ends of justice.'

7 Preventive detention laws in Bangladesh, their exercise during the five proclamations of emergency and judicial response to such exercise*

7.1 Introduction

The *Constitution of Bangladesh*, as pointed out earlier in Section 3.9.2.3, did not originally contain any provisions permitting the exercise of the power of preventive detention. However, the *Constitution (Second Amendment) Act*, 1973, which inserted provisions concerning the proclamation of emergency and suspension of the enforcement of fundamental rights during the continuance of emergency, replaced the original Article 33 with one that empowers the Parliament to pass laws concerning preventive detention.[1]

In this chapter, first an endeavour will be made to evaluate the provisions concerning preventive detention contained in the *Constitution of Bangladesh* and Bangladeshi statutes – both permanent and temporary. After that, light will be shed on the exercise of the power of preventive detention during declared periods of emergency in Bangladesh and the judicial response to the exercise of such power.

7.2 The *Constitution of Bangladesh* and provisions concerning preventive detention

It is striking that following in the footsteps of the framers of the *Constitution of India*, 1950 and, the 1956 and 1973 Constitutions of Pakistan, as explained in Sections 3.9.2.1, 3.9.2.2.1 and 3.9.2.2.3, lawmakers in Bangladesh have also placed provisions concerning preventive detention in the Part entitled 'Fundamental Rights' of the Constitution. Thus, the very Part of the Constitution that is supposed to guarantee the enjoyment of fundamental liberties contains provisions permitting their encroachment.

However, the inserted Article 33, which permits the enactment of laws concerning preventive detention, does offer certain safeguards to a detainee. Clauses (4) and (5) of this Article provide:

> (4) No law providing for preventive detention shall authorise the detention of a person for a period exceeding six months unless an Advisory

Board consisting of three persons, of whom two shall be persons who are, or have been, or are qualified to be appointed as, Judges of the Supreme Court and the other shall be a person who is a senior officer in the service of the Republic, has, after affording him an opportunity of being heard in person, reported before the expiration of the said period of six months that there is, in its opinion, sufficient cause for such detention.

(5) When any person is detained in pursuance of an order made under any law providing for preventive detention, the authority making the order shall, as soon as may be, communicate to such person the grounds on which the order has been made, and shall afford him the earliest opportunity of making a representation against the order.

Provided that the authority making any such order may refuse to disclose facts which such authority considers to be against the public interest to disclose.

An attempt will now be made to examine to what extent these procedural safeguards mitigate the harshness of laws concerning preventive detention.

a) Absence of any guidance as to the circumstances that can warrant the exercise of the power of preventive detention
Unlike the Constitutions of India and Pakistan, which, as pointed out earlier in Sections 3.9.2.1 and 3.9.2.2, permit the enactment of laws for preventing the commission of activities, *inter alia*, detrimental to the integrity, security or defence of the nation, foreign or external affairs, and public order, the provisions inserted in Article 33 of the *Constitution of Bangladesh* make no mention of the circumstances which can warrant exercise of the power of preventive detention. It is therefore evident that these provisions allow significant leeway to the Parliament to pass laws that can allow the executive to exercise the powers concerning preventive detention for extraneous purposes without the precondition of an emergency threatening the security of the nation.
b) Review of a detention order by an advisory board
As mentioned above, the *Constitution of Bangladesh* in clause 4 of Article 33 provides that an individual cannot be kept in preventive custody for a period exceeding six months without the concurrence of an Advisory Board.

It is evident from the above provision that the Constitution does not provide for the formation of a review body for the scrutiny of every detention order made by the executive. Rather the question of such scrutiny by an Advisory Board arises only when there is a necessity to keep an individual in preventive custody for more than six months. In other words, the executive has the absolute authority to deprive an individual of his liberty without any trial or review for a period up to six months. This provision is significantly harsher than those contained in the Constitutions of India and Pakistan, since the Constitutions of India and Pakistan, as pointed out earlier in Sections 3.9.2.1 and 3.9.2.2.3, provide that any law providing for preventive detention cannot permit the detention of an individual without the approval of an Advisory Board for periods longer than two months and one month respectively.

Furthermore, unlike the *Constitution of India*, 1950, and *Constitution of Pakistan*, 1973 (see Sections 3.9.2.1 and 3.9.2.2.3), the *Constitution of Bangladesh* does not confine the membership of the Advisory Board solely to persons who 'are or have been or are qualified' for appointment as judges of superior courts. Rather, following in the footsteps of the 1962 Constitution of Pakistan, which as pointed out earlier in 3.9.2.2.2 was formulated by a military dictator, the *Constitution of Bangladesh* also provides for inclusion in the Advisory Board of a civil servant, who can hardly be expected to be objective due to the influence of the executive.

It should also be pointed out here that according to clause 4 of Article 33 of the Constitution, the Advisory Board can recommend either the release or continuation of the detention of an individual. However, the Advisory Board has not been given the power to express an opinion as to how much longer than six months the detainee should be kept in preventive custody if it is found that there are reasons for continuing the detention.

c) Communication of the grounds of detention to the detainee and his right of representation

The *Constitution of Bangladesh* in clause 5 of Article 33 imposes two obligations on the detaining authority, namely, 1) the duty to communicate to the detainee, as soon as may be, the grounds of his detention, and 2) the obligation to afford the detainee the opportunity to make a representation against the detention order. The obligation to furnish the grounds of detention to the detainee in clean and clear terms is inextricably linked to the facilitation of an effective representation by the detainee against his detention order. In this context, the observations of Justice Kemaluddin Hossain in *Abdul Latif Mirza v Government of Bangladesh [1979] 31 DLR (AD) 1* are relevant. He remarked:

> Grounds [to be communicated to the detainee] … must be clear, precise and give such information to the detenu[2] that he could make a representation; it must not be vague or indefinite and that the grounds must be relatable to the existing facts (10).

However, it should be pointed out here that, unlike the 1973 *Constitution of Pakistan*, as detailed in Section 3.9.2.2.3, the *Constitution of Bangladesh* does not provide for a specific time-frame for communicating the grounds of detention to a detainee. Rather, the Constitution has kept the time limit for informing the detainee of the grounds of detention unspecified by using the vague expression 'as soon as may be'. The use of this vague expression grants significant leeway to the detaining authority to withhold the grounds of detention and, as such, weakens the enforcement of the detainee's right to make an effective representation against the detention order.

d) Non-disclosure of facts related to the detention
In the same manner as the *Colonial Anarchical and Revolutionary Crimes Act*, 1919, and the *Constitution of India*, 1950, which were discussed in Sections 3.9.1.2.3 and 3.9.2.1, the *Constitution of Bangladesh* seeks to qualify the above safeguards concerning the communication of grounds and the right to make representation. For the proviso to clause 5 of Article 33 confers on the detaining authority the wide discretion to withhold the grounds of the detention order if disclosure is considered to be against the public interest.
  The vesting of wide discretion in the executive to withhold the grounds of the detention from the detainee renders the right of making an effective representation meaningless. For the decision of the executive to withhold the grounds for reasons of public interest may be exercised arbitrarily and the Constitution does not offer any guarantee for the scrutiny of the discretion of the executive in order to ascertain whether it was exercised 'arbitrarily, capriciously or mala fide' (*Sushila Madiman v Commissioner of Police [1951] AIR (Bombay) 252*, 254).

e) Absence of a provision barring detention incommunicado:
A close perusal of clauses 4 and 5 of Article 33 of the Constitution reveals that a detainee has not been afforded any opportunity to communicate with lawyers and family members. The isolation of the detainee from the outside world for prolonged periods of time, as pointed out earlier in Section 4.4.5, in turn facilitates the torture of detainees kept in preventive custody, in particular those who are detained for political purposes.

f) Absence of a time limit for keeping a detainee in preventive custody
The *Constitution of Bangladesh* also does not prescribe the maximum period for keeping an individual in preventive custody. It is noteworthy that the provisions concerning preventive detention were incorporated in the *Constitution of Bangladesh* on 22 September 1973 through the *Constitution (Second Amendment) Act* – five months and 10 days after the adoption of the 1973 Constitution of Pakistan, which fixes the maximum period for keeping individuals in preventive custody at 12 months. However, instead of inserting such a safeguard, the *Constitution of Bangladesh* follows in the footsteps of the *Constitution of India*, 1950, and the 1956 and 1962 Constitutions of Pakistan, as had been mentioned in Sections 3.9.2.1, 3.9.2.2.1 and 3.9.2.2.2, giving the Parliament free rein to stipulate by law the maximum period of preventive detention.

Only four months and 12 days after the amendment of Article 33 of the 1972 *Constitution of Bangladesh*, on 5 February 1974, the *Special Powers Act* was passed by the Parliament which combined the laws relating to preventive detention and punitive detention. An attempt will now be made to examine the provisions concerning preventive detention as enshrined in this Act.

7.2.1 The Special Powers Act (SPA), 1974

The SPA, which is still in force in Bangladesh, was enacted apparently to 'provide for special measures for the prevention [among other things] of certain prejudicial activities' (preamble paragraph). The following acts are deemed prejudicial by Section 2(f) of the SPA:

(i) intention or likelihood of prejudicing the sovereignty or defence of Bangladesh or its relations with foreign states;
(ii) intention or likelihood of prejudicing the security of Bangladesh or public safety or the maintenance of public order or administration or maintenance of law and order;
(iii) intention or likelihood of creating or exciting feelings of enmity or hatred or fear or alarm among the public;
(iv) intention or likelihood of prejudicing the maintenance of supplies and services essential to the community;
(v) intention or likelihood of prejudicing the economic or financial interests of the State.

Thus, the Parliament followed the Indian and Pakistani traditions of authorising the exercise of the extraordinary power of preventive detention on vague and general grounds (see Sections 3.9.2.1.1, 3.9.2.1.2, 3.9.2.1.3, 3.9.2.2.4.1, and 3.9.2.2.4.2). It is evident that the executive has been afforded significant leeway to bring any situation within the purview of these vague grounds and consequently to misuse the extraordinary power of preventive detention for purposes other than that of protecting the legitimate interests of the state.

It should be pointed out here that the SPA was enacted at a time when there was no grave emergency threatening the life of the nation. However, the government of the day claimed that it was necessary to put down the violent threat posed to the security of the nation from radical left-wing parties. In this context, it can be argued that if preventive detention was indeed necessary for dealing with the deteriorating law and order situation, then the SPA could have been enacted as temporary legislation, whose continuation would then be subject to periodic review by the Parliament, as had been done in the case of the Indian *Preventive Detention Act*, 1950 (see Section 3.9.2.1.1).

It is pertinent to mention here that unlike the Indian *Preventive Detention Act*, 1950, and the *Maintenance of Internal Security Act*, 1971 – both of which despite the absence of any guidance from the Constitution of India fixed the maximum period of preventive detention at one year – the SPA provides for preventive detention for an unlimited period of time.

Furthermore, Section 34 of the SPA purports to bar the jurisdiction of all courts from questioning any order of preventive detention. It provides:

> Except as provided in this Act, no order made, direction issued, or proceeding taken under Act, or purporting to have been so made, issued or taken, as the case may be, shall be called in question in any court, and no suit, prosecution or other legal proceeding shall lie against the Government or any person for anything in good faith done or intended to be done under this Act.

However, this restriction does not extend towards challenging the *mala fide* exercise of the power of preventive detention or detention orders that are passed abusing or violating the provisions providing for preventive detention. For the Constitution in Article 102(2)(b)(i) provides that the

> High Court Division may, if satisfied that no other equally efficacious remedy is provided by law … on the application of any person, make an order… directing that a person in custody be brought before it so that it may satisfy itself that he is not being held in custody without lawful authority or in an unlawful manner.

In this context, the observations of Chief Justice Kemaluddin Hossain in the case of *Abdul Latif Mirza v Government of Bangladesh [1979] 31 DLR (AD) 1* are pertinent:

> The Constitution … has cast a duty upon the High Court to satisfy itself, that a person in custody is being detained under an authority of law, or in a lawful manner. The purpose of the Constitution is to confer on the High Court with the power to satisfy itself that a person detained in custody, is under an order which is lawful … The Bangladesh Constitution, therefore, provides for a judicial review of an executive action … The High Court, therefore, in order to discharge its constitutional function of judicial review, may call upon the detaining authority to disclose the materials upon which it has so acted, in order to satisfy itself that the authority has not acted in an unlawful manner.
>
> (9–10)

The SPA affords certain safeguards to the detainee, which can be summarised as follows:

a) Communication of the grounds for detention
   The SPA in Section 8(2) provides that:

> In the case of a detention order, the authority making the order shall inform the person detained under that order of the grounds of his detention at the time he is detained or as soon thereafter as is practicable, but not later than fifteen days from the date of detention.

It is evident that, although clause 5 of Article 33 of the Constitution by using the expression 'as soon as may be', as mentioned above in Section 7.2, does not prescribe the time-frame for furnishing the grounds of detention to the detainee, Section 8(2) of the SPA specifies a maximum period of 15 days for communicating the grounds. This provision obviates the possibility of the detaining authority abusing the vagueness of the phrase 'as soon as may be', as employed in the Constitution.

b) Review of a detention order and the representation made by the detainee

The SPA, in line with clause 4 of Article 33 of the Constitution, provides for the review of a detention order by an Advisory Board, consisting of a Chairman – a person who 'is, or has been, or is qualified to be appointed as, a Judge of the High Court [Division]' – and two members – one a person who is or has been or is qualified to be appointed as a Judge of the High Court Division and the other 'a senior officer in the service of the Republic'.[3] Section 10 provides:

> In every case where a detention order has been made under this Act, the Government shall, within one hundred and twenty days from the date of detention under the order, place before the Advisory Board constituted… the grounds on which the order has been made and the representation, if any, made by the person affected by the order.

It is evident that although the detainee should be informed of the grounds within 15 days in order to facilitate his right to make representation, the maximum period for placing the detention order and the representation of the detainee before the Advisory Board for its review has been fixed at 120 days. This time limit of 120 days for keeping a person in preventive custody without the concurrence of an Advisory Board is excessive and incongruous with the safeguard afforded to the detainee in Section 8(2).

Furthermore, Section 11(4) of the SPA deprives the detainee of the right to be represented before the Advisory Board by a legal practitioner, which impedes the ability of the detainee to make an effective and meaningful representation against his detention order.

c) Authority of the Advisory Board to make recommendations

In pursuance of Section 12(1) of the SPA, the Advisory Board can recommend to the detaining authority the continuation of the detention order if, in its opinion, there is sufficient cause for such continuation. Since neither the Constitution nor the SPA stipulates the maximum period for keeping an individual in preventive custody, it remains open to the executive to take advantage of this lacuna and consequently continue the detention for an indefinite period.

However, if the Advisory Board, in terms of Section 12(2) of the SPA, reports to the Government that there is 'no sufficient cause for the detention of the person concerned, the Government shall revoke the detention order and cause the person to be released forthwith'. Ascribing mandatory force to the opinion of the Advisory Board provides the detainee with an important safeguard against the arbitrary exercise of power by the executive. However, since the Advisory Board as prescribed by the SPA provides for inclusion of a representative of the executive as a member, it can be argued that he might be tempted to carry out the wishes of the executive and influence the decision of the Board in not releasing the detainee.

Although during parliamentary debate on the *Special Powers Bill* in 1974, an MP from the Awami League termed the SPA as the 'whitest law',[4] a perusal of the provisions of the SPA reveals that the safeguards afforded to detainees are not sufficient to prevent arbitrary encroachment on their liberty.

7.3 Preventive detention laws enacted during the proclamations of emergency in Bangladesh and their exercise

Bangladesh, as noted earlier in Chapter 5, experienced proclamations of emergency on five occasions, namely, in 1974, 1981, 1987, 1990 and 2007, during which new laws providing for preventive detention were enacted by the government of the day despite the existence of the SPA – the permanent piece of legislation concerning preventive detention. An attempt will now be made to examine these laws and their exercise during the five periods of emergency.

7.3.1 Enactment of preventive detention law and its exercise during the first proclamation of emergency (1974–1979)

The President of Bangladesh, as pointed out earlier in Section 5.2, on the advice of Prime Minister Mujib proclaimed an emergency for the first time in the history of Bangladesh on 28 December 1974 on the ground of internal disturbance. The *Emergency Powers Act*, which was enacted on 25 January 1975 replacing the *Emergency Powers Ordinance*, in Section 2 empowered the Government to make rules on a wide range of issues. It provided that:

> (1) The Government may … make such rules as appear to it to be necessary or expedient for ensuring the security, the public safety and interest

> and for protecting the economic life of Bangladesh, or for securing the maintenance of public order, or for maintaining supplies or services essential to the life of the community.
> (2) Without prejudice to the generality of the powers conferred by sub-section (1), the rules may provide for, or may empower any authority to make orders providing for …
> (viii) the apprehension and detention of any person with respect to whom the authority empowered by or under the rules to apprehend and detain is of the opinion that this apprehension and detention are necessary for the purpose of preventing him from acting in a manner prejudicial to Bangladesh's relation with foreign powers, or to the security, the public safety or interest of Bangladesh, the maintenance of supplies and services essential to the life of the community or the maintenance of peaceful condition in any part of Bangladesh;
> Explanation – For the avoidance of doubt it is hereby declared that the sufficiency of the grounds on which such opinion as aforesaid is based shall be determined by the authority forming such opinion; …
> (xi) the apprehension and detention in temporary custody of any person whom the authority empowered by or under the rules to apprehend and detain suspects on grounds appearing to such authority to be reasonable of having acted, acting, being about to act, being likely to act in any such prejudicial manner as is mentioned in clause (viii).

Subsequently, in pursuance of Section 2, the Government formulated the *Emergency Powers Rules*, which contained provisions concerning preventive detention in Rule 5. Rule 5 provided that:

> (1) The Government, if satisfied with respect to any person that with a view to preventing him from acting in a manner prejudicial to the security, the public safety or interest of Bangladesh, Bangladesh's relation with any foreign power, the maintenance of public order, the maintenance of peaceful conditions in any part of Bangladesh or the maintenance of supplies and services essential to the life of the community it is necessary so to do, may make an order –
> (a) directing that such person be detained;
> …
> (4) A person who is ordered to be detained under sub-rule (1)(a) shall be detained in such place and under such conditions as to maintenance, discipline and punishment for breaches of discipline as the Government may from time to time determine.
> …
> (6) An order under sub-rule (1)(a) may be executed at any place in Bangladesh in the manner provided to the execution of warrants of arrest under the Code.

The provisions contained in Rule 5(1) and 5(1)(a) were reproduced from Rule 32(1) and 32(1)(b) of the *Defence of Pakistan Rules*, 1965, which was discussed in detail in Section 3.9.2.2.5.1. The provision contained in Rule 5(4) was a reproduction of the provision contained in Rule 32(4) of the same *Defence of Pakistan Rules*, 1965.[5] Furthermore, Rule 5(1) empowered the Government to pass detention orders on the same grounds that were already the grounds for passing such an order, as pointed out earlier in Section 7.2.1, under Section 2(f) of the SPA.

7.3.1.1 Absence of constitutional safeguards concerning preventive detention in the Emergency Powers Rules, 1975

It is striking that although the *Emergency Powers Rules*, which were framed by a civilian Government in January 1975, provided for the exercise of the power of preventive detention, these Rules did not incorporate any of the safeguards, such as the communication of the grounds to the detainee, the constitution of an Advisory Board and the right to make a representation against the order of detention, as required under the Constitution.

7.3.1.2 Exercise of the power of preventive detention by the regime of Mujib

The wide powers concerning preventive detention under the *Emergency Powers Rules* and the SPA were used to stage a crackdown on political leaders belonging to the extreme leftist political parties, who had posed violent opposition to the regime of Mujib. Although the Government never published any information concerning the number of individuals kept in preventive custody, reports of non-governmental organisation and media reports reveal that as many as 383 opposition political leaders were detained within the first few months of the invocation of the emergency (Amnesty International, 1975). Another 8320 persons were detained by the regime until 14 August 1975, a half of this number being political detainees (Bari, 2015). It seems that the constitutional safeguards concerning preventive detention were deliberately not inserted in the *Emergency Powers Rules* so that the Government could use the power of preventive detention as an effective tool for indefinitely detaining its political adversaries and subsequently perpetuating its survival in power.

7.3.1.3 Incorporation of the constitutional safeguards concerning preventive detention in the Emergency Powers Rules, 1975, by the martial law regime

As mentioned earlier in Section 5.2.1, although martial law was imposed throughout Bangladesh following the assassination of premier Mujib on 15 August 1975, the emergency and the emergency regulations were continued by the martial law regime. Subsequently on 18 August 1977, the martial law regime of General Zia in line with the constitutional requirements incorporated certain safeguards in the *Emergency Power Rules.* These safeguards can be summarised as follows:

1 communication of the grounds of detention order as soon as possible but not later than 15 days from the date of detention to enable the detainee to make a written representation against the detention order (r 5(5A);
2 review of a detention order within 120 days of the detention by an Advisory Committee, consisting of a Chairman – a sitting Judge of the High Court Division of the Supreme Court of Bangladesh – and two members – one a senior civil servant and the other a person who had held judicial office in the territory of Bangladesh for not less than 10 years (r 5(5B) and (5C).

It is striking that although the democratically elected government of Mujib did not incorporate safeguards concerning preventive detention in the Emergency Powers Rules, the extra-constitutional martial law regime took the salutary step of incorporating these safeguards in order to secure compliance with clauses 4 and 5 of Article 33 of the Constitution.

7.3.1.4 The exercise of the power of preventive detention by the martial law regime and the release of detainees by the government of Zia

After the imposition of martial law, Khandaker Moshtaque Ahmed, who had assumed the office of the President, in an address to the nation on 3 October 1975 announced the regime's decision to release the detainees who had been detained by the previous regime. He stressed that in order to facilitate the creation of a congenial political environment, the extraordinary powers concerning preventive detention would not be used to persecute individuals holding political beliefs contrary to that of the government. Furthermore, he announced the formation of a review board consisting of three former judges of the Supreme Court of Bangladesh to examine charges brought against political detainees (Bari, 2015). If the review board found the charges brought against a detainee to be unfounded then such a detainee would be released.

In the same vein, Justice A. M. Sayem, within one day of succeeding Khandaker Moshtaque Ahmed as the President of Bangladesh, on 7 November 1975 announced that the detainees who had been kept in preventive custody for political reasons would be released immediately.

However, despite these commitments from the two Presidents, the martial law regime used the power of preventive detention as a tool for political oppression to strengthen its grip on power. For instance, on 25 November 1975, the regime detained 19 political leaders. Out of the 1498 individuals who were preventively detained in 1976 under the *Special Powers Act*, 1974, and *Emergency Powers Rules*, 1975, several were politicians and former members of the Parliament. In 1977, another 1057 persons were taken into preventive custody – of whom 17 were activists belonging to the left-wing East Pakistan Communist Party (Bari, 2015).

The ascension of General Zia to the office of the Chief Martial Law Administrator on 30 November 1976 and subsequently to the office of the President on 21 April 1977 finally marked the beginning of a change in attitude towards the exercise of the power of preventive detention for political purposes. For, in the first place, the regime of General Zia, as pointed out earlier in 7.3.1.3, inserted the constitutional safeguards concerning preventive detention into the *Emergency Powers Rules*, 1975. Second, on 30 November 1978, it was claimed by his regime that it had released as many as 10,135 persons who had been kept in preventive custody since the declaration of emergency on 28 December 1974 (Bari, 2015). This was followed by the release of another 621 detainees in two steps – 249 detainees were released in December 1978 and 372 were freed in January 1979. In addition to these detainees released by the martial law regime on its own initiative, another 178 detainees were released by the regime in pursuance of the directions of the High Court Division of the Supreme Court of Bangladesh. Thus the total number of detainees released from preventive custody stood at 10,934. However, despite the release of so many individuals from preventive custody and the absence of an emergency threatening the life of the nation, a substantial number of detainees including political detainees continued to be kept in preventive custody. The Home Minister told the Parliament on 26 May 1979 that a total number of 339 detainees – 338 under the *Emergency Powers Rules*, 1975 and one under the Special Powers Act, 1974 – were kept in preventive custody (Bari, 2015).

7.3.1.5 Judicial approach towards the challenge of the exercise of the power of preventive detention during the emergency

It is evident from the discussion above in 7.3.1.2 and 7.3.1.4 that during the continuation of the emergency, a cavalier attitude was adopted by the successive governments – the Awami League Government and the martial law regime – towards the liberty of individuals in detaining an enormous number of individuals during the continuation of the emergency. However, on many occasions, the Supreme Court of Bangladesh protected the detainee by adopting an objective test. The origin of this approach can be traced back to the non-emergency case of *Aruna Sen v Government of Bangladesh [1974] 3 CLC (HCD) 1*, where the High Court Division (HCD) in line with relevant decisions in India and Pakistan[6] held that:

> [T]he well settled principle of law endorsed by a long line of judicial authorities [is that] … any person charged with the authority of taking

> decisions affecting the rights and liberties of the citizens of the State has the corresponding duty of acting judicially and the superior courts having supervisory jurisdiction over such person have the power to see whether the said person conformed to the judicial norms applicable to the case. Apart from the aforesaid general principle, the constitutional obligation imposed upon the High Court Division under Article 102(2) of the Constitution ... is clearly to make an objective assessment of the materials on which the necessary satisfaction of the detaining authority had been based and to be satisfied that an average prudent man could reasonably be so satisfied.
>
> (28)

However, unlike the Indian Supreme Court and Pakistan Supreme Court (see Sections 3.9.2.1.4.4 and 3.9.2.2.5.2), the Supreme Court of Bangladesh did not confine the application of the objective test to peacetime only. Rather by extending the operation of this test, during the continuation of the emergency of 1974, it issued release orders in respect of many of the detainees in consequence of writ petitions challenging their orders of detention. An endeavour will now be made to discuss some of these cases, where the courts set aside the orders of detention due to:

a) vagueness of the grounds of detention;
b) non-existence of the grounds of detention; and
d) detention persecuting political views.

7.3.1.5.1 SETTING ASIDE OF DETENTION ORDERS DUE TO VAGUENESS OF THE GROUNDS

In *Amresh Chandra Chakrabarty v Bangladesh and Others [1979] 31 DLR (AD) 240*, the issue before the Court was that the order of detention served on the detainee did not specify the prejudicial act which the detainee might have committed if he were to remain at large. Instead, it merely made reference to the prejudicial acts contained in Rules 2(e) and 5(1) of the *Emergency Powers Rules*, 1975. The Government in its affidavit-in-opposition stated that: a) the detainee due to his association with the Awami League, which governed Bangladesh prior to the imposition of Martial Law on 15 August 1975, obtained a licence for a dealership in government rations in the city of Khulna, and b) the detainee became a visa agent of the Indian High Commission in Dhaka and thus had close association with the High Commission. These associations of the detainee were construed by the Government as prejudicial activities. The Court found that the detention order was passed without proper application of mind, which is evident from the fact that the detaining authority did not definitively mention the grounds of detention, mere affiliation with the Indian High Commission for monetary gains being construed as a prejudicial activity.

In delivering the judgment of the Appellate Division (AD) of the Supreme Court, setting aside the order of detention, Chief Justice Kemaluddin Hossain observed that:

> The [detention] order merely refers to Rule 2(e) of the Emergency Powers Rules and then invokes the power under Rule 5(1)(a) in passing the order of detention against the detenu. It is to be noticed that Rule 2(e) defined prejudicial acts wherein there are included sixteen different species of activities which come within a generic expression 'prejudicial act', but Rule 5(1) includes only some of the activities which could be a ground for passing the detention order. Unfortunately in this particular case excepting making a casual and careless reference to the numbers of two clauses nothing has been mentioned in the detention order which could at all be said to be an order passed under Rule 5(1) of the Emergency Powers Rules ... no ground whatsoever has been mentioned excepting repeating the number of two clauses and on this ground alone apart from anything else the order of detention must be struck down as invalid as the very manner of articulation shows a total lack of application of the mind of the detaining authority. It is declared that the order of detention is without lawful authority and the detenu is being held in unlawful custody. It is directed that the detenu be released forthwith.
>
> (241)

In the case of *Md Faruque Reza v Government of Bangladesh and Others [1977] 29 DLR (HCD) 4*, the order of detention was passed with a view to preventing the detainee from committing a prejudicial act under Rules 2(e)[7] and 5(1) of the *Emergency Powers Rules*, 1975. Justice M. H. Rahman of the HCD pointed out that the reference to Rule 2(e) in the detention order demonstrated that it was passed without any due process of thought and consideration since Rule 2(e) did not confer any power on the Government to pass an order of detention. Rather the power of the Government to pass detention orders, as pointed out earlier in Section 7.3.1, was 'strictly limited' to the prevention of the prejudicial acts as contained in Rule 5(1) of the Emergency Power Rules, 1975 (5–6). Thus the order of detention was set aside by the Court.

In *Saleha Begum v the Government of Bangladesh [1977] 29 DLR (HCD) 59*, it was alleged by the Government in its affidavit-in-opposition that on 26 June 1976 – a day prior to the detention of the petitioner – some miscreants with prejudicial printed materials were arrested at the residence of the petitioner in his absence. It was further claimed by the Government that the arrested persons were underground armed cadres of the leftist *Jatiya Samajtantrick Dal* (JSD) and as such '[the detainee's] house was a den of miscreants'. The advocate for the detainee argued before the Court that 'the order of detention is vague, indefinite and ... it does not indicate that the order was passed on proper application of mind and on satisfaction as contemplated under Rule 5(1)(a) of the *Emergency Powers Rules*, 1975'. It was further argued by him that the alleged miscreants, who were local boys and neighbours of the detainee, were merely watching a boxing match on television in the out-house of the detainee when police surrounded the house and arrested them for possession of prejudicial materials. Furthermore, most of these boys were subsequently released. Thus, the circumstances of the arrest of these persons from the residence of the detainee could not be said to be tantamount to giving shelter to them, as had been claimed by the Government. Justice Ruhul Islam of the HCD in accepting the contentions of the advocate observed:

> From the order of detention it appears that the Additional District Magistrate passed the order merely at the instance of the police report, because, excepting the police report no other materials were placed before him. If the grounds as mentioned in the impugned order are considered vis-à-vis the police reports and the instances of prejudicial activities as enumerated in the affidavit in opposition, it becomes clear that the order of detention cannot be said to have been passed in conformity with the law. Even if it is accepted that the detenu entertained some young boys alleged to be the members of the so-called armed cadre of Jatiya Samajtantrick Dal with food etc., that by itself, in the absence of any specific activity ascribed to the detenu, is not sufficient to bring the case within the scope of 'prejudicial act' as enumerated in Rule 2(e) and as such he cannot be described as a 'miscreant' endangering the public security, far less, injuring the interest of the People's Republic of Bangladesh. Mere recovery even of some prejudicial printed materials from his house does not bring the case within the scope of Rule 5(1)(a) of the Emergency Powers Rules, 1975. Categorical statement made by the petitioner that the police rounded up some boys when they were enjoying the television show at night along with many others, has not been controverted in the affidavit in opposition does not justify the impugned action of treating the detenu as a miscreant ... In our opinion the extra-ordinary power of preventive detention provided under Rule 5(1)(a) was not properly exercised by the detaining authority, and as such detention ... [of the detenu] is wholly illegal and without lawful authority.
>
> (61–62)

It is evident from the above decisions that the vagueness of the grounds of detention led the Supreme Court to set aside the detention orders. Such vagueness denies the detainee the right to make a meaningful representation against the detention order. As the HCD observed in *Humayun Kabir v State [1976] 28 DLR (HCD) 259*:

> the fundamental rights of the citizen cannot be defeated or reduced to meaninglessness or purposelessness, by communicating some grounds vague, indefinite and non sufficient to afford to the detainee any reasonable opportunity of making any effective representation against his detention order.
>
> (276)

7.3.1.5.2 SETTING ASIDE OF DETENTION ORDERS BY THE SUPREME COURT DUE TO NON-EXISTENCE OF THE GROUNDS OF DETENTION

In *Abdul Latif Mirza v Bangladesh [1979] 31 DLR (AD) 1*, the detainee was an activist of the JSD, a political party whose principal objective was to overthrow the Awami League Government, which, as noted earlier, was in power prior to the imposition of Martial Law on 15 August 1975. It was alleged that the detainee had committed prejudicial activities at various places in order to implement the political agenda of the JSD. However, the detention order made no attempt to detail the nature of these activities. Furthermore, although the Awami League Government was ousted from power by the *coup d'état* of 15 August 1975, the detainee continued to be kept in preventive custody by the martial law regime without the realisation that the removal of the Awami League from power rendered the grounds for keeping him in preventive custody non-existent. As Chief Justice Kemaluddin Hossain in declaring the order of detention unlawful observed:

> the principal ground [of detention] was that the detenu belonged to a political party whose object was to overthrow the government established by law. This was in 1974 when the composition of the government was different. The then government has been overthrown and a new government installed. There have been some changes in the Constitution as well. Judicial notice of these facts can be taken. The detenu, we find, is in continuous detention from 22 April 1974 till today [that is till 2 September 1977, the day of the delivery of the judgment by the court] and this change has taken place during the period of his continued detention. The moot question is, whether the basis of the ground that was existent in 1974, is still existing … The ground clearly stated that the aim of the party was directed against the political government of the day, but it has now been overthrown … The main basis of the grounds of detention has, in the present context of facts, become non-existent, and therefore the principal ground has lost its cogency and has become irrelevant. It is to be remembered that this ground was the foundation of all other grounds, and the rest are but superstructures. The foundation having gone, the superstructures must collapse.
>
> (11–12)

7.3.1.5.3 SETTING ASIDE OF DETENTION ORDERS PERSECUTING POLITICAL BELIEFS

The HCD during the continuation of the emergency also invalidated detention orders passed for victimising individuals for expressing their political views. For instance, in *Md Anwar Hussain v State [1977] 29 DLR (HCD) 15*, the HCD had to examine the lawfulness of the detention of someone who had been preventively detained under the SPA for alleging that the regime of Mujib could not live up to promises it had made prior to the election. The HCD held that 'an accusation that the ruling party had failed to fulfil its election commitment' could not be considered a 'prejudicial act' that could warrant the exercise of the power of preventive detention under the SPA (19).

7.3.1.5.4 UNWILLINGNESS OF THE DETAINING AUTHORITY TO COMPLY WITH THE DIRECTIONS OF THE HCD

In some cases, political detainees who were released in accordance with the orders of the HCD were re-arrested immediately at the prison gate, usually for prevention of other offences under the *Emergency Powers Rules*. However, the HCD on many occasions took into account the Government's defiance of the directions of the Court and invalidated the continued detention of the individual on fabricated charges. In this context, an evaluation of the case of *Shamsun Nahar Begum v Bangladesh [1978] 30 DLR (HCD) 33* is relevant. Mrs Shamsun Nahar's brother Mr Khaliquzzaman, who was the President of a branch of the JCD, was arrested by the Awami League regime on 18 March 1974. Subsequently, on 27 March 1974, a preventive detention order was served on him under the SPA for preventing him from committing any act prejudicial to the security of the state, public safety and maintenance of law and order. In pursuance of a writ petition challenging the detention order, the HCD on 20 January 1977 found Mr Kaliquzzaman's detention to be illegal.[8] In accordance with the order of the HCD, the detainee was released from Dhaka Central Jail on 28 January 1977. However, a fresh detention order was served on him at the prison gate and he was taken back to custody under Rule 30(1) of the *Emergency Powers Rules*, which empowered an Additional Magistrate to detain an individual for a period of 15 days. The new detention order, in the same manner as the previous detention order under the SPA, contended that Mr Khaliquzzaman was 'acting' in a manner which was prejudicial to security or interest of Bangladesh, and to the public safety and the maintenance of law and order. Although Rule 30(1) of the *Emergency Powers Rules* empowered the Additional Magistrate to detain an individual for a maximum of 15 days, Mr Khaliquzzaman was kept in preventive custody for nearly two and a half months from 28 January to 10 April 1977.

It is evident that the detention order served on the detainee on 28 January

1977 was a clear example of an arbitrary and *mala fide* exercise of the power of preventive detention. For Mr Khaliquzzaman was never set free and the question of him 'acting' in a manner prejudicial to the interest of the state, as claimed in the detention order, did not arise at all. Justice Badrul Haider Chowdhury in delivering the judgment of the Court observed:

> The argument ... that when this impugned order was passed the detenu was a free man is not tenable because the whole affair was idle ceremony. While the court said his detention is illegal [in pursuance of the Writ Petition No. 1493/74] the Government obeyed so by bringing him up to the jail gate; then allowing the detenu to have a glimpse of outside world promptly another order was served and this was under Emergency Powers Act [*sic*]. How it can be said that when the order of detention was served he was a free man? To say the least, it is mere words and since the words only mean to convey ideas, the least can be said is the detaining authority paid little regard to the declaration that was made by the court in Writ Petition No. 1493 of 1974 ... [T]o say that security or interest of Bangladesh or public safety and maintenance of law and order is being threatened by the action of a prisoner who is detained in jail is to bring the proposition to an absurdity and such proposition should not be allowed to be argued ... certainly the provisions of the Emergency Powers Act [*sic*] are not available to respondents for detaining such a person who is already in jail ... The opinion [of this Court] is that the detention of Khalequzzaman is illegal and without lawful authority. In the result ... it is directed that the respondents should set Khalequzzaman at liberty forthwith.
>
> (37–40)

The decisions of the Supreme Court show that during the continuance of the emergency, in some cases, the orders of detention were passed in a casual or cavalier manner without due process of thought and consideration. The grounds themselves were vague and in the most general terms. Thus the wide, frequent and arbitrary use of preventive detention in Bangladesh in the absence of an actual emergency showed the indifference and insensitivity of the Awami League regime and the subsequent martial law regime to the serious encroachment on the personal liberty of the individual. In this context, the observations of Justice Badrul Haider Chowdhury in *Shamsun Nahar Begum v Bangladesh [1978] 30 DLR (HCD) 33* are worthy of quote. As he observed:

> Liberty of a citizen ... can only be circumscribed by arriving at a decision that it is so necessary to preventing him from acting prejudicially. The degree of consideration, the degree of care, the degree of duty that is cast on the respondents is of highest order and slightest deviation from such care, from such consideration, from such duty will render the act as

> not a good one ... We conclude by saying that the respondents have displayed utter carelessness and deviated from their duties and the degree of carelessness renders the action as colourable exercise of power. (40)

7.3.2 Enactment of preventive detention law and its exercise during the second proclamation of emergency (1981)

An emergency was proclaimed in Bangladesh for the second time on 30 May 1981, following the assassination of President Zia (see Section 5.3). The *Emergency Powers Rules*, which were enacted in pursuance of Section 2 of the *Emergency Powers Ordinance*, 1981, contained similar provisions to its 1975 predecessor concerning the power of preventive detention. However, unlike the emergency regime of Mujib, the emergency regime of 1981 did not exercise the power of preventive detention as a means for victimising its political adversaries. Furthermore, unlike the continuation of the emergency measures for five years during the first emergency, the limitations imposed on the liberty of individuals by the power of preventive detention under the *Emergency Powers Rules*, 1981, were short-lived. They were revoked after 111 days on 21 September 1981.

7.3.3 Enactment of preventive detention law and its exercise during the third proclamation of emergency (1987)

On 27 November 1987, an emergency was declared in Bangladesh for the third time on the ground of internal disturbance to deal with the threat posed to the life of the regime of Ershad from opposition political parties (see Section 5.4). This was followed by the promulgation of the *Emergency Powers Ordinance*, 1987, which in Section 7(1)(a) replaced the original Section 2(f) of the SPA, which provided for a list of prejudicial acts that could warrant the exercise of the power of preventive detention (see Section 7.2.1), with a new section that was to remain in force for the duration of the emergency. The new Section 2(f) significantly enlarged the list of prejudicial acts. The following vague prejudicial acts were inserted in addition to the prejudicial acts already contained in the original Section 2(f):

> a) acts which cause disaffection among, or prejudice, prevent or interfere with the discipline of, or the performance of duties by, members of the armed forces or public servants;
> b) acts which induce any member of such forces or any public servant to fail in the performance of his duties as such;
> c) acts which cause fear or alarm to the public or to any section of the public;
> d) acts which impede, delay or restrict the means of transport or locomotion or the supply or distribution of any essential commodity;

e) acts which cause, or instigate or incite, directly or indirectly, the cessation of work by a body of persons employed in any undertaking or establishment, except in furtherance of an industrial dispute as defined in the Industrial Relations Ordinance, 1969 (XXIII of 1969), with which such body of persons is directly concerned;
(f) acts which encourage or incite any person or class of persons, or the public generally, to refuse or defer payment of any tax, rate, cess or other dues or amount payable to the Government or to any local authority;
(g) acts which instigate, directly or indirectly, the use of criminal force against public servants generally or any class of public servants or any individual public servant.

Sections 9, 10, 11 and 12 of the SPA, which as noted earlier in Section 7.2.1, provide for the constitution and functions of the Advisory Board, were also omitted by the *Emergency Powers Ordinance* for the duration of the emergency (s 7(1)(c)). Thus, the *Emergency Powers Ordinance* not only extended the ambit of the exercise of the power of preventive detention but also empowered the government to exercise such power for keeping an individual in preventive custody under the SPA indefinitely, without any requirement for the detention to be examined by a quasi-judicial body. Consequently, the autocratic regime of Ershad used the sweeping powers of preventive detention to detain opposition political and student leaders in order to ensure its survival in power. As many as 2465 persons were preventively detained during the continuation of the emergency (Bureau of Democracy, Human Rights and Labour, 1987). Begum Khaleda Zia and Sheikh Hasina – the leaders of the two major opposition parties, BNP and BAL – were among those who were kept in preventive custody.

Since the life of the emergency was not extended by the Parliament, the emergency became inoperative after 120 days, which in turn resulted in the original provisions of the SPA being reinstated.

7.3.4 Enactment of preventive detention law and its exercise during the fourth proclamation of emergency (1990)

In order to put down the popular uprising against the regime of Ershad, an emergency on the ground of internal disturbance was once again declared on 27 November 1990 (see Section 5.5). The proclamation of emergency was followed by the issuance of the Emergency Powers Ordinance on the same day. The *Emergency Powers Ordinance*, 1990, was a complete reproduction of its predecessor – the *Emergency Powers Ordinance*, 1987. It also replaced Section 2(f) of the SPA with one that significantly enlarged the list of prejudicial acts and deleted the requirement under the SPA for the composition of a quasi-judicial body – the Advisory Board – for reviewing detention orders (s 7(1)(a) and (c)). However, these powers did not yield the desired result for Ershad, as in the face of opposition from people of all walks of life, he was forced to relinquish power on 6 December 1990. The Emergency was withdrawn on the same day.

It is ironical that the SPA, which was resorted to by Ershad as the tool for keeping the critics of his regime in preventive custody, was used by the interim Government of Chief Justice Shahabuddin on 12 December 1990 to preventively detain Ershad and prominent members of his former regime (Bureau of Democracy, Human Rights and Labour, 1990).

7.3.5 Enactment of preventive detention law and its exercise during the fifth proclamation of emergency (2007–2008)

An emergency was invoked on the ground of internal disturbance for the fifth time in Bangladesh on 11 January 2007 following the political unrest surrounding the composition of the interim 'Care-taker' Government, and in particular its head (see Sections 5.6 and 5.6.1). Although the political unrest came to an end with the installation of a new 'Care-taker' regime on 12 January 2007, the emergency was nevertheless continued and furthermore the regime, in pursuance of Section 3(1) of the *Emergency Powers Ordinance*, framed the *Emergency Powers Rules* on 25 January 2007.

The *Emergency Powers Rules*, 2007 did not confine the exercise of the power of preventive detention only to prejudicial acts as defined in the SPA. Rather it extended the ambit of the exercise of the power of preventive detention under the SPA to prevent the commission of any of the offences under the *Emergency Powers Rules*,[9] e.g. organising demonstrations and assemblies (r 3), convening *hartal*, strike and lockout (r 4), publication of politically motivated and provocative news (rs 5 and 6), income tax, corruption and money laundering offences (r 15), hoarding, black-marketing, smuggling and sabotage (r 14). It appears difficult to justify incorporating more draconian provisions into the *Emergency Powers Rules* concerning preventive detention when the powers available to the Government under the SPA were sufficient to meet the exigencies of the situation. Furthermore, Rule 19E of the *Emergency Powers Rules* deprived a detainee of the right to seek any remedy from the courts during the continuance of the emergency.

Subsequently, these wide powers concerning preventive detention were used to stage an unparalleled crackdown on senior political leaders belonging to both the major political parties, the BNP and BAL. At least 929 senior politicians were kept in preventive custody, which included former Prime Ministers Begum Khaleda Zia and Sheikh Hasina (Odhikar, 2008). The preventive detention of senior political figures once again exposed the political ambition of the military-backed 'Care-taker' regime to perpetuate its rule in contravention of the constitutional requirement of holding general elections within 90 days of its formation. Furthermore, the exercise of the power of preventive detention by the regime was not only confined to the victimisation of political leaders. Innocent civilians were also brought within the purview of this power often without any criteria or basis for detention. A staggering 230,074 persons were preventively detained during the continuation of the emergency (Asian Forum for Human Rights Development, 2007; Ain o Salish Kendro (ASK), 2008). The government of the day failed to realise that frequent use or misuse of the power of preventive detention makes a mockery of the liberty of the individual in a democratic state.

7.3.5.1 Judicial response to the exercise of the power of preventive detention during the emergency of 2007

From the very outset of the declaration of emergency, the HCD in line with its earlier tradition of acting in a proactive manner during an emergency issued release orders in respect of a number of detainees under Article 102(2)(b)(i) of the Constitution, which empowers the HCD to offer efficacious remedy to individuals if it is satisfied that they are held in custody unlawfully or arbitrarily (see Section 7.2.1). For instance, within 45 days of the invocation of the emergency, the HCD declared former Awami League MP Kamal Majumder's preventive detention order under the SPA unlawful.[10] It rejected the argument of the Attorney General, who is the highest law officer of the Republic, that the *Emergency Powers Rules*, 2007, in Rule 19E curtailed the jurisdiction of the HCD to grant relief to petitioners. The HCD forcefully held that its inherent constitutional power to offer effective remedy could not be curtailed by an ordinary law even during the continuance of a state of emergency.

Furthermore, the HCD released a number of detainees on bail pending decisions on the legality of their detention orders. However, these detainees were often re-arrested immediately at the prison gate and subsequently fresh detention orders were served on them under the *Emergency Powers Rules*. One of the victims was Abdul Qayum Khan, an activist of the BNP and an elected Commissioner of the Dhaka City Corporation, who had been kept in preventive custody since 12 January 2007. The HCD granted him bail pending a decision on the legality of his detention order. Consequently, he was released on 10 January 2008 only to be re-arrested by the police at the gate of the prison. He was placed in preventive custody for another month but he died in jail due to the inadequacy of proper medical treatment for the 'serious illness he had suffered during his prolonged detention in the unhygienic conditions of the prison' (Asian Legal Resource Centre, 2008).

It should be stressed here that the AD of the Supreme Court adopted a highly deferential attitude towards the executive and overturned almost all the orders of the HCD directing the release of detainees from preventive custody.[11] It did so relying on Section 491(3) of the *Code of Criminal Procedure* (CrPc), 1898, which precludes the authority of the HCD to issue directions of the nature of a habeas corpus 'to persons detained under any law for the time being in force providing for preventive detention'.

It can be argued that the AD overlooked the fact that the authority of the HCD to test the legitimacy of an order of preventive detention exists notwithstanding the ouster clauses contained in the CrPC and the *Emergency Powers Rules*. For the supreme law of the Country – the *Constitution of Bangladesh* – unambiguously authorises the HCD to issue an order releasing a detainee when such detention is illegal and without lawful authority. Furthermore, the decisions of the AD are at odds with its own decision, as discussed in Section 7.2.1, delivered in *Abdul Latif Mirza v. Bangladesh [1979] 31 DLR (AD) 1*, where it held that the HCD in pursuance of Article 102(2)(b)(i) of the Constitution has the authority to set aside *mala fide* detention orders even where an ouster clause is contained in a statute (9).

However, notwithstanding the deferential attitude of the AD, the HCD continued to issue release orders concerning individuals kept in preventive custody in exercise of its constitutional power. The uncompromising attitude of the HCD caused considerable annoyance to the military-backed 'Care-taker' regime, and it subsequently persuaded the Chief Justice to reconstitute the benches of the HCD with a view to precluding the proactive judges from hearing challenges to preventive detention orders ('HC Bench of Justice Nayeem, Shahidul Stripped of Writ Powers' 2008).

It is evident from a perusal of the above-mentioned decisions that while the HCD in line with its earlier tradition afforded effective legal protection to individuals against unlawful deprivation of their liberty, the AD in paying undue deference gave the military-backed 'Care-taker' regime unfettered power in the exercise of emergency and preventive detention measures at the expense of the liberty of individuals.

7.4 References

Ain o Salish Kendro (ASK) (2008) *Human Rights in Bangladesh, 2007*, 36.

Amnesty International (1975) *Amnesty International Annual Report 1974/1975*, 84.

Asian Forum for Human Rights Development (2007) 'Bangladesh: Stop Using Preventive Detention', *Press Release*, 27 June, 1.

Asian Legal Resource Centre (2008) 'Bangladesh: The Prolonged State of Emergency is Resulting in Widespread Violations of Human Rights, A Written Statement Submitted to the 7th Session of the Human Rights Council', Hong Kong: Asian Legal Resource Centre (Working Paper No ALRC-CWS-07-001-2008).

Bari, M. E. (2015) 'Suspension of the Fundamental Rights and the Unrestrained Exercise of the Power of Preventive Detention during the Successive Proclamations of Emergency in Bangladesh: A Legal Study', Doctoral Thesis, Macquarie University, Sydney, 354–356.

Bureau of Democracy, Human Rights and Labour, US Department of State (1987) *Annual Human Rights Report: Bangladesh*, 1114, 1117.

Bureau of Democracy, Human Rights and Labour, US Department of State (1990) *Annual Human Rights Report: Bangladesh*, 1387, 1390.

'Detention of ex-MP Kamal Majumder declared illegal' (2007) *The Daily Star*, 27 February, 1.

Haque, Z. (2010) 'Special Power Act: People or Regime Security', Dhaka: Centre for Alternatives, 2.

'HC Bench of Justice Nayeem, Shahidul Stripped of Writ Powers' (2008) *The Daily Star*, 18 March, 1.

Odhikar (2008) *13 Months of Emergency in Bangladesh: Immediately Lift the State of Emergency*, 3.

Notes

* A significantly edited and truncated version of this chapter has been accepted for publication in the *Oxford University Commonwealth Law Journal* on 7 November 2016. For details, see M. E. Bari (2017) 'Preventive Detention Laws in Bangladesh and Their Increased Use during Emergencies: A Proposal for Reform', *Oxford University Commonwealth Law Journal*, 17(1), available at http://dx.doi.org/10.1080/14729342.2017.1306943.

1 *Constitution (Second Amendment) Act 1973*, Act No. XXIV, s 3.

2 In the 1970s and 1980s, the judges in Bangladesh popularly used the word 'detenu' instead of detainee.

3 SPA s 9(2) and (3).

4 See Zakia Haque, *Special Power Act: People or Regime Security* (Centre for Alternatives, 2010) 2.

5 *Defence of Pakistan Rules*, 1965, in rule 32(4) provided: 'A person who is ordered to be detained under this rule shall be detained in such place and under such conditions as to maintenance, discipline and punishment for breaches of discipline, as the Central Government may from time to time determine.'

6 The HCD in particular referred to the decisions of the Indian Supreme Court in the cases of *Pushkur Mukharjee v State of West Bengal* [[1970] AIR (SC) 157] and *State of Bombay v Atmaram Shridhar Vaidy* [[1951] AIR (SC) 157], and the Pakistan Supreme Court in the cases of *Ghulam Jilani v Government of West Pakistan* [[1967] 19 DLR (SC) 403], *Baqi Baluch v Government of Pakistan* [[1968] PLD (SC) 313] and *Government of West Pakistan v Begum Abdul Karim* [[1969] 21 DLR (SC) 1].

7 *Emergency Powers Rules 1975* in Rule 2(e) merely provided an exhaustive definition of what constitutes a 'prejudicial act' without vesting the detaining authority with any power to pass an order of detention. Rule 2(e) stated:

> "prejudicial act" means any act which is intended or is likely –
> i. to prejudice the sovereignty or defence of Bangladesh;
> ii. to prejudice Bangladesh's relation with any foreign power;
> iii. to prejudice the security or the public safety or interest of Bangladesh;
> iv. to interfere with or encourage or incite interference with the administration of law or the maintenance of law and order;
> v. to cause disaffection among, or to prejudice, prevent or interfere with the discipline of, or the performance of duties by, members of the Armed Forces or public servants;
> vi. to render any member of the Armed Forces or any public servant incapable of efficiently performing his duties as such, or to induce any member of such Forces or any public servant to fail in the performance of his duties as such;
> vii. to bring into hatred or contempt, or to excite disaffection towards, the Government established by law in Bangladesh;
> viii. to promote feelings of enmity or hatred between different communities, classes or section of people;

ix. to cause fear or alarm to the public or to any section of the public;
x. to impede, delay or restrict the means of transport or locomotion or the supply or distribution of any essential commodity;
xi. to prejudice the maintenance of supplies and services essential to the life of the community;
xii. to prejudice the economic or financial interest of the State;
xiii. to cause, or to instigate or incite, directly or indirectly, the cessation of work by a body of persons employed in any undertaking or establishment, except in furtherance of an industrial dispute as defined in the Industrial Relations Ordinance, 1969 (XXIII of 1969), with which such body of persons is directly concerned;
xiv. to undermine public confidence in the national credit or in any Government loan or security or in any notes, coins or token which are legal tender in Bangladesh, or to prejudice the success of any financial or economic measures taken or arrangements made by the Government for the purpose or protecting the economic life of Bangladesh;
xv. to encourage or incite any person or class of persons, or the public generally, to refuse or defer payment of any land revenue, tax, rate, cess or other dues or amount payable to the Government or to any local authority;
xvi. to instigate, directly or indirectly, the use of criminal force against public servants generally or any class of public servants or any individual public servants.

8 [1974] Writ Petition No 1493 [HCD].
9 *Emergency Powers Rules 2007* Rule 21.
10 Unreported case; see 'Detention of ex-MP Kamal Majumder declared illegal', *The Daily Star*, 27 February 2007, 1.
11 Within two months and 16 days of the invocation of the emergency, the Appellate Division stayed 27 orders of the HCD directing the release of detainees from preventive custody. A further 113 writ petitions were overturned by the Appellate Division by the end of 2008.

8 Conclusion

8.1 Introduction

The objective of this chapter is to summarise the key arguments of the preceding seven chapters of this book with a view to shedding light on the weaknesses of the provisions governing the proclamation, administration and termination of a state of emergency and the exercise of the power of preventive detention in Bangladesh. Subsequently, on the basis of these findings, recommendations will be put forward for introducing changes in the constitutional provisions governing the exercise of the powers concerning emergency, suspension of fundamental rights and preventive detention in Bangladesh. A constitutionally entrenched framework providing for effective restraints on the exercise of these powers would prevent the possibility of their abuse and thereby ensure the survival of constitutional government by preventing its lapse into arbitrary dictatorship.

8.2 The quest for a satisfactory model of emergency powers

The reasons for incorporating provisions concerning the proclamation of emergency, suspension of fundamental rights and the exercise of the power of preventive detention into a constitution are conservative. They are conservative in the sense that the emergency measures are to be exercised only to efficiently respond to the serious threats posed to the organised life of a nation with a view to restoring normalcy as soon as possible and not to impose any permanent changes on the legal order. Furthermore, since the exercise of emergency powers entails encroachment on the fundamental rights of individuals, a delicate balance must be maintained between protecting the interests of the State and preventing undue intrusion on the rights of individuals (Tushnet, 2005). However, practice demonstrates that the executive can often overstep the conservative contours of emergency powers, thereby upsetting this delicate balance (see Sections 2.5, 2.6.2.1.1, 2.6.2.1.2, 2.6.2.1.3, 2.6.3.3.1, 2.6.3.3.2, 2.6.3.3.3.4, and Sections 4.4.1 and 4.5).

The supposed inability of constitutional emergency provisions to successfully constrain the executive during emergency situations has led Oren Gross to articulate the 'Extra-Legal Measures Model' (ELM). This model is premised on the ideas that: a) emergency situations cannot be constitutionally conceptualised, and b) emergency-related statutes and precedents are often permitted to remain on the books beyond the termination of the emergency (Gross, 2003). Thus, Gross argues that the rule of law and the sanctity of the legal order can be best maintained if the executive is permitted to operate outside the legal framework to respond to emergency situations (see Section 4.2). Since, according to Gross (2008), no legal limits should be imposed on the executive for governing its actions during an emergency, it therefore follows that the executive should have the sole authority to determine: a) what constitutes an emergency, b) what extra-legal measures are required for containing the alleged emergency, and c) how long the extra-legal measures should continue. In the absence of any effective legal norms guiding and constraining the actions of the executive, it can be concluded that the ELM grants the executive absolute and unfettered power during an emergency, which in turn can contribute towards the institutionalisation of a permanent emergency and, as such, is inconsistent with Gross's claim of maintaining the rule of law (see Section 4.2).

David Dyzenhaus also has reservations about constitutionally entrenched emergency powers. However, his reasons are different from those of Gross. In Dyzenhaus's view, constitutional emergency provisions undermine a substantive conception of the rule of law as they allow judges to rely on these provisions in reviewing executive action during emergencies (Scheuerman, 2008). Instead, he contends that during emergency situations, judges can best uphold a substantive conception of the rule of law by relying on 'the values underpinning the common law' as these values provide them with the criteria for scrutinising executive action (Morss, 2009: 80–81). In articulating a court-centric account based on common law constitutionalism, it seems that Dyzenhaus may have overlooked the conservative tendencies of the common law system, which does not allow judges to keep pace with the ever expanding executive actions during emergency situations (see Section 4.3.1.1). It also seems that Dyznehaus, contrary to his claims, is in fact defending a narrow conception of the rule of law (see Section 4.3.1.1). For a substantive conception of the rule of law not only requires judges to scrutinise the actions of the executive but also requires such actions to be based on clear, specific and prospective legal norms (Scheuerman, 2008).

This book finds that it is the absence of effective constitutional safeguards governing emergency powers – a phenomenon prevalent in the constitutions of most nations, including the democratic ones – that provides the executive with significant leeway to blur the distinction between emergency and ordinary situations, and consequently to use and cling on to these powers for extraneous purposes at the expense of the fundamental rights of individuals. Furthermore, history demonstrates that the absence of detailed constitutional provisions governing the exercise of emergency powers dissuades the judiciary from 'energetic enquiry' into the necessity for the proclamation and continuation of an emergency (see Section 2.6.2.1.1, and Sections 4.3.1.1 and 4.3.1.1.1). Therefore, this book argues in line with the reasoning of democratic formalists, such as Bruce Ackerman and William Scheuerman, that a constitutionally entrenched emergency framework providing for detailed norms concerning the proclamation, administration and termination of an emergency offers the most viable solution to the problem of ensuring the observance of the rule of law and safeguarding the enjoyment of the core rights of individuals during emergencies. For such a constitutional framework enumerating effective mechanisms in turn provides the objective benchmarks for adjudicating whether the actions of the executive during an emergency are within the confines of these defined measures.

This book stresses that a standard constitutional model of emergency powers should contain provisions concerning:

a) the concrete circumstances which truly attain a certain degree of gravity and thereby merit a proclamation of emergency so that the executive is unable to obscure the demarcation between ordinary and emergency situations (see Section 4.4.1);
b) the name of the authority to proclaim and ratify a proclamation of emergency (see Section 4.4.2);
c) the mechanisms, such as the strong version of the 'supermajoritarian escalator' and a maximum time limit on the continuation of an emergency, for ensuring the efficient scrutiny of an emergency and its timely termination respectively (see Sections 4.4.3.1.1, 4.4.3.1.2 and 4.4.3.2);
d) the principles of non-derogation and proportionality for reducing unwarranted restrictions on the rights of individuals (see Section 4.4.4); and
e) the safeguards for obviating the possibility of abuse of the powers concerning preventive detention and also ensuring the humane treatment of those kept in preventive custody (see Section 4.4.5).

8.3 Does Bangladesh have an ideal constitutionally entrenched emergency model?

8.3.1 The invocation and continuation of emergency under the Constitution

The *Constitution of Bangladesh*, as amended on 22 September 1973, empowers the President to proclaim an emergency on the grounds of 'war or external aggression or internal disturbance' (art 141A(1)). The question of parliamentary endorsement of a proclamation of emergency arises only if the emergency is required to continue beyond 120 days (art 141A(2)(c)).

It can be argued that the *Constitution of Bangladesh* does not contain any reliable system of checks and balances to prevent the abuse of the power concerning resort to the extraordinary power of emergency and its subsequent continuation. For, in the first place, it uses the vague phrase 'internal disturbance' as one of the grounds for declaring emergency, which in turn contributes towards blurring the distinction between normalcy and emergency (see Sections 4.4.1 and 5.1). Second, it does not confine the executive authority to act unilaterally with regard to a state of emergency to the shortest possible time because it fails to stipulate that a proclamation of emergency should be subject to a prompt ratification by the Parliament. Third, the Constitution neither contains any efficient mechanisms subjecting a proclamation of emergency to periodic review by increasing supermajorities of the Parliament nor stipulates a time limit on the continuation of an emergency (see Section 5.1).

The weakness of the constitutionally entrenched framework has been reflected during the five proclamations of emergency – on 28 December 1974, 30 May 1981, 27 November 1987, 27 November 1990 and 11 January 2007. In each case, the emergency was declared on the ground of internal disturbance, not a single occasion on the ground of war or external aggression. The governments of the day have resorted to the emergency powers, except in 1981 when emergency was proclaimed immediately after the assassination of the Head of the State by a group of army officers, as the effective means to achieve their chief end of staying in power by repressing threats to the political regime, whether real or perceived. Furthermore, taking advantage of the absence of any reliable system of checks and balances for the effective scrutiny and timely termination of an emergency:

a) the emergency proclaimed on 28 December 1974, which co-existed with Martial Law during the period between 15 August 1975 and 6 April 1979, was continued for nearly five years until 26 November 1979, and
b) the emergency declared on 11 January 2007, during the regime of the Non-Party 'Care-taker' Government, was withdrawn on 17 December 2008 after nearly two years of continuation.

Following the termination of the last emergency, the newly elected Government of the BAL used its overwhelming majority in the Parliament to get the *Constitution (Fifteenth Amendment) Act* passed on 3 July 2011. However, contrary to expectations, the said amendment did not incorporate any meaningful safeguards into the Constitution for addressing the problems concerning the proclamation of emergency and its subsequent continuation.

8.3.2 *The power to suspend the enforcement of the fundamental rights during emergencies under the* Constitution of Bangladesh

Unlike the Constitutions of India and Pakistan, the framers of the *Constitution of Bangladesh* did not originally contemplate any circumstances that could warrant the suspension of any of the 18 fundamental rights guaranteed by the Constitution. However, the *Constitution (Second Amendment) Act*, 1973, which inserted provisions concerning emergency into the Constitution, also affords the executive the unlimited power of suspending the enforcement of all or any of the 18 fundamental rights during an emergency (see Section 6.2). Thus it is evident that the Constitution, as amended in 1973, disregards the necessity for maintaining an appropriate balance between protecting national interests and safeguarding core fundamental rights during a state of emergency.

Consequently, the proclamations of emergency in Bangladesh on five occasions have witnessed suspension of the fundamental rights on a fairly large scale – 12 out of 18 fundamental rights – during the first four periods of emergency and on a full scale (suspension of all the 18 fundamental rights) during the last period of emergency (see Sections 6.2.1, 6.2.2, 6.2.3, 6.2.4 and 6.2.5). The suspension of the enforcement of these rights has also been followed by the violation of the core rights of individuals, such as the right to life and right not to be subjected to torture and cruel or inhuman or degrading treatment (see Sections 6.2.5.1 and 6.2.5.3).

Despite the lacuna in the Constitution, which facilitates the arbitrary deprivation of the fundamental rights of individuals during emergency situations, and the country's accession to the *International Covenant on Civil and Political Rights* (ICCPR) in 2000, the principles of non-derogation and proportionality have not been inserted in the Constitution.

8.3.3 *The power of preventive detention under the* Constitution of Bangladesh

Despite strong reservations about the exercise of the power of preventive detention during the days when Bangladesh was part of Pakistan, the *Constitution of Bangladesh* was amended on 22 September 1973 providing for an enabling clause empowering the Parliament to enact laws concerning preventive detention. Furthermore, in following in the footsteps of the Constitutions of India and Pakistan, the enabling clause concerning preventive detention has also been inserted in the chapter on fundamental rights of the *Constitution of Bangladesh*. Referring to the insertion of the provisions concerning the curtailment of fundamental rights in the same chapter which is supposed to guarantee the enjoyment of fundamental rights, one commentator noted that they were not fundamental rights, but 'fundamental dangers to the citizens' (Bannerji, 1991: 233).

The Constitution does not: a) confine the exercise of the power of preventive detention to formally declared periods of emergency, b) bar detention incommunicado, or c) stipulate a maximum time period for keeping an individual in preventive custody. Moreover, the limited safeguards afforded to detainees by the Constitution, e.g. the right of representation against the detention order and the review of the detention order by a quasi-judicial body – the Advisory Board – are not adequate for preventing arbitrary infringement of detainees' liberty (see Section 7.2). It is evident that the provisions concerning preventive detention as enshrined in the Constitution in essence require the surrender of the liberty of individuals at the discretion of the executive.

In the absence of adequate and effective constitutional safeguards mitigating the harshness of the laws concerning preventive detention, the permanent law – the *Special Powers Act* (SPA), 1974 – and temporary laws concerning preventive detention have in turn been exercised during formally declared periods of emergency in the most arbitrary manner to detain political adversaries of the government of the day (see Sections 7.3.1.2, 7.3.1.4, 7.3.3 and 7.3.5).

Judging by the constitutionally entrenched emergency framework articulated in Section 4.4 and briefly summarised above in Section 8.2, it can be concluded that the emergency framework as contained in the *Constitution of Bangladesh* is by no means ideal.

8.4 Recommendations: a constitutionally entrenched emergency model for Bangladesh providing for detailed norms

The discussion set out in the preceding chapters of the book and summarised above reveals that the emergency provisions contained in the *Constitution of Bangladesh* vest powers of remarkable scope and flexibility in the executive. Consequently, the repeated declarations of emergency in Bangladesh have become a threat to the rule of law and the enforcement of fundamental rights. The abuse of the powers concerning emergency has brought to the fore the need to incorporate the following reforms within the *Constitution of Bangladesh*, 1972, by means of an amendment:

a) Confining the power to proclaim emergency to clearly defined circumstances: Since all the five proclamations of emergency were made on the ground of 'internal disturbance', the ground of internal disturbance in Article 141A(1) of the Constitution should be replaced with 'armed rebellion', as has been done in the case of the Indian Constitution by the *Constitution (44th Amendment) Act*, 1978 (see Section 2.6.2). For, unlike the phrase 'internal disturbance', 'armed rebellion' carries a precise connotation (see Section 4.4.1).
b) Insertion of a reliable system of checks and balances for the effective

scrutiny of an emergency: The absence of a provision in the *Constitution of Bangladesh*, 1972, for ensuring the timely termination of an emergency has provided the executive with significant leeway to take steps towards the institutionalisation of the emergency at the expense of the fundamental rights of the citizens. It is, therefore, submitted that a reliable system of checks and balances should be incorporated within the *Constitution of Bangladesh*, 1972, so that an emergency does not continue beyond the circumstances which gave rise to it.

In particular, the strong version of the supermajoritarian escalator, as detailed in Section 4.3.1.2, should be incorporated in Article 141A(2) of the *Constitution of Bangladesh*. Thus, a proclamation of emergency under Article 141A(1) of the *Constitution of Bangladesh* should be placed before the Parliament for a prompt ratification within 14 days from such proclamation and thereafter be subjected to repeated renewals every two months, requiring each such renewal to be approved by a larger majority of parliamentarians – two-thirds (66.66 per cent) for the first two months and three-quarters (75 per cent) for the next two. Furthermore, a provision should be inserted in Article 141A(2) of the Constitution for ensuring the unhindered continuation of the Parliament during a state of emergency so that the executive cannot dissolve the Parliament in order to avoid the effective scrutiny of a proclamation of emergency through the device of supermajoritarian escalator.

c) Stipulation of a maximum time limit in the Constitution on the continuation of emergency: Regarding the question as to the fate of a proclamation of emergency after receiving the assent of three-quarters of the legislators for continuation beyond four months, the *Constitution of Bangladesh* in Article 141A(2) should prescribe the maximum period of emergency at six months. The sole purpose of inserting a maximum time limit on the continuation of an emergency is to prevent the lingering of these extraordinary powers for political purposes beyond the circumstances which gave rise to them. If, however, the exigencies of an actual emergency require the continuation of a proclamation of emergency for more than six months then in such a scenario, it remains open to the executive upon the termination of an emergency on the completion of six months to proclaim a fresh emergency.
d) Insertion of the principles of non-derogation and proportionality in the Constitution: The indiscriminate suspension of the enforcement of most or all of the fundamental rights guaranteed by the Constitution during the five emergencies proclaimed in Bangladesh, and the continuation of their suspension for prolonged periods, has exposed the tendency of succeeding generations of executive to merely pay lip service to the idea of liberties. Article 141C of the Bangladesh Constitution should, therefore, be amended to incorporate into it the principles of non-derogation and proportionality as enshrined in the ICCPR (to which Bangladesh

acceded in September 2000). The enumeration of non-derogable rights and the principle of proportionality in the *Constitution of Bangladesh*, complemented by the above safeguards, will ensure fewer human rights breaches during a state of emergency.

e) Incorporation of safeguards concerning preventive detention within the *Constitution of Bangladesh*: The declarations of emergency in Bangladesh have witnessed excessive and unjust use of preventive detention without regard to the adverse impact of the exercise of such power on the liberty of individuals. Hence a number of guarantees should be inserted in Article 33 of the Constitution in order to ensure that the exercise of this power does not result in the complete surrender of the freedom of individuals.

In the first place, Article 33 of the Bangladesh Constitution should confine the exercise of the extraordinary power of preventive detention to formally declared emergencies. Second, the vague phrase 'as soon as may be', contained in Article 33(4) as the time frame for communicating the grounds of detention to a detainee, should be replaced and a specific time period should be inserted to the effect that a detainee should be informed of the grounds of his detention within seven days of his/her detention. In this connection, it should also be stressed that the proviso to clause 5 of Article 33 ought to be omitted. For it grants broad discretion to the executive to withhold the grounds of detention for reasons of public interest, which essentially reduces the right of the detainee to make representations to a meaningless practice (see Section 7.2).

Third, neither clause 4 nor clause 5 of Article 33 of the Constitution allows a detainee to communicate with his lawyer and family members, which in turn carries the danger of facilitating torture of detainees, especially political detainees. Thus a provision barring detention incommunicado should be inserted in Article 33 to prevent such a prospect. Fourth, the period for which a person can be preventively detained without reference to an Advisory Board under Article 33(4) of the Constitution should be reduced from six months to a timeframe between 10[1] to 30 days.[2] Furthermore, the present inclusion of a civil servant in the Advisory Board, who might influence the proceedings to the detriment of the liberty of the detainee, should be done away with. Instead, the composition of the Advisory Board should be confined solely to persons who are or have been judges of the Supreme Court, as has been done in the *Constitution of Pakistan*, 1973 (see Section 3.9.2.2.3).

Fifth, an overall time limit of six months for keeping a person in preventive custody should be inserted in Article 33 of the Constitution so that a better balance is struck between the liberty of the citizen and the legitimate interest of the State.

Sixth and finally, since Bangladesh has ratified the ICCPR, the provision of providing for monetary compensation for the unlawful deprivation of the right of personal liberty as laid down in Article 9 of the ICCPR, should be incorporated into Article 33 of the *Constitution of Bangladesh*, especially in cases of gross abuse of the power of preventive detention. The provision for providing compensation would act as a check on the executive's tendency to arbitrarily detain an enormous number of individuals during emergency situations (see Section 4.4.5).

f) Incorporation of a provision concerning the inquiry into a state of emergency by a quasi-judicial commission after its termination: In addition to the above safeguards, the Constitution in Article 141A should also provide for the establishment of a quasi-judicial commission, headed by a retired Chief Justice, after the termination of a state of emergency to inquire into any blatant abuse of powers during the emergency. Such a provision would have the potential of acting as a check on the executive. For the executive will be mindful of the fact that any abuse of powers that might be perpetrated during the emergency would not be shrouded under a veil of secrecy for long. The usefulness of the formation of such a commission can be evidenced from the working of the Shah Commission, which was appointed by the Janata Party Government in 1978 to investigate the excesses that had been committed during the emergency rule of Mrs Indira Gandhi between 25 June 1975 and 21 March 1977 (Iyer, 2000). The Commission made public through an official report the gravity of the abuses that had been committed by the regime of Mrs. Gandhi under the guise of an emergency (see Section 4.4.3.3).

g) Maintenance of the rule of law by the judiciary during an emergency: The superior judiciary of Bangladesh, in particular the High Court Division (HCD), has shown greater willingness during emergency situations than its Indian and Pakistani counterparts to safeguard the liberty of individuals by setting aside preventive detention orders passed in a cavalier manner. The HCD has done so by relying on Article 102(2)(b)(i) of the Constitution, which in unambiguous terms empowers it to release a detainee from preventive custody if it is satisfied that he is being held in custody without lawful authority or in an unlawful manner, notwithstanding the ouster of its jurisdiction under the SPA or the *Emergency Powers Rules*. It follows that if the Constitution contains detailed provisions providing for the abovementioned checks and balances concerning the exercise of emergency powers, then the judges will have the means to hold the executive accountable for any breaches of the rule of law during the continuation of the emergency.

If the emergency model devised, stipulating legal limits on the power of the executive as to the proclamation, administration and termination of emergency, were to be incorporated into the *Constitution of Bangladesh*, then it would not only reduce the possibility of the abuse of the emergency powers but also ensure the maintenance of the rule of law and enjoyment of the core fundamental rights of individuals. In this context, the observations of Justice Michael Kirby (2004: 1) are worthy of quote:

> There is no doubt that nurturing good governance is essential to ensuring respect for human rights. Without the rule of law, independent courts and the other institutions of a modern society – essential components of good governance – the promise of human rights may remain just that: a promise unfulfilled. Enforcement of fundamental freedoms when it matters may be impossible. The lesson of history is that transparent, responsible, accountable and participatory governance is a prerequisite to enduring respect for human dignity and the defence of human rights.

It should be further pointed out here that unlike the constitutions of some of the democratic nations, such as the Constitutions of the USA[3] and Australia[4] – both of which provide for complex procedures to amend the Constitution – the *Constitution of Bangladesh* provides for a relatively simple procedure for amending its provisions. Article 142(1)(a) of the Constitution states that any proposed bill for amendment to the Constitution can be passed by the votes of 'two-thirds of the total number of members of the Parliament'. Thus, all that is required is for the politicians of the country to come to the realisation that retaining provisions that assist in resorting to arbitrary action under the guise of an emergency defeats one of the essential democratic virtues on which the country was founded, as is evidenced from the third preamble paragraph of the Constitution: '[I]t shall be a fundamental aim of the State to realise through the democratic process a … society … free from exploitation – a society in which the rule of law, fundamental human rights and freedom … will be secured for all citizens'.

8.5 References

Bannerji, S. (1991) 'Colonial Laws – Continuity and Innovations', in A. R. Desai (ed.), *Expanding Governmental Lawlessness and Organized Struggles*, Bombay: Popular Prakashan, vol. 3, 233.

Gross, O. (2003) 'Chaos and Rules: Should Responses to Violent Crises Always be Constitutional', *Yale Law Journal*, 112: 1011, 1034, 1097.

Gross, O. (2008) 'Extra-Legality and the Ethic of Political Responsibility', in V. V. Ramraj (ed.), *Emergencies and the Limits of Legality*, Cambridge/New York: Cambridge University Press, 71.

Iyer, V. (2000), *States of Emergency: The Indian Experience*, New Delhi: Butterworths, 152.

Kirby, M. (2004) 'Human Rights – Essential for Good Governance', paper presented at the *Seminar on Good Governance Practices for the Promotion of Human Rights*, 15 September 2004, Seoul, Korea, 1.

Lillich, R. B. (1985) *The Paris Minimum Standards of Human Rights Norms in a State of Emergency 1984* art 5(2)(d), 'Current Developments: The Paris Minimum

Standards of Human Rights Norms in a State of Emergency', *American Journal of International Law*, 79: 1072–1079.

Morss, J. R. (2009) 'Facts, Threats and Reds: Common Law Constitutionalism and the Rule of Law', *Deakin Law Review*, 14(1): 80, 81.

Scheuerman, W. E. (2008) 'Presidentialism and Emergency Government', in V. V. Ramraj (ed.), *Emergencies and the Limits of Legality*, Cambridge/New York: Cambridge University Press, 284–285.

Tushnet, M. (2005) 'Controlling Executive Power in the War on Terrorism', *Harvard Law Review*, 118: 2673.

Notes

1 *Constitution of South Africa 1996* s 37(6)(e).

2 *Paris Minimum Standards of Human Rights Norms in a State of Emergency 1984* art 5(2)(d); *Constitution of Pakistan 1973* art 10(4).

3 *Constitution of the USA 1787* in art V states that 'The Congress, whenever two thirds of both Houses shall deem it necessary, shall propose Amendments to this Constitution, or, on the Application of the Legislatures of two thirds of the several States, shall call a Convention for proposing Amendments, which, in either Case, shall be valid to all Intents and Purposes, as Part of this Constitution, when ratified by the Legislatures of three fourths of the several States, or by Conventions in three fourths thereof, as the one or the other Mode of Ratification may be proposed by the Congress; Provided [that no Amendment which may be made prior to the Year One thousand eight hundred and eight shall in any Manner affect the first and fourth Clauses in the Ninth Section of the first Article; and] that no State, without its Consent, shall be deprived of its equal Suffrage in the Senate.'

4 *Commonwealth of Australia Constitution Act 1900* s 128 requires any proposed amendment to be passed: a) by an absolute majority of both Houses of the Federal Parliament or by one House twice, and, b) at a referendum by a majority of the people as a whole and by a majority of the people in a majority of states.

Index

For Product Safety Concerns and Information please contact our EU representative GPSR@taylorandfrancis.com
Taylor & Francis Verlag GmbH, Kaufingerstraße 24, 80331 München, Germany

www.ingramcontent.com/pod-product-compliance
Ingram Content Group UK Ltd.
Pitfield, Milton Keynes, MK11 3LW, UK
UKHW010957180926
475701UK00004B/413
* 9 7 8 0 3 6 7 5 9 4 9 0 9 *